Probing the Limits of Categorization

War and Genocide

General Editors: Omer Bartov, Brown University; A. Dirk Moses, University of Sydney

In recent years there has been a growing interest in the study of war and genocide, not from a traditional military history perspective, but within the framework of social and cultural history. This series offers a forum for scholarly works that reflect these new approaches.

The Berghahn series Studies on War and Genocide *has immeasurably enriched the English-language scholarship available to scholars and students of genocide and, in particular, the Holocaust.* **—Totalitarian Movements and Political Religions**

Recent volumes:

Volume 27
Probing the Limits of Categorization: The Bystander in Holocaust History
Edited by Christina Morina and Krijn Thijs

Volume 26
Let Them Not Return: Sayfo—The Genocide Against the Assyrian, Syriac, and Chaldean Christians in the Ottoman Empire
Edited by David Gaunt, Naures Atto, and Soner O. Barthoma

Volume 25
Daily Life in the Abyss: Genocide Diaries, 1915–1918
Vahé Tachjian

Volume 24
Microhistories of the Holocaust
Edited by Claire Zalc and Tal Bruttmann

Volume 23
The Making of the Greek Genocide: Contested Memories of the Ottoman Greek Catastrophe
Erik Sjöberg

Volume 22
Genocide on Settler Frontiers: When Hunter-Gatherers and Commercial Stock Farmers Clash
Edited by Mohamed Adhikari

Volume 21
The Spirit of the Laws: The Plunder of Wealth in the Armenian Genocide
Taner Akçam and Ümit Kurt

Volume 20
The Greater German Reich and the Jews: Nazi Persecution Policies in the Annexed Territories 1935–1945
Edited by Wolf Gruner and Jörg Osterloh

Volume 19
The Dark Side of Nation-States: Ethnic Cleansing in Modern Europe
Philipp Ther

Volume 18
Judging "Privileged" Jews: Holocaust Ethics, Representation, and the "Grey Zone"
Adam Brown

For a full volume listing, please see the series page on our website: http://berghahnbooks.com/series/war-and-genocide

PROBING THE LIMITS OF CATEGORIZATION

The Bystander in Holocaust History

Edited by Christina Morina and Krijn Thijs

berghahn
NEW YORK · OXFORD
www.berghahnbooks.com

First published in 2019 by
Berghahn Books
www.berghahnbooks.com

© 2019, 2020 Christina Morina and Krijn Thijs
First paperback edition published in 2020

Support for finalizing this volume came from the
Duitsland Instituut Amsterdam/German Studies Institute Amsterdam.

All rights reserved. Except for the quotation of short passages
for the purposes of criticism and review, no part of this book
may be reproduced in any form or by any means, electronic or
mechanical, including photocopying, recording, or any information
storage and retrieval system now known or to be invented,
without written permission of the publisher.

Library of Congress Cataloging-in-Publication Data
Names: Morina, Christina, 1976- author. | Thijs, Krijn, author.
Title: Probing the Limits of Categorization: The Bystander in Holocaust
 History / Morina Christina and Krijn Thijs.
Description: First edition. | New York: Berghahn Books, [2018] | Series: War
 and Genocide; 27 | Includes bibliographical references and index.
Identifiers: LCCN 2018041887 (print) | LCCN 2018042145 (ebook) | ISBN
 9781789200942 (ebook) | ISBN 9781789200935 (hardback: alk. paper)
Subjects: LCSH: Holocaust, Jewish (1939-1945)--Moral and ethical aspects. |
 Bystander effect--Europe--History--20th century. |
 Accomplices--Europe--History--20th century.
Classification: LCC D804.7.M67 (ebook) | LCC D804.7.M67 M67 2018 (print) |
 DDC 940.53/18--dc23
LC record available at https://lccn.loc.gov/2018041887

British Library Cataloguing in Publication Data
A catalog record for this book is available from the British Library.

ISBN 978-1-78920-093-5 hardback
ISBN 978-1-78920-811-5 paperback
ISBN 978-1-78920-094-2 ebook

Contents

List of Illustrations	vii
Introduction: Probing the Limits of Categorization *Christina Morina and Krijn Thijs*	1

Part I. Approaches

Chapter 1 Bystanders: Catchall Concept, Alluring Alibi, or Crucial Clue? *Mary Fulbrook*	15
Chapter 2 Raul Hilberg and His "Discovery" of the Bystander *René Schlott*	36
Chapter 3 Bystanders as Visual Subjects: Onlookers, Spectators, Observers, and Gawkers in Occupied Poland *Roma Sendyka*	52
Chapter 4 "I am not, what I am": A Typological Approach to Individual (In)action in the Holocaust *Timothy Williams*	72
Chapter 5 The Many Shades of Bystanding: On Social Dilemmas and Passive Participation *Froukje Demant*	90
Chapter 6 The Dutch Bystander as Non-Jew and Implicated Subject *Remco Ensel and Evelien Gans*	107

Part II. History

Chapter 7
Photographing Bystanders 131
Christoph Kreutzmüller

Chapter 8
The Imperative to Act: Jews, Neighbors, and the Dynamics of
Persecution in Nazi Germany, 1933–1945 148
Christina Morina

Chapter 9
Martin Heidegger's Nazi Conscience 168
Adam Knowles

Chapter 10
Natura Abhorret Vacuum: Polish "Bystanders" and the Implementation
of the "Final Solution" 187
Jan Grabowski

Chapter 11
Defiant Danes and Indifferent Dutch? Popular Convictions and
Deportation Rates in the Netherlands and Denmark, 1940–1945 206
Bart van der Boom

Chapter 12
The Notion of Social Reactivity: The French Case, 1942–1944 224
Jacques Semelin

Part III. Memory

Chapter 13
Ordinary, Ignorant, and Noninvolved? The Figure of the Bystander in
Dutch Research and Controversy 247
Krijn Thijs

Chapter 14
Hidden in Plain View: Remembering and Forgetting the Bystanders of
the Holocaust on (West) German Television 266
Wulf Kansteiner

Chapter 15
Stand by Your Man: (Self-)Representations of SS Wives after 1945 291
Susanne C. Knittel

Chapter 16
"Bystanders" in Exhibitions at the United States Holocaust Memorial
Museum 309
Susan Bachrach

Epilogue I: A Brief Plea for the Historicization of the Bystander 336
Norbert Frei

Epilogue II: Saving the Bystander 343
Ido de Haan

Index 355

Illustrations

Figure 3.1.	Józef Charyton, *Egzekucja* (Execution), 1945–1963. (From the collection of the Emanuel Ringelblum Jewish Historical Institute, Warsaw.)	61
Figure 3.2.	Józef Charyton, *Żydówki przed egzekucją. Wys-Lit 1942* (Jewish Women before the Execution. Wys-Lit 1942), 1945–1963. (From the collection of the Emanuel Ringelblum Jewish Historical Institute, Warsaw.)	62
Figure 3.3.	*Fotografowanie na pamiątkę* (Photographing for a keepsake), 1945–1963. (From the collection of the Emanuel Ringelblum Jewish Historical Institute, Warsaw.)	64
Figure 4.1.	Typology of action in genocide. Highlighted areas are those types most usefully pointing toward a zone in which bystanders are positioned. (Figure created by author.)	79
Figure 7.1.	Photo by an unknown press photographer, Berlin, 10 November 1938, *New York Times*, 11 November 1938. (AP Images/Hollandse Hoogte.)	132
Figure 7.2.	Photo by Josef Friedrich Coeppicus, Baden-Baden, 10 November 1938. (Stadtmuseum/-archiv Baden-Baden.)	137
Figure 7.3.	Photo by Josef Friedrich Coeppicus, Baden-Baden, 10 November 1938. (Stadtmuseum/-archiv Baden-Baden.)	138
Figure 7.4.	Photo by Josef Friedrich Coeppicus, Baden-Baden, 10 November 1938. (Bundesarchiv.)	139
Figure 15.1.	*The Woman at His Side* (post-performance Q&A), Filmtheater 't Hoogt, Utrecht, 1 September 2016. *From left:* Sabine Werner, Inga Dietrich, Joanne Gläsel. (Photo: Kári Driscoll.)	303

Figure 16.1. The "wall of the rescuers" in the museum's permanent exhibition lists the names of the "righteous" who helped Jews. (United States Holocaust Memorial Museum. Photo: Miriam Lomaskin.) 311

Figure 16.2. Visitors study the Niemöller "bystander" quotation in the museum's permanent exhibition. (United States Holocaust Memorial Museum. Photo: Max Reid.) 312

Figure 16.3. A panel from *Some Were Neighbors* provokes visitors' reflection on the role of ordinary people—here, German customs and tax officials—in the Nazi persecution of Jews. (United States Holocaust Memorial Museum. Photo: David Y. Lee.) 317

Figure 16.4. A display from *Some Were Neighbors* evokes the registries of cards containing the names and addresses of Jews. Such registries aided police during the roundups of Jews in France and other countries where officials collaborated with the Germans. (United States Holocaust Memorial Museum. Photo: Miriam Lomaskin.) 322

Figure 16.5. A display from *Some Were Neighbors* that includes a quotation from the diary of a Dutch shopkeeper imposed over a photograph of a roundup of Jews in Amsterdam. The shot was taken clandestinely from someone's apartment window. (United States Holocaust Memorial Museum. Photo: Joel Mason-Gaines.) 323

Figure 16.6. One of the historic films in *Some Were Neighbors* showed young people participating in the shaming of their neighbors, Bronia and Gerhard, who violated racial decrees prohibiting their relationship. (United States Holocaust Memorial Museum. Photo: Miriam Lomaskin.) 324

Introduction
Probing the Limits of Categorization

Christina Morina and Krijn Thijs

The term "bystander" has gained as much traction as it has stirred controversy in recent years. The reasons for this surged interest are manifold. In part, they stem from the fact that among the three categories used to analyze the role of individuals in the Holocaust—perpetrators, victims, and bystanders—the category of the bystander is the broadest and vaguest. At the same time, it hints at an elemental aspect of human life, namely that people in conflict situations take on various, often ambiguous roles. A scene in Erich Maria Remarque's novel *The Night in Lisbon* (1964) aptly captures this ambiguity by steering the reader's view away from the perpetrator and the victim toward the hesitant "onlooker"—Joseph Schwarz, the author's fictionalized alter ego:

> The SS men cast furious, challenging glances at me as they passed, and the prisoner stared at me out of paralyzed eyes, making a gesture that seemed to be a plea for help... It was a scene as old as humankind: the minions of power, the victims, the eternal third, the onlooker, who doesn't raise a finger in defense of the victim, who makes no attempt to set him free, because he fears for his own safety, which for that very reason is always in danger.[1]

Remarque's story draws attention to the potentially crucial and inherently fragile position of "the eternal third," and, aware of the gravity of Schwarz's predicament, he refrains from passing judgment. After all, Schwarz is himself a fugitive from Nazi Germany, which underscores the hybridity of the bystander position in processes of systemic violence. Nonetheless, the notion of bystanding always seems to carry assumptions about the personal responsibility and culpability of "the other"—assumptions that have both inspired and hampered the historiographical analysis of the role of the non-Jewish populations during the Holocaust.

When Raul Hilberg introduced the category of the bystander in 1992, neither the concept itself nor its inherent complexities were therefore new. Yet, without dwelling much on its earlier uses in public discourses on *Mitläufer* (onlookers, or literally: hangers-on, fellow travelers) in Germany and former Nazi-occupied countries, Hilberg did so to underline an obvious, painstaking fact: the Holocaust was a crime of historic proportions precisely because it had unfolded amid millions of people across the European continent.[2] By raising bystanders to the level of the two other groups, he sought to include in his account the many contemporaries who were neither victims nor perpetrators but who "saw or heard something" of the persecution and murder of the Jews and thus were "a part of this history," too—and thus equally relevant to the story.[3] Many scholars have since relied on Hilberg's triangulation to examine the wealth of historical experiences under Nazi rule. Yet, while it seems relatively easy to define who belonged to the category of perpetrator and victim, analyzing the thoughts and actions of the *other* contemporaries, and thus their role in the unfolding of the crimes, remains a challenging endeavor in international historiography. The fact that historians keep introducing various alternative, more or less sharply defined terms such as neighbors, ordinary people, auxiliaries, accomplices, or profiteers speaks to the fact that this challenge is far from being resolved.[4]

The chapters combined in this volume provide the first comprehensive attempt to map the field of bystander studies. They each not only offer conceptual reflections on the bystander category in general but also suggest ways in which the concept can be modified and applied to specific historical contexts, both in Nazi Germany and in several occupied countries across Europe. Probing the bystander category in such a way deepens our understanding of the Holocaust as a crime not limited to the intentions of a single dictator or a few elites but as the result of a "dynamic interaction between state and society."[5] Recent studies on the daily experiences of non-Jews' interactions with Jews have shown, however, that bystander attitudes and actions cannot be pinpointed easily. The National Socialist seizure of power in 1933 and its expansion into the annexed and occupied countries confronted many non-Jewish Europeans with a defining moment, or rather a series of defining moments, forcing them to a *Stellungnahme*—to take a stand.[6] It created million-fold individual imperatives to position oneself and to react in one way or another to what was happening to the persecuted. These reactions ranged from looking away, turning around, doing "nothing"—which is never doing nothing—to expressing a word of solidarity or hostility, signaling the willingness to help or refusing to denounce, to turning in neighbors and participating in violent assaults. They were often spontaneous, born in a particular moment and under particular circumstances. As "implicated subjects," contemporaries took on shifting roles, oscillating between active and passive participation in the events and adapting to circumstances in various and varying ways.[7] Thus, like scholars of other momentous historical events, Holocaust historians face a surfeit of human experiences, with thousands of individual stories from diverse sources. In their analysis and writing, however, they remain dependent on (by definition, static) categories to depict extremely dynamic social processes.[8]

Precisely because the term "bystander" itself is so ambiguous, it seems that it captures this hybrid spectrum between indirect and direct involvement rather well. However, while exploring the diverse experiences of the "eternal third" in various local and national contexts, historians remain skeptical of schematic categorizations. They grapple with the conceptual and methodological challenges arising from the use of "bystander" as a fixed category. They stress the changeability of people's individual involvement in processes of discrimination, exclusion, and murder. Consequently, as the chapters published here illustrate, the concept's multiple meanings, translations, and contestations in different national contexts themselves have emerged as fascinating subjects of study—regarding not only history but also memory and memorial cultures, in which historians themselves play myriad roles.[9]

Aside from these general challenges emerging from recent Holocaust scholarship, the concrete impulse for this book arose from the latest in a series of controversies in the Netherlands on the role of "ordinary people" in the persecution of their Jewish compatriots. They concern the "Dutch paradox," a key question in Dutch contemporary history, namely how it was possible that in a country of relatively limited antisemitism about 75 percent of Jews were killed in the Holocaust, by far the highest rate in Western Europe.[10] In the 2000s, several works had somewhat shifted focus from the fate of the Jews to the "gray history" of the non-Jewish majority, some (implicitly) challenging the

Holocaust's centrality in Dutch World War II history and memory.[11] In 2012, a book by Bart van der Boom on the alleged lack of knowledge of "ordinary Dutchmen" about the methods used to kill Jews in Eastern Europe triggered the latest round of discussions on this subject.[12] The question of guilt took center stage yet again, with the author arguing that the "guilty bystander" was a "myth" that finally had to be deconstructed. Issues of history and memory once more proved inextricably interwoven. Moreover, the debate highlighted the necessity to reflect on the historians' personal, more or less conscious identifications and (perceived) subject positions as they, with the wider public often listening closely, address the most controversial aspects of Holocaust history. Some of the main protagonists of the Dutch controversy are among the authors of this volume, yet their contributions seek to overcome the confines of recent Dutch memory debates. All other authors in this volume relate to these issues in various implicit or explicit ways without ever suggesting that they adhere to a shared sense of identification or perspectivity.

The issues addressed in this debate concern not just Dutch World War II history. Even though such controversies usually evolve within national boundaries—with Dutch semantics operating in a Dutch tradition of scholarship and memory, Dutch moral connotations and implications, and probing Dutch identities—throughout Europe, studies on local Holocaust histories have raised similar concerns and caused similar polarizations. France debates the history and legacies of Vichy time and again.[13] In Denmark, Bo Lidegaard's widely discussed *Countrymen and the Rescue of Jews* weighed the potential and limits of "patriotism" under a peculiar German occupation regime as a motive for action/inaction.[14] In Poland, Jan Gross's work on *Neighbors* and on the so-called *Golden Harvest* caused deep divisions among scholars as in the wider public,[15] and, in Germany, several works on the reach and structural complicity of the *Volksgemeinschaft* (people's community) have shattered long-lingering assumptions about the *Mitläufer* society.[16]

All these debates allude to comparable moral, historiographical, and national identity discourses and simmer at the intersection between history and memory. They center on the role played by the seemingly uninvolved majorities in Nazi Germany and occupied Europe on the road to genocide. Everywhere, one of the archetypical categories framing these controversies—subtly or outspoken—is that of the bystander. Derived from Hilberg, the impact of the bystander concept can thus be observed in virtually every national context as the proximity or distance of the non-Jewish populations are being measured vis-à-vis processes of exclusion, segregation, expropriation, and murder. Various literal or rough translations of the English term circulate, ranging, for example, from the French and Polish "witness" to the German "onlooker" and the Italian "spectator." Each translation carries succinct, culturally coded meanings and connotations as the term is adapted to and shaped by different, mostly nationally framed narratives of war, occupation, and genocide. Consequently, the analytical value, historiographical operationalization, and moral implications of the category vary widely.

The chapters assembled in this volume explore these translations, applications, and contestations by combining conceptual thinking and empirical research.[17] The essays' contributors first shared their research with one another in Amsterdam in 2015, focusing on reviewing old and probing new ways in which the concept of the bystander is being used in Holocaust historiography. Thoroughly revised under a set of common goals and priorities, we have grouped the chapters into three parts. The first part, "Approaches," discusses concepts and methods derived from different academic disciplines to analyze the role of bystanders in processes of mass violence. Focusing largely on Nazi Germany, Mary Fulbrook draws a distinction between individually motivated acts of violence and contexts shaped by systemic, state-sanctioned violence. In the latter case, she argues, virtually everyone present is in one way or another pulled into the dynamics of violence, and no one can plausibly claim to be standing "outside" the conflict. René Schlott zooms in on the early roots of the concept within Holocaust historiography. He analyzes Hilberg's "discovery" of the bystander as an autonomous category in the 1980s until the publication of *Perpetrators Bystanders Victims* in 1992. Schlott highlights the relevance of Hilberg's conversations with Claude Lanzmann for *Shoah* and, based on Hilberg's correspondence with his publishers, reconstructs some of the problems surrounding the book's—and therefore the bystander concept's—translation into other languages and national contexts. Roma Sendyka proposes to study "onlookers" as visual subjects. Using both textual and visual evidence from two Polish Holocaust observers, she closely examines their "scopic activities" and introduces an alternative categorization by exploring how contemporaries acquired knowledge by seeing. Approaching the field from a comparative political science perspective, Timothy Williams introduces a typology of action and inaction based on the proximity and actual impact of people present in contexts of genocidal violence. His classification breaks down the broad categories "perpetrators," "bystanders," and "rescuers" into a spectrum of fourteen subcategories to account more realistically for the various shades of participation and impact. Froukje Demant explores the potential of social scientific concepts such as bullying, pluralistic ignorance, and false enforcement of unpopular norms for studying bystander behavior in history. Using evidence from the Dutch-German border region in the 1930s, her chapter focuses on the period of social exclusion before the actual expulsions and killing. In the final contribution of this part, Remco Ensel and Evelien Gans reconstruct the emergence of the bystander as non-Jew, both in Dutch Holocaust history and historiography. Studying the historical roots and growing relevance of the divide between Jews and non-Jews in the Netherlands prior to and during the 1930s, they argue that the bystander in its "embryonic" form emerged long before the Nazi occupation and remained crucial in shaping the fate of the few surviving Dutch Jews well into the postwar years.

The second part, "History," presents six case studies on the relations between the majority populations and Jewish minorities during the Holocaust in Nazi Germany and occupied Europe. Closely examining a series of photographs taken during the roundup of Jews in Baden-Baden in November 1938, Christoph Kreutzmüller analyzes the function of onlookers as complicit "audience." By pausing to watch and even to cheer, by blocking escape routes, or by taking pictures, as the photographer himself, bystanders validated and in fact aggravated the spectacle of violence executed by local Gestapo and SS forces. Christina Morina examines how Jewish diarists viewed bystanders in their immediate surroundings in Nazi Germany. Focusing on the shift to war in 1939, she argues that Jews sought and—at least temporarily—found some comfort in the subjunctive solidarity ordinary Germans seemed willing to offer in turn for acknowledgment of their own sufferings in the wake of the ever-worsening war. In a third case study on Germany, Adam Knowles discusses Martin Heidegger's attempts at establishing the Nazi revolution in German academia. Sidelined in 1934, the philosopher stylized himself as a thinker purer than the Nazi movement, who felt he was "standing by on 'the invisible front of the secret spiritual Germany'" while, in fact, condoning the Nazis' aggressive policies and murder of the Jews. Turning to the occupied countries, Jan Grabowski argues that in Poland, where knowledge of the Holocaust among the local population was widespread, few people offered help to the Jews. Faced with a range of options, moved by various motives and fears, most non-Jews took actions, which transformed them into active participants in the genocidal process unleashed by the German occupiers. Bart van der Boom builds on his work on ordinary Dutchmen and the Holocaust and compares the Dutch case to the events in Denmark. He questions that bystander attitudes and actions account for the fact that 75 percent of Dutch Jews died, while 99 percent of Danish Jews survived. Instead of pointing to the bystanders' "mind-set," he argues that these radically different outcomes are overwhelmingly rooted in the contrasting roles played by the occupying and local authorities. Analyzing the French case, Jacques Semelin introduces the notion of social reactivity, which led many ordinary citizens to form a fragile and informal, yet effective network of support for the persecuted. Based on postwar Jewish testimony, he sees this network as the result of a relatively widespread spirit of non-collaboration and disobedience, expressed in an infinite range of small, often spontaneous gestures and acts of assistance.

The third part, "Memory," explores the historiographical application and public contestation of the concept of the bystander after 1945 in various national contexts and memorial cultures. Krijn Thijs recounts the recent controversy in the Netherlands on "ordinary Dutchmen" and their knowledge of the Holocaust. Reviewing the contrasting positions and the underlying assumptions about the relationship between scholarship and collective memory, he interprets the Dutch debate as a case study that highlights the tensions and challenges confronting Holocaust historiography in general at the beginning of the twenty-first century. Wulf Kansteiner explores how the "narrative square" of German, European, and US film and television programs about the Nazi era has evolved since the 1960s. Productions exploring the bystander (and perpetrator) realms emerged rather slowly and with limited resonance. Only since the 1990s has television developed a more persistent interest in exploring the experiences of "ordinary" men and women, perhaps not coincidently as documentary formats simultaneously have lost relevance. Susanne Knittel's contribution focuses on a German theatrical performance that depicts the wartime biographies and self-representations of prominent SS wives based on their autobiographical accounts as a test case to explore the apologetic functionality of the bystander category. Informed by literary theory, Knittel argues that only an "affirmative" critique of these texts can fully unearth their epistemological implications and ethical abysms. Finally, Susan Bachrach reconstructs how permanent and special exhibitions in the United States Holocaust Memorial Museum have depicted and narrated bystanders since 1993. Reflecting newer developments in Holocaust historiography as well as the dynamics of the public memory and civil society discourses in the United States, a special exhibition entitled *Some Were Neighbors* opened in 2013. It can be considered the most sophisticated attempt yet to capture the complexity of human behavior during the Holocaust in a popular history setting. Its reception by visitors from around the world suggests that bystander history—understood as the attempt to relate individual predicaments to larger, systemic contexts—indeed offers some valuable lessons.

The volume closes with two critical comments by Ido de Haan and Norbert Frei on the potentials and limits of future bystander research. Combined, the chapters in this volume thus seek to deepen our understanding of individual agency in instances of mass violence and suffering and—fully aware of the sobering privilege of hindsight and continuing massive human rights violations in the world—to realize which experiences are worth learning from and which forms of behavior we should see to "unlearn."[18]

In Memoriam
While finalizing this volume, one of our authors, the eminent Dutch historian Evelien Gans, passed away. Her scholarly dedication, critical voice, and civil courage will be greatly missed.

Christina Morina is DAAD Visiting Assistant Professor at the Amsterdam Institute for German Studies. Her research focuses on major themes in nineteenth- and twentieth-century German and European history, political and memory culture, the history of Marxism, and the history of historiography. She received a PhD from the University of Maryland in 2007. Her dissertation was published as *Legacies of Stalingrad: Remembering the Eastern Front War in Germany since 1945* (Cambridge University Press, 2011). Her second monograph is a group portrait of the first generation of European Marxists, entitled *Die Erfindung des Marxismus: Wie eine Idee die Welt eroberte* (Siedler Verlag, 2017). She is also coeditor of *Das 20. Jahrhundert erzählen: Zeiterfahrung und Zeiterforschung im geteilten Deutschland* (Wallstein, 2016, with Franka Maubach).

Krijn Thijs is Senior Researcher at the Amsterdam Institute for German Studies and Lecturer at the University of Amsterdam. He has published on political history, memory cultures, and historiography in Germany and the Netherlands. In 2006, he received his PhD from Amsterdam Free University. His dissertation about Berlin master narratives in the twentieth century was published as *Drei Geschichten, eine Stadt: Die Berliner Stadtjubiläen 1937 und 1987* (Böhlau Verlag, 2008). Currently, he is working on a book on professional and biographical upheavals in East German historiography after 1989. He also publishes on the experiences of Wehrmacht soldiers in the occupied Netherlands and on controversies in Dutch historiography.

Notes

1. Erich Maria Remarque, *The Night in Lisbon* (New York, 1964), 91. We thank Christoph Kreutzmüller for bringing this passage to our attention.
2. See, with a focus on Germany, the classic exploration by Karl Jaspers, *The Question of German Guilt*, ed. E. B. Ashton (New York, 2001), 57–64; see also Gesine Schwan, "Der Mitläufer," in *Deutsche Erinnerungsorte*, vol. 1, ed. Étienne François and Hagen Schulze (Munich, 2001), 654–669; for an up-to-date introduction into approaches to bystander history beyond the German case, see Henrik Edgren, ed., *Looking at the Onlookers and Bystanders: Interdisciplinary Approaches to the Causes and Consequences of Passivity* (Stockholm, 2012).
3. Raul Hilberg, *Perpetrators Victims Bystanders: The Jewish Catastrophe, 1933–1945* (New York, 1992), xi–xii.
4. For a recent overview on Holocaust research and narration, see Frank Bajohr and Andrea Löw, eds., *Der Holocaust: Ergebnisse und neue Fragen der Forschung* (Bonn, 2015); Norbert Frei and Wulf Kansteiner, eds., *Den Holocaust erzählen: Historiographie zwischen wissenschaftlicher Empirie und narrativer Kreativität* (Göttingen, 2013); Paul Betts and Christian Wiese, eds., *Years of Persecution, Years of Extermination: Saul Friedlander and the Future of Holocaust Studies* (London, 2010). On the concurrent widening of the category of the perpetrator, see Frank Bajohr, "Neuere Täterforschung, Version: 1.0," *Docupedia-Zeitgeschichte*, 18 June 2018, http://docupedia.de/zg/Neuere_Taeterforschung.
5. Frank Bajohr, "The 'Folk Community' and the Persecution of the Jews: German Society under National Socialist Dictatorship, 1933–1945," *Holocaust and Genocide Studies* 20, no. 2 (2006): 183.
6. Michael Wildt, *Volksgemeinschaft als Selbstermächtigung: Gewalt gegen Juden in der deutschen Provinz 1919 bis 1939* (Hamburg, 2007), 10. See also most recently Susanna Schrafstetter and Alan Steinweis, eds., *The Germans and the Holocaust: Popular Responses to the Persecution and Murder of the Jews* (New York, 2015); Doris Bergen, Andrea Löw, and Anna Haikova, eds., *Alltag im Holocaust: Jüdisches Leben im Grossdeutschen Reich 1941–1945* (Munich, 2013); Jan Grabowski, *Hunt for the Jews: Betrayal and Murder in German-Occupied Poland* (Bloomington, 2013); Peter A. Fritzsche, *Life and Death in the Third Reich* (Cambridge, MA, 2008).
7. On this approach see, e.g., Mary Fulbrook, *Dissonant Lives: Generations and Violence through the German Dictatorships* (Oxford, 2011); Grabowski, *Hunt for the Jews*; Götz Aly, *Hitler's Beneficiaries: Plunder, Racial War, and the Nazi Welfare State* (New York, 2007); Tim Cole, "Writing 'Bystanders' into Holocaust History in More Active Ways: 'Non-Jewish' Engagement with Ghettoisation, Hungary 1944," *Holocaust Studies* 11, no. 1 (2005): 55–74; Tanja Penter, *Die lokale Gesellschaft im Donbass unter deutscher Okkupation 1941–1943* (Göttingen, 2003); Wolf Gruner et al., eds., *Die Verfolgung und Ermordung der europäischen Juden durch das nationalsozialistische Deutschland 1933–1945*, 16 vols. (Munich, 2008ff.); on the notion of "implicated subjects," see Michael Rothberg, "Multidirectional Memory and the Implicated Subject: On Sebald and Kentridge," in *Performing Memory in Art and Popular Culture*, ed. Liedeke Plate and Anneke Smelik (New York, 2013), 39–58.
8. On the Holocaust as social process, see recently Frank Bajohr and Andrea Löw eds., *The Holocaust and European Societies: Social Processes and Social Dynamics* (London, 2016).
9. Some of these issues are explored in Edgren, *Looking at the Onlookers and Bystanders*.

10. For the broader context, see Bob Moore, *Victims and Survivors: The Nazi Persecution of the Jews in the Netherlands 1940–1945* (London, 1997); Ido de Haan, "Imperialism, Colonialism and Genocide: The Dutch Case for an International History of the Holocaust," *BMGN-LCHR* 135, nos. 2–3 (2010): 301–327; Katja Happe, *Viele falsche Hoffnungen: Judenverfolgung in den Niederlanden 1940–1945* (Paderborn, 2017).
11. Krijn Thijs, "Kontroversen in Grau: Revision und Moralisierung der niederländischen Besatzungsgeschichte," in *Täter und Tabu: Grenzen der Toleranz in deutschen und niederländischen Geschichtsdebatten*, ed. Nicole Colin, Matthias M. Lorenz and Joachim Umlauf (Essen, 2011), 11–24.
12. Bart van der Boom, *"Wij weten niets van hun lot": Gewone Nederlanders en de Holocaust* (Amsterdam, 2012); Christina Morina, "The 'Bystander' in Recent Dutch Historiography," *German History* 32, no. 1 (2014): 101–111.
13. Sarah Fishman, Robert Zaretsky, Ioannis Sinanoglou, Leonard V. Smith, and Laura Lee Downs, eds., *France at War: Vichy and the Historians* (Oxford, 2000).
14. Bo Lidegaard, *Countrymen: The Untold Story of How Denmark's Jews Escaped the Nazis, of the Courage of Their Fellow Danes—and of the Extraordinary Role of the SS* (New York, 2013).
15. Jan T. Gross and Irena Grudzinska-Gross, *Golden Harvest: Events on the Periphery of the Holocaust* (New York, 2012); Jan T. Gross, *Neighbors: The Destruction of the Jewish Community in Jedwabne, Poland* (Princeton, NJ, 2000).
16. Wildt, *Volksgemeinschaft als Selbstermächtigung*; Bajohr, "The 'Folk Community'"; Aly, *Hitler's Beneficiaries*.
17. Thus, the volume's title was inspired by the premises of the conference "Probing the Limits of Representation: Nazism and the 'Final Solution'" held by Saul Friedländer and colleagues in 1990 in Los Angeles. See Saul Friedländer, ed., *Probing the Limits of Representation: Nazism and the "Final Solution"* (Cambridge, MA, 1992).
18. This thought draws on a comment made by Wulf Kansteiner during a discussion in Amsterdam in 2015.

Bibliography

Aly, Götz. *Hitler's Beneficiaries: Plunder, Racial War, and the Nazi Welfare State.* New York: Metropolitan, 2007.
Bajohr, Frank. "Neuere Täterforschung, Version: 1.0." *Docupedia-Zeitgeschichte*, 18 June 2013. http://docupedia.de/zg/Neuere_Taeterforschung.
———. "The 'Folk Community' and the Persecution of the Jews: German Society under National Socialist Dictatorship, 1933–1945." *Holocaust and Genocide Studies* 20, no. 2 (2006): 183–206.
Bajohr, Frank, and Andrea Löw, eds. *Der Holocaust: Ergebnisse und neue Fragen der Forschung*. Bonn: Bundeszentrale für politische Bildung, 2015.
———, eds. *The Holocaust and European Societies: Social Processes and Social Dynamics*. London: Palgrave Macmillan, 2016.
Bergen, Doris, Andrea Löw, and Anna Haikova, eds. *Alltag im Holocaust: Jüdisches Leben im Grossdeutschen Reich 1941–1945*. Munich: Oldenbourg, 2013.
Betts, Paul, and Christian Wiese, eds. *Years of Persecution, Years of Extermination: Saul Friedlander and the Future of Holocaust Studies*. London: Continuum, 2010.
Boom, Bart van der. *"Wij weten niets van hun lot": Gewone Nederlanders en de Holocaust*. Amsterdam: Boom, 2012.

Cole, Tim. "Writing 'Bystanders' into Holocaust History in More Active Ways: 'Non-Jewish' Engagement with Ghettoisation, Hungary 1944." *Holocaust Studies* 11, no. 1 (2005): 55–74.
Edgren, Henrik, ed. *Looking at the Onlookers and Bystanders: Interdisciplinary Approaches to the Causes and Consequences of Passivity*. Stockholm: Forum för levande histori, 2012.
Fishman, Sarah, Robert Zaretsky, Ioannis Sinanoglou, Leonard V. Smith, and Laura Lee Downs, eds. *France at War: Vichy and the Historians*. Oxford: Berg, 2000.
Frei, Norbert, and Wulf Kansteiner, eds. *Den Holocaust erzählen: Historiographie zwischen wissenschaftlicher Empirie und narrativer Kreativität*. Göttingen: Wallstein Verlag, 2013.
Friedländer, Saul, ed. *Probing the Limits of Representation: Nazism and the "Final Solution."* Cambridge, MA: Harvard University Press, 1992.
Fritzsche, Peter A. *Life and Death in the Third Reich*. Cambridge, MA: Belknap Press, 2008.
Fulbrook, Mary. *Dissonant Lives: Generations and Violence through the German Dictatorships*. Oxford: Oxford University Press, 2011.
Grabowski, Jan. *Hunt for the Jews: Betrayal and Murder in German-Occupied Poland*. Bloomington: Indiana University Press, 2013.
Gross, Jan T. *Neighbors: The Destruction of Jewish Community in Jedwabne, Poland*. Princeton, NJ: Princeton University Press, 2001.
Gross, Jan T., and Irena Grudzinska-Gross. *Golden Harvest: Events on the Periphery of the Holocaust*. New York: Oxford University Press, 2012.
Gruner, Wolf, et al., eds. *Die Verfolgung und Ermordung der europäischen Juden durch das nationalsozialistische Deutschland 1933–1945*. 16 vols. Munich: Oldenbourg, 2008ff.
Haan, Ido de. "Imperialism, Colonialism and Genocide: The Dutch Case for an International History of the Holocaust." *BMGN-LCHR* 135, nos. 2–3 (2010): 301–327.
Happe, Katja. *Viele falsche Hoffnungen: Judenverfolgung in den Niederlanden 1940–1945*, Paderborn: Schöningh, 2017.
Hilberg, Raul. *Perpetrators Victims Bystanders: The Jewish Catastrophe, 1933–1945*. New York: HarperCollins, 1992.
Jaspers, Karl. *The Question of German Guilt*. Edited by E. B. Ashton. New York: Fordham University Press, 2001.
Lidegaard, Bo. *Countrymen: The Untold Story of How Denmark's Jews Escaped the Nazis, of the Courage of Their Fellow Danes—and of the Extraordinary Role of the SS*. New York: Knopf, 2013.
Moore, Bob. *Victims and Survivors: The Nazi Persecution of the Jews in the Netherlands 1940–1945*, London: Arnold, 1997.
Morina, Christina. "The 'Bystander' in Recent Dutch Historiography." *German History* 32, no. 1 (2014): 101–111.
Penter, Tanja. *Die lokale Gesellschaft im Donbass unter deutscher Okkupation 1941–1943*. Göttingen: Wallstein, 2003.
Remarque, Erich Maria. *The Night in Lisbon*. New York: Harcourt, 1964.
Rothberg, Michael. "Multidirectional Memory and the Implicated Subject: On Sebald and Kentridge." In *Performing Memory in Art and Popular Culture*, edited by Liedeke Plate and Anneke Smelik, 39–58. New York: Routledge, 2013.
Schrafstetter, Susanna, and Alan E. Steinweis, eds. *The Germans and the Holocaust: Popular Responses to the Persecution and Murder of the Jews*. New York: Berghahn Books, 2015.
Schwan, Gesine. "Der Mitläufer." In *Deutsche Erinnerungsorte*, vol. 1, edited by Étienne François and Hagen Schulze, 654–669. Munich: Beck, 2001.

Thijs, Krijn. "Kontroversen in Grau: Revision und Moralisierung der niederländischen Besatzungsgeschichte." In *Täter und Tabu: Grenzen der Toleranz in deutschen und niederländischen Geschichtsdebatten*, edited by Nicole Colin, Matthias M. Lorenz and Joachim Umlauf, 11–24. Essen: Klartext-Verlag, 2011.

Wildt, Michael. *Volksgemeinschaft als Selbstermächtigung: Gewalt gegen Juden in der deutschen Provinz 1919 bis 1939*. Hamburg: Hamburger Edition, 2007.

Part I

Approaches

Chapter 1

Bystanders

Catchall Concept, Alluring Alibi, or Crucial Clue?

Mary Fulbrook

The notion of bystander has become an established part of the way we talk about conflict situations.[1] The concept is widely used to discuss situations in which people are in proximity to a situation of conflict and questions arise about moral responsibility to intervene. Both classic and recent approaches to bystanders suggest that it has functioned as a catchall concept, and something of a residual category that is inherently unstable. The term may, however, be an appealing alibi, relevant to understanding self-representations in accounts since 1945. Moreover, a focus on the conditions under which bystanding behaviors are prevalent may assist historians in understanding the dynamics of persecution in a wider context. The correlate is that we must also develop a more differentiated analysis of those "on the perpetrator side," as well as victims.

The initial categories of the classic triad must, in a sense, be "rethought together." They are relational terms predicated on a particular model of a system in which it is possible in some way to be "outside" the act of violence; this was not the case in Nazi-dominated Europe. In particular, key questions arise regarding the distinctions between individually motivated acts of violence, and state-ordained or state-sanctioned collective violence. The situation with respect to individual incidents of, for example, rape, robbery, or bullying, in which the institutions of power and authority are opposed to the violence, is very different to a situation in which the forces of repression are on the side of those committing violence. Moreover, while the former may be viewed as discrete incidents in which perpetrators and victims constitute a core conflict situation and bystanders in some sense "stand outside," the system of violence in the latter encompasses larger numbers of people over extended periods of time and territory. It is harder to identify what might legitimately be seen as "outside" the specific conflict situation.

Catchall Concept: An Inherently Unstable Category of Analysis

In relation to the Nazi persecution of the Jews, the notion of bystander has become firmly entrenched as one of the three elements of the triad highlighted by the eminent pioneer of Holocaust historiography Raul Hilberg in his book on *Perpetrators Victims Bystanders*, first published in 1992.[2] For all the criticism levied at the book even immediately on publication, the triptych in the title has subsequently gained wide currency as a standard analytic framework.

The concept of bystander is not only used by historians but is also used widely in everyday life to discuss situations in which people find themselves in close proximity to a situation of conflict and the question arises as to an individual's moral responsibility to intervene. The Massachusetts Institute of Technology, for example, defines "bystander" as "a person who observes a conflict or unacceptable behavior." This behavior "might be something serious or minor, one-time or repeated, but the Bystander knows that the behavior is destructive or likely to make a bad situation worse."[3] The implication is that the bystander has a moral duty to act in some way on behalf of the victim. This is central to some of the issues around its use as a concept for historical analysis, yet the focus on the actors in the trilogy tends to deflect attention from the context of action.

Definition of the term should be straightforward. A bystander is "standing by" but not involved in a significant situation of conflict between a perpetrator and a victim (or groups of each). It is in effect not the person but the context that defines the role: the person happens to be close to something that is in essence part of someone else's history. The bystander is by definition "outside" the real dynamics of the situation. It is notable that definitions do not generally embed the discussion in any wider contextual analysis. The *Merriam-Webster Dictionary*, for example, states that a bystander is "one who is present but not taking part in a situation or event."[4] The *Oxford Dictionary* agrees that a bystander is a "person who is present at an event or incident but does not take part." It goes on to give as an example, "water cannons were turned on marchers and innocent bystanders alike."[5] Or, in the somewhat fuller definition of the sociologist Victoria Barnett: "The bystander is not the protagonist, the person propelling the action; nor is the bystander the object of the action. In a criminal case, the bystander is neither victim nor perpetrator; his or her legally relevant role is that of witness—someone who happened to be present and could shed light on what actually occurred."[6] The bystander in these decontextualized versions, where the conflict situation is itself bounded and discrete, appears initially to be a neutral role, that of a person who sees but is not an intrinsic part of a conflict situation.

"Bystanding" and "standing by" are inherently problematic terms. They are attributes not of the people themselves but rather of their location in relation to where the conflict is taking place. Bystanders are defined by virtue of proximity to a situation in which they are not involved; it is the very fact of *not* being part of the conflict that actually defines them as "bystanding," even if it is not necessarily possible to be "not involved." Therefore, at the same time, bystanding is an inherently unstable term, with a heightened moral freighting. Where others are inevitably situated on one side or another, as perpetrators or victims, bystanders alone appear to have a choice as to which side they choose to be on, or whether to avoid taking sides—which in itself is not a morally neutral decision either, since inaction on behalf of the victims effectively condones or favors the power of the dominant group. As Barnett puts it, "bystanders are confronted by a wide range of behavioral options, and they bear some responsibility for what happens."[7]

Intervention and failure to intervene are inherently loaded acts. Nonintervention effectively reinforces the perpetrator's behavior, allowing an advantage over the victim and condoning or even reinforcing violence. Intervention may succeed in challenging violent norms and behaviors, thus tipping the balance in the victim's direction, but it might also mean that bystanders risk becoming victims themselves. In this analysis of situational dynamics, there is no real possibility of "innocence," but rather only one of asking, "Whose side are you on?"

In a sense, then, the "innocence" of bystanders is only one possibility; guilt is equally possible, as is heroism, or indeed foolhardiness. All these imply both a pragmatic and a moral evaluation of the choices made by bystanders about the ways in which they did or did not become involved.

It is the moral weighting of the term, and particularly the question of presumed innocence, on which most approaches agree that we need to focus our attention. But we can only do this fruitfully if we build in distinctions between individual and collective violence, between isolated incidents and systemic violence, which have, to date, largely escaped adequate attention.

What, then, of the use of the term by historians? Hilberg, the great pioneer of Holocaust historiography, essentially divided the world into three: victims, perpetrators, and bystanders. In the third edition of his three-volume work *The Destruction of the European Jews*, Hilberg pointed out the relevance of the behavior of local populations in determining the outcome of persecution as "witnesses distanced themselves from the victims, so that physical proximity no longer signified personal closeness."[8] Hilberg contended that "local bystanders formed a human wall around the Jews entrapped in laws and ghettos."[9] An evaluation of local bystander attitudes and likely behavior was crucial in weighing options on the part of victims: "Escape meant risk of denunciation or extortion. Anyone could be dangerous and help was uncertain."[10] Bystanders were, after all, part of the situational dynamics, helping to determine differing outcomes in different areas. These insights were, as we shall see, crucial, but Hilberg went on to extend the concept massively, losing the conceptual precision essential to historical analysis. In *Perpetrators Victims Bystanders*, he included under "Bystanders" chapters on "Nations in Adolf Hitler's Europe," "Helpers, Gainers and Onlookers," "Messengers," "Jewish Rescuers," "The Allies," "Neutral Countries," and "The Churches."[11] Many of his examples could be categorized as victims, facilitators, collaborators, or resisters; few were really "bystanders" in any sense that does not presuppose intrinsic involvement in the dynamics of the situation.

Michael Marrus suggested that the notion of "bystander" for Hilberg was more an accusatory than an analytical category, commenting that Hilberg "seems less a pathfinder than a conscience."[12] Reflecting in his autobiographical work, *The Politics of Memory*, Hilberg was bitterly disappointed at this reception: the "triptych" mattered desperately as a critique of failures to intervene when intervention might have made a difference.[13] For him and many others, the notion of bystanding is intrinsically rooted in the reproach that those who saw and knew what was going on could have intervened on the side of the victims but failed to do so.

But is such a catchall concept really a useful analytic—as opposed to moral—tool? Recent uses tend not to apply the concept across more or less the whole world, with states, governments, institutions, and organizations all coming under the blanket category of bystanders, but more commonly address situations in which people witnessed events unfolding before their eyes. The term "bystanders" is generally used to refer to people within Nazi-controlled areas, and specifically those who could personally see the interactions of persecutors and persecuted.

Again, the moral evaluation seems intrinsic to the definition. Bystanders could, it is generally implied, have made some difference to the outcome of specific situations if they had been less indifferent. The question of potentially tipping the balance is evident, for example, in the United States Holocaust Memorial Museum's 2013 exhibition *Some Were Neighbors*, revealingly subtitled "Collaboration and Complicity in the Holocaust."[14] The issue is not so much that "bystanders" were not involved but rather that they were not *necessarily* involved and had a degree of *choice*—which might in practice be very limited—about which side to become involved in, or whether to become involved at all. Yad Vashem's Holocaust Resource Center similarly points up the moral implications of the term. It defines "bystanders" in terms of those people "in Germany and occupied Europe" who "were aware, to at least some extent, of how the Nazi regime was treating the Jews." Yad Vashem offers as explanation not only "antisemitic sentiments" but also and indeed "primarily" a sense "that it was an assault not on them but on 'an other,' even if this 'other' was a neighbor, partner or acquaintance." It emphasizes both fear and profit, pointing not only to the "Nazi policy of terror" but also to "the benefits that many people received through the dispossession and murder of the Jews."[15] Yad Vashem's documents used to support the study of "bystanders" overwhelmingly relate to local populations in areas of persecution. Interactions range from perceived indifference—including failure to provide small forms of help, such as food on a death march—to materially benefitting through profits from property, goods, and clothing.[16] Bystander reactions are portrayed negatively: willful failure to help, morally questionable profiting at the expense of the Jews, or collaboration with persecutors. We need, then, a more differentiated spectrum. In some cases, terms such as "beneficiaries" and "collaborators" might be more helpful—insofar as we want to use a noun at all for a category of person.

Many scholars, however, now question the use of nouns, categories into which individuals can be neatly slotted, as the best way of proceeding. A "social process" approach that concerns how people become involved in acts of perpetration has been developed, but it is initially less easy to see how such a processual approach could be applied to bystanding. In contrast to becoming involved in an act of perpetration, being a bystander is arguably only possible at the start, not the end point, of the social dynamics of a conflict situation. The inherent instability of the bystanding position means that soon the balance tips toward one side or another. Time is simply flowing in a different direction for this situationally defined status. Unlike "becoming" a perpetrator over time, one "leaves" the status of being a bystander.

Another way of avoiding use of a noun is to limit the focus to behavior at a specific point in time. The social psychologist Dan Bar-On, for example, proposes the concept of "bystanding behavior" in place of "bystander," seeing "bystanding behavior as contextual, situational rather than in terms of a personality trait."[17] Bar-On points out that there are "many forms of bystanding behaviors," and raises questions about widespread lack of awareness of the moment when "constructive inaction" becomes "destructive" and about the conditions under which people may move into "becoming rescuers" or "getting involved in resistance." He suggests that there are different positions, including "eyewitnesses, distant listeners, those far away who should be concerned," and "different levels of exposure to the victimization process," yet very few become "rescuers" or perform "acts of resistance."[18] Bar-On's approach may provide a helpful way forward in examining the dynamics of particular situations, at least as far as psychological rather than historical dynamics are concerned.

The simplest recent usage on the part of historians is to define anyone in a given locality as bystanders if they are neither direct perpetrators in any obvious or strong sense (SS, Gestapo) nor targeted victims of Nazi persecution, such as inmates of concentration camps or fugitive Jews. Bystanders defined in this way are sometimes seen in quite positive terms, as in Jack Morrison's work on Ravensbrück concentration camp for women, largely based on survivors' accounts.[19] By contrast, Gordon Horwitz focuses on Mauthausen concentration camp, as well as the nearby euthanasia center in Schloss Hartheim, and highlights how members of the local population participated in the functioning of the camp and benefitted from plundering the dead.[20] Local residents were also sufficiently hostile to prisoners to assist in hunting down any who escaped.[21] Others who lived nearby were determined, despite clear evidence, to "not see" and "not know" what was going on. Horwitz draws on the work of the philosopher Mary Midgley, arguing that "'deliberate avoidance [of knowing] is a responsible act.'"[22] The concept of bystanding is intrinsically an ethical and moral concept.

When we look at historical dynamics in more depth, we soon encounter issues concerning sources. These relate to different understandings of not only what it means to be a bystander but also what it means to be a perpetrator. We therefore need to look closely at precisely why the concept of being "merely a bystander" might be alluring to those who were implicated in a system of collective violence without being perpetrators in a narrow or legal sense of the term.

Alluring Alibi: Or, Bystanders Are Not Perpetrators

People who lived through these times and were not themselves victims have a personal interest in not being classed among the perpetrators. Just as we refine the concept of perpetrator, we need to be aware of the multiple ways in which people sought to ensure a less contaminated place for themselves in the category of "innocent bystanders." For many who were tainted, the claim has served as a convenient means of establishing a clear conscience.

Many people later claimed innocence through ignorance: they alleged that they "had never known anything about it" (*davon haben wir nichts gewusst*). In this formulation, what is meant by "it" slides into ever-increasing distance: for those living far enough away, "it" is reduced to the death camps of occupied Poland; for those living close to such camps, "it" can be reduced to "just" the gas chambers, or the "function" of extermination rather than "merely" incarceration and hard labor. "Ignorance" is a claim even mounted by those at incredibly close quarters who talk of "suspicion" rather than "knowledge" of what "might" be going on.[23]

People who had demonstrably "known" but not intervened on behalf of the victims were put on the defensive in a later era. In later accounts, such individuals sought to justify their former passive onlooker status in a variety of ways. One way of casting oneself in the role of "innocent bystander" was to misrepresent the situation. By focusing on the immediate clash of physical forces, it was possible to downplay or even deny one's own role in the system of which these forces were but one manifestation. This alibi was prevalent in West Germany in the 1950s, when the definition of "perpetrator" was narrowed repeatedly. Starting with statements by German Chancellor Konrad Adenauer, "perpetrators" were defined largely in terms of Hitler and his henchmen, plus the brute forces of the SS, the Gestapo, and a few sadists and thugs. "Normative demarcation" (in Norbert Frei's phrase) indicated clear disapproval of those held to be guilty while also reintegrating those who were to be rehabilitated in service of a new, functioning democratic system—even at the expense of others who had opposed, challenged, or been excluded from the Nazi system.[24] Meanwhile, professional groups—the civil service, the medical profession, the judiciary, even the army—portrayed their own former roles in a far more benign light. They may have "known" about violent and illegal acts, atrocities, and what were often written off as "excesses," but they themselves were effectively "bystanders," not really responsible. This approach was rooted in a widely held misrepresentation of the structure of the Nazi state. It can be found at all levels of the hierarchy and across different areas of activity, including among members of the civilian administration who played a role in stigmatization and ghettoization of Jews and then disassociated themselves from any responsibility for the subsequent deportations and deaths that their actions had facilitated.[25]

There were other ways of later constructing a self-image as someone who was intrinsically good but lacking in agency or adequate understanding at the time. For example, Melita Maschmann, a former German Youth leader in the *Bund Deutscher Mädel*, wrote a memoir in the form of letters to a school friend of Jewish descent; this "reckoning" with her "former self" was supposedly not an attempt at self-justification but was, in essence, precisely that. Recounting her experiences in the newly occupied and annexed territories of Poland, Maschmann vividly depicts the suffering of Jews in the ghettos of Kutno and Łódź. Implicitly anticipating the reader's outraged reaction, she defends herself by pointing to the power of ideology. She suggests it was possible to "see without seeing," blinded by an ideology that allegedly exerted particular power over idealistic young people such as her.[26] She not only suppressed any sympathy but even criticized Jews for not engaging in productive work. She understood that to get Jews to hand over their possessions, it would be necessary to cut their rations—without questioning these policies.[27] Moreover, she told herself that her private feelings of sympathy, particularly for suffering and starving children, should be suppressed in view of the larger necessity of "driving out the Jews," essential "if the Warthegau was to become a German land."[28] In this attempt to understand and portray her past—telling us more about the mentality of a former Nazi in 1960s West Germany than about the views of middle-class girls in the 1930s and early 1940s—Maschmann constructs a would-be sympathetic picture of an idealistic youngster taken in by those in authority, navigating a fine line between innocent bystander and complicit actor. Portraying herself as effectively the puppet of others, she presents a person mobilized against her instincts rather than motivated by her own intentions. She is therefore neither fully responsible for her actions nor really guilty by virtue of her failure to see what turned out to be the wrong side of history.

If Maschmann claimed lack of agency through the power of ideology and if others claimed lack of agency by a misrepresentation of the system, a further means was to split the self between outer behavior and inner authenticity. This strategy was successful in many West German trials. Defendants were cleared of the charge of murder if they could prove that they had been "merely obeying orders" under such constraints that they could not have acted otherwise, or had at least thought this at the time, even if this was a misperception. Lack of evidence about subjective attitudes could get them off the hook—as indeed was the case for many defendants who had so successfully participated in mass murder in Bełżec.[29]

There were many other cases where perpetrators claimed they were in reality just bystanders, eyewitnesses without agency. For example, Heinz Schubert, a former adjutant of Otto Ohlendorf in Einsatzgruppe D, which had murdered Jews, Gypsies, and "partisans" in the southern Ukraine and Caucasus in 1941 and 1942, was unwittingly interviewed by Claude Lanzmann for the latter's film *Shoah*. In footage that was filmed surreptitiously (not included in *Shoah*), Schubert made great play of the difference between the German words for "supervise" (*beaufsichtigen*) and "see" (*besichtigen*). He claimed that he had only "observed," but not had responsibility for, acts of killing: he was in his self-presentation merely an innocent bystander.[30] Examples like these, precisely in their extremity, underscore the way in which an understanding of the wider system and the demarcation of bystanders from perpetrators are essential if we are to make progress with the term as an analytic tool for historians.

Crucial Clue

The problem with the exhaustive triad—perpetrators, victims, bystanders—is that it is not fit for historical analysis of a system of state-ordained violence over a long period of time. When authorities are also against the offence being committed, bystanders can in principle call for help. But bystanders within a system of state-sanctioned violence cannot necessarily act in the same way. In such situations, momentary "bystanders" to a particular "node" of acutely concentrated violence were themselves part of a broader field of multiple, conflicting forces: there is no "outside." In contexts infused with collective violence, the world is more complicated than it is in relation to one-off acts of individual violence in an essentially benign wider context. And in a system changing over time, sometimes very rapidly, it is more complex still.

The question is therefore twofold. First, it is a question of adequate differentiation between different roles and behaviors in a wider system that was in itself violent, whether symbolically, structurally, or physically. Second, we must build in the dimension of time: we need to understand changing behaviors in evolving situations, with key shifts in power structures, social roles and relations, cultural understandings, and individual responses. Systemic violence was punctured by incidents and episodes within a wider sea, in the course of which all protagonists were changing.

So, the primary task is to understand better the multiple ways in which an intrinsically violent system was established, expanded, and sustained. This means that we cannot be restricted by everyday understandings or legal definitions of the word "perpetrator" but need to think harder about the variety of behaviors that contributed to making mass persecution possible. Beyond the top-level initiators of policy and the murderers on the ground, people acted to sustain the system in many different ways, whether or not they felt they were internally opposed to it and regardless of however much they retained a sense of inner distance. There were of course different degrees of responsibility (and culpability), but certain distinctions can be made. In Germany, the willingness of so many people to distance themselves from former friends and neighbors of Jewish descent was a precondition for later policies to be put into effect. In the occupied territories, a combination of fear and profiting affected people's willingness to collaborate or benefit from German occupation. Everywhere, people were in some way affected by the Nazi regime.

On only the most cursory of occasions—when referring to a specific incident lasting a delimited period of time—could people readily be classed as "bystanders." Depending on circumstances, they could be described as "eyewitnesses," or even "spectators," "onlookers." These categories too embody their own problems, as when Jews were forced to spectate at public hangings, alongside Germans who came to enjoy the spectacle. The categories do not really map onto that of bystander in these cases, nor would one really want to lump the groups together. The notion of "bystander" is at best useful when we have a snapshot—perhaps literally a photograph—of an incident and we know nothing at all about those who are watching in the background.[31] When considered over longer periods of time, however, even those who were neither active members of the persecuting community nor obvious targets of persecution were nevertheless affected by and implicated in the system of terror in one way or another. Whether it is helpful to lump them all together as "bystanders" needs to be addressed in more detail.

Let us take some examples from contemporary sources. Consider, for example, the diary of Zygmunt Klukowski, the surgeon and doctor in charge of the Zamość County hospital in the small Polish town of

Szczebrzeszyn.[32] It is clear from the very start just how badly not only the Jewish residents but also the local Polish population were affected by the invasion of Poland in September 1939. Over the ensuing years, curfews, numerous restrictions, food shortages, robberies, constant violence, reprisals, uncertainties, and humiliation made Klukowski feel that he and his fellow Poles were living in a state of almost unbearable "slavery" (his term). While the treatment of the Jews was worse than that of non-Jewish Poles—and the Jews were eventually targeted for total extermination, mass murder—the defeated Polish population was also a victim of Nazi occupation. Poles were, then, not only "bystanders" to the Jewish catastrophe but also themselves victims of Nazi oppression. Even so, they had somewhat greater leeway for choice over how to respond to the Nazi persecution of the Jews. They not only were victims of German rule but might also have been collaborators, perpetrators, and beneficiaries of Nazi persecution of the Jews. The massacre of the Jews of Jedwabne by their neighbors has become infamous, but it is arguably still insufficiently recognized that all across the country Poles were responsible for the identification, betrayal, and often even murder of their former Jewish neighbors.[33] Klukowski provides horrific examples of Polish involvement: helping to kill escaping Jews with axes, laughing during a massacre.[34] The mass murder of the Jews could not have taken place without the involvement of many ordinary Polish people in hunting down and "rendering" Jews to the Germans to enrich themselves.[35]

The fact that the state backed violence that the Germans had themselves initiated was important in the dynamics of increasing lawlessness. Klukowski commented bitterly, following his report on the day's attacks and robberies on 21 May 1942, "The attackers are laughing and telling people to notify the German police."[36] By 19 September 1942, Klukowski noted that the "the number of bandits and robbers is growing… It appears they are laughing at the gendarmes and police." This situation affected other people living in the locality: "Some of the people have been broken and lost their will to fight for survival. Everyone's hope is to survive until the end of the war."[37] At the other end of the spectrum, some Poles were involved in oppositional activities that often ended in their own arrest or even execution, and partisan bands roaming the countryside posed limits to the Germans' power in the area. Even Klukowski's eleven-year-old son tried to join the Polish underground but was sent home by a forest ranger.[38] However courageous some of these partisans might have been, fighting the Germans did not necessarily make them any friendlier toward Jews, and many groups excluded Jews from partisan activities or betrayed them to the Germans. Yet, even so, some Jews were successfully able to hide and survive precisely because of a few courageous Poles—for whom the penalty was execution, of not only themselves but also their whole families.

The very mixed and often totally unpredictable responses of local Polish people become evident in, for example, the early postwar accounts of Jewish children who survived "on the Aryan side," thanks to the compassion, for whatever reason, of people who were often complete strangers to them.[39] Some of these rescuers were paid, some accepted the children's labor and found them to be reliable farmworkers, and others appear to have acted out of sheer kindness—but any willingness to hide Jews could turn suddenly into something quite different if fear of adverse consequences struck.

Of course, the local Poles were in some sense "bystanders," as when Klukowski tells us that some of them stood around laughing when they watched Jews being massacred, while others seized the opportunity to enrich themselves, but they were also very much active participants, one way or another. Klukowski himself, who might—in his role as observer and diarist—be seen as the classic bystander, was deeply affected by the period through which he lived. His responses to particular situations, such as having to refuse medical treatment to Jews on the order of the Germans, reveal the constraints under which he was operating. He too was a part of a wider system that made it impossible for Jews to receive appropriate assistance at a crucial time, but only because to have opposed the German ban would have meant certain arrest and likely execution. Clearly, to explore the changing perceptions and reactions of those who were part of the wider system does help us to understand the dynamics of persecution. To focus on isolated incidents of nonintervention is not always helpful, as becomes evident when considering the roles played by individuals over time.

To take another example of a contemporary diary writer, we can consider the journalist Ruth Andreas-Friedrich in Berlin. She had many friends who, like herself, sought to provide assistance and shelter to Jews in hiding or evading deportation. She was horrified at the reports of the fate of Jews who had been deported, and noted rumors of the killings—"mass shootings and death by starvation, tortures, and gassings"—in her diary as early as 2 December 1942.[40] Her main effort, in the small resistance group of which she was a part, was to provide food and lodging to imperiled Jews. But from another perspective, she might have been considered a bystander when she watched but did not intervene on occasions when Jews were being grabbed off the streets and thrown into trucks for deportation. As she pointed out in her entry of 28 February 1943, any intervention in such incidents would have been entirely senseless and counterproductive. She noted, aghast, that people were being loaded onto "overcrowded trucks with blows of gun butts," like "human cargo ... penned in and jostled about like cattle going to the stockyards." But, she reflected: "The SS is armed; we aren't. No one is going to give us weapons, either; and if anyone did, we wouldn't know how to use them. We just aren't 'killers.' We revere life. That is our strength—and our weakness."[41]

In different ways, both Klukowski and Andreas-Friedrich were acute observers of events, and bystanders to particular incidents of violence. But because we know more about them, their activities and roles over time, their reasons for engaging in certain types of action and not others, we would not likely want to call them bystanders. Rather, we would seek a more differentiated approach to understanding the ways in which they engaged in a longer-term system of terror and coercion, which affected them deeply and in which they were highly constrained, having very little freedom to choose precisely how to respond at particular moments in the light of their morals, their principles, and the practical realities of any given situation.

Moreover, much depended not only on the views of a particular individual at a specific time but also on how people thought others might react. It is worth noting that when large numbers of people were willing to cooperate in an act of resistance, it was more likely to be successful—and possible to pull others on board for action—than when only isolated individuals were involved. The case of saving the Jews of Denmark provides the simplest illustration.[42] Microcosms of perception, interpretations, and discourse were as important as the realities in any given situation. Again, change over time is a crucial feature to be taken into consideration here.

Interestingly, in the third edition of *The Destruction of the European Jews*, Hilberg engaged in a discussion on "neighbors" (not related to Jan Gross's use of this term).[43] Hilberg makes some extremely perceptive comments about the significance of the surrounding population—those living and working in or passing through territory where perpetrator-victim dynamics were taking place—for the outcome of such dynamics. As Hilberg puts it, "All the prewar divisions between Jews and non-Jews were deepened as the non-Jewish neighbors turned their concerns inward for the sake of material and mental stability," affecting their responses to those now seen in a quite different light.[44] Even "bystanders" were themselves transformed by the changing situation in which they were living. Changes taking place in the character of the bystander population over a period of time—longer or shorter, depending on location—could tragically affect the outcome of situations for the victims. Bystanders were not some static category, happening to be on the scene as ready-made, two-dimensional figures at the time of action, but were themselves people who changed and developed.

It was not only individuals who shifted their horizons, aspirations, and priorities in changing circumstances, although this was highly significant in areas that remained somewhat stable. In some areas, the composition of bystander populations also changed to a greater or lesser extent, particularly with Nazi policies of resettlement and "Germanization." Moreover, the social and political contexts changed rapidly, affecting what local bystanders might take into account in acting in one way or another. So, the question of bystanding under Nazism must be considered within changing contexts over longer stretches of time (and not just as a one-off situation that presupposes relatively stable wider parameters and conditions). Within a system of collective violence, we cannot treat bystanders as individual actors, defined by proximity to a specific incident within an essentially neutral context. We might rather reconceive them as part of the wider field of forces, where the authorities not merely support but actively produce (and indeed are) the perpetrators. "Bystander populations" are formed and transformed over time within a constantly evolving situation.

Nazism changed who it was that the bystanders were, in three significant ways: in terms of individual attitudes and outlooks; in terms of the composition of the population; and in terms of the broader contexts of action or inaction. When viewed in this more differentiated manner, bystanders could provide crucial clues to the outcomes of specific situations. The character of the local bystander population could be particularly significant in areas where sheer physical survival or the chances of escape, rescue, or resistance were dependent on the character of the local population, as many escapees from ghettos and camps discovered.[45]

A more differentiated analysis of variations among local bystander populations reveals interesting distinctions.[46] It is, for example, perhaps a desperate and certainly rather sad undertaking to compare the slim chances of survival in the two largest ghettos, Warsaw in the General Government and Łódź (Germanized as Litzmannstadt) in the Reichsgau Wartheland, incorporated into the Greater German Reich. In both ghettos, many tens of thousands of people died from starvation and disease even before deportation to the death camps. Many factors were involved in determining daily death rates within the ghettos and in affecting chances of escape. The roles of the respective Jewish Councils, and particularly of their leaders—the controversial Chaim Rumkowski in Litzmannstadt and the more reputable Adam Czerniaków in Warsaw— have been endlessly debated. The slightly differing German policies toward each of these ghettos also played a significant role. The overwhelming majority of the people trapped in these ghettos could not survive the combination of brutal conditions resulting in diseases and starvation, or later deportation to the death camps. The existence of the sewer system in Warsaw also meant that it was physically less easy to seal off from the outside world than was the ghetto of Litzmannstadt, where escape was far more difficult. But for a few, the character of the bystander population could prove to be highly significant in heightening or restricting their chances of survival. Even contemporaries were aware of the fact that it was slightly easier to smuggle in additional foodstuffs and, eventually, weapons from areas surrounding the Warsaw Ghetto, where among the local population of cowed Poles there could be found a significant number who were sympathetic to the plight of the ghetto inhabitants, than it was in the somewhat more Germanized surroundings of Litzmannstadt. It was also easier to smuggle people out and to find hiding places for those who escaped the Warsaw Ghetto—something that again did not work for those trapped in the more Germanized environment around Łódź.

The character of local populations also affected possibilities for survival in less tangible ways. Moral support—words of encouragement, acts of solidarity or friendship, willingness to listen or soothe—might restore faith in humanity as well as assistance in physical survival. There is a form of "relational support" that is distinct from "rescue" or "resistance" but might for some be equally important at key moments in their lives—or rather, near deaths, as on the occasions when people threw bread or handed water to people on the death marches. There are numerous such stories in survivor testimonies.[47] An analysis of how victims perceived those they only knew as bystanders might genuinely help in understanding some crucial aspects of the dynamics of Nazi persecution and the roles of others who were not in the same category as the particular groups of victims at key moments in their lives.

Conclusions

If bystander is effectively used as a catchall concept for anyone who was neither a perpetrator nor a victim in a particular situation, the notion of guilt and the dynamics of violence are effectively reduced to a rather small circle of actors. Such an approach also tends to restrict the concept of violence to discrete actions or episodes, in specific places and for limited periods. It may work for particular moments of individual acts, but it is far from clear that it is equally relevant when talking about systemic, collective violence over sustained periods of time and exerted in multiple ways. If applied to a system of state-ordained violence, the triad can easily function to provide alibis of innocence for some and to cast a guilty shadow over others—both equally undeserved. In a sustained system of collective violence, virtually everyone was in one way or another constrained to develop a relationship—perhaps changing over time—to the driving dynamics of violence. Some were more contaminated by the relationships they chose than were others.

The notion of bystander retains some value as a residual category for short-term purposes. It is clearly applicable to those who witnessed or were demonstrably present at certain events but about whom we know too little to say more than that they did not intervene on that specific occasion. It is potentially also applicable at an early moment of time for those who became involved in the dynamics of collective violence by virtue, initially, of simple proximity. But once we build in the dimension of time and the evolution of the system, these people develop behaviors that either serve to underscore and sustain the system or to challenge and undermine it, potentially shifting roles and allegiances over time.

The initial three categories of the classic triad must, in a sense, be "rethought together." They are relational terms predicated on a particular model of a system in which it is possible in some way to be "outside" the act of violence; this was not the case in Nazi-dominated Europe. "Perpetrator" is both a legal and a moral category, with implications for justice. "Victim" too is a contested category: recognition may be implicated in terms of justice, reparations, compensation, entitlement to some form of "making good again." It may be argued that "bystander" here rightly implies that one is somehow outside this legal and moral framework. But this is not necessarily the case even in terms of legal systems. It is certainly not so in moral terms.

Perhaps we should not start from the standard triad as a means of trying to encompass all those involved. Rather, we should begin by recognizing the distinction between individual incidents within a system that does not condone such acts, and participation in a system of collective violence that is initiated and driven by the state. We need to recognize violence across the system and over time, and analyze the ways in which the system itself produces the roles in which people find themselves. Rather than categorizing individual persons, we also need to make distinctions between outer behaviors and inner states at different times—as the diaries of Ruth Andreas-Friedrich and Zygmunt Klukowski remind us.

Can we, or even should we, try to devise other concepts and categories that might be more useful? Certainly, there is much mileage to be gained from looking, for example, at collaborators, beneficiaries, functionaries and facilitators, and other roles on the "perpetrator side," such that the restrictive notions characteristic of German evasions of justice no longer dominate the historiographical landscape or even the landscape of public history. Moreover, some people were supportive, others terrified, while others just tried to keep their heads down and survive. There is so much more to be explored about ways of living through the system of violence that cannot adequately be captured by a simple trilogy.

Are there, nevertheless, ways of making the notion of bystander less of a catchall concept, less of an alibi, and more analytically fruitful? Further questions can be posed about the ways in which people developed responses in a range of directions in changing contexts. Such a discussion might first, for example, take into account the moral choices people make in the light of both ethical and practical considerations, and consider on whose behalf they are acting. Second, we might look at spectrums relating to the context and ask how the wider situation affects people's choices: how likely is an intervention to be effective, and what are the risks of intervening either to oneself or to other people? The latter could include people dear to one, such as members of one's own family, or even other people one is hiding, as in the case of Andreas-Friedrich. Third, the wider context includes the question of how many others would be likely to act in the same way. Choices depend not only on individual morals and politics, as well as weighing up of risks, but also on the likelihood of other people acting in sufficient numbers. Fourth, we may want to pose questions around how later justifications relate to earlier actions (or inaction). Some self-representations might tend to exaggerate claims about risks or about benefits of the ways they acted. If we can systematically compare perceptions at the time (of risk or of capacity for intervention) with later statements, we may unlock many clues to the legacies of collective violence for later self-understandings and evasions—for feelings of guilt, shame, and responsibility.

The exploration of "bystanders," if coupled with a differentiation of "perpetrators" and a recognition of the significance of changing locations within a constantly evolving system of collective violence, could in fact prove highly rewarding. It will take a seismic shift in the historiography to achieve such a transformation, but if this can be achieved, it may help us to understand not only the violence of the times but also the dynamics it unleashed for decades to come.

Mary Fulbrook, FBA, is Professor of German History at University College London. A graduate of Cambridge and Harvard, she is the author or editor of some twenty-five books. Recent major publications include *Reckonings: Legacies of Nazi Persecution and the Quest for Justice* (2018), the Fraenkel Prize–winning *A Small Town near Auschwitz: Ordinary Nazis and the Holocaust* (2012), and *Dissonant Lives: Generations and Violence through the German Dictatorships* (2011; two vols., 2017), all published by Oxford University Press. She has written widely in other areas, including *Historical Theory* (Routledge, 2002) and *German National Identity after the Holocaust* (Polity, 1999), as well as two best-selling overviews of German history, *A Concise History of Germany* (Cambridge University Press, 3rd ed., 2018) and *A History of Germany 1918–2014* (Blackwell, 3rd ed., 2014). Among other professional roles, she currently serves on the Academic Advisory Board of the Buchenwald and Mittelbau-Dora Memorials Foundation.

Notes

1. This is an amended and shortened version of a chapter first published in Mary Fulbrook, *Erfahrung, Erinnerung, Geschichtsschreibung: Neue Perspektiven auf die deutschen Diktaturen* (Göttingen, 2016).
2. Raul Hilberg, *Perpetrators Victims Bystanders: The Jewish Catastrophe 1933–1945* (New York, 1993).
3. Active Bystander Program and Mediation@MIT, "Active Bystanders: Definition & Philosophy," accessed 28 June 2018, http://web.mit.edu/bystanders/definition/index.html.
4. *Merriam-Webster Dictionary*, s.v. "bystander," updated 27 June 2018, http://www.merriam-webster.com/dictionary/bystander.
5. *Oxford Dictionary*, s.v. "bystander," accessed 28 June 2018, http://www.oxforddictionaries.com/definition/english/bystander.
6. Victoria Barnett, *Bystanders: Conscience and Complicity during the Holocaust* (Westport, CT, 1999), 9.
7. Ibid., 10.
8. Raul Hilberg, *The Destruction of the European Jews*, vol. 3, 3rd ed. (New Haven, CT, 2003), 1123.
9. Ibid., 1125.
10. Ibid., 1126.
11. Hilberg, *Perpetrators Victims Bystanders*.
12. Michael R. Marrus, "Acts That Speak for Themselves," *New York Times*, 20 September 1992.
13. Raul Hilberg, *The Politics of Memory: The Journey of a Holocaust Historian* (Chicago, 1996), 189–194.
14. On this, see Susan Bachrach, this volume.
15. Yad Vashem: The World Holocaust Remembrance Center, "Holocaust > The Holocaust Resource Center > Bystanders," accessed 28 June 2018, http://www.yadvashem.org/yv/en/holocaust/resource_center/item.asp?gate=2-52#!prettyPhoto.
16. E.g., Edi Weinstein, "Survivor Edi Weinstein on Germans Selling Jewish Stolen Property to the Poles," in *Quenched Steel: The Story of an Escape from Treblinka*,

ed. Noah Lasman, trans. Naftali Greenwood (Jerusalem 2002), 89–90; Fritzi Schiffer, "From the Testimony of Fritzi Schiffer about the Daily Conditions and the Local Jews of Tashkent during the War," Yad Vashem Archives 0.3-7873, accessed 28 June 2018, http://www.yadvashem.org/odot_pdf/Microsoft%20Word%20-%203845.pdf.
17. Dan Bar-On, "The Bystander in Relation to the Victim and the Perpetrator: Today and during the Holocaust," *Social Justice Research* 14, no. 2 (2001): 127.
18. Ibid., 130.
19. Jack G. Morrison, *Ravensbrück: Everyday Life in a Women's Concentration Camp 1939–45* (Princeton, NJ, 2000); Gordon J. Horwitz, "Places Far Away, Places Very Near: Mauthausen, the Camps of the Shoah, and the Bystanders," in *The Holocaust and History: The Known, the Unknown, the Disputed, and the Reexamined*, ed. Michael Berenbaum and Abraham J. Peck (Bloomington, IN, 1998), 409–420.
20. Gordon J. Horwitz, *In the Shadow of Death: Living Outside the Gates of Mauthausen* (New York, 1990), 43–44; Horwitz, "Places Far Away, Places Very Near," 412.
21. Horwitz, "Places Far Away, Places Very Near," 413.
22. Mary Midgley, *Wickedness* (London, 2001), 62–63, quoted in Horwitz, "Places Far Away, Places Very Near," 416.
23. See also Mary Fulbrook, *Reckonings: Legacies of Nazi Persecution and the Quest for Justice* (Oxford, 2018); Susanne Knittel, this volume.
24. Norbert Frei, *Adenauer's Germany and the Nazi Past* (New York, 2002).
25. See, e.g., the case of Udo Klausa, discussed in Mary Fulbrook, *A Small Town near Auschwitz: Ordinary Nazis and the Holocaust* (Oxford, 2012).
26. Melita Maschmann, *Fazit: Kein Rechtfertigungsversuch* (Stuttgart, 1963), 90.
27. Ibid., 88–89.
28. Ibid., 86.
29. Michael Bryant, *Eyewitness to Genocide: The Operation Reinhard Death Camp Trials, 1955–1966* (Knoxville, TN, 2014), 35–70; more generally, see Fulbrook, *Reckonings*, part 2.
30. Interview in Ahrensburg, Germany, 1979, United States Holocaust Memorial Museum (USHMM), Claude Lanzmann Shoah Collection, Heinz Schubert, Story RG-60.5013, Film IDs 3216, 3217, 3218, 3219.
31. For an exploration of photographs as snapshots of such situations, see Christoph Kreutzmüller, this volume.
32. Zygmunt Klukowski, *Diary from the Years of Occupation 1939–44*, ed. Andrew Klukowski and Helen Klukowski May, trans. George Klukowski (Urbana, IL, 1993).
33. Jan T. Gross, *Neighbors: The Destruction of the Jewish Community in Jedwabne, Poland, 1941* (London, 2003); Antony Polonsky and Joanna Michlic, eds., *The Neighbors Respond: The Controversy over the Jedwabne Massacre in Poland* (Princeton, NJ, 2004); Anna Bikont, *The Crime and the Silence: A Quest for the Truth of a Wartime Massacre*, trans. Alissa Valles (London, 2015).
34. Klukowski, *Diary*, 197, 220.
35. In detail, see Jan Grabowski, *Hunt for the Jews: Betrayal and Murder in German-Occupied Poland* (Bloomington, IN, 2013); Jan Grabowski, this volume.
36. Klukowski, *Diary*, 198.
37. Ibid., 216.
38. Ibid., 194.
39. See, e.g., the accounts in Maria Hochberg-Mariańska and Noe Grüss eds., *The Children Accuse*, trans. Bill Johnstone (London, 1996).
40. Ruth Andreas-Friedrich, *Berlin Underground 1938–1945*, trans. Barrows Mussey (New York, 1947), 83.
41. Ibid., 90–91.

42. See Bart van der Boom, this volume.
43. Hilberg, *Destruction of the European Jews*, 1119–1126.
44. Ibid., 1123.
45. See also ibid., 1125.
46. In fact, Hilberg himself engages in just such a more differentiated analysis—picked up also (if not actually plagiarized) by Hannah Arendt, *Eichmann in Jerusalem: A Report on the Banality of Evil* (New York, 1963).
47. See also Fulbrook, *Reckonings*.

Bibliography

Andreas-Friedrich, Ruth. *Berlin Underground 1938–1945*. Translated by Barrows Mussey. New York: Henry Holt & Co., 1947.

Arendt, Hannah. *Eichmann in Jerusalem: A Report on the Banality of Evil*. New York: Viking, 1963.

Barnett, Victoria. *Bystanders: Conscience and Complicity during the Holocaust*. Westport, CT: Greenwood Press, 1999.

Bar-On, Dan. "The Bystander in Relation to the Victim and the Perpetrator: Today and during the Holocaust." *Social Justice Research* 14, no. 2 (2001): 125–148.

Bikont, Anna. *The Crime and the Silence: A Quest for the Truth of a Wartime Massacre*. Translated by Alissa Valles. London: William Heinemann, 2015.

Bryant, Michael. *Eyewitness to Genocide: The Operation Reinhard Death Camp Trials, 1955–1966*. Knoxville: University of Tennessee Press, 2014.

Frei, Norbert. *Adenauer's Germany and the Nazi Past*. Translated by Joel Golb. New York: Columbia University Press, 2002.

Fulbrook, Mary. *Erfahrung, Erinnerung, Geschichtsschreibung: Neue Perspektiven auf die deutschen Diktaturen*. Göttingen: Wallstein Verlag, 2016.

———. *Reckonings: Legacies of Nazi Persecution and the Quest for Justice*. Oxford: Oxford University Press, 2018.

———. *A Small Town near Auschwitz: Ordinary Nazis and the Holocaust*. Oxford: Oxford University Press, 2012.

Grabowski, Jan. *Hunt for the Jews: Betrayal and Murder in German-Occupied Poland*. Bloomington: Indiana University Press, 2013.

Gross, Jan T. *Neighbors: The Destruction of the Jewish Community in Jedwabne, Poland, 1941*. London: Random House, 2003.

Hilberg, Raul. *The Destruction of the European Jews*. Vol. 3. 3rd ed. New Haven, CT: Yale University Press, 2003.

———. *Perpetrators Victims Bystanders: The Jewish Catastrophe, 1933–1945*. New York: HarperCollins, 1993.

———. *The Politics of Memory: The Journey of a Holocaust Historian*. Chicago: Ivan R. Dee, 1996.

Hochberg-Mariańska, Maria, and Noe Grüss, eds. *The Children Accuse*. Translated by Bill Johnstone. London: Vallentine Mitchell, 1996.

Horwitz, Gordon J. *In the Shadow of Death: Living Outside the Gates of Mauthausen*. New York, 1990.

———. "Places Far Away, Places Very Near: Mauthausen, the Camps of the Shoah, and the Bystanders." In *The Holocaust and History: The Known, the Unknown, the Disputed, and the Reexamined*, edited by Michael Berenbaum and Abraham J. Peck, 409–420. Bloomington: Indiana University Press, 1998.

Klukowski, Zygmunt. *Diary from the Years of Occupation 1939–44*. Edited by Andrew Klukowski and Helen Klukowski May. Translated by George Klukowski. Urbana: University of Illinois Press, 1993.
Maschmann, Melita. *Fazit: Kein Rechtfertigungsversuch*. Stuttgart: Deutsche Verlags-Anstalt, 1963.
Midgley, Mary. *Wickedness*. London: Routledge, 2001.
Morrison, Jack G. *Ravensbrück: Everyday Life in a Women's Concentration Camp 1939–45*. Princeton, NJ: Markus Wiener, 2000.
Polonsky, Antony, and Joanna Michlic, eds. *The Neighbors Respond: The Controversy over the Jedwabne Massacre in Poland*. Princeton, NJ: Princeton University Press, 2004.
Weinstein, Edi. "Survivor Edi Weinstein on Germans Selling Jewish Stolen Property to the Poles." In *Quenched Steel: The Story of an Escape from Treblinka*, edited by Noah Lasman, translated by Naftali Greenwood, 89–90. Jerusalem: Yad Vashem, 2002.

Chapter 2

Raul Hilberg and His "Discovery" of the Bystander

René Schlott

Prologue

According to the memoirs of Raul Hilberg, the origins of his 1992 book *Perpetrators Victims Bystanders*[1] lie in the city of Amsterdam, more than half a century ago. In 1961, shortly after publishing his seminal work *The Destruction of the European Jews,* Hilberg traveled through Europe for the first time since the end of World War II. He spent a month in Italy, France, Austria, Denmark, and the Netherlands visiting the cities' great museums, such as the Rijksmuseum in Amsterdam.[2] As he recalled in his memoirs, published in 1996, Hilberg was especially interested in Renaissance portrait paintings. While studying these images, a new idea came to him: he would create a Holocaust book not about structures, like his first book, but about people. Among other works, the triptychs and paintings of the Christian trinity in the Rijksmuseum inspired him to divide this coming book into three parts that nevertheless belonged together to tell a complete story—to write three seemingly separate sections, which by the end formed a single unit.

Inspiration

In general, the historian needs to be critical with the narratives in autobiographies. Every memoir is a retrospective testimony written years or—like in the case of Raul Hilberg—decades after the actual event. Autobiographical accounts are often highly stylized and constructed.[3] Still, Hilberg's anecdote about the inspiration for his influential "triangle" from a painting belongs to the beginnings of some of the most influential categories in Holocaust research. In this chapter, I will reconstruct Hilberg's introduction of the bystander term into his own work and its subsequent adaption and critique within Holocaust historiography. A third section examines the revealing debates surrounding the manifold translations of the term soon after *Perpetrators Victims Bystanders* was initially published. It shows that the term has both inspired and challenged a thorough reckoning with the role of non-Jewish populations during the Holocaust all across Europe. A brief discussion of criticism closes the chapter.

Interestingly enough, Hilberg did not refer in his memoir to his own experiences with bystanders during his early years in Vienna to explain his interest in the subject. Born in 1926 in Austria's capital, he witnessed as a young boy the mockery of Jews in his hometown. Shortly after the *Anschluss* in March 1938, Jewish Viennese were forced to clean the streets on their knees surrounded by numerous ordinary people watching them.[4] Half a century later, and thirty years after his visit to the Amsterdam museum, the idea of a Holocaust triptych inspired a book about the causes and contexts of the mass murder of the European Jews. Before that, Hilberg himself had "walked through" the different parts of the three-part painting cum grano salis, like the Holocaust historiography after the end of World War II.[5] Following the Nuremberg trials in the 1940s and the evidence that came to light there, his first book, *The Destruction of the European Jews*, based on his Columbia University dissertation of 1955, focused on the perpetrators. He noted in the preface: "This is a book about the people who destroyed the Jews. Not much will be read about the victims. The focus is placed on the perpetrators."[6]

Nevertheless, Hilberg touched upon many "bystander"-related issues in this early work, even though the term itself was not used, as Christopher Browning has concluded:

> One finds in Hilberg little-noted references to the famous Riegner telegram, the obstruction of the State Department, the Morgenthau Report leading to the creation of the War Refugee Board, the failure to bomb Auschwitz

or the rail lines, the Brand mission and the Saly Mayer-Kurt Becher negotiations, and a questioning of the adequacy of the American Jewish leadership's response. In short, virtually every topic of the subsequent debate on the "bystanders" was touched upon by Hilberg.[7]

In the 1970s, Hilberg changed his research in part to focus on the victims.[8] After six years of work, in 1979 he edited the diary of Adam Czerniakow, head of the Jewish Council in the Warsaw ghetto from 1939 to 1942.[9] After the US TV series *Holocaust* was broadcast in 1978, the victims were brought to the forefront of public attention in a general way. However, according to Hilberg, interest in the Holocaust had already been rising slowly since the early 1970s. This development was, in his opinion, a consequence of the Vietnam War. The Holocaust had become a "reference point" some years before the homonymous TV series itself, and the bystander attained urgency in the public conscience of US society when it was faced with the atrocities committed by its own military in Southeast Asia.[10]

The word "bystander" has a longer tradition in Holocaust historiography, even if the term was not widely used before Hilberg's book was published in 1992. Hilberg himself admitted that research on the bystander category was actually initiated by a non-historian much earlier, namely in 1963, with Rolf Hochhuth's *Der Stellvertreter*—released in English under the title *The Representative*—referring to Pope Pius XII (1939–1958), whom Hilberg had called the "supreme bystander."[11] A variation of the triangulation *Perpetrators Victims Bystanders* appeared in 1979 for the first time at a conference in the United States about the *Kirchenkampf* (church struggle), entitled "Human Responses to the Holocaust: Perpetrators and Victims, Bystanders and Resisters."[12] Finally, in his book *The Holocaust in History* published in 1987, Michael Marrus gathered the Allies, the neutral powers, the Vatican, and the Jews of the "free world" under the title "bystanders"—similar to the categorization that Hilberg would adopt.[13]

To my knowledge, Hilberg used the triangle for the first time in December 1985 during a three-day seminar at the International Center for Holocaust Studies in New York City. On that occasion, he also participated in a symposium entitled "Who Was an Accomplice?" next to Frances Henry, the author of *Victims and Neighbors: A Small Town in Germany Remembered* (1984). In 1987, he presented another public paper entitled "The Holocaust in Retrospect: Perpetrators, Victims, Bystanders."[14] By the late 1990s, "bystander" had found entry into the relevant encyclopedias. For example, according to the *Encyclopedia of Genocide* (1999), "bystanders are individuals and groups, including nations that are witnesses to events and choose to ignore them ... The passivity of bystanders significantly increases the likelihood of genocide ... The potential power and therefore responsibility of bystanders is great."[15] In the same year, the American theologian Victoria Barnett published the first monograph dedicated solely to bystanders, proposing the first analytical framework for the varieties of bystander behavior during the Holocaust.[16]

With this brief review of the spread of the concept since the mid-1980s in mind, let us now turn to the genesis of Hilberg's thinking on bystanders. In the revised, second edition of *The Destruction of the European Jews*, published in 1985, he finally extended his view to include the use of "bystander" in his analysis of the Holocaust. He believed that understanding the "'how' of the event is a way of gaining insights into perpetrators, victims, and bystanders. The roles of all three will be described in this work."[17] Yet, even though the subject of the bystander was announced so prominently, it was not treated in more depth in the book—for the time being. Only in the extended, third edition of *The Destruction of the European Jews*, published in 2003, did Hilberg add a new subchapter called "The Neighbors" to his conclusion in chapter 10.[18] The same chapter in the two previous editions only contained a summary of the behavior of perpetrators and victims. According to Hilberg, the neighbors' reactions toward the fate of the Jews were characterized mainly by passivity and indifference. To quote his laconic commentary about the lack of solidarity with the persecuted Jews in occupied France, which he saw as typical for most other European countries: "The intellectuals of Paris could be found in their customary coffee houses. In that city Pablo Picasso went on painting, and Jean-Paul Sartre wrote his plays."[19] I will come back to this remarkable shift toward equating bystanders with neighbors over the course of a decade. In any case, the added chapter was never translated into German. The only available German edition of *The Destruction of the European Jews* is still based on the 1961 manuscript—a fact rarely noticed, as the book indeed remains "the greatest book about the Holocaust that is the least read."[20]

It appears that Hilberg himself discovered—or, taking into account the anecdote about the Amsterdam triptych from his memoirs, rediscovered—bystanders as a group through Claude Lanzmann's *Shoah*.[21] In this documentary, both men can be seen in Hilberg's home in Burlington, Vermont, in January 1979, where they recorded more than six hours of conversation. *Shoah* was released in 1985 and was the first documentary to depict the now commonly used method of triangulation. Hilberg was the only expert whom Lanzmann included in his film besides the perpetrators, victims, and—some German, but mainly

Polish—bystanders themselves. In his memoirs, Hilberg referred to the trichotomy of Lanzmann's documentary to tell the genesis story of his book, and he acknowledged Lanzmann as the first filmmaker who interviewed bystanders for a Holocaust documentary.[22] Moreover, the "Bystanders" section in Hilberg's book is introduced by a quote from Czesław Borowi, a Polish man shown in Lanzmann's film who had lived near Treblinka. When asked by Lanzmann whether he and his fellow farmers feared not only for their own safety but also for that of the Jews, the translator relayed the following response: "Well, he says, it's this way: if I cut my finger, it doesn't hurt him."[23] Hilberg used this sentence to highlight the extent of passivity and indifference among most bystanders.

Composition

In his first appearance in *Shoah*, Hilberg declares:

> In all of my work I have never begun by asking the big questions, because I was always afraid that I would come up with small answers; and I have preferred to address these things which are minutiae or details in order that I might then be able to put together in a gestalt a picture which, if not an explanation, is at least a description, a more full description, of what transpired.[24]

This reflects the character of the bystander section in *Perpetrators Victims Bystanders*. Hilberg does not judge the people who saved Jews or who remained apathetic. In fact, he tries to describe the different reactions and types of behavior. Thus, "bystander" in his work is not an explicit normative term teaching the reader which reaction was wrong and which was right. Nevertheless, the definition of an individual as a bystander has implicit moral connotations. Accordingly, in response to the question, "What can you learn from the history of the Holocaust?" Hilberg answered in 1993, "You can learn to look on."[25] He added that, from 1933 to 1945, besides a small group of perpetrators and a much larger group of victims, bystanders had been the majority—and still, he noted critically, Holocaust scholars had long ignored the mass of bystanders. Yet, he himself had hesitated for a long time to publish anything about bystanders. In January 1986, Hilberg answered a letter asking him to contribute to a book about this subject: "I do not wish to have my preliminary thoughts about bystanders in print. More thought and more research is needed before I can be confident enough to formulate some final conclusions. This cannot be done in the next ten days; I will need a couple of more years."[26] Indeed, it would take six more years of research and writing before he considered these thoughts ripe enough to be printed.

In 1992, shortly after his retirement from the Department of Political Science at the University of Vermont, where he had taught uninterrupted since 1956, the sixty-six-year-old published *Perpetrators Victims Bystanders: The Jewish Catastrophe 1933–1945*. It was only his second book after the publication of the dissertation more than thirty years earlier, and according to Hilberg, this was a book that was "so easy to read, but ... so difficult to write."[27] Hilberg divided the "Bystanders" section in his monograph into seven parts and included widely differing groups, such as helpers, gainers, messengers, rescuers, the Allies, neutral countries, and churches, in fact using "bystander" as an "umbrella term." The book consists of twenty-four subchapters, which Hilberg thought were readable "in any number and any order." Consequently, there is not necessarily a connection between the different chapters.[28]

"Bystanders" is the study's shortest section, spanning sixty-five pages, while the longest section is dedicated to the perpetrators, reflecting Hilberg's main research interest. As art historians point out, the middle part of a triptych is the most important one with the two sidepieces complementing the center. From this perspective and assuming that Hilberg was indeed inspired to use the triptych as a metaphor for his analysis, we can surmise that he consciously decided to put the victims in the center framed by perpetrators and bystanders to concede them a special relevance in this book. The fact that the "Victims" section has, with nine, the most subchapters underlines this idea. The "Bystanders" section begins with an overview concerning the collaboration of different nations in the persecution of their Jewish minorities. What seems banal to us today was important to stress at the time when the book was published: "In each nation, specific historic, cultural and situational factors" must be taken into consideration.[29] Thus, Hilberg walks the reader through German-occupied Europe from East to West, providing insight into prewar Gentile-Jewish relations, the deteriorating conditions under German occupation, and the mass deportations, killings, or occasional rescue of the Jews. The cases of Poland and the Netherlands are discussed in greater detail because of the high Jewish death rate in these countries. However, Polish and Dutch rescuers are mentioned too, and Hilberg stresses how dramatically the two cases differed on the consequences helpers faced if caught by German authorities. While the policy of tracking down hidden Jews in Poland meant death for the helping family, those hiding or saving Jews in the Netherlands would not be executed.

Interestingly, most of the individual rescuers remain anonymous in this chapter or are portrayed only briefly. For example, Hilberg did not mention Raoul Wallenberg (instead, "Sweden" appears in the subchapter "Neutral Countries" as the rescuer of Hungarian Jews), and he dedicates only one sentence to Oskar Schindler and his efforts. The first detailed biographical study appears in the "Messengers" subchapter dedicated to the SS officer Kurt Gerstein. His case shows how difficult it is to place an individual within one single category. Granted, Gerstein was a messenger informing foreign diplomats in the Reich of what he had seen in Belzec and Treblinka in August 1942. On the other hand, he remained in the SS until the end of the war and continued to deliver Zyklon B to Auschwitz. In an even more problematic way, Hilberg portrayed Jan Karski as messenger even though he was married to a Jewish woman, lost his in-laws during the Holocaust, and thus could belong into the victim category too. Throughout his work, Hilberg makes every effort to quantify his findings, concluding that within the bystander group, onlookers were the most numerous, followed by a smaller group of profiteers and still fewer helpers: "Gainers outnumbered givers in the Jewish catastrophe."[30] The motivations for helping, he also points out, were extremely varied, ranging from greed to humanitarianism.

Almost half of the "Bystanders" section is taken up by a subchapter entitled "The Jewish Rescuers," dealing with the activities of different Jewish organizations during World War II. It remains unclear why he placed them here, because these organizations did not stand by but rather took action, as Hilberg describes in detail, even though most of their actions focused on raising attention for the fate of European Jewry in countries such as the United States and the United Kingdom failed. In contrast, Hilberg accuses the "Allies" in his homonymous subchapter of passivity because of their unwillingness to help the Jews even after several "messengers" had informed them about the crimes committed on the Eastern Front.

Translation

In the United States, HarperCollins printed thirty-five thousand copies of the first edition of *Perpetrators Victims Bystanders* in 1992. A year later, S. Fischer Verlag put out fifteen thousand copies of the German translation in Frankfurt.[31] These are impressive numbers for a nonfiction title. They reflect both an increased public interest in the Holocaust and Hilberg's grown reputation in both countries.

From 1989 to 1992, Hilberg and Fischer's editor Walter Pehle were engaged in lengthy discussions around the question of how to translate the English term "bystander" into German. Several translations were considered during this publication process, among them *Unbeteiligte*[32] (noninvolved), *Gaffer*[33] (gazer), *Volksgenossen*[34] (comrades), *Umstehende*,[35] *Zeitgenossen*[36] (contemporaries), and *Gleichgültige*[37] (indifferents). The translator, Hans Günter Holl, opposed the last term because, in his opinion, *Gleichgültige* could be considered too normative and did not apply to the content of the book's bystander section.[38] It is noteworthy that the German editors, according to the written sources, never considered the well-established German term *Mitläufer*[39] (follower) or other expressions like *Mittäter* (co-perpetrators), *Mithelfer* (co-helper), or *Mitwisser* (accomplices) as the best translation. Finally, it was decided to translate the word "bystander" as *Zuschauer*[40] (onlooker). Thereupon, a discussion followed whether to use it with quotation marks on the book cover.[41] Eventually, *Zuschauer* appeared unqualified, yet, unlike in the English original, the three terms were separated by commas.

The monograph was subsequently published in many other languages, and the unique English word "bystander" was translated very differently. In the French and Polish editions, "bystanders" became "witnesses" (*témoins*,[42] *świadkowie*[43]); in the Italian translation, "spectators" (*spettatori*),[44] like in the German and Czech editions (*Zuschauer*, *diváci*).[45] In Dutch, "bystanders" became *omstanders*,[46] and in Lithuanian, "observers" (*stebėtojai*).[47] This reflects not only how broad and vague the original term is—only the Dutch *omstander* matches the English "bystander." The varied translations also raise questions about the Holocaust memorial cultures of these different—formerly German occupied—countries. To witness an event is, in terms of responsibility, quite different than to observe or simply watch it.[48]

Hilberg himself was aware of the particular national contexts his work was translated to. The dedications vary from edition to edition. The English edition of *Perpetrators Victims Bystanders* was dedicated to Hilberg's second wife, Gwendolyn, who kept him free for the work on the book. The French translation *Exécuteurs, victimes, témoins: La catastrophe juive 1933–1945* was inscribed to Claude Lanzmann. Finally, the German translation *Täter, Opfer, Zuschauer: Die Vernichtung der Juden 1933–1945* was dedicated to German Prior Bernhard Lichtenberg.[49] The book, in fact, ends with a biopic of Lichtenberg as a nontypical bystander, who prayed openly for the persecuted Jews in Berlin's most important Catholic church and, after being arrested by the Gestapo in October 1941, died during a prisoner transport in November 1943.[50]

Critics

Hilberg's 1992 book was published during resonant contemporary events. A wave of xenophobia attacks occurred in Germany in 1992—including murders of immigrants, as happened in the city of Moelln—frequently encouraged and cheered on by large groups of bystanders, as observed in Rostock-Lichtenhagen. Some reviews mentioned this coincidence.[51] Hilberg himself also considered in a letter to his French editor, "The events in Germany have pushed interest in the book to a peak."[52] In June of the same year, a civil war broke out in Bosnia, and Europe and the United States were challenged not to look on as Yugoslavian forces and Bosnian Serbs were killing thousands of Bosnian civilians. The context for the reception of the book was thus marked by dramatic events involving issues of perpetration and bystanding as human beings were once again being victimized on a massive scale.

Most of the reviews at that time saw Hilberg's book as a supplement to his thirty-year-old classic *The Destruction of the European Jews* and judged it benevolently. The German Holocaust scholar Eberhard Jäckel in *Die Zeit* reviewed the book's idea as "groundbreaking" (*umstürzend*).[53] Jäckel regrets the German translation *Zuschauer* for "bystander," precisely because most bystanders did not look on but looked away. John K. Roth stated in *Holocaust and Genocide Studies* that Hilberg generally concluded for the bystanders that "too little was done too late by too few."[54] Shortly after its publication, Michael Marrus reviewed the book in the *New York Times*, underlining its accusatory tone.[55] This criticism was not new to Hilberg, as he had experienced the same with his first book when an anonymous reviewer called him a "polemical prosecutor."[56] Still, the reading of Marrus's review hurt him.[57] Hilberg's autobiography begins with a gloomy chapter titled "The Review," meaning Marrus's *New York Times* article in which Marrus called Hilberg "less a pathfinder than a conscience."

Mary Fulbrook recently recurred to Marrus's criticism and sees Hilberg's notion of bystander as more an accusatory than an analytical category.[58] There is some truth in this appraisal, but I do not think that Hilberg's bystander chapter is so one-dimensional. First, the portrayal of figures likes Bernhard Lichtenberg, Jan Karski, or Gerhart M. Riegner is not at all accusatory. Their behavior is in fact an example of great courage in a world of indifference. Second, Hilberg offers, in my opinion, the notion "bystander" primarily as an analytical category, as the "necessary third party" besides perpetrators and victims.

To Hilberg, the indifference of most of this "third party" was a conditio sine qua non for the destruction process. If the Germans or the Dutch had protested in masses against the deportations of their neighbors, the process would have been disrupted. What if the churches had reminded every single Christian clear and loud of the Bible's fifth commandment or the allies had destroyed the railroads? In Hilberg eyes, the silence in most of the occupied societies made them accomplices. Only their indifference had made the "final solution" possible. To state this could indeed be seen as an accusation, but it should foremost be read as a way to explain the crucial role of the "bystanders" as the "third party" in the destruction process.

Others, like Efraim Zuroff, criticized the book for Hilberg's treatment of the Jewish councils and accused him of minimizing the Jewish resistance. Zuroff closed his review in *The Jerusalem Report* with the cynical remark: "One can only hope that in the future Hilberg will concentrate on the perpetrators."[59]

With Lanzmann's *Shoah* (1985), with Christopher Browning's *Ordinary Men* (1992), and finally with Hilberg's second book, a new phase perhaps began that focused on ordinary people and their testimonies in Holocaust literature while the perpetrator research was also flourishing with authors like Ulrich Herbert, Omer Bartov, and Götz Aly.[60] Hilberg's approach to analyze the Holocaust from at least three—but actually many more—points of view could be seen also as one of the first steps toward an integrated history of the Holocaust qualified by a multidimensional perspective of the people in their time.[61] In 1997, Saul Friedländer implemented this idea most consistently when he published the first part of his magnum opus, in which he spent more time on the victims and their records.[62]

The discussion about Hilberg's triangulation began right after the publication. In his preface, Hilberg himself admitted that the trichotomy concept of his work was not infallible and certainly too schematic, as "in some areas, bystanders became perpetrators themselves."[63] In the course of its gradual adaption, the triptych was often extended, and other categories that modified the term "bystander" were added. For example, the American psychologist Ervin Staub added the category of "heroic helpers."[64] He also made a distinction between internal and external bystanders depending on whether they belonged to the perpetrator society.[65] Some added "rescuers" to Hilberg's triangle,[66] or referred to "bystanders" as "semiactive participants."[67] Still others, like Harald Welzer, argued that there was no such thing as a bystander, because even passive and indifferent Germans became part of a dualistic social constellation of perpetrators and their victims.[68]

Moreover, the fact that Hilberg, as noted earlier, titled his subchapter in the 2003 edition of *Destruction* "Neighbors" and not "Bystanders," points to his own conceptual insecurity and could be interpreted as a sign that he was aware of the difficulties that the term caused as he had used it in *Perpetrators Victims Bystanders* in 1992. Apparently, he grew so uncomfortable with it that he became reluctant to repeat it a decade later.

Epilogue

To close the chapter, I will return to the place where it opened: Amsterdam. The city is mentioned five times in Hilberg's *Perpetrators Victims Bystanders*. Not surprisingly, Amsterdam figures prominently in the bystander section:

> Unlike the Jews who spoke Yiddish in Warsaw, or the Jews who spoke Ladino in Salonika, the Jews of Amsterdam and all the other Dutch cities conversed in the language of their neighbors. Yet they died in proportions that recall the fate of Eastern and Balkan Jews... How could it have happened to such an extent on Netherlands soil?[69]

With this question, also called the "Dutch paradox," and with his entire book, Hilberg established a new standard in Holocaust research. He set the beginning for ongoing discussions, not offering a real theoretical approach but proposing to think about new classifications to reveal the dynamics of destruction in societies confronted with the National Socialists' anti-Jewish policies. Despite the many reasonably objections pleaded by other Holocaust scholars in the past twenty-five years since the publication of the book, Hilberg's triad *Perpetrators Victims Bystanders* remains an important albeit contested point of departure for seeking answers to the fundamental questions raised by human behavior during the Holocaust and offers a more sophisticated historiography of the bystanders, as demanded by some scholars.[70] For those who were neither victims nor perpetrators, Hilberg's introduction of the "catchall" term "bystander" became a classic of Holocaust literature. Furthermore, Hilberg's book offers a systematics for the variety of social behaviors involved in the Holocaust: a dramatis personae facing the genocide. Even if some historians currently state that in different situations, the same person could be victim, perpetrator, or "bystander" in one.[71]

Finally, the vagueness of Hilberg's categorization provided a continuing impulse for other researchers to explore the bystander issue more thoroughly and to ask new questions. What is for sure, though, is the incompleteness of any neat categorization of the people who were ensnared in the Holocaust. Even if we were to differentiate the categories or modify the terms, we would still lack the appropriate words to capture the immensity of the extermination process and its countless participants. And unlike what many critics suggest, Hilberg knew very well, that the "complexity cuts across perpetrator, victim and bystander," as he admitted in 1990 at a conference at the Vrije Universiteit Amsterdam.[72]

René Schlott is a historian and researcher at the Centre for Contemporary History in Potsdam and teaches history at the universities of Potsdam and Berlin. He received his PhD in 2011 from the University of Giessen and is currently working as a postdoc on the first biography of life, work, and legacy of Raul Hilberg. In 2017, he was awarded a three-year scholarship (*Habilitationsstipendium*) from the Konrad-Adenauer-Stiftung for his research project. He is coeditor, with Walter H. Pehle, of *Anatomie des Holocaust: Essays und Erinnerungen von Raul Hilberg* (S. Fischer Verlag, 2016).

Notes

1. Raul Hilberg, *Perpetrators Victims Bystanders: The Jewish Catastrophe, 1933–1945* (New York, 1992).
2. Raul Hilberg, *The Politics of Memory: The Journey of a Holocaust Historian* (Chicago, 1996), 189.
3. Michaela Holdenried, "Biographie vs. Autobiographie," in *Handbuch Biographie: Methoden, Traditionen, Theorien*, ed. Christian Klein (Stuttgart, 2009), 41.
4. See photograph no. 03741 in the collection of the United States Holocaust Memorial.
5. See Saul Friedländer, "The Extermination of the European Jews in Historiography: Fifty Years Later," in *Thinking about the Holocaust: After Half a Century,* ed. Alvin H. Rosenfeld (Bloomington, IN, 1997).
6. Raul Hilberg, *The Destruction of the European Jews: A Documented Narrative History* (Chicago, 1961), v.
7. Christopher R. Browning, "The Revised Hilberg," *Simon Wiesenthal Annual* 3 (1986), http://motlc.wiesenthal.com/site/pp.asp?c=gvKVLcMVIuG&b=395051. Browning refers to Hilberg, *Destruction*, 718–722.
8. Cf. Federico Finchelstein, "The Holocaust Canon: Rereading Raul Hilberg," *New German Critique*, no. 96 (2005): 29.
9. Raul Hilberg, Stanislaw Staron, and Josef Kermisz, eds., *The Warsaw Diary of Adam Czerniakow* (New York, 1979).
10. Raul Hilberg, "Working on the Holocaust," *Psychohistory Review* 14, no. 3 (1986): 10.
11. Hilberg, *Perpetrators Victims Bystanders*, xi.

12. Michael D. Ryan, ed., *Human Responses to the Holocaust: Perpetrators and Victims, Bystanders and Resisters—Papers on the 1979 Bernhard E. Olson Scholars' Conference on The Church Struggle and the Holocaust* (New York, 1981).
13. Michael R. Marrus, *The Holocaust in History* (Hanover, NH, 1987).
14. Raul Hilberg, "The Holocaust in Retrospect: Perpetrators, Victims, Bystanders," paper presented at the Stevens Institute of Technology, Hoboken, NJ, 21 April 1987.
15. Ervin Staub, "Bystanders to Genocide," in *Encyclopedia of Genocide*, vol. 1, ed. Israel W. Charny (Santa Barbara, CA, 1999), 127–128.
16. Victoria J. Barnett, *Bystanders: Conscience and Complicity during the Holocaust* (Westport, CT, 1999), xvi.
17. Raul Hilberg, *The Destruction of the European Jews*, vol. 1, 2nd ed. (New York, 1985), ix.
18. Raul Hilberg, *The Destruction of the European Jews*, vol. 3, 3rd ed. (New Haven, CT, 2003), 1119–1126.
19. Ibid., 1122.
20. Doris L. Bergen, "Out of the Limelight or In: Raul Hilberg, Gerhard Weinberg, Henry Friedlander, and the Historical Study of the Holocaust," in *The Second Generation: Émigrés from Nazi Germany as Historians*, ed. Andreas W. Daum, Hartmut Lehmann, and James J. Sheehan (New York, 2016), 230.
21. Claude Lanzmann, dir., *Shoah* (Paris, 1985).
22. Hilberg, *Politics of Memory*, 191; Douglas Century, "Hilbergs 'Rashomon,'" *Forward*, 2 October 1992, 10.
23. Hilberg, *Perpetrators Victims Bystanders*, 193.
24. Claude Lanzmann, *Shoah: An Oral History of the Holocaust* (New York, 1985), 70.
25. "Gespräch in Drei," Klaus Schulz in a conversation with Raul Hilberg, *Sender Freies Berlin 3*, 8 May 1993.
26. Raul Hilberg to Dennis Klein, 2 January 1986, Raul Hilberg Papers, University of Vermont, box 5, folder 36.
27. Discussion with Raul Hilberg, Literaturhaus Wien November 1992, Record Archive Walter Pehle.
28. Hilberg, *Perpetrators Victims Bystanders*, xii.
29. Ibid., 195–196.
30. Ibid., 214.
31. Walter Pehle to Raul Hilberg, 25 June 1993, Archive S. Fischer Verlag.
32. Walter Pehle to Raul Hilberg, 12 March 1992, Archive S. Fischer Verlag.
33. Handwritten notice by Walter Pehle dated 31 January 1989, after a meeting with Raul Hilberg in Frankfurt, Archive S. Fischer Verlag.
34. Walter Pehle to Raul Hilberg, 30 October 1991, Archive S. Fischer Verlag.
35. Raul Hilberg to Walter Pehle, 9 November 1991, Archive S. Fischer Verlag.
36. Raul Hilberg to Walter Pehle, 15 December 1991, Archive S. Fischer Verlag.
37. Walter Pehle to Raul Hilberg and Hans Günter Holl, 30 March 1992, Archive S. Fischer Verlag.
38. Hans Günter Holl to Walter Pehle, 31 March 1992, Archive S. Fischer Verlag.
39. Gesine Schwan, "Der Mitläufer," in *Deutsche Erinnerungsorte*, vol. 1, ed. Étienne François and Hagen Schulze (Munich, 2001), 654–669.
40. Walter Pehle to Raul Hilberg, 6 March 1992, Archive S. Fischer Verlag.
41. Walter Pehle to Raul Hilberg, 12 March 1992, Archive S. Fischer Verlag.
42. Raul Hilberg, *Exécuteurs, victimes, témoins: La catastrophe juive 1933–1945* (Paris, 1994).
43. Raul Hilberg, *Sprawcy, Ofiary, Świadkowie: Zagłada Żydów, 1933–1945* (Warsaw, 2007).

44. Raul Hilberg, *Carnefici, vittime, spettatori: La persecuzione degli ebrei 1933–45* (Milan, 1994).
45. Raul Hilberg, *Pachatelé, oběti, diváci: Židovská katastrofa 1933–1945* (Prague, 2002).
46. Raul Hilberg, *Daders Slachtoffers Omstanders: De joodse catastrofe 1933–1945* (Haarlem, 1993).
47. Raul Hilberg, *Nusikaltėliai, aukos, stebėtojai: Žydų tragedija 1933–1945* (Vilnius, 1999).
48. Cf. Roma Sendyka, this volume.
49. Raul Hilberg, *Täter, Opfer, Zuschauer: Die Vernichtung der Juden 1933–1945* (Frankfurt, 1992), 7.
50. Hilberg, *Perpetrators Victims Bystanders*, 268.
51. E.g., Christian Semler, "In Übereinstimmung mit der Führung," *Die Tageszeitung*, 30 September 1992, xiv. In this newspaper, the book is wrongly entitled "Täter, Opfer, 'Unbeteiligte.'"
52. Raul Hilberg to Eric Vigne, 5 December 1992, Archive Gallimard Paris.
53. Eberhard Jäckel, "Wie es geschehen konnte," *Die Zeit*, no. 41 (1992): 119.
54. John K. Roth, "Review to Raul Hilberg: Perpetrators Victims Bystanders," *Holocaust and Genocide Studies* 8, no. 2 (1994): 280.
55. Michael R. Marrus, "Acts That Speak for Themselves," *New York Times*, 20 September 1992.
56. Henry H. Wiggins to Raul Hilberg, 29 December 1958, Institutional Archive of the United States Holocaust Memorial Museum.
57. Hilberg, *Politics of Memory*, 15–18.
58. See Mary Fulbrook, this volume.
59. Efraim Zuroff, "The Mystery of Evil, the Quality of Mercy," *The Jerusalem Report*, 3 December 1992, 48.
60. Frank Bajohr, "Täterforschung: Ertrag, Probleme und Perspektiven eines Forschungsansatzes," in *Der Holocaust: Ergebnisse und neue Fragen der Forschung*, ed. Frank Bajohr and Andrea Löw (Frankfurt, 2015), 167–185.
61. Saul Friedländer, "Den Holocaust beschreiben: Auf dem Weg zu einer integrierten Geschichte," in *Den Holocaust beschreiben: Auf dem Weg zu einer integrierten Geschichte*, ed. Saul Friedländer (Göttingen, 2007), 7–27. Cf. Michael Wildt, "Raul Hilberg and Saul Friedländer: Two Perspectives on the Holocaust," in *Years of Persecution, Years of Extermination: Saul Friedländer and the Future of Holocaust Studies*, ed. Christian Wiese and Paul Betts (London, 2010), 111: "Hilberg and Friedländer have more in common than the first glance might suggest." Cf. Ulrich Herbert, "Holocaust-Forschung in Deutschland: Geschichte und Perspektiven einer schwierigen Disziplin," in Bajohr and Löw, *Der Holocaust*, 57: "Friedländers Postulat von der integrierten Geschichte des Holocaust ... wurde von Raul Hilberg mit den Kategorien Täter-Opfer-Bystander operationalisiert."
62. Saul Friedländer, *The Years of Persecution, 1933–1939* (New York, 1997).
63. Hilberg, *Perpetrators Victims Bystanders*, xi.
64. Ervin Staub, "The Psychology of Bystanders, Perpetrators, and Heroic Helpers," *International Journal of Intercultural Relations* 17 (1993): 315–341.
65. Staub, "Bystanders to Genocide," 127.
66. Adam Jones, ed., *Genocide, Vol. 3: Perpetrators, Victims, Bystanders, Rescuers* (Los Angeles, 2008).
67. Ervin Staub, "The Psychology of Bystanders, Perpetrators, and Heroic Helpers," in Jones, *Genocide*, 17.

68. Harald Welzer, "Vom Zeit- zum Zukunftszeugen: Vorschläge zur Modernisierung der Erinnerungskultur," in *Die Geburt des Zeitzeugen nach 1945*, ed. Martin Sabrow and Norbert Frei (Göttingen, 2012), 37.
69. Hilberg, *Perpetrators Victims Bystanders*, 210.
70. Donald Bloxham and Tony Kushner, *The Holocaust: Critical Historical Approaches* (Manchester, 2005), 176.
71. Cf. Anna-Raphaela Schmitz, "Report to the Conference 'The Holocaust and European Societies: Social Processes and Social Dynamics,'" *H-Soz-Kult*, 24 January 2015, http://www.hsozkult.de/conferencereport/id/tagungsberichte-5789. Hilberg expressed the same idea in an interview in *Süddeutsche Zeitung*, 10–11 July 1993, 14.
72. Raul Hilberg, "The Discovery of the Holocaust," paper presented at the symposium "De Holocaust en heden," Amsterdam Vrije Universiteit, 11 September 1990, Raul Hilberg Papers, University of Vermont, box 2, folder 17.

Bibliography

Bajohr, Frank. "Täterforschung: Ertrag, Probleme und Perspektiven eines Forschungsansatzes." In Bajohr and Löw, *Der Holocaust*, 167–185.
Bajohr, Frank, and Andrea Löw, eds. *Der Holocaust: Ergebnisse und neue Fragen der Forschung*. Frankfurt: S. Fischer, 2015.
Barnett, Victoria J. *Bystanders: Conscience and Complicity during the Holocaust*. Westport, CT: Greenwood Press, 1999.
Bergen, Doris L. "Out of the Limelight or In: Raul Hilberg, Gerhard Weinberg, Henry Friedlander, and the Historical Study of the Holocaust." In *The Second Generation: Émigrés from Nazi Germany as Historians*, edited by Andreas W. Daum, Hartmut Lehmann, and James J. Sheehan, 229–243. New York: Berghahn Books, 2016.
Bloxham, Donald, and Tony Kushner. *The Holocaust: Critical Historical Approaches*. Manchester: Manchester University Press, 2005.
Browning, Christopher R. "The Revised Hilberg." *Simon Wiesenthal Center Annual* 3 (1986). http://motlc.wiesenthal.com/site/pp.asp?c=gvKVLcMVIuG&b=395051.
Finchelstein, Federico. "The Holocaust Canon: Rereading Raul Hilberg." *New German Critique*, no. 96 (2005): 3–48.
Friedländer, Saul. "Den Holocaust beschreiben: Auf dem Weg zu einer integrierten Geschichte." In *Den Holocaust beschreiben: Auf dem Weg zu einer integrierten Geschichte*, edited by Saul Friedländer, 7–27. Göttingen: Wallstein 2007.
———. "The Extermination of the European Jews in Historiography: Fifty Years Later." In *Thinking about the Holocaust: After Half a Century*, edited by Alvin H. Rosenfeld, 3–17. Bloomington: Indiana University Press, 1997.
———. *The Years of Persecution, 1933–1939*. New York: HarperCollins, 1997.
Herbert, Ulrich. "Holocaust-Forschung in Deutschland: Geschichte und Perspektiven einer schwierigen Disziplin." In Bajohr and Löw, *Der Holocaust*, 31–79.
Hilberg, Raul. *Carnefici, vittime, spettatori: La persecuzione degli ebrei 1933–45*. Milan: Mondadori, 1994.
———. *Daders Slachtoffers Omstanders: De joodse catastrofe 1933–1945*. Haarlem: Becht, 1993.
———. *The Destruction of the European Jews: A Documented Narrative History*. Chicago: Quadrangle Books, 1961.
———. *The Destruction of the European Jews*. Vol. 1. 2nd ed. New York: Holmes & Meier, 1985.

―――. *The Destruction of the European Jews*. Vol. 3. 3rd ed. New Haven, CT: Yale University Press, 2003.
―――. *Exécuteurs, victimes, témoins: La catastrophe juive 1933–1945*. Paris: Éditions Gallimard, 1994.
―――. *Sprawcy, Ofiary, Świadkowie: Zagłada Żydów, 1933–1945*. Warsaw: Wydawnictwo Cyklady, 2007.
―――. *Nusikaltėliai, aukos, stebėtojai: Žydų tragedija 1933–1945*. Vilnius: Mokslo ir enciklopedijų leidybos institutas, 1999.
―――. *Pachatelé, oběti, diváci: Židovská katastrofa 1933–1945*. Prague: Argo, 2002.
―――. *Perpetrators Victims Bystanders: The Jewish Catastrophe, 1933–1945*. New York: HarperCollins, 1992.
―――. *The Politics of Memory: The Journey of a Holocaust Historian*. Chicago: Ivan R. Dee, 1996.
―――. *Täter, Opfer, Zuschauer: Die Vernichtung der Juden 1933–1945*. Frankfurt: S. Fischer Verlag, 1992.
―――. "Working on the Holocaust." *Psychohistory Review* 14, no. 3 (1986): 7–20.
Hilberg, Raul, Stanislaw Staron, and Josef Kermisz, eds. *The Warsaw Diary of Adam Czerniakow*. New York: Stein and Day, 1979.
Holdenried, Michaela. "Biographie vs. Autobiographie." In *Handbuch Biographie: Methoden, Traditionen, Theorien*, edited by Christian Klein, 37–43. Stuttgart: Metzler, 2009.
Jäckel, Eberhard. "Wie es geschehen konnte." *Die Zeit*, no. 41 (1992): 119.
Jones, Adam, ed. *Genocide, Vol. 3: Perpetrators, Victims, Bystanders, Rescuers*. Los Angeles: Sage, 2008.
Lanzmann, Claude, *Shoah*. Paris: Fayard, 1985.
―――. *Shoah: An Oral History of the Holocaust*. New York: Pantheon, 1985.
Marrus, Michael R. *The Holocaust in History*. Hanover, NH: University Press of New England, 1987.
Roth, John K. "Review to Raul Hilberg: Perpetrators Victims Bystanders." *Holocaust and Genocide Studies* 8, no. 2 (1994): 276–280.
Ryan, Michael D., ed. *Human Responses to the Holocaust: Perpetrators and Victims, Bystanders and Resisters—Papers on the 1979 Bernhard E. Olson Scholars' Conference on the Church Struggle and the Holocaust*. New York: E. Mellen Press, 1981.
Schmitz, Anna-Raphaela. "Report to the Conference 'The Holocaust and European Societies: Social Processes and Social Dynamics.'" *H-Soz-Kult*, 24 January 2015. http://www.hsozkult.de/conferencereport/id/tagungsberichte-5789.
Schwan, Gesine. "Der Mitläufer." In *Deutsche Erinnerungsorte*, vol. 1, edited by Étienne François and Hagen Schulze, 654–669. Munich: C. H. Beck, 2001.
Staub, Ervin. "Bystanders to Genocide." In *Encyclopedia of Genocide*, edited by Israel W. Charny, 127–128. Santa Barbara, CA: ABC-CLIO, 1999.
―――. "The Psychology of Bystanders, Perpetrators, and Heroic Helpers." *International Journal of Intercultural Relations* 17 (1993): 315–341.
―――. "The Psychology of Bystanders, Perpetrators, and Heroic Helpers." In Jones *Genocide*, 4–32.
Welzer, Harald. "Vom Zeit- zum Zukunftszeugen: Vorschlage zur Modernisierung der Erinnerungskultur." In *Die Geburt des Zeitzeugen nach 1945*, edited by Martin Sabrow and Norbert Frei, 33–48. Göttingen: Wallstein, 2012.
Wildt, Michael. "Raul Hilberg and Saul Friedländer: Two Perspectives on the Holocaust." In *Years of Persecution, Years of Extermination: Saul Friedländer and the Future of Holocaust Studies*, edited by Christian Wiese and Paul Betts, 101–113. London: Continuum, 2010.

Chapter 3

Bystanders as Visual Subjects
Onlookers, Spectators, Observers, and Gawkers in Occupied Poland

Roma Sendyka

"Out of Sight"

The well-known precautions taken by Germans to hide the "final solution" from view suggest that no other sense was so obsessively controlled as the sense of sight.[1] On the one hand, any activity that might have rendered visual testimony was prohibited (i.e., viewing, photographing). The camps were built in woods; crematoria were curtained with bushes. The roundups took place in the early morning hours—windows were shut, blinds drawn, and cars sealed, and locals were ordered to stay indoors. The processes of visual control were developed not only outside but also inside the bystanders' community: the *voyeurs* were "not welcomed," the *watching* "indecent," the *spectacle* an "irritant," the *scene*—regardless if "repelling or attracting"—was considered "a threat."[2] On the other hand, many forms of atrocities were (made) excessively visible. As Patrick Desbois, an expert on the "Holocaust by bullets," writes: "I had always been told that the Jews had been murdered in secret in the middle of the woods, far from view. In other words,

I had the greatest difficulty accepting that they had been killed in the middle of the village and believing the veracity of the testimonies I was gathering."[3]

These observations, which remain at the core of discussions on bystanders, serve as basis for the hypothesis that any conceptualization of bystanders must embrace their faculty of being visual subjects. In other words, there is an urgent need to augment the bystander's ontology through the theory of spectatorship, expanding definitions, which are merely based on topographical or temporal closeness to events. Following Jan T. Gross, I will go against the assumption that "a bystander is a person who just accidentally happens to be nearby." Instead, I stress the importance of examining the bystander's scopic decisions. As Gross notes, "a bystander could just as well be someone who turns his back on the event, occupied by his own concerns, or a person who is standing on her tiptoes in the crowd of gawkers."[4] Efforts to define bystanders usually acknowledge the diversity of a group (individuals, institutions, nations) and often follow Raul Hilberg's functional approach in discussing the different types of actions taken in the face of the Holocaust.[5] Discussions since then have further complicated the act of "being present," allegedly passive, into one of "facilitating"[6] and "benefiting,"[7] and even characterized as "upstanding," "taking messages," "rescuing," "documenting," not to mention "provoking" and "legitimizing."[8] I would suggest that the bystanders' faculty of "watching the Holocaust" needs similar scrutiny leading to more specific and varied approaches. The act of looking is central in this regard (Victoria J. Barnett has noted the "individual act of silently watching the public humiliation of local Jews"[9] or the "observant passivity"[10] of bystanders). The synonyms provided in lexicons only reinforce the visual faculty of being a bystander: a bystander is synonymous with onlooker, passerby, spectator, witness, observer, viewer, looker-on, watcher, eyewitness,[11] voyeur, or rubbernecker.[12] If so many and various actions are implicated in the act of bystanding, the field of visual culture studies can provide useful tools for critically analyzing seemingly self-evident behavior.[13]

Genealogy of Visuality

Since at least 1987, when W. J. T. Mitchell published his *Iconology: Image, Text, Ideology*,[14] a new interdisciplinary field called visual culture studies, or simply visual culture, grew into a complex approach for analyzing vision and visuality.[15] Over the next three decades, the body of knowledge has accumulated, and it is now impossible to refer to acts of visual activity as being merely explainable by optics, as "an easy and naturally acquired skill."[16] Instead, there are now sophisticated, culture-dependent protocols of "double coding." Visual field scholars call them visual literacies—"highly cultivated and trained experiences and techniques of visual observation."[17] In his influential *Picture Theory* (1995), Mitchell famously identifies the need to "realize that spectatorship (the look, the gaze, the glance, the practices of observation, surveillance, and visual pleasure) may be as deep a problem as various forms of reading (decipherment, decoding, interpretation, etc.),"[18] which seems especially appropriate for those analyzing bystanders' and witnesses' testimonies. Yet, it is rare to find attempts that merge the theory of visual culture with historical investigations of bystanders.[19]

Relying on the findings of visual culture scholars, I argue that critical analysis of four terms regularly used as mere synonyms for the "viewing subject"[20] may change the parameters of investigating bystanders. As I will demonstrate for the "onlooker," the "spectator," the "observer," and the "gawker," etymological criticism may sharpen the conceptual tools and make the taxonomies more nuanced. Yet, I will not go into a separate discussion of the "witness" or the "eyewitness," as this is since antiquity a person who appears in court as a third party, ready and able to give testimony.[21] The visual subject I define here precedes the able-to-speak subject. When observing bystanders as visual subjects and not yet witnesses, we may gain the access to the primary experience of bystanding: when the violence has been perceived but leaves the person dumbed or still, unable to formulate opinion. The visual path into researching the bystander allows for an understanding of the pre-semantic, nonsymbolic, affective, and somatic part of the bystander experience. I now turn to four central terms of viewing.

The "onlooker," meaning someone who *looks on* something, is etymologically derived from the Old English *locian* meaning the "use of the eyes." In Old English, the verb "looking" was used with the preposition *on*; the use of *at* began in fourteenth century. The term *on*looker (since the noun *at*looker was not devised) therefore has an archaic flair, morphing the onlooker into a historical and even primordial figure who does as much as opens his eyes, directing the optical organ toward an object. The proverbial "they look, but they don't really see," from Matthew 13:13, suggests that the onlooker is not processing the data acquired. The onlooker, one may say, is simply a camera with open lenses, certainly not an automatic one: "We only see what we look at. *To look is an act of choice*,"[22] wrote the influential theorist of gaze John Berger. Visual culture scholars stress an important aspect of this seemingly neutral optical action: the *right to look*[23] is differentiated socially, racially, gender-, and class-wise. As Griselda Pollock put it, visual theory helped develop a "critique of the kinds of ideologies that imagine there is a pure realm of vision that exist before gender, race, class and all other social influences."[24] Marita Sturken and Lisa Cartwright called for a nuanced socially oriented analysis of acts of looking: "Through looking we negotiate social relationships and meanings. Looking is a practice much like speaking, writing or singing ... [and] involves relationships of power."[25]

The term "spectator" comes from Latin *spectare*, which is from the earlier *spectō*. It designates someone who watches a *spectaculum*, or a public event. From Aristotelian times, it has been connected with theatrical performances and therefore connotes a strong affective component. A spectator is thus a member of a community, already organized around an object, with preexisting protocols on how to refer to it: the script is applied to the spectator's senses, body movements, and behavior. For that reason, a spectator cannot provide a fully individual and independent account of what they see: a preexisting public/institutional scenario will always be part of their report. Nineteenth-century connotations made spectators passive and pleasure-driven, as Jacques Rancière[26] had put it: submissive, ignorant, immobile, stultified—or bored. This again suggests that affects are here the main receptive channel. The seminal, polemical 1967 *Society of the Spectacle* by Guy Debord connected the spectator with passive consumerism. Here spectators are alienated by the powers of the capitalist market, but bound together in a relation to a dominant spectacle.[27] Moreover, a spectator is also a gendered figure: the word *spectatress* and the more classically correct *spectatrix* were used since the early 1600s; the contemporary domination of a noun used for male subjects might reveal the presumption, almost imperceptible today, that the normative spectator figure is male.

The "observer," as discussed by Jonathan Crary in his 1992 *Techniques of the Observer*, is the most complicated figure so far. The observer in the sixteenth century was one who keeps a rule, custom, and so on; the meaning of "one who watches and takes notice" was a later development. The observer sees, analyses, and uses external protocols for this procedure. *Observare* means "to conform one's action, to comply with," so an observer is tethered by external rules, never able to act of their own accord. Again, it is a situation in which one is not able to produce an individualized account of a scene, but an observer exists "only as an *effect* of an irreducibly heterogeneous system of discursive, social, technological, and institutional relations. There is no observing subject prior to this continually shifting field."[28] The observer's attitude is the most "scientific" and emotionless: the frame here is mostly cognitive. The observer works with calculated precision, calmly deliberating their actions: they are able to take notes, compare, and analyze as a subject working in a laboratory, observing samples and specimens. Similar to the figures of onlooker and spectator, the observer is "both the historical product and the site of certain practices, techniques, institutions, and procedures of subjectification."[29]

The visual genealogy of the concept of bystanders may be extended even further and indeed should be, encompassing other scopic terms. The fourth and final notion to be highlighted is one much used lately in Poland in discussions about Polish bystanders. In a powerful book *Polski teatr Zagłady* (Polish theater of the Shoah), the theater critic Grzegorz Niziołek formed the strong thesis that postwar Polish culture was generally a culture of "'witnesses,' 'observers' or even 'gawkers'" (*gapie*).[30] It is hard to find a close enough equivalent to translate the Polish derogative, even contemptuous word *gapie*: *les badauds* and *Schaulustige* are close to the core meaning of the term describing those who look with passive, thoughtless pleasure on someone else's misfortune. In Polish, the word is commonly used in the plural form. The aforementioned gives the possibility of defining gawkers as those who have spontaneously gathered, bonded by guilty pleasure, driven by morbid curiosity, rubbernecking to have a better view, away from direct danger: a hybrid, multipersonal visual subject with no will of its own, just passive subservience to primitive desires—the context here would be bodily, libidinal, even erotic. Niziołek's definition is dispersed throughout the chapter entitled "Gawkers' Theatre" and could be reconstructed into a description that portrays gawkers as a crowd, a common, initially neutral gathering of passersby, which turns into an audience by a sudden occurrence of a Jew in a public view, whose misery is so evident that it becomes an irresistible visual anchor. The behavior of individuals might be different: "The view of this dark, dirty, gaunt figure in the bright light of day instigates on the street even more intense stir and interest. Someone spits, someone laughs, someone casts a hurtful phrase. Someone expresses helpless sympathy. Not all recognize him at once as a Jew—thinking that he might be blind or a lunatic."[31] The community generated by this sudden event—even if individuals express different attitudes—is indifferent: the refusal of sympathetic action is not neutral, however. In the context of war atrocities, it turns into hostility.[32] Gawkers are apathetic, thoughtless, their indifference based not on "not-looking" but on "not-feeling for the victim."[33] Therefore, the crowd of gawkers ought to be characterized by an excess of scopic activity with the simultaneously affective deficit in empathy.

To sum up the above, I would stress that any extension of the terms for the ocular-centric bystander must be done while carefully weighing the context and being aware that the aforementioned scopic positions are not entirely voluntarily acts. The viewer—as seen within visual culture—is never autonomous. A bystander, viewed through the theory of spectatorship, is therefore always motivated by externally inherited cultures, ideologies, and complexes of desire and anxiety, power, and interest. "There never was or will be a self-present beholder to whom a world is transparently evident," Crary writes. "Instead there are more or less powerful arrangements of forces out of which the capacities of an observer are possible."[34] Indeed, a viewer, after the pictorial turn, must be seen as a "complex interplay between visuality, apparatus, institutions, discourse, bodies, and figurality."[35] The bystander as a visual subject should thus be carefully analyzed within a broader net of relationships with pre-imposed cultural scripts, social and institutional relations, technologies, and somatic reactions.

Case Study No. 1: *Look at It, Look at It* (Jan Karski)

The four terms mentioned above form four vertices of a polygon that mark out a space for many other transitive forms of the scopic subject, understood in mechanical, social, affective, institutional, cognitive, or libidinal/somatic ways. To further develop this line of analysis and rethink the scopic faculties of a bystander, we must take into account that witnessing is a time-bound process. We should therefore consider onlooking, spectating, observing and gawking as actions with inner dynamism and not as stable demarcated phenomena contained within a momentous event. To explain my point, I refer to a famous bystander's account, well known after thirty years that have passed since the premiere of *Shoah*.[36]

In Jan Karski's[37] thirty-nine-minute monologue in the eighth hour of Claude Lanzmann's documentary, one observes many attempts to recreate the eyewitness's visual experience of the Holocaust. With each such attempt, there is a shift in rhetoric, namely the narration jumps from the past to the present tense. The first such jump happens when Karski recounts the moment of crossing the tunnel into the Warsaw Ghetto. From the darkness, the protagonist emerges into an open space, which can be understood literally as well as figuratively, as emerging from repressed ("dark")[38] memories into an open scene where testimony is finally possible. The first image, carefully chosen, after a longer moment of silence, is striking. Karski pronounces a strong nominal sentence, highlighting by the avoidance of a verb the dominance of an image over the action in his account. He says, "Naked bodies on the street." The viewer (Karski, but also the viewer of the documentary) is struck by white objects, standing out sharply from the background. In the next instance, he is able to look around. Karski provides a general view of the ghetto, stressing the indiscernible multitude of objects: "Everybody offering something to sell." The zoom-out changes then into a zoom-in and we get a detail: "Three onions, two onions, some cookies." Karski continues to pronounce his observations as nominal sentences, as frozen frames or snapshots: "Women with their babies," "babies with crazy eyes." The scene of scanning the area turns into a scene of running into a house and witnessing the wanton killings committed by Hitlerjugend boys. Karski, the narrator, is then urged by his Jewish guide, "Look at it, look at it!" In this moment, his position as a visual subject is confirmed and reinforced. The scene concludes his first visit to the ghetto. The visual subject has not fulfilled his mission: "You didn't see everything. You didn't see too much... I want you to see everything," says his guide. The second visit is clearly different. "I was more conditioned, I felt other things," says Karski. The initial sense impressions on entering the ghetto are indeed different the second time around, especially for the olfactory sense: "stench everywhere, suffocating." The walk is interrupted many times by the guide's urging, "look at it," concluded by an order, "remember!" The visitor and his guide stop at the sight of a motionless Jew. "He is dying. Look at him, tell them!" comes the explanation and instruction. The visit ends with Karski feeling physical ill.

It is clear from this recapitulation that the experience of eye witnessing the Shoah is a dynamic and not a stable visual "process." The subject is oftentimes blinded, distracted, or disoriented. The eye movements are rapid, unplanned, working under incredible stress. The position of an onlooker ("a camera zooming in and out," a recording mechanism working to transport the images to the outside world) is abandoned under the urge to understand and memorize. However, Karski's effort to make sense of what he is seeing (and thus to become an observer) fails ("It was not a world. It was not humanity."). The views were incomparable; there was no external protocol at hand to help the observer to locate his viewing within a predefined order ("I never saw [something like that in] any theatre, I never saw any movies").[39] The analytical position would be most desired—it could sooth the terror by introducing an emotional distance—but it turns out to be unattainable. The affective load is enormous, so the most probable choice of viewing position is now the spectator. However, the view is nothing but unbearable. The cognitive processes stop and the body takes over. The action of absorbing the horrid externality abruptly ends and the abject reality literally is expelled when the body vomits.

Karski remembers and recounts his experience of becoming a visual subject of the Shoah as a gradual transition from being mechanical, objective, to being emotional, before he finally admits the impossibility of assuming the position of visual subject at all. There is no way to assign one term to what he recreates in his interview. Concluding from that, I would claim that a bystander as a visual subject is an unstable, precarious "condition." Such a visual subjectivity, shaky and agitated, can never be stable. Cognitive powers are shuttered, and what gets through the invalidated channels of perception is highly emotionalized and somatized. It is clear, then, that any understanding of the visual subject of the Shoah requires a most careful and meticulous analysis of the processes the subject enters, and any singular attribution may prove to be a gross attempt to avoid complexity by merely essentializing.

What is more, Karski's example makes it clear that any oral account of the act of viewing the Holocaust is bound to be most inaccurate. Such an account attempts to narrate a highly affect-loaded event. The work of narration certainly stabilizes the experience and reorganizes it; the effort to organize the narrated experience is clear in Karski's monologue. Yet, the frantic shifting of assumed positions is still very noticeable. We may surmise that the whole experience of viewing the ghetto was even more chaotic and so was the flow of assumed perspectives. To test that hypothesis, non-textual material is needed. Since it is impossible to retrieve an image from the visual cortex of a viewing subject, a visual representation fashioned by such a subject may become the second-best object of analysis.

Case Study No. 2: *Camera Dropped from My Hands* (Józef Charyton)

I would like to look at another response to the Holocaust, studying the works of a relatively unknown, self-taught artist from eastern Poland, Józef Charyton.[40] His works are a rare example of taking immediate visual notes of the Shoah, in this case a small-town ghetto and its annihilation. Charyton was born in 1909. Trained briefly in the Academy of Fine Arts in Kraków, he worked as a fresco painter, decoration artist, and photographer in Wysokie Litewskie.[41] He befriended the poet Mojżesz Teitelbaum and contributed to the local Jewish artistic life by illustrating publications and preparing scenography for a theater. During the war, he worked shortly as a provisional councilor to the magistrate and a manager of the town's economic activities, officially taking stands against the harassments of Jews, which won him respect from the ghetto community.⁴² Both his public service and the location of his apartment that overlooked the ghetto gave him an opportunity to witness events behind the wall closely:

> I watched the Jews build the Ghetto with their own hands. I knew then that some horrific trap was being prepared. I kept a diary, I checked all the facts, and I felt compelled to be everywhere and see everything, even though this took me to some very dangerous places. Some irresistible desire was pushing me to witness the History. At times, this desire placed me in situations dangerous to my own life. On the outside, I was calm. I never gave any reason for suspicion to the authorities, and—under various pretexts—I kept on visiting the Ghetto.⁴³

Charyton sketches are in his own account immediate visual notes, equivalents of photographs: "I observed the life of the stifled Jewish community and I returned to my studio, where I sketched compositions which I intended to serve for future works in oil."⁴⁴ The works today give access to what is lost in oral postwar accounts; we may assess the vantage point taken, the mode of observation: its angle, its perspective, and finally, the type of subject present. Today, that amounts to invaluable material to analyze bystanders as visual subjects.

In 1963, the Jewish Historical Institute (JHI) bought 185 of Charyton's works.⁴⁵ Many others are in private collections, and four are part of the permanent exhibition in Yad Vashem (YV).⁴⁶ The sketches owned by the JHI are mostly of similar dimensions, approximately forty-two by thirty centimeters. Crafted in ink on random material (drawing or photographic paper), they are usually titled and dated. The JHI archive cards identify two periods: 1942–1943 and the 1960s. This vast body of work has not been researched enough to state clearly, if we are dealing with the immediate sketches mentioned in the oral account (as YV's description suggests) or later works done to catch haunting "afterimages" (which is what the archive cards at the JHI suggest). Since both cases refer us to the "image imprinted on the visual cortex" (as an immediate picture or afterimage retrieved later from memory), the question need not be settled for the purposes of the current discussion.

I am deliberately choosing here three works of very different aesthetics. Figure 3.1 represents the most emotional works by Charyton: hasty, expressionistic, affect-loaded; figure 3.2 is sketchy but precise, more readable—the manner of painting is definitely more composed and calm. Figure 3.3 is closest to the aesthetics of a documentary drawing, with more recognizable facial features. However, here the simplified manner of figurations is strikingly reminiscent of a poetics of a caricature. They

Figure 3.1. Józef Charyton, *Egzekucja* (Execution), 1945–1963. (From the collection of the Emanuel Ringelblum Jewish Historical Institute, Warsaw.)

Figure 3.2. Józef Charyton, *Żydówki przed egzekucją: Wys-Lit 1942* (Jewish women before the execution: Wys-Lit 1942), 1945–1963 (From the collection of the Emanuel Ringelblum Jewish Historical Institute, Warsaw.)

depict scenes from the ghetto (fig. 3.3), scenes observed on liquidation of the ghetto outside its walls (marches, killings—fig. 3.1), and scenes he reconstructed from others testimonies (fig. 3.2).[47]

If we concentrate on the three sketches from the JHI collection (figs. 3.1–3.3), we may at first define the viewer as an observer: he is cold, calm, and composed, giving precise dates (fig. 3.2) and informing us in writing on the nature of the ongoing event (figs. 3.1–3.3). He gives us a full frame and a clear view (figs. 3.2 and 3.3). However, we soon realize that the "rationalized" mode of giving an impartial account is broken by the very technique (or—techniques, since they vary) used. The paper is of a random choice; the hand seems shaky and rushed (esp. fig 3.1). The perspective is not linear; the image is flat, with no depth, resembling the poetics of a snapshot. The sketch is hasty (fig 3.1); letters fall into each other as if there was too much ink on the brush and the painter had no time to see to details. The analytical, scientific mode encapsulated by the precise, cold captions and the very effort of documenting crimes in the numerous aquarelle depictions (more than two hundred objects can be counted today) portraying different types of torment are strangely counterpoised by emotional mode of painting.

The figures have hardly recognizable faces; the perpetrators usually turn their backs to the viewer (figs. 3.1 and 3.3): the "snapshots" will not incriminate them if taken to court as evidence.[48] The victims seem so similar to each other as if the viewer was unable to look them in their faces (esp. fig. 3.1)—so in the end they seem paradoxically deindividualized (fig. 3.2). Yet, a compassion directed toward them is patently visible. The scenes capture moments of high emotional tensions: the women are frightened and ashamed (fig. 3.2), the men helpless (fig. 3.1).

The affective component draws the image toward the "spectatorial" mode. Some other incongruent features make the sketches inherently broken: for instance, when painting a naked female body, Charyton seems to be unable to drop conventional "nude" representations (fig. 3.2) with all their libidinal connotations. He thus "observes" external protocols, failing—in part—to capture the horrid realism. Thus, his works in fact would be dismissed in any court case: forensic in intent, the sketches become too personal, revealing too much of the viewer's inner emotional state. Again, within one frame we have the same effect of instability we observed in Karski's case: modes of emotionless recounting by a professional observer, followed by emotion-driven portrayals of a spectacle (seen here no doubt as a tragedy), and finally an individual mode full of authentic sympathy. The visual documentation of "bystanding" is consistently inconsistent, containing multiple modes of viewing. Again, I must therefore claim that any one-sided interpretation

Figure 3.3. *Fotografowanie na pamiątkę* (Photographing for a keepsake), 1945–1963. (From the collection of the Emanuel Ringelblum Jewish Historical Institute, Warsaw.)

of being a bystander (passively?) witnessing the Shoah is in danger of being simplistic.

The flatness of the composition, its clear focus, reduced background, the multiplication of frames, the similarity of formats, its monochromaticity—all those features suggest a photographical mode as reference (figs. 3.2 and 3.3). A photograph indeed was the desired image that Charyton intended for his forensic documentation: "One night I was awakened by the rattle of a machine gun. In the morning, I saw a few corpses lying before my windows. The same thing happened in other parts of the town. From that point on I began to carry a camera, which—unfortunately—I never used at the right moment." There is no sign in the Polish archives[49] of his photographs. Were they available, we would have priceless material for analyzing bystanders as visual subjects as well as powerful additional proof of the "Holocaust by bullets." Charyton testifies about his effort to provide visual documentation for Nazi crimes:

> After checking the ditch in the evening, I would lock myself up for the night and wait for the morning. In the morning, I cleared the frost on the glass window and *waited with my camera. I had a very good field of observation:* ... *I had a panoramic view*, and *I could see all* the activities on the roads leading to the ditch, which was about 20 meters from my position.

What he also recounts is his failure to produce photographical evidence. The reason why it happened is crucial for further discussions on bystander as a viewing subject: *"I could not use my camera because I considered it worthless in comparison with the lost lives and the camera dropped from my hands.* Only shortly afterwards I took a few pictures, when victims' blood was steaming in the cold."[50]

It seems that, when exposed to the Jewish suffering at its most extreme, Charyton intuitively decided that photographing it amounted to something improper, indecent ("I considered it worthless"), inhumane ("in comparison with the lost lives"). Indeed, holding a camera is not a neutral gesture, as Susan Sontag proved in her powerful *Regarding the Pain of Others*: the very fact of holding a recording tool in one's hands distances the photographer from the suffering person: "It is felt that there is something morally wrong with the abstract of reality offered by photography; that one has no right to experience the suffering of others at a distance, denuded of its raw power."[51] Charyton's sketch picturing German soldiers taking photos of Jews seems to prove his not fully articulated intuition that the recording of suffering turns the viewer into a voyeur, guilty of not helping, of being passive, mixing the feelings of horror with ones of relief (the threat is targeted elsewhere), or even morbid pleasure.[52] The act of dropping the camera can therefore be read as a conclusion that "doing-nothing in the face of the Holocaust" and taking visual record associates you with the perpetrator. The latter is the one who is able to hold the camera (fig. 3.3).

Conclusion

Concluding from the above, it could be argued that the ultimate position of a bystander-as-visual-subject would be theoretically a person with a camera who would pass on to posterity through the composition of the photograph her position, point of view, emotions, observational faculties, and attitudes, which can turn the bystander into a witness who can give testimony. Charyton's choice—to drop the camera and return to the remembered scenes only later—may lead us to a paradox. There can be no doubt that the analysis of a bystander as a visual subject can provide valuable insight into his precarious position at the scene of the Holocaust. However, it is also true that there is no ultimate access to the bystander as "the one who saw." Therefore, it is not only the conglomerate of a "complex interplay between visuality, apparatus, institutions, discourse, bodies, and figurality" that separates us from the un-predetermined bystander as visual subject, but also the fact that the very act of viewing places the bystander closer to the position of a perpetrator. At the same time, the act of turning their eyes away from the scene makes them similarly guilty of hostility through indifference. The scopic conceptualization of a bystander therefore would leave us with a paradoxical figure: momentarily, assuming transitional and changing points of view (moving from onlooker to observer to spectator, etc.), dependent on the context of events and forms of violence, ontologically of a precarious nature.

Moreover, the visual approach to Shoah would need further research as Mary Fulbrook writes: "Jews were forced to spectate at public hangings, alongside Germans who came to enjoy the spectacle."[53] Indeed, acts of spectatorship need to be considered, to further calibrate the baffling category of bystanders and its relation to concepts of perpetrators and victims. What is more, gaze exchange is a dynamic process; its participants can switch agency within very short periods of time (an observer can be absorbed by a mob to become momentarily a gawker, but in an instant, they can regain control over the movements of their body and turn their eyes away from the scene of torment. Thus, they would become someone who actually—and paradoxically—sees the situation in its full meaning. A complete visual analysis of bystanding would therefore require a refined methodology capable of capturing the interpersonal, cross-linked, dynamic, unstable exchanges of multiplying, fleeting, uncoordinated, and intersecting scopic acts.

Roma Sendyka is Associate Professor in the Faculty of Polish Studies and Director of the Research Center for Memory Cultures at the Jagiellonian University in Kraków, Poland. Her work combines memory studies, visual culture, and literary anthropology. She researches cultural and societal functions of abandoned sites of trauma in Central and Eastern Europe. Another focus of her work is the response of visual arts and vernacular visual culture to the Holocaust.

Notes

1. Georges Didi-Huberman, *Images in Spite of All: Four Photographs from Auschwitz* (Chicago, 2008), 23. Didi-Huberman reconstructs how the Nazi "machinery of disimagination" worked to keep the Holocaust outside the visual field. The thesis of "hiding the Final Solution from view," that is, the effort to run the death camps clandestinely, holds true both for Western and Eastern Europe. However, there were significant differences in how the killing was hidden from public attention.
2. Raul Hilberg, *Perpetrators Victims Bystanders: The Jewish Catastrophe, 1933–1945* (New York, 1993), 214–215.
3. Patrick Desbois, *The Holocaust by Bullets: A Priest's Journey to Uncover the Truth behind the Murder of 1.5 Million Jews* (New York, 2009), 64.
4. Jan Tomasz Gross, "Sprawcy, ofiary i inni," *Zagłada Żydów*, no 10 (2014): 885.
5. David Cesarani and Paul A. Levine, *"Bystanders" to the Holocaust: A Re-evaluation* (London, 2014); Victoria J. Barnett, *Bystanders: Conscience and Complicity during the Holocaust* (Westport, CT, 2000).
6. Mary Fulbrook, *A Small Town Near Auschwitz: Ordinary Nazis and the Holocaust* (Oxford, 2013), 27.
7. Gross, "Sprawcy, ofiary i inni," 886.
8. Ibid., 885–886.
9. Victoria J. Barnett, "Reflections on the Concept of 'Bystander,'" in *Looking at the Onlookers and Bystanders: Interdisciplinary Approaches to the Causes and Consequences of Passivity*, ed. Henrik Edgren, (Stockholm, 2012), 36.
10. Barnett, *Bystanders*, 8.
11. *Collins Dictionary*, s.v. "bystander," accessed 28 June 2018, http://www.collinsdictionary.com/dictionary/english/bystander.
12. WordReference.com, s.v. "bystander," accessed 29 July 2016, http://www.wordreference.com/synonyms/bystander.
13. So far, the overly presentist approaches developed within visual culture studies did not produce too many analyses reflecting on scopic relations between subjects in a specific historical moment. Jonathan Crary, *Techniques of the Observer: On Vision and Modernity in the Nineteenth Century* (Cambridge, MA, 1992) is a notable exception. The recent Nicholas Mirzoeff, *The Right to Look: A Counterhistory of Visuality* (Durham, NC, 2011) debates large-scale social visual processes changing in the course of history, not individual acts of viewing developed by visual artists.

14. W. J. Thomas Mitchell, *Iconology: Image, Text, Ideology* (Chicago, 1987).
15. See Hal Foster, ed., *Vision and Visuality* (Seattle, WA, 1988).
16. W. J. Thomas Mitchell, "Visual Literacy or Literary Visualcy?" in *Visual Literacy*, ed. James Elkins (New York, 2007), 13.
17. Ibid., 14.
18. W. J. Thomas Mitchell, *Picture Theory: Essays on Verbal and Visual Representation* (Chicago, 1995), 16.
19. An excellent exception is Ernst van Alphen, *Caught by History* (Stanford, CA, 1997), which criticizes the alleged unmediativity of history and historical narrative and privileging it over visual accounts; the chapters on Armando offer insightful applications of visual criticism on the figure of the bystander. Additionally, Mieke Bal, *Of What One Cannot Speak: Doris Salcedo's Political Art* (Chicago, 2011) analyzes Doris Salcedo's art using the bystander concept and visual analysis.
20. With the notion of "visual subject," I mean the subject seen from the point of view of visual culture: someone endowed with the agency (= subject) to choose his or her scopic action (= visual). Mirzoeff defines a visual subject as "a person who is both constituted as an agent of sight and as the effect of a series of categories of visual subjectivity." Nicholas Mirzoeff, ed., *The Visual Culture Reader* (London, 2002), 10.
21. Giorgio Agamben, *Remnants of Auschwitz: The Witness and the Archive* (New York, 1999), par. 1.3, 17. It is important to note, that in Polish the dominant translation of Hilberg's "bystander" is "witness." For many commentators this is misleading. If a term "witness" suggests ability to give testimony and be willing/able to be reviewed in court, the bystanders are not so willing to be implicated into the evaluation of the violent act. They tend to be "more neutral," "indifferent" to the events. See Gross, "Sprawcy, ofiary i inni," 885.
22. John Berger, *Ways of Seeing: Based on the BBC Television Series* (London, 1990), 8, emphasis added.
23. Mirzoeff, *The Right to Look*.
24. Griselda Pollock, *Looking Back to the Future: Essays on Art, Life and Death* (Amsterdam, 2001), 23.
25. Marita Sturken and Lisa Cartwright, *Practices of Looking: An Introduction to Visual Culture* (Oxford, 2001), 10.
26. Jacques Rancière, *The Emancipated Spectator*, trans. Gregory Elliott (London, 2011), 12.
27. Guy Debord, *Society of the Spectacle*, trans. Donald Nicholson-Smith (New York, 1995), 23. This approach was more recently adopted by Jonathan Crary, who saw spectacular culture as "not founded on the necessity of making a subject see, but rather on strategies in which individuals are isolated, separated, and inhabit time as disempowered. Crary, *Techniques*, 3.
28. Ibid., 6.
29. Ibid., 5.
30. Grzegorz Niziołek, *Polski teatr Zagłady* (Warszawa, 2014), 53. "Witness" here means "bystander." Ibid., 27.
31. Ibid., 41.
32. As Gross puts it, "doing-nothing in the face of the Holocaust is also an action." Gross, "Sprawcy, ofiary i inni," 886.
33. Niziołek, *Polski teatr*, 49.
34. Crary, *Techniques*, 6.
35. Mitchell, *Picture Theory*, 16.
36. Claude Lanzmann, dir., *Shoah*, 1985. In 1978, Jan Karski met Lanzmann for two days. In the first day, he recalled the Warsaw Ghetto in the middle of 1942 and the

meeting with two Jewish leaders (Menachem Kirszenbaum and Leon Fajner) with whom he secretly entered the ghetto premises twice (through a secret passage under a townhouse on Muranowska Street No. 6). The second day was focused on Karski's meetings with Western officials. Lanzmann used only some sequences from this material (approx. 40 minutes). In 2010, Lanzmann returned to the interview from 1978 in his forty-eight-minute documentary, *Le Rapport Karski*.

37. Jan Karski to Hilberg was a paradigmatic bystander; Hilberg pointed to his actions to illustrate the category of bystanders-messengers. Hilberg, *Perpetrators Victims Bystanders*, 221–224.
38. When giving the interview to Lanzmann, Karski returned to his wartime memories after many years of not mentioning the subject.
39. All citations from Claude Lanzmann, *Shoah: The Complete Text of the Acclaimed Holocaust Film* (New York, 1995), 159–161.
40. There is no significant scholarly analysis of Charyton's work so far. The only exception is Norbert Mojżyn, "Symboliczna wartość obrazowania zagłady w malarstwie Józefa Charytona" [Symbolic value of picturing the Holocaust in Józef Charyton's work], *Studia Teologiczne*, no. 22 (2004): 295–315. Stowarzyszenie Bioregion collects materials on Charyton's work and life. His account in English can be found in Wysokie Litewskie, "Charyton's Holocaust Memoir: My Youth in Wysokie Litewskie," last updated 22 December 2009, http://www.wysokie-litewskie.org/CharytonReport/youth.i.html. Charyton is a protagonist of a short story written by one of the most renown Polish-Jewish writers of historical reportage: Marian Brandys, *Strażnik Królewskiego Grobu: Opowiadanie o Józefie Charytonie z Siemiatycz* (Warsaw, 1984).
41. Charyton died in 1975. After the war, his works on the other cycle, *Jewish Faces*, gained popularity. The Jewish portraits and other cycle: shtetl scenes were often exhibited. However, devoid of wartime details, the serene and realistic paintings were not fully unrelated to war: Charyton claimed to be forced to paint faces of people he used to know and who now "visit his studio and did not leave until I finish painting." Some five hundred works of "Jewish faces" is known to exist. See Stowarzyszenie Bioregion, "Biografia Józefa Charytona," accessed 28 June 2018, http://www.nawschodzie.pl/bio.html.
42. All the information given above follows Charyton self-assessment in his testimony written for the Jewish Historical Institute, 6 February 1963, doc. no. 301/6133.
43. Wysokie Litewskie, "Charyton's Holocaust Memoir: The Ditches," last updated 22 December 2009, http://www.wysokie-litewskie.org/CharytonReport/ditches.i.html. Translation of the oral testimony done for the Jewish Historical Institute in Warsaw, 6 February 1963, doc. no. 301/6133.
44. Ibid. Charyton stresses that his notes are immediate and hasty—as snapshots. He evidently wants to highlight his effort to work as an "indexical machine" free from possible deformations that stem from artistic poetics, media ramifications, effects of time passing, and later emotional reworking.
45. For a sum of 10,000 Polish zloty, which approximately equaled more than five average monthly wages. The works were sold directly by the painter. Charyton produced and kept the works for decades, hence the uncertain dating. On the sketches, one can usually (but not always) see a note on a date and place, like: "Wys. Lit., 1942" (Wysokie Litewskie, 1942).
46. They are presented as a part the main exhibition in the section highlighting killing sites.
47. As he admits in his testimony, Jewish Historical Institute, 6 February 1963, doc. no. 301/6133, 57

48. Charyton claims that his aim in pursuing the large Holocaust cycle was "to recreate the most horrid scenes on big-scale canvas for the purpose of history. However, personal economic troubles, the forced relocation [from Wysokie Litewskie, which became part of postwar Belarus, to Siematycze in Poland], lack of proper housing and many other adversities [Charyton might relate here to his conjugal problems] wrecked these endeavors." Testimony, Jewish Historical Institute, 6 February 1963, doc. no. 301/6133. His goal was thus more generally humanistic than directly judicial.
49. Information from the interview with Marcin Korniluk from Stowarzyszenie Bioregion, Obrazy pamięi: Józef Charyton, accessed 28June 2018, http://www.nawschodzie.pl/obrazy_pamieci.html. There are also no photo works by Charyton in the Jewish Historical Institute archives.
50. Wysokie Litewskie, "Charyton's Holocaust Memoir: The Ditches," emphasis added.
51. Susan Sontag, *Regarding the Pain of Others* (New York, 2004), 118.
52. On the act of photographing, see Christoph Kreutzmüller, this volume.
53. On precarious ontology of the figure bystander, see Mary Fulbrook, this volume.

Bibliography

Agamben, Giorgio. *Remnants of Auschwitz: The Witness and the Archive*. New York: Zone Books, 1999.
Alphen, Ernst, van. *Caught by History*. Stanford, CA: Stanford University Press, 1997.
Bal, Mieke. *Of What One Cannot Speak: Doris Salcedo's Political Art*. Chicago: University of Chicago Press, 2011.
Barnett, Victoria J. *Bystanders: Conscience and Complicity During the Holocaust*. Westport, CT: Praeger, 2000.
———. "Reflections on the Concept of 'Bystander.'" In *Looking at the Onlookers and Bystanders: Interdisciplinary Approaches to the Causes and Consequences of Passivity*, edited by Henrik Edgren, 35–52. Stockholm: Living History Forum, 2012.
Berger, John. *Ways of Seeing: Based on the BBC Television Series*. London: Penguin, 1990.
Brandys, Marian. *Strażnik Królewskiego Grobu: Opowiadanie o Józefie Charytonie z Siemiatycz*. Warsaw: Iskry, 1984.
Cesarani, David, and Paul A. Levine. *"Bystanders" to the Holocaust: A Re-evaluation*. New York: Routledge, 2014.
Crary, Jonathan. *Techniques of the Observer: On Vision and Modernity in the Nineteenth Century*. Cambridge, MA: MIT Press, 1992.
Debord, Guy. *Society of the Spectacle*. Translated by Donald Nicholson-Smith. New York: Zone Books, 1995. Originally published as *La société du spectacle* (Paris: Buchet-Chastel, 1967).
Desbois, Patrick, *The Holocaust by Bullets: A Priest's Journey to Uncover the Truth behind the Murder of 1.5 Million Jews*. Translated by Paul A. Shapiro. New York: Palgrave Macmillan, 2009.
Didi-Huberman, Georges. *Images in Spite of All: Four Photographs from Auschwitz*. Chicago: University of Chicago Press, 2008.
Foster, Hal, ed. *Vision and Visuality*. Seattle, WA: Bay View Press, 1988.
Fulbrook, Mary. *A Small Town Near Auschwitz: Ordinary Nazis and the Holocaust*. Oxford: Oxford University Press, 2013.
Gross, Jan Tomasz. "Sprawcy, ofiary i inni." *Zagłada Żydów*, no. 10 (2014): 885–888.
Hilberg, Raul. *Perpetrators, Victims, Bystanders: The Jewish Catastrophe, 1933–1945*. New York: Harper Perennial, 1993.

Lanzmann, Claude. *Shoah: The Complete Text of the Acclaimed Holocaust Film*. New York: Da Capo Press, 1995.
Marrus, Michael R. *The Holocaust in History*. Hanover, NH: University Press of New England, 1987.
Mirzoeff, Nicholas. *The Right to Look: A Counterhistory of Visuality*. Durham, NC: Duke University Press, 2011.
―――, ed. *The Visual Culture Reader*. London: Routledge, 2002.
Mitchell, W. J. Thomas. *Iconology: Image, Text, Ideology*. Chicago: University of Chicago Press, 1987.
―――. *Picture Theory: Essays on Verbal and Visual Representation*. Chicago: University of Chicago Press, 1995.
―――. "Visual Literacy or Literary Visualcy?" In *Visual Literacy*, edited by James Elkins, 11–14. New York: Routledge, 2007.
Mojżyn, Norbert. "Symboliczna wartość obrazowania zagłady w malarstwie Józefa Charytona." *Studia Teologiczne*, no. 22 (2004): 295–315.
Niziołek, Grzegorz. *Polski teatr Zagłady*. Warsaw: Wydawnictwo Krytyki Politycznej, 2014.
Pollock, Griselda. *Looking Back to the Future: Essays on Art, Life and Death*. Amsterdam: G&B Arts International, 2001.
Rancière, Jacques. *The Emancipated Spectator*. Translated by Gregory Elliott. London: Verso, 2011.
Sontag, Susan. *Regarding the Pain of Others*. New York: Picador, 2004.
Sturken, Marita, and Lisa Cartwright. *Practices of Looking: An Introduction to Visual Culture*. Oxford: Oxford University Press, 2001.

Chapter 4

"I am not, what I am"
A Typological Approach to Individual (In)action in the Holocaust

Timothy Williams

When Max Koegel came home from his position as *Kommandant* at Ravensbrück concentration camp, his wife, Anna, was waiting for him. Anna herself did not engage in any acts of brutality, nor is she known to have been prominent in any organizational capacity, yet she lived with her husband in a house within the compounds of a concentration camp. As she physically harmed no one herself, but was physically present, she could be described as a bystander. Yet, one can also argue that her presence in the home did in fact have an impact on the violence in the camp, as her presence normalized the space for her husband and precisely her inaction signaled assent. Thus, her lack of resistance to Koegel's actions will have encouraged him in seeing his actions as legitimate, if not laudable.[1]

In Sobibór, Stan Szmajzner was a twelve-year-old boy who was saved by Franz Stangl, *Kommandant* of this death camp. Stangl allowed him to stay alive in order to work as a goldsmith and process the gold stolen from the murdered Jews, and Stangl is even said to have given him extra rations because he liked the boy.[2] This description of people who saved someone from execution by giving them a job is reminiscent of the case of Oskar Schindler, who saved hundreds of Jews by arguing their necessity for the war effort.³ It strikes one as absurd to say that the term "hero," which is so easily accepted for Schindler, could also be chosen for Stangl who is one of those characters who epitomizes the system of destruction and is thus understood as a perpetrator.

Iago's exclaim "I am not, what I am" at the beginning of Shakespeare's *Othello* is the title for this chapter precisely because it hints at this parallel simplicity and complexity of attempting to conceptually untangle the definitional web of actors in genocide and mass violence. Franz Stangl as a rescuer, a bystander, or a perpetrator? Anna Koegel as a bystander with influence? People who are commonly referred to as perpetrators also engaged in acts of resistance and rescue, which they performed in the context of their other daily duties within the Nazi system. Occasionally, bystanders, through their inaction, even create the conditions under which perpetration can occur. What are these individuals to be labeled as? Rescuers, perpetrators, bystanders? This chapter argues that such a broad classification is a valid starting point but that for a fuller understanding of the process of genocide, these categories can be interrogated in a more nuanced way and differentiated in more detail.

The category of the bystander remains the most enigmatic and under-researched, yet the concept of the bystander cannot be understood without reference to other categories of actors in genocide. To understand what constitutes a bystander is to understand what participation or perpetration is, to understand what victimhood is, to understand what action and inaction, resistance and support are. Perpetration can only be understood in its demarcation from resisters, rescuers, or heroes. The boundaries between perpetrator and bystander and between bystander and rescuer become blurry when looking more closely at the actions of individuals during the Holocaust and other genocides. Building on these propositions and in an effort to further our conceptual thinking about genocidal processes, this chapter develops a typology for classifying action in a genocidal context. The typology is not particularly parsimonious but in its complexity captures the relevance of various "gray zones" conceptually and locates them comparatively, thus deepening our understanding of bystanders in relation to each other, as well as to perpetrators and to rescuers. As such, an "exploration of 'bystanders,' if coupled with a differentiation of 'perpetrators,' and a recognition of the significance of changing locations within a constantly evolving system of radical collective violence, could in fact prove highly rewarding."⁴

Such a typology is useful for anyone studying the Holocaust and other genocides, as it can function as an intermediary between individual empirical examples on the one hand and broader theoretical models and generalizable historical patterns on the other. The proposed categories within the typology serve to identify and group certain individual actions as similar, expecting them to have similar causes or consequences. Even where this turns out to be inaccurate vis-à-vis the historical record, a typology can act as a starting point for theorizing the similarities and differences between cases. It allows researchers to start their empirical endeavors from a conceptual standpoint and a comparative perspective with other similar types of action and then tease out the nuances particularly constitutive of this individual case.

Before embarking on this endeavor, it should be clarified that this chapter is based on a relatively narrow understanding of genocide, understood as "a form of one-sided mass killing in which a state or other authority intends to destroy a group, as that group and membership in it are defined by the perpetrator."[5] Thus, it focuses on the act of killing during the Holocaust and participation in it, not as a broader process of social exclusion and group destruction.[6] However, it is important to recognize that processes of social exclusion and group destruction, such as legal discrimination, ghettoization, arrests, deportation, securing of sites for massacring, and so forth, predate the acts of the actual mass killing. Thus, the Holocaust and participation in it as a perpetrator, bystander, and rescuer is not limited to the sites of massacre in concentration camps or the countryside of Eastern and Southeastern Europe, but begins—in a narrower sense—with the deportations from Germany and the occupied countries of Western as well as Eastern and Southeastern Europe. While the increasing discrimination of Jews and other victim groups in the 1930s is also important, this chapter zooms in on manifest steps in a causal chain of orchestrated physically violent actions culminating in the killing itself.

This chapter will first introduce the case study of Reserve Police Battalion 101 from which several empirical examples will be drawn throughout the rest of the chapter regarding the diversity of action during the Holocaust. Then I will argue that previous attempts at categorization have failed to grasp these nuances because they have focused on the actors rather than the actions in which these actors engage. Thus, mine is a typology, which approaches bystanding, perpetrating, and rescuing rather than bystanders, perpetrators, and rescuers. The typology along two axes of impact on the genocidal process and proximity is then presented and its utility demonstrated for several of the empirical examples. The chapter ends with a short reflection of how the typology can be used in future research on bystanders.

The Diversity of Action Roles: The Example of Reserve Police Battalion 101 in Józefów

I have already alluded to three examples—Anna Koeger, Franz Stangl and Oskar Schindler—which the typology will seek to categorize. This section will introduce several more individuals, drawing on the example of Reserve Police Battalion 101. Given how broadly this unit has been studied,[7] this section will only briefly introduce it and focus on highlighting the variety of roles its members took on. A focal point of many discussions of this Order Police battalion, including Christopher Browning's seminal book *Ordinary Men*, are the initial fatal actions of the unit in Józefów in which they, without having previously killed any Jews, murdered around 1,500 Jewish men, women, and children in just one day. From July 1942 onward, this battalion participated in several massacres, killing at least 38,000 Jews and helping to deport another 45,200 to the extermination camp Treblinka.[8]

When hearing in advance about the planned massacre at Józefów, Heinz Buchmann, commander of First Platoon of the battalion's First Company, categorically ruled out participating in the killing of women and children, asking for a different assignment. His superior allowed Buchmann to instead be in charge of escorting male Jews who had been selected out of the village's population to be taken to Lublin as "work Jews."[9] With the first light of day, the commander of the battalion, Major Wilhelm Trapp, assembled his men and informed them of the orders to round up and shoot the Jewish population of the town. While he subsequently dispensed orders to his various subordinates and ordered the action, he was visibly uncomfortable with the implementation of this task, and he gave his men the option of refusing it. The first of around a dozen men to step forward and opt out of participating was Otto-Julius Schimke.[10] He and others were not required to kill in this or other *Judenaktionen*, but they were nonetheless present and required to participate in the fight against partisans.[11]

In the ensuing division of labor, two platoons of Third Company surrounded the village and were ordered to shoot anyone trying to escape. Noncommissioned officers, such as Georg K. or Karl S. were divided into small groups, which combed the Jewish part of Józefów, sending any Jews they found to the marketplace and shooting the immobile, the elderly, and infants. Others guarded the streets and then under the command of Trapp's adjutant Lieutenant Hagen separated about 300 men to be deported as forced laborers from the remaining 1,500 who were to be killed that day.[12]

Members of Second Company and Third Platoon of Third Company were responsible for loading the Jews onto trucks and transporting them from the marketplace to the forest. Here, most of the members of First Company, including Friedrich B., had been instructed by the battalion physician, Dr. Schönfelder, how to kill their victims most effectively. They thus formed a firing squad, actually implementing the killing orders with First Sergeant Arthur Kammer issuing the commands to the Jews to lie down and his men to shoot.[13]

During all this action, some officers like Paul H. requested to be released from executing the order as the true nature of this action dawned on them, and most superiors granted the requests. Others did not officially ask to be released from these actions but instead sought to avoid participation by hiding (e.g., Heinrich Bl.), putting down their weapons and slipping off to lurk around the trucks, helping to unload the Jews (e.g., Paul M.) or taking as long as possible to search houses for Jews so that they would not be reassigned to a firing squad (e.g., Alfred L.).[14] It is this diverse variety of actions, exemplified here in the case of Reserve Police Battalion 101 and their mission in Józefów, which the typology now seeks to adequately categorize and classify.

Categorizing Actors and Action in the Holocaust and Other Genocides

Before arguing the case for approaching the topic not from an actor-centric perspective but instead by focusing on individual actions, a brief review of the existing categorizations seems in place. The departure point for many scholars when thinking about different types of actors in the Holocaust is Raul Hilberg's trichotomy of perpetrators, bystanders, and victims.[15] Hilberg's differentiation is based primarily on positions within the system, and he identifies both individuals and organizations as perpetrators[16] and bystanders.[17] Kai Ambos has also developed a typology based on the position of an individual in the system, which is, however, very different to Hilberg's. Ambos differentiates more systematically between low-, middle- and high-level individuals and state and non-state actors.[18] The problem with such typologies is, however, that they focus on the official position of the actor rather than what actions a person engages in, so two different individuals can play two completely different roles even though they hold the same position, ranging from actually killing (even if it is not part of their official assignment), to not fulfilling their role to the fullest and standing idly by, or even to rescuing people.

Next, Eric Markusen[19] has argued for complicity as a useful classificatory condition, and various categorizations by motivations have been suggested by Michael Mann, Alette Smeulers, and others in their most comprehensive form and by Gerhard Paul and Herbert Jäger in a more rudimentary variation.[20] While the issue of motivation is extremely important for the study of Holocaust bystanders, perpetrators, and rescuers, the problem with categorizing actors by their motivations is that the same motivation can be the reason people engage in different types of action. For example, greed can be a motivator across all types of actions, as rescuers can be motivated by financial interests, profiting from slave labor from Jews they had saved; a bystander can refrain from intervening because of financially profiting from Jews saved by someone else or from the deportation of Jews by others; plundering perpetrators can be motivated by greed as they participate in order to steal jewelry while clearing the ghetto or before shooting their victims. Motivations are thus only a second analytical step that can help us understand why people engage in action, but first it is necessary to understand what this action is.

Thus, a categorization is needed that allows us to focus on the actions comprising the Holocaust and then study their motivations and the positions from which they were executed. The closest categorization to this approach has been provided by Lee Ann Fujii in her work on the Rwandan genocide, differentiating between leaders, collaborators, joiners, survivors, rescuers, evaders, witnesses, and resisters.[21] However, while her approach offers more nuance, she does not differentiate the categories from each other using defining criteria, and her categories are not exhaustive. The typology I present here allows us to differentiate more precisely between various individuals who have been labeled perpetrators, bystanders, or rescuers, making the gray zones between them clearer. The typology does this not by looking at the individual actors but by disaggregating even further and categorizing the actions that these individuals engage in.[22] This typology departs from Hilberg's trichotomy of perpetrators, victims, and bystanders, replacing victims with rescuers, because it focuses on those who have an impact on the genocidal violence, the subjects who account for the violence (albeit to varying degrees), whereas the victims are objects of this violence. Naturally, victims' actions can impact the way in which the genocide occurs, but my typology focuses on those perpetrating the genocide, those who have the capacity and willingness to implement it, halt it, or stand by.

This approach will also assist in bringing bystanders in from the analytical fringes, where they have remained thus far. Their action and inaction is important for understanding the occurrence and dynamics of the Holocaust: their action and inaction were not without consequences, so it is important to relate their impact on the genocidal process to other kinds of perpetrators and rescuers. With this focus, it will be possible to study in more depth people who engage in various forms of action at different times without being limited to one label. As Mary Fulbrook stresses, the actions of bystanders are very diverse and they can—depending on the precise context and how it changes over time—have varying impact, sometimes tacitly supporting the system and giving it legitimacy, at other times allowing certain people to survive by not denouncing or even rescuing them.[23]

Typology of Action in Genocide

The following typology of action in genocide is defined along two dimensions: the individual impact on the genocide and proximity to the killing. First, I define individual impact on the genocide as the consequences that an individual's actions have on the actually realized mass murder—that is on the mass killing of the victim group. What would have been different had the individual not acted the way they did? This criterion of individual impact ranges from preventing to causing the occurrence of mass murder at all, with being responsible for preventing or causing individuals' deaths, and influencing the situation and the efficiency of the system in between. Right in the middle is a category in which the individual has no impact on the genocide at all.

Second, I bring a spatial dimension to defining genocidal action and define proximity as the distance which separates an individual from the killing. Proximity is defined physically, asking whether an acting individual is geographically close to the locus of killing. This highlights that various actions can have a similar impact on the genocide even though some occur closer to the killing and others further away. Thus, I differentiate between close and distant in the typology.

Bringing these two axes together produces the fourteen-field typology in figure 4.1. In the following, I will briefly explain each type and relate it to the empirical examples discussed earlier. First, there are those actions that have the most significant impact and without which the genocide itself would not occur. In places distant from the actual sites of killings, *agitating* occurs when the political or legal framework or the ideological underpinnings of the genocide are created and propagated; these include such notorious actors as Adolf Hitler and Joseph Goebbels. Conversely, *commanding* is when the action is closer to the killing, giving the orders for mass killing and overseeing their implementation, as was the case

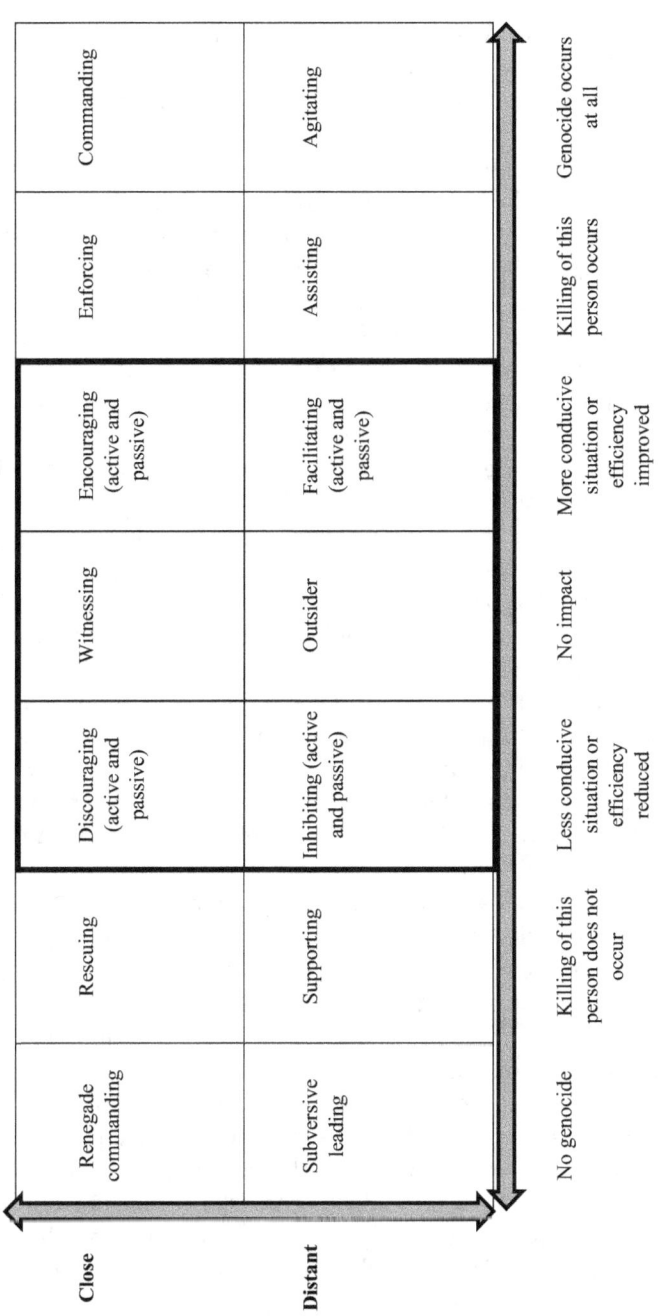

Figure 4.1. Typology of action in genocide. Highlighted areas are those types most usefully pointing toward a zone in which bystanders are positioned. (Figure created by author.)

for the actions of Major Wilhelm Trapp in Józefów, Franz Stangl in Sobibór and Treblinka, or the even more proximate actions of Arthur Kammerer who gave the orders to shoot again and again in the forests near Józefów.

Enforcing is an action, which is most closely associated with perpetration, as it is the actual execution of the orders to kill, actions such as Friedrich B.'s actual shooting of the Jews who had been transported to the woods. *Assisting* is an action that logically precedes enforcing and without which the killing could not occur either. These are actions such as those performed by Georg K. or Karl S. who rounded up the Jews of Józefów and were involved in transporting them to the killing site. Without these actions, there would have been no one to kill, even if they do not necessarily take place at the killing site.

Next, some actions create an environment more conducive to genocide occurrence or improve the efficiency of the system; this is possible through actions as well as inaction. For example, when close to the locus of killing, *active encouraging* occurs—that is, individuals take photographs, cheer or clap to spur on the killing process—and as such bystanding becomes an active form of participation. Or consider Dr. Schönfelder who taught the officers at Józefów how "best" to shoot their Jewish victims, making the murder more efficient and rendering it more legitimate through the medical semblance of a "humane" mode of killing. These actions do not actually prepare the killing but rather create an environment in which it becomes (much) easier to kill and to push the people enforcing orders forward. *Passive encouraging* is when the inaction of an individual is close to the killing—for instance, someone watching and not expressing protest at the proceedings and thus tacitly legitimizing the killing and creating a more conducive atmosphere. Anna Koegler's actions in her presence in the camp normalized the killing for her husband; she maybe even actively encouraged him. More distant from the killing sites, the same occurs at a societal level with *passive facilitating* manifesting itself in people's silence about discrimination and genocide when they witness it and thus allowing these acts to become more normal. *Active facilitating* from a distance is seen in actions designed to optimize the system, such as Adolf Eichmann's coordination of the deportations to the East, as these logistically enhanced the killing process; a further example is the development and production of Cyclone B by the company Degesch (and respectively the individuals working there) that made the killing process in the death camps more efficient.

Witnessing and *outsiders* are actions close to and distant from the killing that have no impact on the genocidal dynamics, respectively. An example of witnessing could have been people like Heinrich Bl., Paul

M., or Alfred L. whose nonparticipation went unnoticed and who were close to the locus of violence but not actually part of it. Should their (in)actions, however, have been noticed by their comrades, it is then unlikely that this would have had no impact on the situation.

The typology follows a similar pattern for the remaining categories, although these refer to actions, which hinder—or at least are intended to hinder—the attempts at mass murder. *Discouraging* is an action located close to the violence which makes enforcing less likely. An example of passive discouraging is Otto-Julius Schimke's refusal to take part in the mass killings of Józefów, which will have raised questions for his comrades as to why he refused and thus make them possibly question their own participation. More distant from the killing, people can engage in passive or active *inhibiting*, actions that make the general environment less conducive to the genocide or which make the system less effective.

An action that leads to the avoidance of an individual victim's death can be called rescuing or supporting, depending on whether it is close to or more distant from the killing, respectively. Two examples of *rescuing* are Oskar Schindler's actions, which saved hundreds of Jews from death, as well as Franz Stangl's saving of Stan Szmajzner at Sobibór death camp. While these two individuals differ significantly in their overall culpability regarding mass murder in the Holocaust, these specific actions are comparable. A further controversial example would be to classify Lieutenant Hagen's sorting out of 300 men as *Arbeitsjuden* as a rescuing action. In effect, it did save these men's lives (at least for the time being), but by sorting these men out, Hagen was also condemning the other 1,500 to death, so he simultaneously rescued and enforced. *Supporting* applies itself to the process and does not remove someone from the grips of death itself but aims to assist this effort from further afar, providing logistical or other forms of support, for example, Heinz Buchmann's actions of refusing to participate in the Jewish killings and transporting the *Arbeitsjuden* away to Lublin.

Finally, *subversive leading* and *renegade commanding* are actions committed by high-level individuals who manage to oppose genocidal legislation, propaganda, and action, or its implementation at an operational level, respectively. These types of action are the genocide-defying equivalents to agitating and commanding.

The Typology's Analytical Utility

How do these types link back to the classical distinction of perpetrators, bystanders, and rescuers, and what precisely is the analytical value of a differentiation of *actors* based on their performed *actions*? The proposed typology of actions during genocide is not parsimonious but allows for a fine-grained analysis of different forms of action that compete with and complement each other and altogether create the dynamics, which underlay the Holocaust.

One can unequivocally label actions of outsiders and witnessing as actions, which are associated with the classical treatment of a bystander as a person with no influence on the genocide, someone who is present but apart from it. Agitating, commanding, and enforcing are associated with perpetrators, and subversive leading, renegade commanding, and rescuing are action types connected to rescuers. However, all other categories are more ambivalent and difficult to allocate. Actions of assisting would fall under a broad understanding of perpetration, as will some forms of facilitating and encouraging, particularly with regards to individuals such as Adolf Eichmann or people involved in pushing victims from the trains to the gas chambers or clearing the ghettoes. So how should one categorize people who stand by and urge those enforcing the genocidal orders? Are they perpetrators or bystanders? What about those whose quiet acquiescence without active involvement furnishes the system with legitimacy and prevents any counter-discourse from emerging so that perpetrators see no alternative to participation?

These gray zones between bystanders and rescuers and bystanders and perpetrators are not captured in the threefold distinction of perpetrators, bystanders, and rescuers but are fundamental for a full understanding of the Holocaust. With the proposed typology, it is possible to tease out these differences in impact in a more nuanced way. Thus, above all, it primarily helps to systematically approach the various facets of action and impact of bystanders. The six categories that one could label as a "bystander zone" highlight that bystanders are not neutral but do have an impact on the genocide and its unfolding. They are barely ever simply "'outside' the real dynamics of the situation,"[24] but instead their actions can have a decisive impact on the genocidal process, shaping it and how various actors perceive of it. In this way, I would define bystanders not through their proximity to the situation and lack of action but instead by the *lower* impact their actions have on the genocide.

Another crucial aspect is that one person can and often does engage in various actions, thus playing varying roles, so their behavior fits into different fields of the typology. For example, Franz Stangl epitomizes the persona of a perpetrator in his leadership role in the Sobibór and Treblinka death camps, and in his role in the T4-program before that, in all three cases engaging in commanding roles. Yet, his actions toward Stan Szmajzner are those of a rescuer. By refocusing our attention on the actions of the individual, it becomes easier to incorporate such solitary actions of rescuing in a general tendency of commanding and enforcing. Overall and in the aggregation of his actions, Stangl can certainly be seen as a perpetrator, but it is precisely this detailed study of his various actions that allows us a more nuanced understanding of his varying actions instead of a more black-and-white portrayal. Equally, some individuals shift between phases of enforcing, assisting, and facilitating, moving between roles of bystanders and perpetrators, at times possibly also inhibiting or discouraging. This need be seen not only as contradictory but also as complementary, as different circumstances may make various actions more attractive or plausible to the individual within the constraints and opportunities of that specific situation. There need not be any a priori assumption of value consistency over time, yet this could be studied in a more nuanced way by interrogating the attitudes and values attached to the various actions an individual engages in.

Finally, it is interesting to contemplate the middle two categories of outsider and witnessing and to ask how realistic these are empirically. Are there even any actions (or inactions) that truly have no impact? I would argue that these two categories are possibly redundant because every person engages in actions, which together create and sustain a larger system. Otto-Julius Schimke's decision not to join in the massacre at Józefów had a discouraging effect on others and actually created a space in which refusal became more possible, an option about a dozen other men subsequently chose; yet, the fact that others did not step forward after Major Trapp's offer had a facilitative effect as it stipulated that this was the norm and gave it legitimacy. Acting and not acting alike impact the situation and an individual's peers' perception of their (in)action in it. In this situation of the roll call, there was no third option, no action in between these two: either one steps forward in refusal, or one does not. Only if others do not perceive the action of an individual at all will they not be influenced by it. Alternatively, an action remains without impact if it is perceived to be unrelated to the genocide. Thus, only if Heinrich Bl., Paul M., or Alfred L.'s nonparticipation had remained unnoticed would it have had no impact on the killing process, and thus simply have been witnessing; otherwise, such behavior has—if only the slightest—discouraging effect as it questions the inevitability and normalcy of participation.

A Comparative Perspective: Action in the Khmer Rouge Genocide in Cambodia

One key advantage of this typology is its level of abstraction, which allows us to apply it not just to the Holocaust but to other cases of genocide as well. Thus, it encourages comparative studies across multiple contexts, potentially shedding light on more generalizable dynamics underlying the human capacity of genocide and mass murder. Particularly, this is helpful for researchers who want to understand how various contexts can have similar impacts on different individuals and their relevant actions.

For example, the typology helps us approach the gray zones of perpetrators, bystanders, and rescuers for the case of the Cambodian genocide instigated by the Khmer Rouge in the late 1970s, as it allows to better understand the actions of certain individuals in this case.[25] The killing itself was carried out by a very small group of cadres who had no other responsibilities but to kill[26] and whose actions can be classified as enforcing. However, the executions were preceded by a long process of identification, arrest, guarding, and interrogating—assisting actions necessary for the "enemies of the revolution" to end up on the killing fields where they were executed.[27]

However, at the same time, any actions of discouraging or inhibiting, no matter how passive, such as refusing to work in the fields or evacuate the cities, was seen as evidence that a person was an enemy of the revolution and should thus be killed.[28] This strong degree of coercion limits the possible actions within the "bystander zone," truncating it toward only accepting bystander actions, which favored the genocide or are without impact. In essence, most actions of ordinary people who complied with the commands of the system were thus facilitating, as they seemingly supported the overall system.

This highlights an interesting tension within the Cambodian case, as the truncation of the "bystander zone" toward only impact-neutral actions or facilitating and encouraging suggests a very limited possibility of tacitly undermining the system and thus implicates most actors as (if only implicitly) legitimizing the system, even if they remained passive. At the same time, while implicating them, this does not strip these people of the possibility of having simultaneously been victims of the regime. As I had explicitly ruled victims out of the typology, it is conceptually possible for any action to coincide also with a victim status. For example, the facilitating bystanders in Cambodia are often also victims, as they experience the coercive nature of the regime (which itself even created the truncation of the "bystander zone" and ruled out inhibiting or discouraging actions). Going further, many of those engaged in assisting, as well as even some of those who committed actions of enforcing feel that they belong to the victim group, because they, too, feared for their lives, experienced dire hunger and terrible living conditions and were brutally overworked during the regime.[29]

Implications for Bystander Research

This chapter has presented a typology of action within the Holocaust and other genocidal contexts. The typology is two-dimensional, defining actions by the impact, which they have on the genocide and their proximity to the killing, allowing a broad array of actions to be located within the typology and categorized in relationship to each other and thus enhancing our understanding of such acts of collective violence by humans against humans. The additional example of the Cambodian genocide, in which various actions that forwarded the genocide coexisted with the status of victimhood, demonstrates that the possibility of people engaging in contradictory actions within the typology as has been discussed here for perpetrators, rescuers, and bystanders, can also be expanded further to allow people to engage in these actions and at the same time be classified as victims. This statement, as well as the gray zones described throughout the chapter, obviously has strong normative implications. Yet, my aim is not to open up a moral framework for describing or analyzing various forms of action and inaction within a genocidal context, but instead to propose a new classification of these in relationship to each other.

Given the little attention bystanders have received thus far, this typology is important, as it reminds us that the actions of those who are not perpetrators or rescuers but nonetheless are members of a society in which genocide is being perpetrated must be included in the analysis of genocidal dynamics. These individuals' actions—and their inactions—are not independent of the actions of others but are located along a continuum of actions that in turn influence the occurrence and process of genocide to varying degrees. This typology departs from a black-and-white-trichotomy of helping, killing, or doing nothing and opens up spaces for understanding the gray zones in between these absolutes. The various forms of actions depend on each other and are related in how they have varying but mutually facilitating or inhibiting effects on the overall situation. I have posited that many forms of actions by bystanders, which others have classed as being irrelevant, are actually important for our understanding of the Holocaust and other genocides.

From here, other researchers can take the typology as a starting point to understand how certain types of actions come to occur, how they are enforced, what consequences they have, how they relate temporally to an individual engaging in other types of actions, and many other questions. This typology is not the answer to any of these questions but instead an analytical tool to help with a more nuanced approach to answering them. A typology is not designed as an end in and of itself but will have to face the test of empirical application. It is meant not as a mere grid into which individual forms of action are pressed but as a starting point for thinking about how the actions of various actors are related to each other and how diverse actions during the Holocaust were. Ideally, it becomes possible to compare the action of one person in one context with other actions elsewhere, which have a functionally similar impact and proximity. In this way, perpetration, bystanding, and rescuing become more comparable and more comprehensible across the various loci in which the Holocaust played out. By focusing on *actions* instead of *actors*, my typology can allow for a more fine-grained perspective on the dynamics of genocide. Moreover, such a theoretically grounded analysis makes it possible to relate what we know from the Holocaust to the actions of individuals in other contexts and times, in other cases of genocide and mass violence.

Timothy Williams is a postdoctoral research fellow at the Center for Conflict Studies at the University of Marburg, Germany, where he also concluded his PhD in 2017 that has since been acknowledged with two awards: one by the University of Marburg, the other by the German Peace Psychologist Association. His research deals with violence, perpetrators, and victims, focusing on the consequences for postconflict societies and transitional justice, as well as dynamics during violence at the micro level. He has conducted extensive field research in Cambodia and was awarded the Emerging Scholar Prize of the International Association of Genocide Scholars in 2017. He has published in, among others, *Terrorism and Political Violence*, *International Peacekeeping*, *Genocide Studies and Prevention*, and *Transitional Justice Review* and has coedited, with Susanne Buckley-Zistel, *Perpetrators and Perpetration of Mass Violence: Action, Motivations and Dynamics* (Routledge, 2018).

Notes

1. On the roles of such SS wives and their postwar (self-)perceptions, see also Susanne Knittel, this volume.

2. Gitta Sereny, *Into that Darkness: From Mercy Killing to Mass Murder* (London, 1977), 131.
3. David Crowe, *Oskar Schindler: The Untold Account of His Life, Wartime Activities, and the True Story Behind the List* (Cambridge, MA, 2004).
4. See Mary Fulbrook, this volume.
5. Frank Chalk and Kurt Jonassohn, *The History and Sociology of Genocide: Analyses and Case Studies* (New Haven, CT, 1990), 26.
6. While there is no academic consensus on these issues, it would go beyond this chapter's scope of interest to go into these discussions in any depth; for a fuller discussion, see, among many others, Adam Jones, *Genocide: A Comprehensive Introduction* (London, 2006); A. Dirk Moses, "Raphael Lemkin, Culture, and the Concept of Genocide," in *The Oxford Handbook of Genocide Studies*, ed. Donald Bloxham and A. Dirk Moses (Oxford, 2010), 19–41; Christopher Powell, "What Do Genocides Kill? A Relational Conception of Genocide" *Journal of Genocide Research*, no. 9 (2007): 527–547; Martin Shaw, "Sociology and Genocide," in Bloxham and Moses, *Oxford Handbook of Genocide Studies*, 142–162; Scott Straus, "Contested Meanings and Conflicting Imperatives: A Conceptual Analysis of Genocide," *Journal of Genocide Research* 3, no. 3 (2001): 349–375.
7. See, among many others, Christopher Browning, *Ordinary Men: Reserve Police Battalion 101 and the Final Solution in Poland* (New York, 1992; New York, 2001), 2 (citations refer to the 2001 edition); Stefan Kühl, *Ganz normale Organisationen: Zur Soziologie des Holocaust* (Berlin, 2014). I adopt the pseudonyms as they appear in Browning, *Ordinary Men*.
8. Browning, *Ordinary Men*, 225.
9. Ibid., 56.
10. Ibid., 57.
11. Ibid., 67, 129.
12. Ibid., 59–60.
13. Ibid., 57, 61.
14. Ibid., 62–63.
15. Raul Hilberg, *Perpetrators Victims Bystanders: The Jewish Catastrophe, 1933–1945* (New York, 1992).
16. Adolf Hitler; the establishment; old functionaries; newcomers; zealots, vulgarians, and bearers of burdens; physicians and lawyers; non-German governments; and non-German volunteers. Ibid.
17. Nations in Adolf Hitler's Europe; helpers, gainers, and onlookers; messengers; the Jewish rescuers; the Allies; neutral countries; the churches. Ibid.
18. Kai Ambos, "Criminologically Explained Reality of Genocide, Structure of the Offence and the 'Intent to Destroy' Requirement," in *Collective Violence and International Criminal Justice*, ed. Alette Smeulers (Antwerp, 2010), 153–173.
19. Eric Markusen, "Mechanisms of Genocide," in *Will Genocide Ever End?* ed. Carol Rittner, John K. Roth, and James M. Smith (St. Paul, MN, 2002), 83–89.
20. Herbert Jäger, *Verbrechen unter totalitärer Herrschaft: Studien zur nationalsozialistischen Gewaltkriminalität* (Olten, 1967; Frankfurt, 1982); Michael Mann, *The Dark Side of Democracy: Explaining Ethnic Cleansing* (Cambridge, 2005), Gerhard Paul, "Von Psychopaten, Technokraten des Terrors und 'ganz gewöhnlichen' Deutschen: Die Täter der Shoah im Spiegel der Forschung," in *Die Täter der Shoah: Fanatische Nationalsozialisten oder ganz normale Deutsche?* ed. Gerhard Paul (Göttingen, 2002), 13–92; Alette Smeulers, "Perpetrators of International Crimes: Towards a Typology," in *Supranational Criminology: Towards a Criminology of International Crimes*, ed. Alette Smeulers and Roelof Haveman (Antwerp, 2008), 233–265; Alette

Smeulers and Lotte Hoex, "Studying the Microdynamics of the Rwandan Genocide," *British Journal of Criminology* 50, no. 3 (2010): 435–454.
21. Lee Ann Fujii, *Killing Neighbors: Networks of Violence in Rwanda* (Ithaca, NY, 2009), 16, 130.
22. On violence as action, see Christian Gudehus, "Violence as Action," in *Perpetrators and Perpetration of Mass Violence: Action, Motivations and Dynamics.*, ed. Timothy Williams and Susanne Buckley-Zistel (London, 2018), 36–57.
23. See Fulbrook, this volume.
24. Ibid.
25. These insights are based on six months of fieldwork I conducted in Cambodia in 2014 and 2015, which encompassed interviews with fifty-eight former cadres of the Khmer Rouge in ten provinces of the country.
26. Interview with a former chief of a hard labor site, Battambang province, August 2014.
27. For a more detailed discussion of the killing process under the Khmer Rouge, see David Chandler, *Voices from S-21: Terror and History in Pol Pot's Secret Prison* (Chiang Mai, 2000); David Chandler, *A History of Cambodia* (Boulder, CO, 2008); Ben Kiernan, *The Pol Pot Regime: Race, Power, and Genocide in Cambodia under the Khmer Rouge* (New Haven, CT, 1996).
28. Interview with a former soldier, bodyguard, and then district committee member in charge of the economy, Kampong Chhnang province, August 2014; interview with a former collective committee chief, Kampong Chhnang province, August 2014; interview with a former S-21 guard, Kampong Chhnang province, September 2014; interview with a former S-21 guard, Takéo province, October 2014.
29. See also Timothy Williams, "Perpetrator-Victims: How Universal Victimhood in Cambodia Impacts Transitional Justice Measures," in *Understanding the Age of Transitional Justice: Crimes, Courts, Commissions, and Chronicling*, ed. Nanci Adler (New Brunswick, NJ, 2018), 194–212; Erin Jessee and Timothy Williams, "Perpetrators as Victims? Individual Narratives of the Genocidal Continuum in Cambodia and Rwanda," (forthcoming).

Bibliography

Ambos, Kai. "Criminologically Explained Reality of Genocide, Structure of the Offence and the 'Intent to Destroy' Requirement." In *Collective Violence and International Criminal Justice*, edited by Alette Smeulers, 153–173. Antwerp: Intersentia, 2010.
Bloxham, Donald, and A. Dirk Moses, eds. *The Oxford Handbook of Genocide Studies*. Oxford: Oxford University Press, 2010.
Browning, Christopher. *Ordinary Men: Reserve Police Battalion 101 and the Final Solution in Poland*. New York: Penguin, 2001. First published 1992 by HarperCollins (New York).
Chalk, Frank, and Kurt Jonassohn. *The History and Sociology of Genocide: Analyses and Case Studies*. New Haven, CT: Yale University Press, 1990.
Chandler, David. *A History of Cambodia*. 4th ed. Boulder, CO: Westview Press, 2008.
———. *Voices from S-21: Terror and History in Pol Pot's Secret Prison*. Chiang Mai: Silkworm, 2000.
Crowe, David. *Oskar Schindler: The Untold Account of His Life, Wartime Activities, and the True Story Behind the List*. Cambridge, MA: Westview Press, 2004.

Fujii, Ann Lee. *Killing Neighbors: Networks of Violence in Rwanda*. Ithaca, NY: Cornell University Press, 2009.
Gudehus, Christian. "Violence as Action." In *Perpetrators and Perpetration of Mass Violence: Action, Motivations and Dynamics*, edited by Timothy Williams and Susanne Buckley-Zistel, 36–57. London: Routledge, 2018.
Hilberg, Raul. *Perpetrators, Victims, Bystanders: The Jewish Catastrophe, 1933–1945*. New York: HarperCollins, 1992.
Jäger, Herbert. *Verbrechen unter totalitärer Herrschaft: Studien zur nationalsozialistischen Gewaltkriminalität*. Frankfurt: Suhrkamp, 1982. First published 1967 by Walter Verlag (Olten).
Jessee, Erin, and Timothy Williams. "Perpetrators as Victims? Individual Narratives of the Genocidal Continuum in Cambodia and Rwanda." Forthcoming.
Jones, Adam. *Genocide: A Comprehensive Introduction*. London: Routledge, 2006.
Kiernan, Ben. *The Pol Pot Regime: Race, Power, and Genocide in Cambodia under the Khmer Rouge*. New Haven, CT: Yale University Press, 1996.
Kühl, Stefan. *Ganz normale Organisationen: Zur Soziologie des Holocaust*. Berlin: Suhrkamp, 2014.
Mann, Michael. *The Dark Side of Democracy: Explaining Ethnic Cleansing*. Cambridge: Cambridge University Press, 2005.
Markusen, Eric. "Mechanisms of Genocide." In *Will Genocide Ever End?* edited by Carol Rittner, John K. Roth, and James M. Smith, 83–89. St. Paul, MN: Paragon House, 2002.
Moses, A. Dirk. "Raphael Lemkin, Culture, And the Concept of Genocide." In Bloxham and Moses, *Oxford Handbook of Genocide Studies*, 19–41.
Paul, Gerhard. "Von Psychopaten, Technokraten des Terrors und 'ganz gewöhnlichen' Deutschen: Die Täter der Shoah im Spiegel der Forschung." In *Die Täter der Shoah: Fanatische Nationalsozialisten oder ganz normale Deutsche?* edited by Gerhard Paul, 13–92. Göttingen: Wallstein, 2002.
Powell, Christopher. "What Do Genocides Kill? A Relational Conception of Genocide." *Journal of Genocide Research* 9, no. 4 (2007): 527–547.
Sereny, Gitta. *Into that Darkness: From Mercy Killing to Mass Murder*. London: Picador, 1977.
Shaw, Martin. "Sociology and Genocide." In Bloxham and Moses, *Oxford Handbook of Genocide Studies*, 142–162.
Smeulers, Alette. "Perpetrators of International Crimes: Towards a Typology." In *Supranational Criminology: Towards a Criminology of International Crimes*, edited by Alette Smeulers and Roelof Haveman, 233–265. Antwerp: Intersentia, 2008.
Smeulers, Alette, and Lotte Hoex. "Studying the Microdynamics of the Rwandan Genocide." *British Journal of Criminology* 50, no. 3 (2010): 435–454.
Straus, Scott. "Contested Meanings and Conflicting Imperatives: A Conceptual Analysis of Genocide." *Journal of Genocide Research* 3, no. 3 (2001): 349–375.
Williams, Timothy. "Perpetrator-Victims: How Universal Victimhood in Cambodia Impacts Transitional Justice Measures." In *Understanding the Age of Transitional Justice: Crimes, Courts, Commissions, and Chronicling*, edited by Nanci Adler, 194–212. New Brunswick, NJ: Rutgers University Press, 2018.

CHAPTER 5

THE MANY SHADES OF BYSTANDING
ON SOCIAL DILEMMAS AND PASSIVE PARTICIPATION

Froukje Demant

When Hitler came to power on 30 January 1933, nothing immediately changed for Alfred and Sophie Süskind, a Jewish couple from Fürstenau, a small town in the Emsland. Although they were nervous about the virulent antisemitic rhetoric of the Nazis, they hoped and expected that the Nazi regime would have to leave the political stage soon. One non-Jewish neighboring household, with whom they had cordial contact—helping each other out with daily chores, keeping spare keys of each other's houses—tried to reassure them: "Don't worry, it is nothing personal. This is about the 'big' Jews: the bankers and other people in important positions. You have nothing to be afraid of." In later months and years, these neighbors upheld their friendly relationship with the Süskinds, even though they had party membership and uniforms. It was only after almost three years, when the Nuremberg Laws came into force in the fall of 1935, that they changed their manner: when they encountered the Süskinds in public, they crossed the street and looked the other way. Then the owner of the local *Gastwirtschaft* (tavern) came to the house of the Süskinds to tell Alfred that he was not welcome anymore at the *Stammtisch* (pub table). He explained to Alfred that he had come to tell him this personally in order to avoid a painful situation in public.

Over the years, the Süskinds lost contact with almost all their neighbors and friends. In public, they were ignored and isolated. After dark, however, they regularly found food in front of their door, left behind by anonymous helpers. And one person always stayed in touch with the family: a dear family friend who had been the witness at the wedding of the Süskinds. Yet, during the so-called *Kristallnacht*, the pogrom of 9 November 1938, this friend came by unexpectedly and asked for Alfred. When he did not find him home, he took Bernard, the seventeen-year-old son, out into the street and handed him over to SA men, saying, "Here, I found another Jew."[1]

According to Raul Hilberg's famous triad of perpetrators, victims, and bystanders, all the neighbors, acquaintances, and friends of the Süskinds, with their very different and variable behavior toward the Jewish family, fall under the category of the bystanders. They were no perpetrators as Hilberg defined them, as they played no specific part in the formulation and implementation of the anti-Jewish measures.[2] And they were no victims, because these measures were not intended for them. They were the "other" contemporaries, present to, and witness of, the events.[3]

Hilberg's description is archetypical to the bystander that returns time and again in academic and popular representations of violent interactions: the passive witness who observes, or looks away from, the violence. This passive figure is also a classic object of study in the field of social psychology.[4] Yet, historians of the Holocaust have come to realize that this archetype does not suffice to capture the complex and changing positions of those who were neither perpetrators nor victims of the Nazi persecution of the Jews. Therefore, various new categories and concepts have been introduced, such as beneficiaries, onlookers, accomplices, and helpers. These enable a more differentiated analysis, but they still cannot capture the dynamic nature of the bystander position. Moreover, scholars grapple with the problem that by defining and explaining bystanders, they are immediately confronted with questions regarding responsibility and culpability, as well as the legacies of persecution and mass violence. On the one hand, the category of the bystander can be used in self-exonerating strategies of people who were not victims and who have an interest in not being classed among the perpetrators.[5] On the other hand, in recent years, the category of the bystander at times has been used as a synonym for co-perpetrator, and the term "perpetrator society" is gaining ground to describe the society of the Third Reich.[6]

Scholars such as Frank Bajohr, Andrea Löw, and Mary Fulbrook therefore call for a nuanced approach, differentiating between various kinds of roles and behaviors in evolving situations and analyzing the complex social processes that influenced the choices of people in the Nazi era.[7] Such an approach first of all sheds light on the *situational* nature of the bystander. Bystanders are defined not by inner characteristics but by their position in a situation when victimizers inflict harm upon their victims. The bystander is also an inherently *relational* concept: bystanders are by definition part of a social constellation in which they are neither perpetrator nor victim. One could argue that it is the perpetrator who makes others into bystanders, as the perpetrator chooses the setting and the specific victim, thereby involving others.[8] The *factor of time* is of essence in explaining the behavior of bystanders; long-term situations cause a fundamentally different dynamic than unique, short-term incidents of violence. Last but not least, in case the political order sanctions and ordains the violence, and thus the violence is of a *systemic, collective* nature, there is no option of standing outside the arena of conflict; everybody is inherently involved in one way or another.[9]

In this chapter, I will build on the approach proposed by Bajohr, Löw, and Fulbrook, exploring how the behavior of the Süskinds' neighbors and acquaintances, and the changes and ambivalences therein, relate to our understanding of the bystander. Can we find analytical tools to explain their thoughts and actions, attitudes and decisions, and to start at the same time unraveling the complexity of the bystander concept? In order to address these questions, I will make use of social-scientific, especially social-psychological, perspectives on bystanders. While historical perspectives center on the context of historical events and dynamics, social science in contrast searches for commonalities in different contexts and times. Combining these different perspectives enables us to not only review the social-scientific theories in light of a specific historical reality but also to analyze and explain that reality.

First, I will introduce the social-scientific perspective on bystanders by focusing on the case of bystanders of bullying behavior in school classes. Of course, bullying in a classroom cannot, and should not, be equated with the persecution and annihilation of the Jews in the Nazi era. There are, however, interesting parallels that are worth exploring: bullying is a group process that unfolds over time, and children cannot easily escape the group dynamics in their class. The study of the microcosm of the classroom can therefore uncover certain mechanisms that are of relevance for the study of the bystander position in general, especially regarding collective normative shifts. Second, I will describe a specific historical case: the behaviors of non-Jews toward Jews in the

German-Dutch borderland from 1933 to 1941, focusing thus on the years preceding the deportations and physical annihilation. Third, I will connect the social-scientific approaches to the historical case, exploring how the social-psychological insights can help explain the positioning of the non-Jewish population toward the Jews. Finally, I will discuss some broader implications of this approach for the definition and conceptualization of bystanders and their involvement in the Nazi persecution of the Jews.

Bystanding as Social Dilemma

Focusing our attention on the micro level of bullying behavior in a classroom, we can quite clearly see that bullying entails more than a bilateral interaction. Except from the so-called ringleader bully, who initiates the bullying process, and the victim, who is the bully's target, all the children in the classroom are involved in the process in one way or another. They actively help and support the bully, for example, by catching the victim, or they reinforce the bully by providing him or her with positive feedback, for example, by laughing. But there are also children who defend the victim or position themselves as outsiders who observe that classmates are being victimized but do not intervene or pretend that nothing is going on. Even if the majority does not participate, it may behave in ways that make the beginning and continuation of the bullying process possible. Thus, bullying is a group process.[10]

Intuitively, we understand that the behavior of the other children influences the behavior of the bully. Bullies strive to achieve status by dominating classmates, and since the group assigns status to its members, bullies are dependent on the peer group in the realization of their status goal. This influence of the children present to the bullying has indeed been demonstrated on the group level of school classes: studies have shown that the more classmates tend to reinforce the bully, the more frequently bullying takes place in a school class while classroom levels of supporting and defending the victims have an opposite effect.[11]

What makes bullying the more relevant for the study of bystanders is that it is a process unfolding over time and that it often arises and prevails despite the fact that most children are against bullying.[12] Apparently, many children take on positions (supporting or reinforcing the bully, observing without intervening) that are contrary to their own beliefs. To explain this, we need to focus on the social dilemma in which these children find themselves. On one hand, they understand that bullying is wrong and they would like to do something to stop it; on the other hand, they strive to secure their own status and safety in the peer group. By targeting someone else, the aggressive child arouses in others a fear that they themselves may become targets if they do not follow along. It can seem adaptive for children to distance themselves from victims. Behaving aggressively—or at least not friendly—toward the target of bullying becomes like a trend, a way of confirming one's belonging to the peer group. Over time, it becomes a social norm of the group not to like the victim. In this way, new class norms arise: the behavior of the bullies becomes normative in a classroom.[13] Thus, the unpopularity of victims should be understood as both a cause and a result of continuous bullying.

Can we transfer these insights from the micro situation of bullying in a classroom to the complex, multilayered, and long-term process of bystanding during the Nazi persecution of the Jews? Many social-psychological approaches aiming to explain the Holocaust indeed focus on social norms and the psychological mechanisms that allow people to act in breach of these norms.[14] However, insightful as these theories are, they mainly deal with changes in individual attitudes. Yet, following Dennis Kahn, the real question is not what caused bystanders (and perpetrators) to act in breach of social norms but rather how the norms were allowed to shift to such a degree that the exclusion, violence, and annihilation of an entire people became normalized.[15] In order to explain how the initial social dilemma of bystanders leads over time to a collective normative shift, two social-psychological mechanisms appear to be essential: pluralistic ignorance and the false enforcement of unpopular norms.

Pluralistic ignorance refers to a situation in which group members privately reject a norm but at the same time believe that others accept it. When very few individuals publicly challenge the norm or openly communicate their private attitudes to others, the group members might infer that the others subscribe to the norm. They suppress their dissent and copy the behavior of others who are wrongly believed to represent the popular majority, thereby bolstering the false norm in the group.[16]

Whereas pluralistic ignorance can explain the passive compliance of bystanders to a norm they privately reject, the mechanism of false enforcement goes a step further, uncovering why bystanders would also choose to conform actively to an unpopular norm. This mechanism refers to a situation in which group members who do not adhere to a norm privately nonetheless conform to it publicly *and* enforce conformity among others.[17] Why would they take such an active stance if they do not believe in the norm? A study by the sociologists Robb Willer, Ko Kuwabara, and Michael Macy suggests that people enforce an unpopular norm in order to display to others the sincerity of their conformity. In other words, people who privately doubt or even oppose a norm can take an active role in the enforcement of this norm in order to convince others that they are true believers and did not conform simply to secure social approval. In this way, a norm with almost no initial support can snowball into having a powerful apparent majority; it becomes a "false" norm. This mechanism is particularly likely to occur in cases when there is uncertainty about the norm and social pressure is high. Once the trend is set, it becomes increasingly difficult for others not to follow along; the mechanisms of pluralistic ignorance and false enforcement give the group a superficial appearance of cohesion and homogeneity.

The Many Shades of Bystanding

To explore the potential of these social-scientific approaches for the study of bystanders to the Holocaust, I shall briefly introduce the results of a specific historical case study, namely the behaviors of non-Jews toward Jews in the German-Dutch borderland (Westmünsterland, Grafschaft Bentheim and Emsland) from 1933 to 1941.[18] This study offers some insight into the local reality of bystanding in the context of a system of state-ordained violence and is based on different sources: interviews with Jewish and non-Jewish contemporary witnesses, contemporary *Stimmungsberichte* (reports on the mood of the population), postwar memoirs, and local documentations. Although these sources contain the perspectives of the non-Jewish population, the local regime, and the Jewish victims, the perspective of the victims is dominant.[19] Thus, the description of the behaviors of the non-Jews is mainly based on victim accounts.

The exclusion and expulsion of the Jews from German society was a long-term process; nine years lay between the Nazi power takeover at the beginning of 1933 and the first deportations from the border region in December 1941. In these years, the cohabitation of Jews and non-Jews can be described as a constantly changing constellation of interactions, acts, and reactions. In their interactions with Jews, non-Jews could emphasize—or alternatively, minimize—the new power imbalance between themselves and the Jews and thus the degree to which they actively isolated, degraded, exploited, or helped their Jewish acquaintances.

Jewish contemporary witnesses describe how, apart from overtly degrading behavior as scolding and physical violence toward Jewish properties or persons,[20] many non-Jews displayed one or more kinds of isolating behavior. One option was evasion: many people chose to silently withdraw from their relations with Jewish acquaintances. They no longer contacted their friends, did not show up for appointments, avoided places where they might run into one another. Another way to make clear to Jewish friends that further contact was not desired without explicitly saying so was openly ignoring them. This was a very common type of isolating behavior, in cases of both distant acquaintances and close contacts. Others chose to explicitly terminate the contact, sometimes trying to ease their message by assuring that the friendship would continue despite the ending of the relations.[21]

The sources demonstrate that in addition to the isolation, many non-Jews took the opportunity to exploit their Jewish neighbors and acquaintances.[22] The ongoing Nazi policy of exclusion made it very easy for non-Jews to profit from the suffering of the Jews. They purchased Jewish properties at a low price, and some people even went as far as to steal Jewish belongings. On the other hand, some people kept helping Jews over the years, for example, by doing their laundry, bringing food, or offering direct financial support. And while the economic boycott forced most Jewish entrepreneurs to close their doors within a few years of the Nazis coming to power, Jewish cattle dealers could keep their heads above water for a relative long time because the local farmers continued to trade with them in secret.[23]

The conduct of the non-Jews thus encompassed all kinds of active participation, as well as many shades of passive "nonaction." To what extent the daily life of Jews was marked by degradation, isolation, and exploitation could therefore vary from moment to moment and from person to person. I will give two short examples to illustrate this point: the first is on the local level in the years before the pogrom of November 1938; the second is on the individual level and describes the experiences of a Jewish/non-Jewish mixed married couple after the pogrom.

In Ahaus, in the Westmünsterland not far from the Dutch border, the Jewish cattle dealer Adolf de Jong was beaten up by SA men in his own house in 1934.[24] He was severely injured and would remain limp for the rest of his life. His experience is a frightening early example of degradation of and violence against the local Jewish population. However, in the same year, Adolf's three children—Henny, Marga, and Herbert—took part in the *Kinderschützen* party that was organized in their neighborhood. Pictures of the event show the children sitting between other children of the neighborhood, without any sign of trouble or inconvenience. The same is true for the local festivities three years later, in 1937.[25] At that time, non-Jewish boys still helped Jewish cattle dealers with managing their cattle at the station. The boys could earn 10 pfennig through this work and were thus always very happy when "the Jews were back again."[26]

Non-Jewish contemporary witnesses describe how in the same period, a teacher from the *Bernsmannkampschule*, the school for boys in Ahaus, let his pupils march in front of the houses of local Jews, while they sang the song "Wenn's Judenblut vom Messer spritzt" (When the blood of the Jew spurts from the knife). On a sign from the teacher, one pupil had to shout "Juda," after which the rest of the group cried, "Verrecke!" (Jew, die!).[27] At the local school for girls, on the other hand, a school picture could be taken, in 1937, showing the Jewish girl Marga Cohen sitting smiling on the lap of her non-Jewish friend Bärbel Sümmermann.[28]

The second example is provided in the memoirs that Lotte Herz, a non-Jewish woman from the town of Burgsteinfurt who was married to a Jewish man, wrote in 1948. Lotte describes her experiences in the period between the pogrom in November 1938 and the couple's flight out of Germany in October 1940.[29] The couple experienced degradation and exploitation: during the night of the pogrom, Lotte's husband was arrested, and their villa was first ransacked and then burned. The crowd that flocked around the remains of the house afterward did not speak to Lotte at all and did not provide aid in any way. When her husband was released from prison, the couple could not stay at Lotte's mother's house, because they were threatened that it would be set on fire as well. They were also not welcome in the houses of non-Jewish friends and acquaintances. When the couple later was forced to sell their ruined property, interested parties tried to acquire it as cheap farming land.

Parallel to these negative experiences, however, Lotte describes several instances of helping behavior. During the night of the pogrom, two old acquaintances came to grant their aid to Lotte because of the incarceration of her husband. The next day, two women from her neighborhood came to invite her for dinner at their place. A group of older men—former pupils of the local gymnasium—offered financial help in support of her son's studies. They said they wished to compensate him for the harm that the younger generation had inflicted on his family. Finally, when the couple left Burgsteinfurt in October 1940, an acquaintance from the neighboring town of Borghorst came by to bring them food for their journey.

The examples both show the ambiguous and contradictory nature of the Jewish/non-Jewish cohabitation in these years under Nazi rule. The non-Jewish positioning toward the victims of Nazi persecution was an elusive mix of isolating, violent, and exploitative behavior, genuine expressions of affection, and evasive attempts of normalization.

Yet, relations between Jews and non-Jews were not only interlaced with ambiguities; they were also multilayered, as a termination of relationships in the public sphere did not always mean the end of contact. Because of public exclusion, an increasing separation arose between the public and the private spheres. Some non-Jews remained secretly in touch with their Jewish acquaintances—in the dark in the backyard or at home with the shutters closed. Most of the supporting and helping behaviors also took place in secret, in the private sphere of the home or at night under the cover of darkness. This means that non-Jews were inconsistent in their positioning toward Jews: some who ignored their Jewish acquaintances during the day continued friendly contact at night.[30]

Therefore, the positioning of non-Jews toward Jews could best be described as "ambivalent excluding." They were ambiguous and inconsistent in their behavior, yet, at the same time, the majority contributed, in various degrees, to the gradual exclusion of the Jews. Over the years, the Jewish/non-Jewish coexistence degenerated to a situation in which the Jews were harassed, threatened, and exploited by some, ignored in the public space by many, and greeted and helped by only a very few.

The Strength of Unpopular Norms

Most studies on the attitudes of the population in Nazi Germany tend to emphasize either the Germans' antisemitism and enthusiasm for the Nazi concept of a German folk community, or the terror unleashed by the regime that forced the population into compliance. Yet, the ambivalent and multilayered positioning of the non-Jewish population toward the Jews indicates that, at least in the case of the people in the border region, it was not clearly one or the other. The case study shows that non-Jews had to decide repeatedly how to act, how to position themselves within the context of the current situation and within the accompanying possibilities and constraints, as they perceived them. If we now take into account social-psychological dynamics, we gain insight into how, through an interaction between state and society, a system of collective violence can take root in the everyday reality of local communities.

This process took place in the context of high social pressure to conform to the expectations and demands of the regime.[31] Non-Jews who stayed in contact with Jews were pressured in various ways to end the relationship: from public humiliation, open criticism, and recognizable pictures in the antisemitic newspaper *Der Stürmer*, to the threat of decreasing income or job loss, to even arrest. With the introduction of the Nuremberg Laws, keeping relations with Jews became a ground not only for social loss of face but also for very real criminalization. The pressure came not from an abstract, far-away regime but rather from local, and therefore very familiar, actors. So-called block leaders of the Nazi Party, who were responsible for the supervision of a neighborhood, knew the social relations within the local communities very well and were therefore able to notice "undesired conduct." They had both definitional as decisional power: they determined whether specific behavior should be considered unwanted and whether it was worth the trouble to report on it. The same was true for the local postal workers.[32]

The social pressure thus created fertile ground for dynamics of pluralistic ignorance and the enforcement of false norms. Even if a large part of the population initially was not convinced of the virulent antisemitism of the Nazis, it is likely that in the first years of the Third Reich, the illusion took hold that everybody supported the new norm of antisemitic exclusion and persecution. People felt spied on, and for good reason: they spied on each other. A self-policing society arose in which citizens—for various reasons, often more personal and material than political—denounced each other to the Gestapo.[33] People who held up their relationships with Jews, and tried to help and support them, therefore most often chose to do this in secret. Whether this individual undermining of the new norm was unknown to the public or more of an open secret is not always clear, but in both ways an unintended effect of the secrecy was the fostering of the norm of exclusion on the collective level. Furthermore, along with the new norm came new opportunities: one was able, indeed encouraged, to humiliate and exploit others. Stripping Jewish neighbors from their belongings went unpunished, and youngsters grew up in an atmosphere where they could abuse and even assault Jewish people without consequences.[34]

Notably, the existence of a false norm does not rule out the possibility that the perpetual conforming to, and enforcement of, that norm can lead to a real change in individual attitudes over time. Perhaps, initially, one was skeptical about the virulent antisemitism of the Nazis but conformed just to prevent gossip in the neighborhood. Then, as one had repeatedly ignored, degraded, or exploited Jews, the need for cognitive dissonance reduction led to moral disengagement: people convinced themselves that they behaved that way for a reason and that the Jews indeed were lesser creatures that could no longer be tolerated. Through such a convergence of group norms and individual attitudes and opportunities, the social dilemma that non-Jews found themselves in might have become less pressing.

Conclusion

The history of the Jewish/non-Jewish coexistence under Nazi rule draws attention to the ambiguous and multilayered nature of bystanding. The position of the bystanders involved all kinds of (non)action: from active participation in the exclusion, to passive acts of evasion and ignoring, to (secret) help to the victims. Bystanders alternated between very different kinds of behavior depending on the situation, and they shifted their position over time. Yet, regardless their position and degree of participation, they were all part of the social constellation of exclusion, and their presence therefore was never neutral.

Social-scientific approaches to bystanders in different times and contexts provide clues for an analysis and explanation of the complex position of the bystanders of the Nazi persecution of the Jews. They point to the central role of social norms and to the shifts in these norms over time. By focusing on the social dilemmas bystanders find themselves in, and on the dynamics of pluralistic ignorance and the enforcement of false norms, we gain insight into the ways in which moral universes arise, sustain, and shift. Studying the behaviors of historical bystanders through this lens can therefore help to understand both psychological and historical dynamics.

Social science's search for commonalities in different contexts, however, also leads to an overly structured frame that does not render justice to the infinitely more complex (historical) reality. The example of the Jewish/non-Jewish relations in the German border region under Nazi rule illustrates that the social-psychological mechanisms, and thus the normative shifts, were in no way structured, linear processes. In contrast, the relations were marked by ambivalences and contradictions. Yet, notwithstanding the contradictory, nonlinear nature of the process, there was a process indeed: despite all the ifs and buts, over time most Jews were isolated and betrayed by neighbors and friends. By taking into account social-psychological dynamics, we can make progress in an explanation of this process—an explanation that brings us beyond the too simple fear-or-enthusiasm schism that so often dominates debates about the position of the "ordinary" population.

How do these insights relate to the conceptualization of the bystander? Given the contradictory and multilayered reality of bystanding, I would argue that the position of the bystander is even more complex than we have assumed thus far, because almost all behaviors and reactions help to sustain the system in one way or another. Even persons who support the victims on the individual level, for example, by secretly bringing food or providing hiding places, contribute on the collective level to the system, as they do not speak out publicly against the norms of exclusion and persecution and therefore facilitate the illusion that everybody support these norms. Thus, the real problem is not that bystanders are forced to take sides but that these sides are intertwined in perverse ways. In a system of violence where there is no outside, (almost) everybody is inherently implicated.

It is important to stress that this is an analytical rather than a moral statement: the fact that almost everybody inherently contributes to the system in one way or another tells us nothing about agency or the option of choice, and therefore nothing about innocence or guilt. It does not imply that all bystanders are inherently guilty or that they are all innocent because "there was nothing that could be done." In other words, the analysis of how it is (or was) should not be mistaken for a description of how it should have been or of how it could have been. In order to proceed fruitfully in the definition and explanation of bystanders, it is essential to distinguish truly between analytical description and moral weighting—especially in light of the apologetical and self-exonerating potential of the topic of the bystander. A key issue in this regard is how to define and analyze the "involvement" of bystanders in the system of violence. This paradox might be best captured if we, in analogy with the concept of choiceless choices that so aptly describes the situation of the Jews in Nazi Germany,[35] describe their position in terms of uninvolved involvement or passive participation.[36] Yet, reflections on this theme are complicated because terms such as "involvement," "mobilization," and "participation" have themselves strong moral connotations: they suggest co-responsibility and co-culpability.

If there is one thing that has become clear, it is that bystanders *matter*. The presence of parties other than the aggressor and the victim influences the dynamics and the intensity of the violence significantly. Bystanders are more than passive witnesses; they have agency. All acquaintances of the Süskinds had room to decide whether they would continue greeting the family, betray them, or bring them food instead. Yet, they were also part of a wider field of forces that constrained them in very real and in imagined ways. By studying the bystanders in the context of their agency and (perceived) constraints gives insight into the inner workings of the system of violence. Not every individual had the power of change: the system would not have become instable or would have collapsed if one or more individuals would have refused to take up their role. The exclusion was a complex dynamic of actors who were dependent on each other. It is clear that those actors would have been able to redirect, or even stop, the shifts in the existing order. Yet, the question remains: who, when, and how many? We are just at the beginning to unravel the complexity of the bystander position.

Froukje Demant is Senior Researcher at the National Committee for 4 and 5 May (the Netherlands) and Postdoctoral Research Fellow at the Amsterdam Institute for German Studies. She received a PhD from the University of Amsterdam in 2015 for her dissertation "Verre Buren: Samenleven in de schaduw van de Holocaust" (Distant neighbors: Jews and non-Jews in the shadow of the Holocaust). Her research focuses on the social dynamics in Jewish/non-Jewish cohabitation in the German-Dutch border region from the 1920s through to the 1950s. In her research, she explores the relationship between everyday interactions and the experience of normality, and the meaning of silence in the immediate postwar years.

Notes

1. Interview with Bernard Süskind, 23 September 2011.
2. It could be argued, however, that the family friend became a perpetrator at the moment that he betrayed Bernard Süskind—an illustration of the fluidity of the bystander category that will be discussed in more detail here.
3. Raul Hilberg, *Perpetrators Victims Bystanders: The Jewish Catastrophe, 1933–1945* (New York, 1992), ix–xi.
4. John M. Darley and Bibb Latané, "Bystander Intervention in Emergencies: Diffusion of Responsibility," *Journal of Personality and Social Psychology* 8, no. 4 (1968): 377–383; Bibb Latané and John M. Darley, *The Unresponsive Bystander: Why Doesn't He Help?* (New York, 1970); John M. Darley, Allan I. Teger, and Lawrence D. Lewis, "Do Groups Always Inhibit Individuals' Responses to Potential Emergencies?" *Journal of Personality and Social Psychology* 26, no. 3 (1973): 395–399; John M. Darley and C. Daniel Batson, "'From Jerusalem to Jericho': A Study of Situational and Dispositional Variables in Helping Behavior," *Journal of Personality and Social Psychology* 27, no. 1 (1973): 100–108.
5. Mary Fulbrook, *A Small Town near Auschwitz: Ordinary Nazis and the Holocaust* (Oxford, 2012).
6. Frank Bajohr and Andrea Löw, "Beyond the 'Bystander': Social Processes and Social Dynamics in European Societies as Context for the Holocaust," in *The Holocaust and European Societies: Social Processes and Social Dynamics*, ed. Frank Bajohr and Andrea Löw (London, 2016), 3–14. In academic debates on the Holocaust, there is a trend toward the interpretation of bystanders as co-perpetrators. In German literature, phrasings as "resilience" (*Resistenz*) and "the uninvolved" (*Unbeteiligten*) have been replaced by "dictatorship of bottom-up consent" (*Zustimmungsdiktatur*) and "situational complicity" to describe the position of the bystanders. On *Unbeteiligten*, see Dieter Pohl, "Die Holocaust-Forschung und Goldhagens Thesen," *Vierteljahrshefte für Zeitgeschichte* 45, no. 1 (1997): 14. On *Zustimmungsdiktatur*, see Götz Aly, *Rasse und Klasse: Nachforschungen zum deutschen Wesen* (Frankfurt,

2003), 246; Frank Bajohr, "The 'Folk Community' and the Persecution of the Jews. German Society under National Socialist Dictatorship, 1933–1945," *Holocaust and Genocide Studies* 20, no. 2 (2006): 183. On "situational complicity," see Michael Wildt, *Volksgemeinschaft als Selbstermächtigung: Gewalt gegen Juden in der deutschen Provinz 1919 bis 1939* (Hamburg, 2007), 214–15, 371. Yet, this is not only a German trend; see, e.g., Ervin Staub, "The Psychology of Bystanders, Perpetrators, and Heroic Helpers," *International Journal of Intercultural Relations* 17, no. 3 (1993): 315–341; David Bloomfield, Teresa Barnes, and Luc Huyse, eds., *Reconciliation after Violent Conflict: A Handbook* (Stockholm, 2003).
7. Bajohr and Löw, "Beyond the 'Bystander,'" 4–5; see also Mary Fulbrook, this volume.
8. Dan Bar-On, "The Bystander in Relation to the Victim and the Perpetrator: Today and During the Holocaust," *Social Justice Research* 14, no. 2 (2001): 125–148.
9. Bajohr and Löw, "Beyond the 'Bystander,'" 4; see also Mary Fulbrook, this volume.
10. Gijs Huitsing and René Veenstra, "Bullying in Classrooms: Participant Roles from a Social Network Perspective," *Aggressive Behavior* 38, no. 6 (2012): 494–509; Christina Salmivalli, Kirsti Lagerspetz, Kaj Björkqvist, Karin Österman, and Ari Kaukiainen, "Bullying as a Group Process: Participant Roles and Their Relations to Social Status Within the Group," *Aggressive Behavior* 22, no. 1 (1996): 1–15; Jeroen Pronk, "Bullying Contextualized: Changing the Group Process by Changing Outsiders' Involvement" (PhD diss., Vrije Universiteit Amsterdam, 2015); Christina Salmivalli, "Bullying and the Peer Group: A Review," *Aggression and Violent Behavior* 15, no. 2 (2010): 112–120.
11. Salmivalli, "Bullying and the Peer Group," 114.
12. Ibid., 114–115.
13. Ibid., 116–117.
14. Influential theories in this regard are the theory of cognitive dissonance and the theory of moral disengagement. These theories start from the basic assumption that people have a strong motivation to maintain consistency between their cognitions and norms on the one hand and their behavior on the other. In the context of extreme violence, they can employ numerous psychological "neutralization techniques" in order to convince themselves that the regular norms do not apply to the specific situation they find themselves in. These techniques entail, among others, moral justification, euphemistic labeling, diffusion and displacement of responsibility, and victim blaming. Staub, "The Psychology of Bystanders"; Alexander Alvarez, "Adjusting to Genocide: The Techniques of Neutralization and the Holocaust," *Social Science History* 21, no. 2 (1997): 139–178; Albert Bandura, "Moral Disengagement in the Perpetration of Inhumanities," *Personality and Social Psychology Review* 3, no. 3 (1999): 193–209; Linda M. Woolf and Michael R. Hulsizer, "Psychosocial Roots of Genocide: Risk, Prevention, and Intervention," *Journal of Genocide Research* 7, no.1 (2005): 101–128; Dennis Kahn, "Norm Shifting and Bystander Intervention," in *Looking at the Onlookers and Bystanders: Interdisciplinary approaches to the Causes and Consequences of Passivity*, ed. Henrik Edgren (Stockholm, 2012), 67–82.
15. Kahn, "Norm Shifting and Bystander Intervention," 69.
16. Robb Willer, Ko Kuwabara, and Michael W. Macy, "The False Enforcement of Unpopular Norms," *American Journal of Sociology* 115, no. 2 (2009): 455; Salmivalli, "Bullying and the Peer Group," 117.
17. Willer et al., "False Enforcement of Unpopular Norms," 451–490.
18. This study was part of an investigation into the everyday relations of Jews and non-Jews living in the region of the Dutch-German border—on both sides—between the 1920s and 1950s. See Froukje Demant, *Verre buren: Samenleven in de schaduw van*

de Holocaust [Distant neighbors: Jews and non-Jews in the shadow of the Holocaust] (Enschede, 2015).
19. The study is based on interviews with eleven non-Jewish contemporary witnesses and thirty-four Jewish contemporary witnesses; all memoirs were written by victims who survived Nazi persecution.
20. Demant, "Verre buren," 111–113.
21. Ibid., 108–110.
22. Ibid., 113–116.
23. Ibid., 118, 121, 123–125.
24. Christoph Spieker, "Ausgrenzung und Verfolgung jüdischer Mitbürger 1933–1938," in *"Es ist nicht leicht, darüber zu sprechen": Der Novemberpogrom 1938 im Kreis Borken*, ed. August Bierhaus (Borken, 1988), 27–44.
25. Photos of the children at the two parties were published in "Auf der Suche nach Henny de Jong: Brief an eine in Auschwitz ermordete 16-Jährige aus Ahaus" written by students from class 10a of the Anne Frank Realschule (Ahaus, 2005) for the project "Stolpersteine." It is possible that the photos were taken in 1933 and 1938 rather than in 1934 and 1937.
26. Interview with Ludwig Hopp, 18 June 2010.
27. "Auf der Suche nach Marga Cohen und ihrer Familie: Tagebuch einer Annäherung," written by pupils of classes 9a, 10a, and 10d of the Anne Frank Realschule (Ahaus, 2009), 23–24.
28. Published in "Auf der Suche nach Marga Cohen und ihrer Familie."
29. "Bericht von Lotte Herz, geb. Kappesser, 9. November 1938–24. Oktober 1940," in Willi Feld, *"Mir ist, als tropfe langsam alles Leben aus meinem Herzen": Der lange Abschied der Familie Herz aus Burgsteinfurt—Eine Dokumentation: Die Juden in der Geschichte der ehemaligen Stadt Burgsteinfurt Teil III* (Münster, 2008).
30. Demant, "Verre buren," 120.
31. On social pressure in the Third Reich, see also Wildt, *Volksgemeinschaft als Selbstermächtigung*, 214–215, 371.
32. Herbert Wagner, *Die Gestapo war nicht allein ... Politische Sozialkontrolle und Staatsterror im deutsch-niederländischen Grenzgebiet 1929–1945* (Münster, 2004), 252–253.
33. Robert Gellately, who studied social control among the population in Nazi Germany, speaks of a "denunciatory atmosphere." Robert Gellately, "Denunciations in Twentieth-Century Germany: Aspects of Self-Policing in the Third Reich and the German Democratic Republic," *Journal of Modern History* 68, no. 4 (1996): 947–948, 952; see also Wagner, *Die Gestapo war nicht allein*, 612.
34. Wildt, *Volksgemeinschaft als Selbstermächtigung*, 211–213.
35. Lawrence Langer, *Versions of Survival: The Holocaust and the Human Spirit* (Albany, NY, 1982), 72.
36. Ervin Staub speaks in this regard of "semi-active participants." Staub, "The Psychology of Bystanders," 327.

Bibliography

Alvarez, Alexander. "Adjusting to Genocide: The Techniques of Neutralization and the Holocaust." *Social Science History* 21, no. 2 (1997): 139–178.
Aly, Götz. *Rasse und Klasse: Nachforschungen zum deutschen Wesen*. Frankfurt: S. Fischer Verlag, 2003.

Bajohr, Frank. "The 'Folk Community" and the Persecution of the Jews: German Society under National Socialist Dictatorship, 1933–1945." *Holocaust and Genocide Studies* 20, no. 2 (2006): 183–206.

Bajohr, Frank, and Andrea Löw. "Beyond the 'Bystander': Social Processes and Social Dynamics in European Societies as Context for the Holocaust." In *The Holocaust and European Societies: Social Processes and Social Dynamics*, edited by Frank Bajohr and Andrea Löw, 3–14. London: Palgrave Macmillan, 2016.

Bandura, Albert. "Moral Disengagement in the Perpetration of Inhumanities." *Personality and Social Psychology Review* 3, no. 3 (1999): 193–209.

Bar-On, Dan. "The Bystander in Relation to the Victim and the Perpetrator: Today and During the Holocaust." *Social Justice Research* 14, no. 2 (2001): 125–148.

Bloomfield, David, Teresa Barnes, and Luc Huyse, eds. *Reconciliation after Violent Conflict: A Handbook*. Stockholm: International Institute for Democracy and Electoral Assistance, 2003.

Darley, John M., and Bibb Latané. "Bystander Intervention in Emergencies: Diffusion of Responsibility." *Journal of Personality and Social Psychology* 8, no. 4 (1968): 377–383.

Darley, John M., and C. Daniel Batson . "'From Jerusalem to Jericho': A Study of Situational and Dispositional Variables in Helping Behavior." *Journal of Personality and Social Psychology* 27, no. 1 (1973): 100–108.

Darley, John M., Allan I. Teger and Lawrence D. Lewis. "Do Groups Always Inhibit Individuals' Responses to Potential Emergencies?" *Journal of Personality and Social Psychology* 26, no. 3 (1973): 395–399.

Demant, Froukje. *Verre buren: Samenleven in de schaduw van de Holocaust* [Distant neighbors: Jews and non-Jews in the shadow of the Holocaust]. Enschede: Ipskamp Drukkers, 2015.

Feld, Willi. *"Mir ist, als tropfe langsam alles Leben aus meinem Herzen": Der lange Abschied der Familie Herz aus Burgsteinfurt—Eine Dokumentation: Die Juden in der Geschichte der ehemaligen Stadt Burgsteinfurt Teil III*. Münster: LIT Verlag, 2008.

Fulbrook, Mary. *A Small Town near Auschwitz: Ordinary Nazis and the Holocaust*. Oxford: Oxford University Press, 2012.

Gellately, Robert. "Denunciations in Twentieth-Century Germany: Aspects of Self-Policing in the Third Reich and the German Democratic Republic." *Journal of Modern History* 68, no. 4 (1996): 931–967.

Hilberg, Raul. *Perpetrators Victims Bystanders: The Jewish Catastrophe, 1933–1945*. New York: HarperCollins, 1992.

Huitsing, Gijs, and René Veenstra. "Bullying in Classrooms: Participant Roles from a Social Network Perspective." *Aggressive Behavior* 38, no. 6 (2012): 494–509.

Kahn, Dennis. "Norm Shifting and Bystander Intervention." In *Looking at the Onlookers and Bystanders: Interdisciplinary Approaches to the Causes and Consequences of Passivity*, edited by Henrik Edgren, 67–82. Stockholm: Living History Forum, 2012.

Langer, Lawrence. *Versions of Survival: The Holocaust and the Human Spirit*. Albany: State University of New York Press, 1982.

Latané, Bibb, and John M. Darley. *The Unresponsive Bystander: Why Doesn't He Help?* New York: Appleton-Century-Crofts, 1970.

Pohl, Dieter. "Die Holocaust-Forschung und Goldhagens Thesen." *Vierteljahrshefte für Zeitgeschichte* 45, no. 1 (1997): 1–48.

Pronk, Jeroen. "Bullying Contextualized: Changing the Group Process by Changing Outsiders' Involvement." PhD diss., Vrije Universiteit Amsterdam, 2015.

Salmivalli, Christina. "Bullying and the Peer Group: A Review." *Aggression and Violent Behavior* 15, no. 2 (2010): 112–120.

Salmivalli, Christina, Kirsti Lagerspetz, Kaj Björkqvist, Karin Österman, and Ari Kaukiainen. "Bullying as a Group Process: Participant Roles and Their Relations to Social Status within the Group." *Aggressive Behavior* 22, no. 1 (1996): 1–15.

Spieker, Christoph. "Ausgrenzung und Verfolgung jüdischer Mitbürger 1933–1938." In *"Es ist nicht leicht, darüber zu sprechen": Der Novemberpogrom 1938 im Kreis Borken*, edited by August Bierhaus, 27–44. Borken: Kreis Borken, 1988.

Staub, Ervin. "The Psychology of Bystanders, Perpetrators, and Heroic Helpers." *International Journal of Intercultural Relations* 17, no. 3 (1993): 315–341.

Wagner, Herbert. *Die Gestapo war nicht allein ... Politische Sozialkontrolle und Staatsterror im deutsch-niederländischen Grenzgebiet 1929–1945*. Münster: LIT Verlag, 2004.

Wildt, Michael. *Volksgemeinschaft als Selbstermächtigung: Gewalt gegen Juden in der deutschen Provinz 1919 bis 1939*. Hamburg: Hamburger Edition, 2007.

Willer, Robb, Ko Kuwabara, and Michael W. Macy. "The False Enforcement of Unpopular Norms." *American Journal of Sociology* 115, no. 2 (2009): 451–490.

Woolf, Linda M., and Michael R. Hulsizer. "Psychosocial Roots of Genocide: Risk, Prevention, and Intervention." *Journal of Genocide Research* 7, no. 1 (2005): 101–128.

CHAPTER 6

THE DUTCH BYSTANDER AS NON-JEW AND IMPLICATED SUBJECT

Remco Ensel and Evelien Gans*

On Thursday, 6 August 1942, a large-scale raid in Amsterdam took place:

> Assisted by industrious, black NSB police, *Grüne Polizei* invaded all houses and floors to round up Jewish citizens. In front of the street, an old woman with a pale contorted face stood on the sidewalk left to fumble with her black purse, all the while being guarded by a heavy armed constable and gaped at by curious onlookers.[1]

Quoted by the Dutch historian Jacques Presser (1899–1970), this eyewitness account evokes the genocidal configuration of perpetrators, accomplices, victims, and bystanders that is central to this chapter. Terms such as "perpetrator" and "victim," let alone "bystander," are absent, but from expressive verbs and adjectives, we learn about the different subject positions during the raid. Elsewhere in *Ashes in the Wind: The Destruction of Dutch Jewry* (1968), or *Ondergang* in the Dutch

---

* Evelien Gans died in July 2018. This chapter appears as the final piece of a harmonious collaboration and in memory of a committed and generous historian.

original (1965), Presser did "remind the reader that all these events did not take place in a vacuum. There were the Dutch non-Jews. There were Dutch authorities in The Hague and in London. There was the rest of the world."[2] The author of these lines was implicated in the events that were central to his book—he himself narrowly escaped the raid on 6 August, while his wife was caught and later murdered—which might account for his keen eye and occasional acerbic remarks about the role of his fellow Dutchmen.

Ashes in the Wind was not the first narrative that went against the prevailing image of Dutch constancy and resistance in the face of antisemitic terror, but it was the one that made the greatest impression after it was published. To Presser, his account amounted more to a personal closure than to the opening of a new field of study. It was left to a new generation of historians to reconsider and debate the persecution of Jews in the Netherlands, the high percentage of Dutch Jews who were murdered, or the involvement of the authorities and bystanders.[3] In this chapter, we aim to build on Presser's observations by presenting several analytical tools that might help to further our understanding of the genocidal configuration that he tried to fathom in his monumental study. We shall therefore rely on some of the critical comments we made during a recent Dutch controversy on the role of the bystander, in order to provide a context for our approach to analyze the emergence of the bystander as a non-Jew.

Since Presser's book, a large body of work has appeared on the role of higher and lower civil servants and other occupational groups who, even if unintentionally, have played a role in processes of disenfranchisement and persecution of Dutch Jews—people such as mayors, judges, police officers, prison staff, civil servants, notaries, and railroaders.[4] Along with several regional and local studies, this body of scholarship gives more detail as to the behavioral repertoire that was available to citizens when confronted with antisemitic measures and outright persecution.[5] In particular, the broad category of Presser's "curious onlookers" has been addressed after the historian Hans Blom in his inaugural lecture of 1983 called for a thorough examination of the prevailing spirit of a country under occupation.[6]

The term "bystander" does not appear in the work of Presser, or in that of other Dutch historians of his generation like Abel Herzberg (1893–1989) and Loe de Jong (1914–2005).[7] With regard to the aforementioned raid of 6 August 1942 Presser's book presents a witness who confessed it was "so shocking and humiliating that you needed all your self-control to remain a passive bystander."[8] Yet, the Dutch original did not contain the word bystander. It was the translator who had turned a posture (*lijdelijk toezien*, i.e., sit back in resignation) into a subject. Historically, the meaning of the Dutch word *omstander*, commonly used in the plural, varied from "spectator" (*toeschouwer*) to "witness" (*getuige*) to "outsider" (*buitenstaander*). The *omstanders* are close to the action; they observe but remain aloof, maintaining an unbiased position. However, if necessary, the *omstander* intervenes without taking sides. The Dutch "omstander," has, in other words, the potential to act and intervene.

It took probably more than a decade after Blom's lecture for this term to be adopted within Dutch Holocaust studies.[9] A case in point is Ido de Haan's study *Na de Ondergang* (1997), which references Presser's *Ondergang*. With respect to the threatened Jews, De Haan stated unequivocally that "bystanders were witness to their demise" (*omstanders [waren] getuige van hun ondergang*) while mostly remaining deaf to their futile cry for help. Therefore, "Auschwitz" should not be made into a "catchword" of what had happened, because "the persecution of the Jews happened around the corner, on every doorstep and in front of one's house."[10] De Haan did not claim that bystanders bore full responsibility for the persecution. However, the general assumption that this passage suggests regarding the knowledge of "bystanders" differed very much from the proposition the historian Bart van der Boom had appended to his PhD dissertation in 1995: "The fact that the Dutch officials, police officers, and Jews in majority followed the German contracts for the deportations *can only* be understood from the utter unpredictability of Auschwitz."[11] Bystanders were ignorant, and can and should not be held accountable for their actions. About fifteen years later, these different views on the bystander led to an intense and lively public debate.[12]

In this chapter, we do not want to take the concept of the bystander for granted. We will first reconsider the concept by recasting some of the contested issues of this debate, followed by an account of the emergence of the bystander as a non-Jew in the Netherlands, before, during, and after the war. More specifically, we look at the relationship between Dutch Jews and non-Jews during the Shoah, from the perspective of an existing and growing distance between the minority and majority group under discussion. In our approach to the bystander as a non-Jew, the bystander's subject position existed in an embryonic form at the start of the antisemitic policies and persecutions in the Third Reich, and—after the Netherlands were invaded in May 1940—emerged more distinctly and consequentially while still allowing for different possible positionings and strategies for intervention, varying from perpetrator to rescuer, accomplice, or inactive bystander and onlooker. Finally, after the liberation, some of these positions of non-Jews vis-à-vis the persecuted could manifest themselves in an extended distance or even aversion toward Jewish survivors.

The Bystander in Recent Dutch History Writing

After the books of, among others, Presser and De Haan, it is surprising that the one book in recent years that deals with the Dutch bystanders does so mainly to dismiss them as having any relevance for an understanding of the genocidal configuration. In *"Wij weten niets van hun lot": Gewone Nederlanders en de Holocaust*, Bart van der Boom argues that a "myth of the guilty bystander" dominates the historiography on the Shoah. Historians, columnists, and others have supposedly propagated a vision in which bystanders "consciously allowed the Holocaust to happen, remaining passive or lending a hand." Van der Boom furthermore argues this "myth" is generally accepted in "international historiography," referring to the work of the historians Saul Friedländer and Dan Stone. Thus, the guilty bystander has erroneously become "the leading character in the history of the Holocaust."[13] From 2012 to 2014, the study was the subject of intense debate in the Netherlands, layered and diverse, in part because contributions did not only come from academics. We have participated in this debate, presenting a wide variety of critical comments. In what follows, we will specifically discuss Van der Boom's use of the concept of the "bystander" and present our own, alternative approach.

Based on an extensive reading of war diaries, Van der Boom called for the innocence of the bystander. People were not indifferent to but rather involved with the fate of the Jews. Neither bystanders nor accomplices knew the Holocaust (defined as "murder upon arrival" in the gas chamber) was taking place, which provides an important explanation for their behavior. In his book, Van der Boom proposes to use the Jews as a "control group," who, just as the bystanders, had no knowledge of the gas chamber and acted accordingly.[14]

Since the book reduces the Holocaust to the actual extermination in the gas chambers and everything that preceded that—the anti-Jewish ordinances, the isolation, the expropriations, the humiliations, the roundups, the deportations, everything Presser's "curious onlookers" had to witness—does not qualify in this approach, it never quite enters into a discussion with earlier perspectives by Presser, De Haan, or the body of work on all those who were involved in the implementation of the racist policies in the Netherlands. Instead, it is supposed that, if bystanders and accomplices such as police officers, railway personnel, and civil servants had known "it," then they would have been less passive. "I wonder," Van der Boom said in an interview, "whether they would have obeyed just as easily if the Germans had asked: 'Could you draw up a list of names? So that we can gas those people.'"[15] This way, the central argument is driven by speculation. A telling example is the discussion of two diarists. The teacher Mrs. Glazema extensively underpins her refusal to harbor an unknown man. Mrs. Boekholt had to make the same deliberation and actually did offer help to her daughter's Jewish teacher. In the case of Mrs. Boekholt, her assistance is classified as "accidental," whereas Van der Boom explicitly assumes that Mrs. Glazema, if she had known "it," would have made her privacy subservient to giving help. Instead of speculating about what they would have done in other circumstances, we think it is more productive to make an assessment of the relations between bystanders and victims and the circumstances under which people intervene and modify their subject position. These examples show how already-existing ties between Jews and non-Jews aided survival.[16]

Van der Boom makes alternating use of the concepts of bystander and "ordinary Dutchman." In our view, this ordinary Dutchman constitutes an obfuscating category. Both Jews and non-Jews are counted among these—although members of the resistance or of the National Socialist Movement in the Netherlands (Nationaal-Socialistische Beweging, NSB) are not. However, the situation of the Jews was incomparable to that of non-Jews, because the former were persecuted and had to choose between two evils: being deported or going into hiding. In the Dutch debate, various critics rightly highlighted how untenable the concept of "ordinary Dutchman" is.[17] Nevertheless, the problem centers more generally on the notion of the bystander as a veiled empty category, as if it is only filled with the "leftovers" after the historian has identified and tallied the perpetrators, victims, and accomplices. When the bystander is by definition exclusively circumscribed by his absence of involvement, we are left with an incomplete description of the genocidal configuration.

In his *Writing History, Writing Trauma*, Dominick LaCapra observes that "the figures with whom the historian has at least implicitly identified have often been bystanders because the identification with the bystander is at least superficially closest to ... the idea of full objectivity, neutrality, not being a player, not being a participant."[18] If the bystander represents, almost by design, a neutral or even an objective position, this must be because "we" do not wish to see ourselves as the perpetrators, accomplices, or victims. Likewise, Tony Kushner argues that "the bystander represents 'us' in the past."[19] These notes help us to understand the separate positionings in the Dutch debate. For our part, we identified Van der Boom's book as a plea for the innocence of the bystanders. Thus, already on the first page, it stated that "we Dutchmen" are still occupied with the question as to why so many Jews were deported from the Netherlands, because "it immediately touches upon our identity." In the study, Dutch national identity seems not only to have been determined by a constant interest in the Shoah but also to be embodied in the "ordinary" or "average" Dutchman, the same ordinary Dutchman who was blamed wrongfully as guilty bystander. The book can be read as a quest for liberation and redemption from the guilt for which Dutch nationals, and thus for which "we" (i.e., non-Jews), were wrongfully blamed.[20] Responsible for this wrongful accusation were all those maintaining the so-called myth of the guilty bystander, including those historians acting as emotionally motivated commemorators.[21] We would rather argue that every historian engages with the past in multivarious ways, which demands from all of us explicit reflection on the presuppositions and convictions of our research and findings.

The Dutch debate prompted us to look for other ways to investigate the position of the bystander. Rather than to predetermine the bystander in clearly defined categories, it seems more fruitful to think about the bystander as a specific and inherently dynamic subject position that arises in the genocidal process. Accordingly, we propose to think about the potential bystander as an "implicated subject," which, according to Michael Rothberg, allows us to explore "a new category of historical responsibility" applicable to a "range of differentially situated subjects, including bystanders, beneficiaries, latecomers, and others connected to pasts they did not directly experience and to contemporary contexts that might seem distant."[22] The concept invites us to reexamine various forms of involvement, as well as the social and psychological aspects of the bystander position evolving over time.[23] Victoria Barnett takes the argument one step further with the proposal "to understand the term not as a reference to a particular group of individuals or institutions but rather as a process."

We wish to follow up on these propositions by looking at the bystander from a temporal perspective. In this respect, a poignant example of the bystander positioned within a genocidal configuration can be found in the diary of Moshe Flinker (1926–1944). In the well-known passage of 22 January 1943 (15 Sjevat 5703), the seventeen-year-old metaphorically imagines the configuration of victim-bystander-accomplice-perpetrator and thereby evokes the gradual formation of social and psychological separations during the German occupation of the Netherlands, through which Jews eventually would end up in a "world of shrinking prospects."[24]

It is like being in a great hall where many people are joyful and dancing and also where there are a few people who are not happy and who are not dancing. And from time to time a few people of this latter kind are taken away, led to another room and strangled. The happy dancing people in the hall do not feel this at all. Rather, it seems as if this adds to their joy and doubles their happiness.[25]

The passage illustrates not only how the figure of the bystander was a constitutive part of the process of persecution and extermination of European Jewry, but also how at least one diarist clearly and unequivocally recognizes the commitment of the bystander in relation to those of victim and perpetrator. After having already been through years of discrimination and persecution, it seems as if at this point in time a new sense of an existential gap between "Jews" and "non-Jews" dawned on Moshe: " I don't know what to think, what to say, what to do. I see in the streets that the Gentiles are happy and gay, and that nothing touches them."[26] We are interested in the history of this configuration of a shrinking world and the distinct emotions it engendered.

The Prewar Years: The Advent of the Embryonic Bystander

In the following, we shall present a tentative outline of some of the social and psychological mechanisms that led to the mutual estrangement and growing social distance between Dutch bystanders and Jews as victims for the duration of three phases: the years preceding, during, and after the occupation of the Netherlands. Becoming a bystander is not just a matter of individual choice but part of a larger sociopolitical process. In theory, beginning with the first anti-Jewish measures, the Nazi regime classified all non-Jews or Gentiles as bystanders. Subsequently, this "embryonic bystander" could develop into perpetrator, rescuer, and resistance fighter or accomplice, or remain a "bystander"—and they could change their position over time.

During the 1930s, the positionings of Dutch Jews were affected by the disastrous developments in Germany. The process of identifying Jews (including those who personally did not identify themselves as such), and singling them out as a target group, thus started affecting Dutch Jews before the German occupation even began. In these prewar years, there existed a great variety in Jewish self-identifications, depending on descent or religious or sociocultural involvement. The position and the representation of Jews as fellow citizens, however, began to change. "The Jew" in itself became a topic of debate and government policy;

antisemitism became more visible. Even the growing concern for the situation of the Jews in Germany and expressions of solidarity with their fate may be interpreted as further evidence of the growing distance between people classified as either "Jews" or "non-Jews." Generally speaking, political language on Jews underwent a change in the course of the 1930s. Affected by the Évian Conference in 1938, political debates on Jewish refugees reveal a change in rhetoric with concepts such as "Aryans," "Eastern Jews," "full Jews," and "half-Jews" being imported from Germany and used by Dutch policy makers, members of the civil service, and even Jewish committees.[27] For example, in the border province of Overijssel, prewar refugee policy "changed from one day to the next" when, without apparent directive, border police officials began registering the "race" of visitors.[28] Likewise, the German ban on marriage between Jews and non-Jews issued in September 1935 was validated and applied to Germans living in the Netherlands.[29]

Thus, the gap between Jews and those non-Jewish "embryonic bystanders" became palpable during the 1930s in many different ways. First, generally, Jews related differently to the antisemitic policies and persecutions in the Third Reich, if only because they had family members in Germany. Their concerns and their identification with what happened across the border were much more direct, intense, and frightening. Second, a classic form of economic competition was crucial for the widening of the gap. One fear was that German Jews would become competitors in an economy that was already in crisis and in which unemployment was rampant. In the political debates, this was the most-heard argument against admitting Jewish refugees. There was already an economic divide between Jews and non-Jews within "Jewish branches" such as the diamond, tobacco, and textile industries and with numerous Jews working as traders in all shapes and sizes. During the economic crisis, these Jewish employees and small shopkeepers were the first to plunge into poverty. On top of this, there was an economic, social, and cultural exclusion: many non-Jewish employers did not like to employ Jews.[30] Third, Dutch social and economic antisemitic stereotyping increased, in part because of the increasing flow of Jewish refugees. Many Dutch Jews did not wholeheartedly welcome the refugees either—especially for fear that the rise of antisemitism encouraged by the arrival of the newcomers would rebound on them. Nevertheless, it was mainly Jewish organizations, individuals, and families who took care of the refugees. To non-Jews, the German and Austrian Jewish refugees were simply "the other"—for Dutch Jews, they were one's own other. Fourth, and as a result, racist political and ideological antisemitism increased during the 1930s. It was primarily propagated by the Dutch national-socialist organizations, of which the NSB was the largest and most influential. The awareness of both the presence and increase of antisemitism can be derived from an initiative that the government took in 1934 to add two new articles to the Dutch Criminal Code, both dealing with group defamation, which until then was not a criminal offense. The government under Christian-conservative Prime Minister Hendrik Colijn explained that the new articles were intended to protect our "Israelite fellow citizens" against hurtful statements, while elsewhere insults even had taken on a kind of "epidemic character."[31] Action against the rise of antisemitism mainly came from the part of Jewish and non-Jewish progressive and leftist intellectuals and artists who came together in a Comité van Waakzaamheid (Commission of Vigilance).[32]

Antisemitism transcended pillarization (*verzuiling*), the typically Dutch division of society into confessional or ideological subcultures and organizations. The Jews fell between not just two but many proverbial stools.[33] Antisemitism should not be seen as a natural consequence of pillarization. Catholic and Protestant newspapers, though certainly opposed to the anti-Jewish policies in Germany, nevertheless denounced the Jews for their seemingly disproportional presence in the press, the economy, and the financial world.[34] Social democracy was not immune to antisemitism either, as was testified by Henri Polak (1868–1943), a well-known Jewish union leader, in a booklet on the countless antisemitic remarks and prejudices he and his Jewish constituents had been confronted with.[35]

With regard to the changing social atmosphere in the 1930s, the historian Ivo Schöffer has concluded that, if only because of all the talk about the persecutions of the Jews abroad, it seemed inevitable that people "paid attention to the Jews, more than ever before, with compassion or yet again with prejudicial disapproval."[36] In hindsight, the aforementioned Abel Herzberg, a survivor of Bergen-Belsen concentration camp, wrote in 1950 that for someone to have compassion does not mean that they are necessarily one of those who suffer. On the contrary, Herzberg contended, compassion is "the twin brother (or, if you wish, the father) of aversion."[37]

The Years of Occupation: Outside the Universe of Obligation

In the Netherlands, the Nazis succeeded in enforcing the civil segregation of Jews and non-Jews by issuing anti-Jewish orders and prohibitions aimed at preventing non-Jews from having any contact with their

Jewish fellow citizens. The occupying regime could benefit from a preexisting, yet not fully developed, social distance between the majority of Jews and non-Jews. As argued above, Jews were often not part of what sociologist Helen Fein has called "the universe of obligation," that is, "that circle of persons toward whom obligations are owed, to whom the rules apply and whose injuries call for expiation of the community."[38] This presented itself as a crucial obstacle when it proved extremely difficult to find hiding places for those people who had lived in close-knit Jewish communities. It proved in any case very difficult to find hiding places—much more for Jews than for non-Jews (who wished to evade forced labor in Germany).[39]

In the course of the German occupation, intentionally and unintentionally, contacts between Jews and non-Jews disintegrated more and more. Both groups began to refer to non-Jews as "Aryan."[40] Non-Jews began to look at the Jews as a "separate group, a strange element within our nation."[41] By 1942, Jews walked down the street in constant fear, as a Jewish survivor recalled: "When we chatted with befriended neighbors, we almost immediately felt a distance between them and us. During the war, there were *'Jews'* and *'People,'* *normal* people."[42] A "double wall of silence," consisting of a mutual act of avoidance and keeping quiet about the avoidance, regulated the relations between "Jews" and "normal people."[43] Dienke Hondius has considered the role of those who watched from behind the curtains as the Jews were deported from their houses and argues that here the curtain functions as both a literal and metaphorical wall between Jews and bystanders as ("curious") onlookers.[44] A striking illustration of the growing divide is the dramatic drop in Jewish/non-Jewish marriages even before this type of marriage was legally forbidden in the Netherlands, causing the loss of a fundamental mechanism for integration, cohesion, and potential help in times of distress.[45]

Though sometimes denied, non-Jews knew very well that Jews were the main target of the Nazis.[46] Moreover, distancing oneself from those who were being isolated, robbed, and humiliated before being removed altogether in a brutal and violent way could cause, consciously or not, feelings of triumphant or shameful relief. Dismissal of Jews, expropriation of their enterprises, and so forth offered—unintended though welcome—new jobs, houses, or, in general terms, opportunities for non-Jews. As the Dutch proverb says: *De een zijn dood is de ander zijn brood* (One man's meat is another man's poison). In psychoanalytical terms, another possible reaction to the anti-Jewish policies was repression or suppression through a process of "moral disengagement"—as a result of cognitive dissonance.[47] The bystander feels that the atrocities are wrong but cannot cope with their own powerlessness. It seems thus easier to accept the persecutions than to deal with the fact that one does not help the victims. Having said that, however, about 20 percent of the Dutch Jews, twenty-eight thousand people, were able to find a hiding place offered by thousands of intervening individuals and families.[48]

The illegal press reported extensively about the increase of antisemitism, which contributed in one way or another to the deportation of the vast majority of Jews. In 1944, the Dutch resistance fighter Gerrit van der Veen (1902–1944) wrote, "a large part of the Dutch population had abandoned their Jewish fellow-countrymen and had even, to make life easier, taken refuge in antisemitism." This was understandable, he contended in an attempt to make sense of the passive if not hostile attitude of his non-Jewish compatriots, because when someone is in misery, you want this to be their own fault: "If you are bad, you are punished. The persecution of the Jews is punishment indeed, therefore the Jews are bad."[49] In other words, during the occupation, antisemitism confirmed and created distance and diminished feelings of empathy as well as of shame and guilt.

After the Liberation: A Continuum of the Jewish/Non-Jewish Gap

Except for those directly involved in assisting Jews who went into hiding and those working together with Jewish resistance fighters, the Dutch had gotten used to a society without Jews. When survivors returned from the camps or came out of hiding after the liberation, they were certainly not only welcomed with kindness. They were often confronted with startled reactions ("we hadn't expected you back"), sometimes combined with reluctance or an outright refusal to return Jewish possessions, ranging from tapestry, tea service, and jewelry to money, houses, companies, jobs, patients, and clients.[50] So here, we find one of many manifestations of a postwar continuum of the Jewish/non-Jewish gap, one in which non-Jews as bystanders became and remained fully implicated in a major aspect of the genocidal process, that is, the redistribution of socioeconomic means.[51] Materialistic motivation, however, was projected back onto the Jews themselves, building on the old stereotype of "stingy Shylock."

As the German sociologist Werner Bergmann put it: "The Jews partly have themselves to blame for the hatred and the persecutions," a form of so-called secondary antisemitism.[52] One recurrent complaint was that the Jews chased their properties rather than mourn their beloved; they dug up their banknotes, drove the biggest cars once more, and were playing the first fiddle again, literally and figuratively. Non-Jewish shopkeepers firmly resisted the abolition of the Nazi ban of Jewish shops opening on Sundays.[53] This was a mix of postliberation economic competition and ethnic and traditional anti-Jewish stereotyping—including the myth that Jews were pulling the strings. We cannot rule out psychological motives for this postliberation antisemitism. Apart from empathy, returning Jews also caused feelings of guilt. These prolonged negative feelings about Jews amounted to what Theodor W. Adorno has coined *Schuld- und Erinnerungsabwehrantisemitismus* (antisemitism based on rejection of guilt and unwelcome memories)—an unwillingness to openly face the history of the Shoah disguised by criticism of Jewish behavior.[54] It was then, during quarrels about—often banal—issues, that the curse "They have forgotten to gas you" popped up frequently as an abuse against Jews: the first post-Holocaust antisemitic stereotype, because it said "the Jew" was there to be gassed.[55]

Jews *and* non-Jews noticed not just the postwar divide but yet another increase in antisemitism, and some took action against both.[56] The Dutch government, however, initially adopted a fallacious argument against a policy that acknowledged the special position of the Jews, by reasoning it did not want to pursue a similar distinction between Jews and non-Jews as the Nazis had done. This approach worked out badly for the Jews. First, it maintained the gap between non-Jews and Jewish survivors who at this stage had hardly anything to fall back on. Second, by arguing that special measures would strengthen what they called "latent antisemitism" among the population, the government tolerated if not facilitated this antisemitism instead of taking a stand against it.[57] So not unlike during the prewar years, an interaction between government policies and the behavior of a part of the non-Jewish population was at play that kept the social and mental distance from Jews alive.

Conclusions

In this chapter, we have tried to outline a process in which the "embryonic bystander" as a "non-Jew" emerged at a time of unease and growing stigmatization in combination with socioeconomic strife and a state policy that kept citizens apart. After 1940, the stigmatization, segregation, and terrorization of the Jews by the Nazi regime turned them into a target group for genocide, creating potential bystanders in the process. After the war, the divide between Jews and non-Jews continued to maintain its force. This can perhaps be explained by acknowledging that this divide remained functional for several purposes. Actually and paradoxically, what the postwar government did was a form of leveling (*nivellering*): reducing former and still existing differences in position, circumstances, motives, and dilemmas, as well as emotions between victims on the one hand and bystanders and accomplices on the other.[58] Many bystanders did so themselves after 1945, claiming—it is a cliché by now—that they had suffered as much as the Jews had. These people preferred to perceive themselves rather as helpless victims than as bystanders of a catastrophe with the capacity to act. Conversely, Jews were accused of passivity and lack of resistance, so their victimhood was cast in a dubious light. People claimed and acted from specific subject positions, as either innocent or guilty bystander or victim for specific social and psychological motives.

Looking back at all the different perspectives since Presser, it becomes ever more clear that it is up to us as historians but also as "implicated subjects"—"connected to pasts we did not directly experience," as phrased by Rothberg—to scrutinize and make sense of our observations with the conceptual tools and sources at our disposal.[59] Jacques Presser not only made it clear from the beginning that he was implicated in the events he described. He also explained why he sided with the victims when he spoke of his "growing awareness of what, in all humility, I felt to be my duty: to speak up for all those thousands now doomed to eternal silence, whose last cries were unheard, and whose ashes no one was allowed to gather up."[60] Confronted with the divergent past relationships that historians hold according to their subject positions, the challenge is to avoid using "routine oppositions" such as references to "objectivity" and "science" versus accusations of partisanship and memory politics. A critical and vibrant historiography depends on communication, dialogue, and debate in full recognition of dissimilar philosophies and practices of scholarship.[61]

Remco Ensel teaches modern history at Radboud University. From 2010 to 2014, he was affiliated with the NIOD Institute for War, Holocaust and Genocide Studies. He has published on the cultural foundations of social inequality, ethnicity, nationalism, and antisemitism.

Evelien Gans (1951–2018) held the chair for Modern Jewish History at the University of Amsterdam. As a senior researcher, she also was affiliated with the NIOD Institute for War, Holocaust and Genocide Studies.

She has written about modern Jewish ideologies and changing Jewish identities (PhD, "De kleine verschillen die het leven uitmaken," 1999) and Jewish family history (*Jaap en Ischa Meijer: Een joodse geschiedenis, 1912–1956*, 2008). She published regularly on (anti-)Jewish stereotypes and antisemitism. With Remco Ensel, she coedited the volume *The Holocaust, Israel and "the Jew": Histories of Antisemitism in Postwar Dutch Society* (2017).

Notes

1. Jacques Presser, *Ondergang: De vervolging en verdelging van het Nederlandse Jodendom, 1940–1945*, 2 vols. (The Hague, 1965), 1:269. This quote by Jaap Hemelrijk, a teacher at a Jewish lyceum in Amsterdam, was not included in the English edition, *Ashes in the Wind: The Destruction of Dutch Jewry*, trans. Arnold Pomerans, (London, 1968), so we have translated it from the Dutch original. All other translations are our own unless otherwise indicated.
2. Presser, *Ashes in the Wind*, 146.
3. On *Ondergang* as closure, see Conny Kristel, *Geschiedschrijving als opdracht: Abel Herzberg, Jacques Presser en Loe de Jong over de Jodenvervolging* (Amsterdam, 1998), 61–62.
4. Guus Meershoek, *Dienaren van het gezag: De Amsterdamse politie tijdens de Bezetting* (Amsterdam, 1999); Ralf Futselaar and Ingrid de Zwarte, "'Rustig en beheerscht': Nederlands gevangenispersoneel tijdens de Duitse bezetting, 1940–1945," *BMGN: Low Countries Historical Review* 129, no. 3 (2014): 27–50; Joggli Meihuizen, *Smalle marges: De Nederlandse advocatuur in de Tweede Wereldoorlog* (Amsterdam, 2010); Peter Romijn, *Burgemeesters in oorlogstijd: Besturen tijdens de Duitse bezetting* (Amsterdam, 2006); Corjo Jansen, *De Hoge Raad en de Tweede Wereldooorlog: Recht en rechtsbeoefening in de jaren 1930–1950* (Amsterdam, 2012); Raymund Schütz, *Kille mist: Het notariaat en de erfenis van de oorlogstijd* (Amsterdam, 2016).
5. On regional studies, see Marjolein J. Schenkel, *De lotgevallen van de joodse bevolking van Hengelo en Enschede tijdens de Tweede Wereldoorlog* (Zutphen, 2003); Marnix Croes and Pieter Tammes, *"Gif laten wij niet voortbestaan:" Een onderzoek naar de overlevingskansen van joden in Nederlandse gemeenten, 1940–1945* (Amsterdam, 2004); Kees Ribbens, *Bewogen jaren: Zwolle in de Tweede Wereldoorlog* (Zwolle, 1995); Froukje Demant, *Het alledaags samenleven van joden en niet-joden in de Nederlands-Duitse grensstreek, 1925–1955* (PhD diss., University of Amsterdam, 2016).
6. J. C. H. Blom, *In de ban van goed en fout? Wetenschappelijke geschiedschrijving over de bezettingstijd in Nederland* (Bergen, 1983).
7. Actually, Herzberg was a jurist, lawyer, and writer. Abel J. Herzberg, *Kroniek der Jodenvervolging, 1940–1945* (Amsterdam, 1978); Loe de Jong, *Het Koninkrijk der Nederlanden in de Tweede Wereldoorlog* (The Hague, 1969–1976).
8. Presser, *Ashes in the Wind*, 152.
9. *Omstander, ommestander, omstaander*. In *Woordenboek van de Nederlandsche taal* (WNT), 1871/2007. References to *omstander* in Dutch literature date back to the seventeenth century in the database Digitale Bibliotheek voor Nederlandse Letteren, www.dbnl.nl.

10. Ido de Haan, *Na de Ondergang: De herinnering aan de jodenvervolging in Nederland, 1945–1995* (The Hague, 1997), 14.
11. Proposition no. 6 to the thesis by Bart van der Boom, *Den Haag in de Tweede Wereldoorlog* (The Hague, 1995), emphasis added.
12. There was however debate about the work by the historian Nanda van der Zee (1951–2014) on, among other things, the role of Queen Wilhelmina, Dutch politicians, and the higher civil service. Nanda van der Zee, *Om erger te voorkomen: De voorgeschiedenis en uitvoering van de vernietiging van het Nederlandse jodendom tijdens de Tweede Wereldoorlog* (Amsterdam, 1997). Bart van der Boom reviewed the book in 1997, introducing the term *"omstander"* (in quotation marks) in "De schuld van bezet Nederland," *De Volkskrant*, 9 May 1997. Central to the 2012–2014 debate was Bart van der Boom, *"Wij weten niets van hun lot": Gewone Nederlanders en de Holocaust* (Amsterdam, 2012); Bart van der Boom, "Ordinary Dutchmen and the Holocaust: A Summary of Findings," in Wichert ten Have, ed., *The Persecution of the Jews in the Netherlands, 1940–1945: New Perspectives* (Amsterdam, 2012), 45–49. See Remco Ensel and Evelien Gans, "We Know Something of Their Fate: Bart van der Boom's History of the Holocaust in the Netherlands," unpublished manuscript, http://www.academia.edu/9835819/We_know_something_of_their_fate._Bart_van_der_Boom_s_history_of_the_Holocaust_in_the_Netherlands. Cf. Krijn Thijs, this volume.
13. Van der Boom, *"Wij weten niets van hun lot,"* 218.
14. Ibid., 313; Van der Boom, "Ordinary Dutchmen," 47.
15. Bas Kromhout, "We hebben het nicht gewusst," *Historisch Nieuwsblad*, no. 5 (2012), 22. Van der Boom, *"Wij weten niets,"* 414–415.
16. Van der Boom, *"Wij weten niets,,"* 406–416; Mark S. Granovetter's "strength of weak ties" was already a topic of discussion in Dutch Holocaust studies. Ido de Haan, "Breuklijnen in de geschiedschrijving van de Jodenvervolging: Een overzicht van het recente Nederlandse debat," *BMGN: Low Countries Historical Review* 123, no. 1 (2008), 31–70.
17. Guus Meershoek, "Een aangekondigde massamoord," *De Groene Amsterdammer* 137, no. 5 (31 January 2013): 30–33.
18. Dominick LaCapra, *Writing History, Writing Trauma* (Baltimore, 2001), 146.
19. Tony Kushner, "'Pissing in the Wind?' The Search for Nuance in the Study of Holocaust 'Bystanders,'" in *"Bystanders" to the Holocaust: A Re-evaluation*, ed. David Cesarani and Paul Levine (London, 2000), 57–76.
20. In an interview, Van der Boom furthermore explained the origins of his study: "But I am not Jewish myself, and as far as I know, I have no relatives who were very good or very evil. This is not personal. Call it an intellectual interest." *Reformatorisch dagblad*, 28 November 2012.
21. Bart van der Boom, "Ook die joodse verraders zijn interessant," *De Groene Amsterdammer* 137, no. 1 (9 January 2013).
22. Michael Rothberg, "On Being a Descendant: Implicated Subjects and the Legacies of Slavery," lecture delivered at Utrecht University, June 21–22 2013; Michael Rothberg, "Multidirectional Memory and the Implicated Subject: On Sebald and Kentridge," in *Performing Memory in Art and Popular Culture*, ed. Liedeke Plate and Anneke Smelik (New York, 2013), 39–58.
23. Cf. Victoria Barnett, "Reflections on the Concept of 'Bystander,'" in *Looking at the Onlookers and Bystanders: Interdisciplinary Approaches to the Causes and Consequences of Passivity*, ed. Henrik Edgren (Stockholm, 2012), 35–52.
24. Alexandra Garbarini, *Numbered Days: Diaries and the Holocaust* (New Haven, CT, 2006), xi.

25. Moshe Flinker, born in The Hague, fled with his family to Belgium in 1940. The family was arrested in 1944 and sent to Auschwitz. All his siblings survived, but Moshe and his parents perished. David Patterson, "Moshe Flinker (1926–1944)," in *Encyclopedia of Holocaust Literature*, ed. David Patterson, Alan L. Berger, and Sarita Cargas (Westport, 2002), 50–51; Moshe Flinker, *Young Moshe's Diary: The Spiritual Torment of a Jewish Boy in Nazi Europe* (Jerusalem, 1965), 71.
26. Flinker, *Young Moshe's Diary*, 71. Van der Boom, *"Wij weten niets,"* 11, considers the employment of the Flinker citation in present-day literature as part of the propagation of the myth of the guilty bystander.
27. Corrie van Eijl, *Al te goed is buurmans gek: Het Nederlandse vreemdelingenbeleid 1840–1940* (Amsterdam, 2005), 180, 214–215.
28. Geertje Mak, "Vluchtelingenbeleid in Overijssel tijdens het Interbellum," *Overijsselse Historische Bijdragen* 115 (2000): 7–32.
29. Evelien Gans, *De kleine verschillen die het leven uitmaken: Een historische studie naar joodse sociaal-democraten en socialistisch-zionisten in Nederland* (Amsterdam, 1999), 160–161.
30. Selma Leydesdorff, "In Search of the Picture: Jewish Proletarians in Amsterdam between the Two World Wars," in *Dutch Jewish History*, vol. 1, ed. Jozeph Michman (Jerusalem, 1984), 320; Jacob Arnon, "The Jews and the Diamond Industry in Amsterdam," in Michman, *Dutch Jewish History*, 309–310; Karin Hofmeester, *Jewish Workers and the Labour Movement: A Comparative Study of Amsterdam, London and Paris, 1870–1914* (Aldershot, 2004); Gans, *De kleine verschillen*, 290–291.
31. Cf. Article 137c of the Dutch Criminal Code; Minutes, States-General of the Netherlands, 1933–1934, 237, 3 (memorandum); Marloes van Noorloos, *Hate Speech Revisited: A Comparative and Historical Perspective on Hate Speech Law in the Netherlands and England & Wales* (Cambridge, 2011), 197.
32. Gans, *De kleine verschillen*, 87–88, 93–94, 109; Frank van Vree, *De Nederlandse Pers en Duitsland. 1930–1939: Een studie over de vorming van de publieke opinie* (Groningen, 1989), 30, 459.
33. One effect of pillarization would be, as Bob Moore has argued, that when the Jews needed help, "there were still social and cultural barriers which had to be broken down." Bob Moore, *Victims and Survivors: The Nazi Persecution of the Jews in the Netherlands, 1940–1945* (London, 1997), 162.
34. Evelien Gans, "The Netherlands in the Twentieth Century," in *Antisemitism: A Historical Encyclopedia of Prejudice and Persecution*, ed. Richard Levy (Santa Barbara, CA, 2005), 499.
35. Henri Polak, *Het "wetenschappelijk" antisemitisme: Weerlegging en betoog* (Amsterdam, 1933).
36. Ivo Schöffer, "Nederland en de joden in de jaren dertig in historisch perspectief," in *Nederland en het Duitse Exil 1933–1940*, ed. Kathinka Dittrich and Hans Würzner (Amsterdam, 1982), 91.
37. Herzberg, *Kroniek der Jodenvervolging*, 252; Evelien Gans, *Gojse nijd en joods narcisme: Over de verhouding tussen joden en niet-joden in Nederland* (Amsterdam, 1994), 32. For the factors "fear" and "aversion," see also Jong, *Het Koninkrijk der Nederlanden*, 8:440–441, 462–463.
38. Helen Fein, *Accounting for Genocide: National Responses and Jewish Victimization during the Holocaust* (1979; repr., Chicago, 1984), 33.
39. Ben Sijes, "Enkele opmerkingen over de positie van de Joden in de Tweede Wereldoorlog in Nederland," in *Jaarboek van de Maatschappij der Nederlandsche Letterkunde te Leiden, 1973–1974* (Leiden, 1975), 35; Loes Gompes, *Fatsoenlijk land: Porgel en Porulan in het verzet* (Amsterdam, 2013), 58.

40. Ies Dikker, *Nergens veilig: Brief uit de onderduik* (Haarlem, 1995), 38, 54.
41. J. W. Matthijsen, afterword to *Antisemitisme in Na-Oorlogstijd. Ervaringen en beschouwingen van een die partij is bij het pro en contra*, ed. J. W. Matthijsen (Barendrecht, 1945), 52.
42. Dick Walda, *Een huilbui van jaren. Episoden uit het leven van Rita Koopman* (Amsterdam, 1979), 26.
43. See also Eviatar Zerubavel, *The Elephant in the Room: Silence and Denial in Everyday Life* (Oxford, 2006), 47–51.
44. Dienke Hondius, "Bystander Memories: Unfolding and Questioning Eyewitness Narratives on the Deportation of the Jews," in Edgren, *Looking at the Onlookers and Bystanders*, 179.
45. Wouter Ultee and Ruud Luijkx, "De schaduw van een hand: Joods-gojse huwelijken en joodse zelfdodingen in Nederland 1936–1943," *Mens en Maatschappij* 72, no. 1 (1997): 55–67.
46. Bart van der Boom, *"We leven nog": De stemming in bezet Nederland* (Amsterdam, 2003), 67; Kromhout, "We hebben het niet gewusst."
47. Dennis T. Kahn, quoted in Henrik Edgren, "The Project 'Bystanders—Does It Matter?'" in Edgren, *Looking at the Onlookers and Bystanders*, 19–20, 23. On this and related concepts for an analysis of normative frames, see Froukje Demant, this volume.
48. Croes and Tammes, *"Gif laten wij niet voortbestaan,"* 174, 471.
49. Gerrit Jan van der Veen, *De Vrije Kunstenaar*, 15 March 1944. We thank Guus Meershoek. See, e.g., Bert Bakker, Dick Hendrik Couvée, and Jan Kassies, eds., *Visioen en Werkelijkheid: De illegale pers over de toekomstige samenleving* (The Hague, 1963), 255; Jozeph Melkman, *Geliefde Vijand: Het Beeld van de Jood in de Naoorlogse Literatuur* (Amsterdam, 1964), 20; Gans, *Gojse nijd en joods narcisme*, 28, 30–34.
50. Evelien Gans, "'They Have Forgotten to Gas You': Post-1945 Antisemitism in the Netherlands," in *Dutch Racism*, ed. Philomena Essed and Isabele Hoving, (Amsterdam, 2014), 71–100. Still, there were plenty examples of "guardaryans" (in Dutch, *bewariërs*, which is a wordplay on the guarding of Jewish property by "Aryans"), who painstakingly guarded the possessions given in keeping.
51. Cf. Keith Lowe, *Savage Continent: Europe in the Aftermath of World War II* (New York, 2012), 200.
52. "Juden wird eine Mitschuld an Hass und Verfolgung gegeben." Werner Bergmann, "Sekundärer Antisemitismus," in *Handbuch des Antisemitismus: Judenfeindschaft in Geschichte und Gegenwart, Bd. 3—Begriffe, Theorien, Ideologien*, ed. Wolfgang Benz (Berlin, 2010), 301.
53. Evelien Gans, "Gojse broodnijd: De strijd tussen joden en niet-joden rond de naoorlogse Winkelsluitingswet 1945–1951," in *Met alle geweld: Botsingen en tegenstellingen in burgerlijk Nederland*, ed. Conny Kristel (Amsterdam, 2003), 195–213; Evelien Gans, "'Vandaag hebben ze niets, maar morgen bezitten ze weer een tientje': Antisemitische stereotypen in bevrijd Nederland," in *Polderschouw: Terugkeer en opvang na de Tweede Wereldoorlog—Regionale verschillen*, ed. Conny Kristel (Amsterdam, 2002), 313–353.
54. Theodor W. Adorno, "Zur Bekämpfung des Antisemitismus heute," in *Theodor W. Adorno. Kritik: Kleine Schriften zur Gesellschaft*, ed. Rolf Tiedemann (Frankfurt, 1971), 107–109.
55. Gans, "'They Have Forgotten to Gas You,'" 71.
56. For example, the foundation by Jewish and Gentile intellectuals of the Werkgroep (*Anti-semietische Stemming in Nederland?*) and several articles, mainly in the

left-wing and Jewish press. Gans, *Gojse nijd en joods narcisme*, 31–32; Dienke Hondius, *Return: Holocaust Survivors and Dutch Anti-Semitism* (Westport, CT, 2003).
57. E.g., Gans, "Gojse broodnijd," 200; Gans, "'They Have Forgotten to Gas You,'" 80.
58. While the term in the sense used here is relatively new, historians have already hinted at the idea behind it. Thus, for instance, according to Deborah Lipstadt, *The Eichmann Trial* (New York, 2011), 161, Hannah Arendt "was incensed when critics accused her of closing the gap between perpetrator and victim."
59. Rothberg, "On Being a Descendant."
60. Presser, *Ashes in the Wind*, xiii.
61. Dominick LaCapra, *Representing the Holocaust: History, Theory, Trauma* (Ithaca, NY, 1994), 64–66.

Bibliography

Adorno, Theodor W. "Zur Bekämpfung des Antisemitismus heute." In *Theodor W. Adorno: Kritik Kleine Schriften zur Gesellschaft*, edited by Rolf Tiedemann, 105–133. Frankfurt: Suhrkamp, 1971.
Arnon, Jacob. "The Jews and the Diamond Industry in Amsterdam." In Michman, *Dutch Jewish History*, 305–313.
Bakker, Bert, Dirk Hendrik Couvée, and Jan Kassies, eds. *Visioen en Werkelijkheid: De illegale pers over de toekomstige samenleving*. The Hague: Daamen, 1963.
Barnett, Victoria. "Reflections on the Concept of 'Bystander.'" In Edgren, *Looking at the Onlookers and Bystanders*, 35–52.
Bergmann, Werner. "Sekundärer Antisemitismus." In *Handbuch des Antisemitismus: Judenfeindschaft in Geschichte und Gegenwart, Bd. 3—Begriffe, Theorien, Ideologien*, edited by Wolfgang Benz, 300–302. Berlin: De Gruyter, 2010.
Blom, J. C. H. *In de ban van goed en fout? Wetenschappelijke geschiedschrijving over de bezettingstijd in Nederland*. Bergen: Octavo, 1983.
Boom, Bart van der. *Den Haag in de Tweede Wereldoorlog*. The Hague: Seapress, 1995.
———. "Ook die joodse verraders zijn interessant." *De Groene Amsterdammer* 137, no. 1 (9 January 2013).
———. "Ordinary Dutchmen and the Holocaust: A Summary of Findings." In *The Persecution of the Jews in the Netherlands, 1940–1945: New Perspectives*, edited by Wichert ten Have, 45–49. Amsterdam: Amsterdam University Press, 2012.
———. *"We leven nog": De stemming in bezet Nederland*. Amsterdam: Boom, 2003.
———. *"Wij weten niets van hun lot": Gewone Nederlanders en de Holocaust*. Amsterdam: Boom, 2012.
Croes, Marnix, and Pieter Tammes. *"Gif laten wij niet voortbestaan": Een onderzoek naar de overlevingskansen van joden in Nederlandse gemeenten, 1940–1945*. Amsterdam: Aksant, 2004.
Demant, Froukje. "Het alledaags samenleven van joden en niet-joden in de Nederlands-Duitse grensstreek, 1925–1955." PhD diss., University of Amsterdam, 2016.
Dikker, Ies. *Nergens veilig: Brief uit de onderduik*. Haarlem: Tuindorp, 1995.
Edgren, Henrik, ed. *Looking at the Onlookers and Bystanders: Interdisciplinary Approaches to the Causes and Consequences of Passivity*. Stockholm: Living History Forum, 2012.

———. "The Project 'Bystanders—Does It Matter?'" In Edgren, *Looking at the Onlookers and Bystanders*, 19–20.

Eijl, Corrie van. *Al te goed is buurmans gek: Het Nederlandse vreemdelingenbeleid 1840–1940*. Amsterdam: Aksant, 2005.

Ensel, Remco, and Evelien Gans. "We Know Something of Their Fate: Bart van der Boom's History of the Holocaust in the Netherlands." Unpublished manuscript. http://www.academia.edu/9835819/We_know_something_of_their_fate._Bart_van_der_Boom_s_history_of_the_Holocaust_in_the_Netherlands.

Fein, Helen. *Accounting for Genocide: National Responses and Jewish Victimization during the Holocaust*. 1979. Reprint. Chicago: Free Press, 1984.

Flinker, Moshe. *Young Moshe's Diary: The Spiritual Torment of a Jewish Boy in Nazi Europe*. Jerusalem: Yad Vashem, 1965.

Futselaar, Ralf, and Ingrid de Zwarte. "'Rustig en beheerscht': Nederlands gevangenispersoneel tijdens de Duitse bezetting, 1940–1945." *BMGN: Low Countries Historical Review* 129, no. 3 (2014): 27–50.

Gans, Evelien. *De kleine verschillen die het leven uitmaken: Een historische studie naar joodse sociaal-democraten en socialistisch-zionisten in Nederland*. Amsterdam: Vassallucci, 1999.

———. "Gojse broodnijd: De strijd tussen joden en niet-joden rond de naoorlogse Winkelsluitingswet 1945–1951." In *Met alle geweld: Botsingen en tegenstellingen in burgerlijk Nederland*, edited by Conny Kristel, 195–213. Amsterdam: Balans, 2003.

———. *Gojse nijd en joods narcisme: Over de verhouding tussen joden en niet-joden in Nederland*. Amsterdam: Arena, 1994.

———. "The Netherlands in the Twentieth Century." In *Antisemitism: A Historical Encyclopedia of Prejudice and Persecution*, edited by Richard Levy, 498–500. Santa Barbara, CA: ABC-CLIO, 2005.

———. "'They Have Forgotten to Gas You': Post-1945 Antisemitism in the Netherlands." In *Dutch Racism*, edited by Philomena Essed and Isabele Hoving, 71–100. Amsterdam: Rodopi, 2014.

———. "'Vandaag hebben ze niets, maar morgen bezitten ze weer een tientje': Antisemitische stereotypen in bevrijd Nederland." In *Polderschouw: Terugkeer en opvang na de Tweede Wereldoorlog—Regionale verschillen*, edited by Conny Kristel, 313–353. Amsterdam: B. Bakker, 2002.

Garbarini, Alexandra. *Numbered Days: Diaries and the Holocaust*. New Haven, CT: Yale University Press, 2006.

Gompes, Loes. *Fatsoenlijk land: Porgel en Porulan in het verzet*. Amsterdam: Rozenberg, 2013.

Haan, Ido de. "Breuklijnen in de geschiedschrijving van de Jodenvervolging: Een overzicht van het recente Nederlandse debat." *BMGN: Low Countries Historical Review* 123, no. 1 (2008): 31–70.

———. *Na de Ondergang: De herinnering aan de jodenvervolging in Nederland, 1945–1995*. The Hague: Sdu Uitgevers, 1997.

Herzberg, Abel J. *Kroniek der Jodenvervolging, 1940–1945*. Amsterdam: Meulenhoff, 1978.

Hofmeester, Karin. *Jewish Workers and the Labour Movement: A Comparative Study of Amsterdam, London and Paris, 1870–1914*. Aldershot: Ashgate, 2004.

Hondius, Dienke. "Bystander Memories: Unfolding and Questioning Eyewitness Narratives on the Deportation of the Jews." In Edgren, *Looking at the Onlookers and Bystanders*, 167–185.

———. *Return: Holocaust Survivors and Dutch Anti-Semitism*. Westport, CT: Praeger, 2003.

Jansen, Corjo. *De Hoge Raad en de Tweede Wereldooorlog: Recht en rechtsbeoefening in de jaren 1930–1950*. Amsterdam: Boom, 2012.
Jong, Loe de. *Het Koninkrijk der Nederlanden in de Tweede Wereldoorlog*. 26 vols. The Hague: Staatsuitgeverij, 1969–1976.
Kristel, Conny. *Geschiedschrijving als opdracht: Abel Herzberg, Jacques Presser en Loe de Jong over de Jodenvervolging*. Amsterdam: Meulenhoff, 1998.
Kromhout, Bas. "We hebben het nicht gewusst." *Historisch Nieuwsblad*, no. 5 (2012).
Kushner, Tony. "'Pissing in the Wind?' The Search for Nuance in the Study of Holocaust 'Bystanders.'" In *"Bystanders" to the Holocaust: A Re-evaluation*, edited by David Cesarani and Paul Levine, 57–76. London: Routledge, 2000.
LaCapra, Dominick. *Representing the Holocaust: History, Theory, Trauma*. Ithaca, NY: Cornell University Press, 1994.
——— . *Writing History, Writing Trauma*. Baltimore: Johns Hopkins University Press, 2001.
Leydesdorff, Selma. "In Search of the Picture: Jewish Proletarians in Amsterdam between the Two World Wars." In Michman, *Dutch Jewish History*, 315–333.
Lipstadt, Deborah. *The Eichmann Trial*. New York: Schocken, 2011.
Lowe, Keith. *Savage Continent: Europe in the Aftermath of World War II*. New York: St. Martin's Press, 2012.
Mak, Geertje. "Vluchtelingenbeleid in Overijssel tijdens het Interbellum." *Overijsselse Historische Bijdragen* 115 (2000): 7–32.
Matthijsen, J. W. *Antisemitisme in Na-Oorlogstijd: Ervaringen en beschouwingen van een die partij is bij het pro en contra*. Barendrecht: Carpe Diem, 1945.
Meershoek, Guus. *Dienaren van het gezag: De Amsterdamse politie tijdens de Bezetting*. Amsterdam: Van Gennep, 1999.
——— . "Een aangekondigde massamoord." *De Groene Amsterdammer* 137, no. 5 (31 January 2013): 30–33.
Meihuizen, Joggli. *Smalle marges: De Nederlandse advocatuur in de Tweede Wereldoorlog*. Amsterdam: Boom, 2010.
Melkman, Jozeph. *Geliefde Vijand: Het Beeld van de Jood in de Naoorlogse Literatuur*. Amsterdam: De Arbeiderspers, 1964.
Michman, Jozeph, ed. *Dutch Jewish History*. Vol. 1. Jerusalem: Tel-Aviv University, 1984.
Moore, Bob. *Victims and Survivors: The Nazi Persecution of the Jews in the Netherlands, 1940–1945*. London: Arnold, 1997.
Noorloos, Marloes van. *Hate Speech Revisited: A Comparative and Historical Perspective on Hate Speech Law in the Netherlands and England & Wales*. Cambridge: Intersentia, 2011.
Patterson, David. "Moshe Flinker (1926–1944)." In *Encyclopedia of Holocaust Literature*, edited by David Patterson, Alan L. Berger, and Sarita Cargas, 50–51. Westport, CT: Oryx Press, 2002.
Polak, Henri. *Het "wetenschappelijk" antisemitisme: Weerlegging en betoog*. Amsterdam: Andries Blitz, 1933.
Presser, Jacques. *Ashes in the Wind: The Destruction of Dutch Jewry*. Translated by Arnold Pomerans. London: Souvenir Press, 1968.
——— . *Ondergang: De vervolging en verdelging van het Nederlandse Jodendom, 1940–1945*. 2 vols. The Hague: Martinus Nijhoff, 1965.
Ribbens, Kees. *Bewogen jaren: Zwolle in de Tweede Wereldoorlog*. Zwolle: Waanders, 1995.
Romijn, Peter. *Burgemeesters in oorlogstijd: Besturen tijdens de Duitse bezetting*. Amsterdam: Balans, 2006.

Rothberg, Michael. "Multidirectional Memory and the Implicated Subject: On Sebald and Kentridge." In *Performing Memory in Art and Popular Culture*, edited by Liedeke Plate and Anneke Smelik, 39–58. New York: Routledge, 2013.

———. "On Being a Descendant: Implicated Subjects and the Legacies of Slavery." Lecture delivered at Utrecht University, June 21–22 2013.

Schenkel, Marjolein J. *De lotgevallen van de joodse bevolking van Hengelo en Enschede tijdens de Tweede Wereldoorlog*. Zutphen: Walburg Oers, 2003.

Schöffer, Ivo. "Nederland en de joden in de jaren dertig in historisch perspectief." In *Nederland en het Duitse Exil 1933–1940*, edited by Kathinka Dittrich and Hans Würzner, 247–310. Amsterdam: Van Gennep, 1982.

Schütz, Raymund. *Kille mist: Het notariaat en de erfenis van de oorlogstijd*. Amsterdam: Boom, 2016.

Sijes, Ben. "Enkele opmerkingen over de positie van de Joden in de Tweede Wereldoorlog in Nederland." In *Jaarboek van de Maatschappij der Nederlandsche Letterkunde te Leiden, 1973–1974*, 14–38. Leiden: Brill, 1975.

Ultee, Wouter, and Ruud Luijkx. "De schaduw van een hand: Joods-gojse huwelijken en joodse zelfdodingen in Nederland 1936–1943." *Mens en Maatschappij* 72, no. 1 (1997): 55–67.

Vree, Frank van. *De Nederlandse Pers en Duitsland, 1930–1939: Een studie over de vorming van de publieke opinie*. Groningen: Historische Uitgeverij, 1989.

Walda, Dick. *Een huilbui van jaren: Episoden uit het leven van Rita Koopman*. Amsterdam: Becht, 1979.

Zee, Nanda van der. *Om erger te voorkomen: De voorgeschiedenis en uitvoering van de vernietiging van het Nederlandse jodendom tijdens de Tweede Wereldoorlog*. Amsterdam: Meulenhoff, 1997.

Zerubavel, Eviatar. *The Elephant in the Room: Silence and Denial in Everyday Life*. Oxford: Oxford University Press, 2006.

Part II

History

CHAPTER 7

PHOTOGRAPHING BYSTANDERS

Christoph Kreutzmüller

For discussing the concept of "bystanders," photos appear to be an ideal source.[1] After all, there are people who are neither "perpetrators" nor "victims" in many pictures taken—especially in the early phases of the persecution of Jews in Germany. Frozen in time, these onlookers are there on paper or on the screen. We can magnify, frame, and scrutinize them, searching for concrete evidence of those who passed by or looked on at a certain incident. Yet, what on first glance might seem obvious might not hold up to a second viewing. Can photos really help us understand more about the fleeting relationship between "perpetrators," "victims," and "bystanders?" Can they help us to grasp what the role of the people not actively involved in persecution was? What is the role of the camera? Why do onlookers or passersby smile? Do they like what they see? Or are they just glad to be having their photograph taken? Is there any way of telling what the people thought and felt—what they mumbled, said, or shouted?[2] Taking these questions as a starting point, this chapter aims to discuss these interwoven layers of photographing "bystanders" by analyzing a series of pictures taken on 10 November 1938 in Baden-Baden.

Like any other source, photos need to be contextualized. Thus, in a first step it will be discussed where and under which circumstances the November pogrom, still sometimes referred to as *crystal night*, was photographed. In a second step, the course that the pogrom in Baden-Baden took will be sketched. What happened in the town? Who took the initiative, and who took the pictures? In a last step, three photos of the series will be analyzed in depth to explore what we can learn about (the concept of) "bystanders" by looking at them.

Photographing the Pogrom

On 11 November 1938, the *New York Times* published the first two pictures of the pogrom that did not yet have a name. Flown from Berlin (via Amsterdam) to London and transferred from there by radio photo across the Atlantic, one pixelated image portrayed a burning synagogue in Berlin, while the other one showed the broken window panes of a lamp shop on the capital's fashionable boulevard, Kurfürstendamm (fig. 7.1).[3] Even though it has been reproduced so often, it has become almost iconic;[4] the most striking fact about the image is what is missing: visible violence.

The photo does not show the act of the destruction itself, the smashing of the windows and the looting of the shop. It only portrays shards,

Figure 7.1. Photo by an unknown press photographer, 10 November 1938, *New York Times*, 11 November 1938. (AP Images/Hollandse Hoogte.)

broken and empty shop windows—that is, the results of the violence against things—and some passersby. Violence against people is left out of the picture, even though it was massive and an unknown—but high—number of people were killed in the pogrom.[5] Therefore, the photo epitomizes what is actually evoked semantically by the phrase "crystal night": the citizens wake up after a good night's sleep and are surprised by the shards. Other, more evocative photos (and other, more evocative labels for the pogrom) were suppressed by the Nazi regime. This reflects the regime's anxiety that these photos could be sent abroad and used by the international press in the same vain as, for example, the photograph of the inmates of an early concentration camp in Berlin had been used.[6] Even though neither the Gestapo nor the Reich Ministry of Public Enlightenment and Propaganda (RMVP) actually banned taking photos in November 1938, spreading negative news about the regime could lead to a serious retribution according to the Treachery Act of 1934.[7] The *Manchester Guardian* reported on 10 November 1938, "photographers who tried to take pictures of the wrecking operation were stopped by the police and one American photographer was arrested but later released."[8] Even the ambassador of Colombia was stopped and (briefly) detained by the police for taking pictures, causing a serious diplomatic incident.[9] Apart from the police—busy arresting Jewish citizens on 10 November—ordinary Germans felt compelled to watch out, too. When the accountant Rudolf Neubauer tried to photograph the destroyed shop underneath his apartment in Berlin Schöneberg around midday on 10 November 1938, he was stopped by passersby and taken to the nearest police precinct. There, his camera and two films were "confiscated."[10] Moreover, the press photographers in Germany knew—and took into account—that photos shedding an all too negative light on the regime would not be printed in Germany or allowed to leave the country anyway. Günter Beukert, one of the four photographers working for the Associated Press in the first night of the pogrom in Berlin, recalled after the war that out of the thirty-four pictures he presented to the RMVP, only a few got clearance for publication.[11] Furthermore, taking photos of SA (*Sturmabteilung*) or SS (*Schutzstaffel*) "in action" was a dangerous endeavor, as the perpetrators often were drunk and/or in a state of hysteria and therefore prone to attack those who stood nearby. Even during the blockade of April Fool's Day in 1933, which was staged for the (international) press in a well-organized, disciplined manner, a film operator filming the scene in Berlin for a German newsreel was attacked by an SA man.[12] Strikingly, today's public archives only contain around two dozen pictures of ransacked Jewish businesses in Berlin—all but one taken after the perpetrators had left.[13] As it was even more difficult and dangerous for them to take photos, none of these was taken by a Jew. As with other crimes scenes from the Holocaust, the view of the persecuted is missing in the visual evidence of the pogrom.[14]

While motifs were restricted in Berlin, non-Jews were usually allowed to take photos more freely in the provinces of the Reich. For their comparative study *Vor aller Augen* (In plain view), Klaus Hesse and Philipp Springer have collected photographs of the pogrom from twenty-four towns—all but two (Essen and Düsseldorf) in the backwaters of Germany where there was no foreign consulate nearby.[15] It is a telling fact that these images mainly depict ransacked shops and the destruction of synagogues. Apart from the photos of that "event" collected by Hesse and Springer, even two 8mm films (from Bielefeld and Bühl) have survived, showing the flames and the reaction of nearby citizens to fires.[16] In contrast, the—rather frequent—acts of humiliation of citizens before their deportation to one of the three main concentration camps for men (Buchenwald, Dachau, and Sachsenhausen) were photographed less often. Hesse and Springer only list seven places. Baden-Baden was one of them.[17]

The Pogrom in Baden-Baden

From 7 November 1938, the day that Herschel Grynszpan shot the German ambassadorial legate Ernst vom Rath in Paris, a deluge of violence and destruction swept over the Reich. With Hitler's consent, this deluge was turned into a full-scale pogrom after Rath died on the evening of Wednesday, 9 November 1938 by the RMVP and head of the Nazi Party in Berlin, Joseph Goebbels. During the following night, SS, SA, Nazi Party officials, sympathizers, and soldiers of fortune committed horrible acts of violence in nearly all the cities, towns, and villages of Germany (including Austria) where Jews were still living.[18]

In contrast, things stayed calm in Baden-Baden, a well-known spa in southwest Germany with approximately thirty-three thousand inhabitants, where Fyodor Dostoyevsky had set his famous novella *The Gambler*. Why nothing happened remains unclear. Baden-Baden was regarded by the Jewish weekly *Der Israelit*.as early as 1930 as a "hotbed for the most horrible agitation against Jews."[19] However, after a series of incidents, public protest formed in the summer of 1930, and the new Nazi mayor agreed to a kind of a truce in 1933 with the influential lobby of hotel and sanatoria owners. As business was running low after the Great Depression, it was agreed to prevent attacks or molestations of Jewish guests and citizens in order not to further weaken the spa business. The relative quiet in Baden-Baden led to a clear rise of Jewish residents—from 310 in 1933 to 385 in 1937. When business was back to normal again in 1937, the policy was changed, and signs reading "Forbidden for Jews" were put up all over the town.[20]

In the early hours of Thursday, 10 November 1938, SS and police forces started arresting Jewish men using lists that the Gestapo had assembled. Eighty men were taken to the precinct. There, they were registered and had to wait for hours. The former high school teacher Arthur Flehinger, who was among the arrested, stated in a report to the Wiener Library in 1955 that he had the impression that they had to wait until the crowd outside was large enough.[21] At about 11 a.m., the Jews were ordered to take off their hats and were led through the streets of the town. On long stretches of the march, the men had to walk through a corridor of people. When they finally reached the synagogue, built in 1899 on a little hill off the road, a crowd had gathered there, too. While being abused, the Jews had to walk up the stairs to the synagogue one by one. They had to enter their place of worship without covering their heads, and Flehinger—who, as a teacher, was harassed even more than the other Jews—was forced to read a passage from Hitler's *Mein Kampf*. When he did not read loud enough, he was beaten by the SS. Subsequently, all bareheaded men were forced to sing the Nazi Party anthem, "Horst-Wessel-Lied."

At about 2 p.m., the men were taken to the nearby Hotel Central, which was (still) owned by a Jew. The group was led by two men carrying a sign in the form of a Star of David onto which was written, "God does not forgive us." After their arrival, those who were ill or over the age of sixty were released, while the others were officially taken into "protective custody" (*Schutzhaft*). Meanwhile, the synagogue was plundered and set afire, and the three remaining businesses in town owned by Jews were ransacked. In the afternoon, fifty-two men were taken to the railway station, put on a fright carriage, and taken to the concentration camp Dachau.[22] Because of the inhumane conditions there, one of them—the fifty-eight-year-old Alfred Kaufmann—died. The others returned home after some very exhausting and disturbing weeks. Most of them emigrated. Many of those who stayed behind were deported to France in October 1940, put into the internment camp Gurs, and ultimately taken from there to Auschwitz Birkenau.[23]

The photos discussed here are part of a series of at least two dozen pictures taken by Josef Friedrich Coeppicus, the owner of a photo studio in Baden-Baden. His daughter told a local newspaper in 1998 that her father had been an opponent of the Nazi regime and had therefore been banned from his profession in 1939.[24] Whether this holds true is difficult to ascertain. There is certainly no membership card of the Nazi Party in the files of the former Berlin Document Center in the German Federal Archives (Bundesarchiv) in Berlin. Therefore, we can assume he was not a member of the party, let alone part of the local Nazi Party inner circle. Yet, he was most certainly not an outspoken critic of the regime. Otherwise, he could not have taken the photos the way he did. The pictures taken inside the synagogue in particular indicate that the photographer was known to and accepted by the local police and SS forces.

In 1965, Coeppicus sold the main body of the picture series to the town museum of Baden-Baden. These pictures are archived on postcard paper in the municipal archive.[25] Whether Coeppicus had made these special prints before or after 1945 is unclear. If he developed his images on postcard paper before 1945, he most probably did so in order to sell them. That would not have been unusual. In the little town of Norden, the local drugstore owner took photos of a public humiliation of so-called race defilers and sold these as postcards, too.[26] Still, it remains unclear whether Coeppicus took the photos to do business with them or just for himself—for documentation. As early as 1950, one of the photos (fig. 7.4) was published in a special half-century edition of the then popular German magazine *Quick*—albeit in context of an article about the effects of the Nuremberg Laws.[27] Since then, this picture has been shown so many times that it has become iconic, even though it has often been presented with contradictory information as to the specific location and events it showed.[28]

Photographing the Pogrom in Baden-Baden

One of the first photos of the series was taken from a balcony of the house opposite the precinct (fig. 7.2). *Polizeihauptwache* can be read over the main entrance. The picture shows the last of the Jewish men— men above middle age, well dressed, with ties and in winter coats, at least two even carrying an umbrella—walking in rows of three just after they had left the precinct. Two of them are still wearing hats; a third one is about to take his off. The men are closely surrounded by twelve SS and five police officers wearing their distinct black leather helmets. The SS apparently had just "reminded" the men of the order to walk bareheaded. On the right side of the column—between SS and the onlookers—there is a group of men with coats and hats. Since they obviously have an official function but do not wear uniforms, they are most probably Gestapo agents. Around them, the onlookers stand in two dense lines up to seven ranks deep, forming a corridor. While what

Figure 7.2. Photo by Josef Friedrich Coeppicus, Baden-Baden, 10 November 1938. (Stadtmuseum/-archiv Baden-Baden.)

seems to be a class of schoolchildren to the right are passively watching from the front row, someone in the back row is making an aggressive gesture, pointing his right hand at the Jews. It looks as if he is shouting. To the left, the line of people is thinner—only three ranks deep. That leaves enough space for people passing through. Several people are sitting on the window ledges of the building from which Coeppicus took the picture, watching relaxed. One, judging from the cap he is wearing, might be a hotel boy, and it looks as if he is preparing to take a photo himself momentarily.

The next photo depicts the events after the march had reached the synagogue (fig. 7.3). One by one, the Jews had to walk up the stairs to the temple—through a corridor formed by (at least) one police officer, some SS men, and the onlookers. While one victim is already near the top, another is waiting at the bottom of the stairs for the signal to move. At the bottom of the picture, the heads of the following victims come into sight. Flehinger remembers swear words being shouted and described the ascent as "running the gauntlet."[29] Looking carefully, one can indeed see a boy or young man leaning forward between two SS men and trying to hit or actually hitting the bald man who is high up

Figure 7.3. Photo by Josef Friedrich Coeppicus, Baden-Baden, 10 November 1938. (Stadtmuseum/-archiv Baden-Baden.)

the stairs. The SS men do not seem to mind; at least in the moment the picture was taken they do not move to interfere.

Again, many onlookers do their very best to get a good view of the scene. Some boys are clutching to the lamppost, while others have mounted the wall of a little park to the left. Others had even gone to the rooftop of the building in the back. The photographer Coeppicus had found an excellent vantage point as well by managing to enter an adjoining house. At the decisive moment, he was even able to get into the synagogue and take pictures of the humiliations as well as the fire-raising.

After taking one photo of the men being led out, capturing another photographer running down the stairs to get a good shot, Coeppicus took the next photo at about 2 p.m. (fig. 7.4). For this photo, Coeppicus positioned himself on the top of the wall, cutting off the synagogue grounds from the little street (marked with an arrow on fig. 7.3). On this third photo of the series—following a near classical composition of the diagonal leading into the picture—the second part of the humiliation march is depicted (fig. 7.4). Unsurprisingly, the older of the Jewish men in particular are looking much more tired and distressed. Hour-long humiliation, fear, and physical exhaustion had already taken their toll. Compared to the other two photos, the number of onlookers has somewhat shrunk; for example, there are now no more than a dozen schoolchildren to be

Figure 7.4. Photo by Josef Friedrich Coeppicus, Baden-Baden, 10 November 1938. (Bundesarchiv.)

seen. Maybe they got bored and went home for dinner or to do their homework.[30] Yet, the remaining approximately eighty adults continue to form a sort of corridor through which the Jews have to walk—even though the symmetry is disturbed by an SS car parking in the curb and some onlookers seem to be moving along. A young boy, too, is following the march right in the space between the SS and the onlookers. On top of the wall, across from Coeppicus, another man is taking a photograph. He too can do so in plain view and—assuming my analysis of the man on the window ledge on the first photo of the series is right—is the fourth photographer of the event. The SS man in the bush to the left of him does not seem to mind and does not move.[31] Just below the SS man, at the entrance of the side street, there are a couple of men smoking. Opposite them, on the other side of the marching group, there are five men in white dresses: painters or glaziers. Behind them is a postman with his bicycle. He very likely has delivered the mail to quite a few of the humiliated men in the past years. It is an interesting fact that one of the Gestapo men to be seen in an earlier scene (fig. 7.2) "reappears" on this photo. On the far left of the cordon of SS and police officers, he is seen wearing a light coat and a dark hat with a very characteristic white hatband. Two more agents stand near him in the column. It is quite obvious that the other agents had not withdrawn from the scene either. They were still around, watching the scene—observing the onlookers.

Bystanders?

Considering that 10 November was a Thursday, a normal workday, it is striking that there are so many onlookers in the photos Coeppicus took. In 1938, there were hardly any unemployed in Germany. Did the people take a day or some time off their work to watch? Whatever the case, those who were there had made an effort to be at the scene. Quite a few took their bikes: they can be seen leaning against the wall on the last photo of the series presented here (fig. 7.4). One bike has a briefcase still strapped to its rack. None of the bikes are locked, so their owners must be nearby. In his 1955 report about the pogrom in Baden-Baden, Flehinger stated: "The decent citizens refrained from showing themselves on the street. The onlookers that were to be seen were mob."[32] Fair enough, there are only about three hundred men, women, and children—that is, about 1 percent of the population of Baden-Baden—seen standing near or around the march of the Jews. In addition, all photos depict people who are keeping a distance to the scene of the humiliation march or just pass by. Especially in the background of the second photo, there are quite a few citizens on the street not moving toward the scene, while there are two women (quite possibly mother and daughter) walking between the house and the line on the first picture of the series (fig. 7.2) and a mail carrier on duty or an elderly lady pushing a pram on the third (fig. 7.4). But these people are a minority—in the pictures. We see, of course, neither the people who decided to stay at home or in their offices or shops, nor those who just watched from behind their window curtains. Yet, we also do not see possible onlookers in the dead angle of the camera. Nonetheless, there is a certain bias—or wishful thinking—in Flehinger's statement. In contrast to what the teachers stated seventeen years after the pogrom, the streets are full of what appears to be fairly ordinary citizens and not an uncontrolled and uncontrollable mob.

Even though there are a few workers—that is, the men dressed in white—men wearing suits, ties, and hats dominate the scene. That workers are underrepresented has probably nothing to do with the (rather romantic) notion that workers opposed the Nazi regime more than the middle class did. Rather, the self-employed and white-collar workers worked in the town's center—where the humiliations took place. In addition, the fact that Baden-Baden was a spa and did not have a large industry certainly played a role. Apart from suits and hats, short trousers can actually be seen very often. If there really is a whole school class in the first photo, the teacher, probably in cooperation with the

Hitler Youth, must have organized the visit to the scene of humiliation as an "outing" or at least granted a special leave. As discipline was strict and penalties were severe, it seems very unlikely that so many pupils simply bunked off.

It is remarkable that some onlookers made a real effort to look, clutching to lampposts, craning their necks, or running toward the scene. They behave as if they are watching a spectacle, a parade, or a carnival procession.[33] Those who sit on the walls and window ledges would have come early, securing a good spot. Most of the onlookers are indeed just looking. Some keep their hands in their pockets; others fold their arms. It is difficult to ascertain what they think as we see some excited and some smiling faces. Yet the majority is rather expressionless and the camera too far away to offer a clearer picture. However, there is one man (fig. 7.4) carrying a child on his arm. He obviously wanted the child to see; apparently, the man did not at all mind what he saw.

Even though only a few people were actually stepping out of the line to shout at or beat the humiliated men, it is obvious that most of the onlookers formed the corridor through which the Jews had to walk. In so doing, they blocked possible escape routes, which in turn made the guarding much easier. In this regard, the onlookers involuntarily became part of the persecution process.[34] Based on eyewitness accounts recorded during a postwar trial against twenty-three citizens accused of actively taking part in the pogrom, Angelika Schindler even goes a step further. In her study on the history of the Jews in Baden-Baden, she argues that the high number of onlookers in front of the synagogue led to a delay of the humiliation march, which in turn led to even more violence against the Jews waiting at the bottom of the stairs.[35]

The perpetrators did not use the direct route from the precinct to the synagogue but instead marched the Jews in a detour through large parts of the town. The march thus aimed to expose the Jewish men to as many onlookers as possible. The humiliation of the men was a public matter. It had to be public because otherwise it simply would not have worked as such.[36] After all, the pillory, too, was a very public space. If the Jews were to be shamed and feel their legal and social exclusion, other members of society needed to be present.[37] Flehinger's notion that the perpetrators waited until a crowd had gathered to watch supports this argument. So does the fact that the Jewish men were forced to walk bareheaded—gravely adding to their humiliation. The predominantly male onlookers, even those who really just watched, were addressed. Willingly or not, they became an audience and thus part of the humiliation procedure. Here, the nexus between ex- and inclusion processes and practices becomes strikingly clear.

The fact that the onlookers were in turn watched by the Gestapo mixing with the crowd reminds us that the audience was under scrutiny, too, and takes the argument into another direction. The borders between onlookers and perpetrators were not as clear-cut as they might seem at first glance. Also, a citizen may or may have not entered the scene of humiliation, but those who came and stopped to watch knew they had to behave, at least act inconspicuously. Any open act of resistance or ostentatious gesture of discontent might have had consequences that were difficult to predict and assess. Still, in the third photo (fig. 7.4), there is one man with a worker's cap behind the car who behaves in an odd way, approaching the formation of the march. Why he did so, alas, we do not know. Still, there is no report of any disruption of the march by onlookers.

What about the pictures and their maker? Was Coeppicus a passive onlooker, a "bystander" himself, or a witness? Since we do not know why he took the photos, this is difficult to ascertain. He seems to have taken most of his photos in a rather detached mode, with a "cold eye."[38] Yet, one cannot deny that taking so many photos of humiliated men—especially those inside the synagogue—also reveals a certain voyeuristic trait. Even worse, within the context of persecution, cameras can become weapons. To come back to the photos taken in Norden, it is clear that the humiliated did not want to be photographed. One woman turned her head down, while the other held her hand in front of her face.[39] A similar reaction cannot be seen in the photos in Baden—simply because the photos were taken from a certain distance and because the (other) onlookers deflected the attention or blocked the view. Most likely, the men did not know that they were photographed. Had they known, this would have undoubtedly added gravely to their humiliation.

To open the concept of "bystanders," we need to consider the different perspectives on the incident. The SS, the Gestapo, and the police addressed the onlookers. As an audience, the onlookers were essential to the process of humiliating the Jews. Even though the crowd could not be completely trusted and was therefore under observation, the silence of the onlookers could be read as consent, legitimizing the perpetrators' deeds. In that—and in blocking possible escape routes—the onlookers and perpetrators became partners in crime. Excluding the Jews was one of the vital elements of the envisioned German *Volksgemeinschaft* (people's community).[40] In its reporting about the events of 10 November 1938, the local Nazi paper even went a step further and portrayed the onlookers as the real perpetrators, claiming that the police and the SS had to stop a nameless crowd from assaulting the synagogue.[41] The individual onlookers, in turn, knew that they were being monitored, too—by the Gestapo and other members of the crowd. Still, just by being there, they saw a final unbridgeable rift opening up between them and their (former) neighbors. To the victims, walking through the streets of their hometown bareheaded, the onlookers functioned as a wall defining the borders of the path they had to walk amplifying the feeling of humiliation. For some, the crowd would have looked like a threatening posture one had to expect to be attacked by. Others knew the audience would protect them to a certain degree. As long as there were onlookers, murder was unlikely to be committed, because the onlookers would have to be regarded as potential witnesses.

By and large, analyzing the photos from the pogrom in Baden-Baden highlights that "bystander" is a rather one-dimensional term. The dividing line between "perpetrators" and "bystanders" was not at all as clear-cut as the concept indicates. The groups were linked in more than one way and their social functions tended to overlap. Yet, we should keep in mind that the term "victim" can be equally unfitting. Hans Hauser, once a Jewish citizen of Baden-Baden who can be seen wearing a light trench coat in the forefront of the third picture (fig. 7.4), was able to emigrate to the United States in time and fought his way back into Germany as a GI. When Hauser visited his hometown at the end of the war, some people of Baden-Baden immediately offered him the post of mayor. He declined.[42]

Christoph Kreutzmüller is working as curator of the new permanent exhibition at the Jewish Museum in Berlin. His book *Fixiert: Fotografische Quellen zur Verfolgung und Ermordung der europaeischen Juden* (with Julia Werner) was recently published by the German Federal Agency for Political Education. Together with Tal Bruttmann and Stefan Hördler, he is currently preparing a critical reconstruction of the Lili-Jacob-Album, the iconic Auschwitz Album. He has also worked as a senior historian at the House of the Wannsee Conference and the Humboldt University of Berlin.

Notes

1. For a general discussion of the importance of photos of the Holocaust see Sybil Milton, "Photography as Evidence of the Holocaust," *History of Photography* 23, no. 4 (1999): 303–312.
2. Cf. Michael Wildt, *Volksgemeinschaft als Selbstermächtigung: Gewalt gegen Juden in der deutschen Provinz 1919 bis 1939* (Hamburg, 2007), 9–10.
3. "Jews Are Ordered to Leave Munich," *New York Times*, 11 November 1938. The *New York Times* published three additional Associated Press photos on 18 November

1938. See "Britain Questions Colonies on Jews," *New York Times*, 18 November 1938. The shop on the photo is the Beleuchtungshaus des Westens run by Wilhem Philippi at Kurfürstendamm 206. After the pogrom, Philippi sold the business to the non-Jew and emigrated to Argentina. Cf. Christoph Kreutzmüller, *Final Sale in Berlin: The Destruction of Jewish Commercial Activity, 1930–1945* (New York, 2017 [2015]), 195.

4. For a discussion of the concept of "icons," see Cornelia Brink, *Ikonen der Vernichtung: Öffentlicher Gebrauch von Fotografien aus Nationalsozialistischen Konzentrationslagern* (Berlin, 1998).
5. Raphael Gross, *November 1938: Die Katastrophe vor der Katastrophe* (Munich, 2013), 122.
6. Irene von Götz and Christoph Kreutzmüller, "Spiegel des frühen NS-Terrors: Zwei Foto-Ikonen und ihre Geschichte," *Fotogeschichte: Beiträge zur Geschichte und Ästhetik der Fotografie* 34, no. 131 (2014): 73–75.
7. Bernward Dörner, *"Heimtücke": Das Gesetz als Waffe—Kontrolle, Abschreckung und Verfolgung in Deutschland 1933–1945* (Paderborn, 1998).
8. "Photographer Arrested," *Manchester Guardian*, 10 November 1938.
9. Hermann Simon, "'Man hatte das Gefühl, dass sich hier ein ganzes Volk schämte': Der Novemberpogrom im Spiegel diplomatischer Berichte aus Berlin," in *Es brennt! Antijüdischer Terror im November 1938*, ed. Andreas Nachama, Uwe Neumärker, and Hermann Simon (Berlin, 2008), 123–124; Christian Dirks and Hermann Simon, eds., *From the Inside to the Outside: The 1938 November Pogrom in Diplomatic Reports from Germany* (Berlin, 2014), 78–79.
10. Landesarchiv Berlin, A Pr. Br. Rep. 030, tit. 95, 21620 (Berichte über politische Vorfälle in Berlin, Bd. 5, 1938–1939).
11. Günter Beukert, "Als Bildjournalist in der 'Reichskristallnacht,'" in *Die Gleichschaltung der Bilder: Zur Geschichte der Pressefotografie 1930–36*, ed. Diethart Kerbs, Walter Uka, Brigitte Walz-Richter (Berlin, 1983), 191–193; Klaus Hesse, "'Vorläufig keine Bilder bringen': Zur bildlichen Überlieferung des Novemberpogroms," in Nachama et al., *Es brennt!* 138–139.
12. Christoph Kreutzmüller, Hermann Simon, and Elisabeth Weber, *Ein Pogrom im Juni: Fotos antisemitischer Schmierereien in Berlin 1938* (Berlin, 2013), 14.
13. See Christoph Kreutzmüller and Bjoern Weigel, *Kristallnacht? Bilder der Novemberpogrome 1938 in Berlin* (Berlin, 2013).
14. Christoph Kreutzmüller and Julia Werner, *Fixiert: Fotografische Quellen zur Verfolgung und Ermordung der Juden in Europa—Eine pädagogische Handreichung*, 2nd ed. (Bonn, 2016), 11. One of the few exceptions is a small series of photos Henry Bauer took of the destruction of his family home in Mannheim. See Museum of Jewish Heritage, New York, Id no. 1901.90. I would like to thank my colleague Aubrey Pomerance, Berlin, for this information.
15. Klaus Hesse and Philipp Springer, *"Vor aller Augen": Fotodokumente des nationalsozialistischen Terrors in der Provinz* (Essen, 2002), 89–116. Cf. Hesse, "'Vorläufig keine Bilder bringen.'" An exception is Munich, where the city administration and Hitler's personal photographer Heinrich Hoffmann took photographs. Cf. Andreas Heusler and Tobias Weger, *"Kristallnacht": Gewalt gegen die Münchener Juden im November 1938* (Munich, 1998), 55–64.
16. See Dieter Klose, ed., *9.11.1938: Reichspogromnacht in Ostwestfalen-Lippe* (Detmold, 2007).
17. Hesse and Springer, *"Vor aller Augen,"* 110–116. Cf. Hesse, "'Vorläufig keine Bilder bringen.'"
18. Gross, *November 1938*, 41–56.

19. "Gegen die Überhandnehmende Judenhetze in Baden-Baden," *Der Israelit*, 31 July 1930.
20. Angelika Schindler, *Der verbrannte Traum: Jüdische Bürger und Gäste in Baden-Baden* (Baden-Baden, 1992), 115–127.
21. Report by Arthur Flehinger, 21 May 1955, in Wiener Library London, 048-EA-0559.
22. Schindler, *Der verbrannte Traum*, 128–144.
23. German Federal Archives, "The Memorial Book of the Federal Archives for the Victims of the Persecution of Jews in Germany (1933–1945)," last updated 2 May 2018, https://www.bundesarchiv.de/gedenkbuch/index.html.en. For a detailed analysis of the photographs of the deportation, see Andreas Nachama and Klaus Hesse, eds., *Vor aller Augen: Die Deportation der Juden und die Versteigerung ihres Eigentums—Fotografien aus Lörrach, 1940* (Berlin, 2011).
24. "Ein Gegner des Regimes," *Badener Tagblatt*, 19 November 1998. Cf. Hesse and Springer, *"Vor aller Augen,"* 113.
25. Kreutzmüller and Werner, *Fixiert*, 28–35.
26. Ibid., 20. Cf. Wildt, *Volksgemeinschaft*, 234–239; Astrid Parisius and Bernhard Parisius, "'Rassenschande' in Norden: Zur Geschichte von zwei Fotos, die das Bild Jugendlicher von der NS-Zeit prägen," in *Ostfreesland 2004: Kalender für Jedermann* (Norden, 2003), 129–137.
27. *Quick*, "50 Jahre Weltgeschehen: Sonderheft zur Halbjahrhundertwende 1900–1950," (1950), 68–69.
28. Gerd Kühling, "Fotografien der Novemberpogrome und die Geschichte eines jahrzehntelangen Irrtums," *Aktives Museum Faschismus und Widerstand: Mitgliederrundbrief* 70 (2014): 6–9.
29. Report by Flehinger, 21 May 1955.
30. German schools in Nazi Germany usually ended around midday. Cf. Wolfgang Keim, *Erziehung unter der Nazi-Diktatur: Antidemokratische Potentiale, Machtantritt und Machtdurchsetzung* (Darmstadt, 1995).
31. For a detailed analysis of the perpetrators, see Kreutzmüller and Werner, *Fixiert*, 33–34.
32. Report by Flehinger, 21 May 1955.
33. Cf. Linda Conze, Ulrich Prehn, and Michael Wildt, "Sitzen, baden, durch die Straßen laufen: Überlegungen zu fotografischen Repräsentationen von 'Alltäglichem' und 'Unalltäglichem' im Nationalsozialismus," in *Fotografien im 20. Jahrhundert: Verbreitung und Vermittlung*, ed. Annelie Ramsbrock, Annette Vohwinckel, and Malte Zierenberg (Göttingen, 2013), 270–298.
34. Wildt, *Volksgemeinschaft*, 176.
35. Schindler, *Der verbrannte Traum*, 137.
36. Wildt, *Volksgemeinschaft*, 9–14.
37. Cf. Mark Roseman, *Barbarians from Our "Kulturkreis": German Jewish Perceptions of Nazi Perpetrators* (Göttingen, 2016), 29.
38. Dieter Reifrath and Viktoria Schmidt-Linsenhoff, "Die Kamera der Täter," in *Vernichtungskrieg: Verbrechen der Wehrmacht 1941–1944—Ausstellungskatalog*, ed. Bernd Boll (Hamburg, 1996), 475–503.
39. Kreutzmüller and Werner, *Fixiert*, 22–25.
40. For a discussion on the concept of the folk community, see Frank Bajohr and Michael Wildt, *Volksgemeinschaft: Neue Forschungen zur Gesellschaft des Nationalsozialismus* (Frankfurt, 2009).
41. "Aktion gegen die Juden," *Neues Badener Tageblatt*, 11 November 1938, reprinted in Schindler, *Der verbrannte Traum*, 143.

42. "Hans Hauser: 'Was sollte ich als Deutscher in Amerika?'"—Stolperstein in der Vincentistraße 26," *SWR*, 9 October 2014, http://www.swr.de/swr2/stolpersteine/ menschen/stolperstein-hans-hauser/-/id=12117596/did=14312030/nid=1211 7596/1lqumiz/index.html.

Bibliography

Bajohr, Frank, and Michael Wildt. *Volksgemeinschaft: Neue Forschungen zur Gesellschaft des Nationalsozialismus*. Frankfurt: S. Fischer Verlag, 2009.

Beukert, Günter. "Als Bildjournalist in der 'Reichskristallnacht.'" In *Die Gleichschaltung der Bilder: Zur Geschichte der Pressefotografie 1930–36*, edited by Diethart Kerbs, Walter Uka, and Brigitte Walz-Richter, 191–193. Berlin: Frölich & Kaufmann, 1983.

Brink, Cornelia. *Ikonen der Vernichtung: Öffentlicher Gebrauch von Fotografien aus Nationalsozialistischen Konzentrationslagern nach 1945*. Berlin: Akademie Verlag, 1998.

Conze, Linda, Ulrich Prehn, and Michael Wildt. "Sitzen, baden, durch die Straßen laufen: Überlegungen zu fotographischen Repräsentationen von 'Alltäglichem' und 'Unalltäglichem' im Nationalsozialismus." In *Fotografien im 20. Jahrhundert: Verbreitung und Vermittlung*, edited by Annelie Ramsbrock, Annette Vohwinckel, and Malte Zierenberg, 270–298. Göttingen: Wallstein, 2013.

Dirks, Christian, and Hermann Simon, eds. *From the Inside to the Outside: The 1938 November Pogrom in Diplomatic Reports from Germany*. Berlin: Metropol Verlag, 2014.

Dörner, Bernward. *"Heimtücke": Das Gesetz als Waffe—Kontrolle, Abschreckung und Verfolgung in Deutschland 1933–1945*. Paderborn: Schöningh, 1998.

German Federal Archives. "The Memorial Book of the Federal Archives for the Victims of the Persecution of Jews in Germany (1933–1945)." Last updated 2 May 2018. https://www.bundesarchiv.de/gedenkbuch/index.html.en.

Götz, Irene von, and Christoph Kreutzmüller. "Spiegel des frühen NS-Terrors: Zwei Foto-Ikonen und ihre Geschichte." *Fotogeschichte: Beiträge zur Geschichte und Ästhetik der Fotografie* 34, no. 131 (2014): 73–75.

Gross, Raphael. *November 1938: Die Katastrophe vor der Katastrophe*. Munich: C. H. Beck, 2013.

Hesse, Klaus. "'Vorläufig keine Bilder bringen': Zur bildlichen Überlieferung des Novemberpogroms." In Nachama et al., *Es brennt!* 136–145.

Hesse, Klaus, and Philipp Springer. *"Vor aller Augen": Fotodokumente des nationalsozialistischen Terrors in der Provinz*. Essen: Klartext, 2002.

Heusler, Andreas, and Tobias Weger. *"Kristallnacht": Gewalt gegen die Münchener Juden im November 1938*. Munich: Münchenverlag 1998.

Keim, Wolfgang. *Erziehung unter der Nazi-Diktatur: Antidemokratische Potentiale, Machtantritt und Machtdurchsetzung*. Darmstadt: Wissenschaftliche Buchgesellschaft, 1995.

Klose, Dieter, ed. *9.11.1938: Reichspogromnacht in Ostwestfalen-Lippe*. Detmold: Landesarchiv NRW, 2007.

Kreutzmüller, Christoph. *Final Sale in Berlin: The Destruction of Jewish Commercial Activity, 1930–1945*. New York: Berghahn Books, 2017 (2015).

Kreutzmüller, Christoph, and Björn Weigel. *Kristallnacht? Bilder der Novemberpogrome 1938 in Berlin*. Berlin: Kulturprojekte Berlin, 2013.

Kreutzmüller, Christoph, Hermann Simon, and Elisabeth Weber. *Ein Pogrom im Juni: Fotos antisemitischer Schmierereien in Berlin 1938.* Berlin: Hentrich & Hentrich, 2013.

Kreutzmüller, Christoph, and Julia Werner. *Fixiert: Fotografische Quellen zur Verfolgung und Ermordung der Juden in Europa—Eine pädagogische Handreichung.* 2nd ed. Bonn: Bundeszentrale für politische Bildung, 2016.

Kühling, Gerd. "Fotografien der Novemberpogrome und die Geschichte eines jahrzehntelangen Irrtums." *Aktives Museum Faschismus und Widerstand: Mitgliederrundbrief* 70 (2014): 6–9.

Milton, Sybil. "Photography as Evidence of the Holocaust." *History of Photography* 23, no. 4 (1999): 303–312.

Nachama, Andreas, and Klaus Hesse, eds. *Vor aller Augen: Die Deportation der Juden und die Versteigerung ihres Eigentums—Fotografien aus Lörrach, 1940.* Berlin: Hentrich & Hentrich, 2011.

Nachama, Andreas, Uwe Neumärker, and Hermann Simon, eds. *Es brennt! Antijüdischer Terror im November 1938.* Berlin: Stiftung Topographie des Terrors, 2008.

Parisius, Astrid, and Bernhard Parisius. "'Rassenschande' in Norden: Zur Geschichte von zwei Fotos, die das Bild Jugendlicher von der NS-Zeit prägen." In *Ostfreesland 2004: Kalender für Jedermann,* 129–137. Norden: Ostfriesland Verlag, 2003.

Reifrath, Dieter, and Viktoria Schmidt-Linsenhoff. "Die Kamera der Täter." In *Vernichtungskrieg: Verbrechen der Wehrmacht 1941–1944—Ausstellungskatalog,* edited by Bernd Boll, 475–503. Hamburg: Hamburger Edition, 1996.

Roseman, Mark. *Barbarians from Our "Kulturkreis": German Jewish Perceptions of Nazi Perpetrators.* Göttingen: Wallstein, 2016.

Schindler, Angelika. *Der verbrannte Traum: Jüdische Bürger und Gäste in Baden-Baden.* Baden-Baden: Elster Verlag, 1992.

Simon, Hermann. "'Man hatte das Gefühl, dass sich hier ein ganzes Volk schämte': Der Novemberpogrom im Spiegel diplomatischer Berichte aus Berlin." In Nachama et al., *Es brennt!* 118–127.

Wildt, Michael. *Volksgemeinschaft als Selbstermächtigung: Gewalt gegen Juden in der deutschen Provinz 1919 bis 1939.* Hamburg: Hamburger Edition, 2007.

CHAPTER 8

THE IMPERATIVE TO ACT
JEWS, NEIGHBORS, AND THE DYNAMICS OF PERSECUTION IN NAZI GERMANY, 1933–1945

Christina Morina

The young, charismatic Joachim Prinz, who held a PhD in philosophy from the University of Giessen and since 1926 served as the rabbi of the Friedenstempel in Berlin, knew the social landscape of his homeland by heart. He had grown up comfortably in the Upper Silesian province and had adjusted well to the vibrant metropolitan habitat of 1920s Berlin. Astutely aware of the relevance and fragility of interpersonal relations between members of any community, he—as both a philosopher and a deeply religious man—continually pondered the possibility of German Jews living to lead a life in relative complacency, a "normal" human existence. After witnessing Nazism's rise to power and the gradual yet radical transformation of the German social fabric that affected his entire personal and professional environment, Prinz offered the following "attempt at a first analysis" of the situation of Germany's Jews in the spring of 1935:

> It is the fate of the Jew to be without neighbor... Everywhere, life knows neighbors. He is not the friend but someone who is chosen to share his life *with* the other, not to make life harder for him, to observe his troubles and strivings with friendly eyes. That's what's missing. The Jews of the big city

don't feel it as much, but the Jews of the small towns who live at the market square without neighbors, whose kids go to school without the neighbors' kids, they feel the isolation ... and in the cohabitation of humans it might be the hardest lot anyone can befall. We wouldn't feel all this with so much pain if it weren't for the feeling that we once *had* neighbors.[1]

What Rabbi Prinz was describing in this passage is a story of progressing separation and distancing within a formerly more or less intact lifeworld. He was referring to not a sudden break-off of relations but rather an incremental deterioration, a process that Jews themselves observed as they were forced to live through it and sought desperately to understand. So the story of the disappearance of the "friendly eyes," as the victims themselves relay it to us, may help us write the history of bystanders in the Holocaust.

Based on the assumption that the murder of six million Jews between 1933 and 1945 was the result of a "dynamic interaction between state and society,"[2] this chapter seeks to contribute to our understanding of the bystanders' role by exploring the perspective of Jewish diarists in Nazi Germany. Based on a close reading of the exceptionally long-running diaries of Willy Cohn and Else Behrend-Rosenfeld and with a particular focus on the shift to war in 1939, it explores the way in which German Jews perceived of the people commonly referred to as bystanders in their immediate social surroundings. Bystanders viewed through the eyes of the victims emerge not as a static category of people and behaviors but rather as an unstable, context-dependent mode of social existence and relatedness within a wider framework of systemic coercion and violence. Such an approach offers a unique perspective, as most Holocaust narratives, even those examining diaries systematically, cite excerpts or produce syntheses from victims' diaries as snapshots of individual experiences and coping strategies rather than search for analytical clues these accounts might also contain.[3]

Only recently have scholars begun to shift the way in which we study Holocaust diaries from using them primarily as illustrations of victims' experiences or as evidence for what people "knew" about the Holocaust toward exploring their analytical potential.[4] As Frank Bajohr has noted, valuable insights can be gained from a close-up perspective on societal and interpersonal behavior captured in diaries, as no other genre of primary sources better reflects the process in the course of which ordinary people, who would not readily identify themselves as Nazis, were mobilized into some form of cooperation.[5]

While the few pioneers in this field are primarily concerned with German-Jewish perceptions of "perpetrators," this chapter seeks to examine how bystanders are being addressed in victims' accounts. By tracing the "interior landscape" of the diaries, it will explore the "variations of an exterior landscape" that also transpire from these accounts.[6] Through the eyes of Cohn and Behrend-Rosenfeld, the gradual exclusion of Jews becomes delineable as the social war waged against them since 1933 turned into an all-out war in 1939. How did their views of German society change over time, and how did they make sense of the various reactions on the part of non-Jewish Germans—friends, colleagues, acquaintances, and neighbors? How did they interpret their compatriots' behavior in response to the anti-Jewish measures ordained by the government and the state's institutions? Finally, what do these accounts tell us about the (changing) nature of interpersonal relations within German society during the Nazi regime and World War II?

Differentiating between the immediate social *Umwelt* and the mediate, wider *Mitwelt*, two key components in Alfred Schütz's phenomenology of the social lifeworld, I argue that after years of defamation, social exclusion, legal segregation, and economic expropriation, the shift from peace to war in 1939 is of particular relevance.[7] With the beginning of the war, the position of the remaining Jews within Germany, alongside the *Volksgemeinschaft*, underwent a major transformation, one that some initially hoped would bring them closer to their estranged compatriots—at least the ones who used to observe with "friendly eyes." The war fundamentally changed German society and to some extent even leveled some of the fundamental differences in the daily experience of the Nazi dictatorship. Its consequences—families separated, allied bombings, food rationings, shortages—seemed to affect non-Jewish Germans' lives as much as those of Jews. At least for a while and despite their already yearlong persecution, the latter hoped that a renewed sense of *Schicksalsgemeinschaft*—of a shared community of fate—would create some common ground for mutual sympathy. Thus, in their view of bystanders—that is, neighbors, acquaintances, (former) colleagues, and passersby in public spaces—Jews oscillated between visions of a hostile and widely supported "Aryan" state (*Mitwelt*) and impressions of an immediate lifeworld (*Umwelt*) that seemed willing to offer some measure of empathy in turn for an acknowledgment of the "Aryan" costs and sufferings of war. Yet, such hope for what I call "subjunctive solidarity" proved ultimately futile as the Nazis radicalized the "small war" against the Jews within the "great war," as Willy Cohn put it in his diary, into a war of total physical extermination.

From Retreat to Removal: The Inner and Outer Landscapes of Two Holocaust Diaries

Willy Cohn was born in 1888 into an old Breslau family. He held a PhD in history, taught German, history, and geography at a *Gymnasium* and was a proud World War I veteran. He was a kind but belligerent man, pious and just as proud of his *Deutschtum* as of his Jewish heritage. Cohn was staunchly critical of Jewish assimilation, supported the Zionist movement, and dreamed of a Jewish homeland in Palestine—if not for himself then for his five children, three of whom managed to emigrate before 1939, while the two young daughters were killed with their parents in Kaunas in late 1941.

Politically, Cohn stood on the left; he was critical of capitalist materialism and consumerism, was a member of the Social Democratic Party of Berlin (SPD), and took note in his diary of the anniversary of Ferdinand Lassalle's death. Among the publications that the Nazis burned in April 1933 in Breslau were the biographical sketches that Cohn had written about Marx, Engels, and Lassalle. In 1933, he was overwhelmed by the speed and ease with which the Nazis were able to initiate the removal (*Entfernung*) of the Jews from German social life as if they were "ingrown hair."[8] He retired in the fall of 1933 and spent much of the later 1930s reading and writing about Jewish history, culture, and religion and seeking to retain his contested influence within the Breslau Jewish community. After being banned from the public library, he—to his great comfort—was able to continue to work in the Catholic *Domarchiv* up until his arrest and deportation in November 1941. And even though he felt as if he was "sitting in his retreat [*Klause*], unaware of what's going on in the world, ... living beside history, ... totally excluded from it," Cohn used his diary to keep record of his times: as a historian, after all, "you want to think and live the times consciously," he noted in October 1939.[9]

Else Behrend-Rosenfeld was born in 1891 in Berlin. She was a historian, too, and had received her PhD from the University of Jena in 1919. As Cohn, she was a member of the SPD and had worked as a social worker in a women's prison in Berlin until 1933. After the Nazis seized power, her husband, Siegfried Rosenfeld, a social-democratic member of the Landtag of Prussia, was threatened by the SA, so they retreated to Bavaria, initially as a temporary solution, but they ended up settling there. The couple had three children who were sent to Argentina and England in the late 1930s, and Siegfried was able to retain a visa and immigrate to the United Kingdom in August 1939, five days before the outbreak of the war. That was the moment when Else Behrend-Rosenfeld started her diary. It was the moment, as she put it in her very first entry, when the "war pushed itself between us and freedom like a great, dark trapdoor,"[10] forcing Siegfried to go alone and leaving Else, who did not get her visa in time, behind. From then on, she recorded her experiences so that Siegfried would later be able to read about it and they could stay connected.

On the first pages of her diary, Behrend-Rosenfeld recounts their hasty move to Bavaria in 1933, first to Berchtesgarden and then to Reichenhall, where they met the full force of a self-empowering *Volksgemeinschaft* in the making.[11] In June 1934, the family was denounced by their landlady, threatened by local SA men, both as Jews and as "communists," and Siegfried was arrested and beaten. After his release in August, they left hastily once again and rented a house in Icking in the Isar Valley. From 1934 to 1938, the family there led a relatively peaceful life.

They abruptly left the idyllic town on 10 November 1938 because "under these circumstances the big city seemed safer to us than some small town."[12] To Behrend-Rosenfeld's horror, this turned out to be a grave misconception. In Munich, she felt as if she had been thrown into a "witches' Sabbath."[13] After her family managed to escape in the following months, she started working for the Jewish *Gemeinde* in Munich. She witnessed and, as managing householder, organized the concentration and "resettlement" of the Bavarian Jews and those from Baden and the Pfalz in central homes. After the deportations had begun in September 1940, she gradually realized that *"Verbannung"* (banishment) meant death. In the spring of 1942, days before being deported herself with the last transport to leave Munich, she went into hiding, first in Berlin and later in Freiburg. Finally, in April 1944 she was able to walk across the Swiss border, breaking her leg but reaching a safe haven after all.

By the fall of 1939, after years of persecution, German Jews had almost disappeared from the public landscape as they were gradually excluded from all aspects of social life. "Even before the war, Jews had experienced social death in German society,"[14] as Marion A. Kaplan has put it. Hundreds had been killed, thousands incarcerated, and tens of thousands had left Germany for good. From 1933 to 1939, 247,000 German Jews were able to emigrate, 80,000 alone between January and September of 1939.[15] At the same time, Jews remained the most prominent target of Nazi propaganda. In a deviously coherent effort, the regime framed Germany's fate and future in terms of Jewish responsibility. Moreover, from September 1939 onward, it presented the war along with the declared intention to "exterminate" the Jews as "part of an overarching war of retaliation and defense."[16]

On an everyday basis, Germans read, heard, and discussed multiple variants of this narrative, and Jews did not fail to pick up the mixed yet clear message the regime spread. After years of social war against the Jews within Germany, the beginning of World War II signaled a dramatic shift toward an actual war fought far beyond its borders and with a previously inconceivable viciousness. Jews were now targeted from within and from without, and most of them felt doubly trapped in ever-worsening circumstances. Yet, some took solace in the fact that the war, in a way, leveled social divisions as it affected *all* people living in Germany. Others felt encouraged to hope that the war soon would lead to the downfall of the Nazi regime.[17] Still, the core message of Goebbels's propaganda machinery by May 1943—"The Jews are guilty of everything!"[18]—was recorded and echoed by many contemporaries throughout the war. While the November pogrom had pushed the remaining Jews to intensify their emigration efforts—and many thousands indeed managed to get out—the beginning of the war aggravated the sense of living in a permanent state of emergency since 1933.

Willy Cohn followed the events of war very closely. Initially, he supported Hitler's motives, noted his first military successes, and admired the discipline and "honor" of the Wehrmacht.[19] He agreed that Versailles needed to be undone. Citing newspapers and hearsay, he commented on most major military events, adding his own analysis in an attempt to connect his daily life with the events unfolding at the military fronts. For instance, he observed that "the shortage of fish is a remainder how strongly the British rule the sea."[20] Cohn sought to fathom the scope and dynamic of events by situating them within world history: the start of the war had initiated an "upheaval" (*Umbruch*) comparable only to 1789—a "universal turn" (*Weltwende*) was underway, with events moving forward at "breathtaking" speed, he noted repeatedly during the war's first year.[21] Moreover, he perceptively examined the nexus between Germany's military operations and the fate of the Jews. All anti-Jewish measures, he noted after hearing about the order to wear the Star of David in September 1941, "show how bad the situation for Germany is and how much they let their anger out against the weakest part of the population!"[22] At the same time, the Nazis fought a "war of revenge" against the Jews, a "psychological war" (*Nervenkrieg*), a "small war" within the great war, and every move to help them or to resist the Nazi onslaught, within or outside Germany, was being turned against them with fatal consequences.[23] Finally, Cohn's own memories of fighting for Germany in World War I resurfaced time and again. He constantly compared the two events, warned of premature victory speeches and dreamed of his frontline experiences. After passing by a military parade on Breslau's Schloßplatz, he even felt the "absurd" desire to be "young again and to be allowed to be part of the fighting, once more."[24]

In contrast, Else Behrend-Rosenfeld mentioned the war only in passing. It dwells beneath her writing. On the one hand, the war was the context of her separation from her family. On the other hand, it served her as pretext for going into hiding in Berlin, as she was able to pose as Fräulein Leonie Maier whose Düsseldorf apartment had been destroyed in an air raid and who now came to live with relatives in Berlin.[25] She occasionally recorded conversations about the progress of the war but was mostly preoccupied with the fate of the hundreds of Jews who were being brought to her *Heim* in Berg am Laim to be deported to "Poland" and who, after initial correspondence, were never being heard of again. Unlike Cohn, Hitler's speeches "deeply frighten[ed]" her, and she pondered how long the war would last—three, four, even five more years?[26] The times seemed "dark" to her in a double sense: dark because of the looming dangers, but also literally as private worlds turned dark following the blackout orders in the wake of the Allied bombings. "I try not to think too much about the future," she ruminated in November 1939, "as it lies ahead of us dark and obscure; yet we have also learned that the dark is soothing [*wohltätig*] and that we should not try to lift it."[27]

How do the two diaries reflect on the way in which people in the immediate surroundings reacted to these changing circumstances? More broadly speaking, did they notice changes in the behavior of non-Jews in light of the deterioration of the situation for most *Volksgenossen* who started to miss the relatively comfortable life in Hitler's *Volksstaat* and where soon to fight a "total war"?[28]

Mitmenschen, Neighbors, Bystanders: Responses to the Nazi Imperative

In the wake of the National Socialist propagandistic, legal, and physical attacks on their Jewish compatriots since 1933, non-Jews were forced to react to the Nazi imperative on a daily basis. They faced, as long as Jews continued to be part of their *Umwelt*, a series of defining moments, forced to react to the myriad assaults waged against their compatriots in plain sight. These reactions were equally myriad, ranging from ignoring events and turning away to expressing gestures and words of empathy or hostility, to actions that transformed bystanders either into rescuers (e.g., offering food stamps or even a hiding place) or perpetrators (e.g., denunciation, physical violence). Very often, such actions were taken spontaneously rather than deliberately, born in a particular moment and under particular circumstances, and the underlying attitudes, safety, and feasibility calculations could change over time.

The diaries of Willy Cohn and Else Behrend-Rosenfeld mirror the instability and hybridity of the responses that led to the destruction of long-existing (however fractured) communities and, ultimately, to the Jews' "removal" by deportation and murder. In their ruminations about the changing interpersonal relations in their everyday life, both diaries capture three distinct yet interrelated social conditions: systemic hate, incidental personal attacks, and a steady stream of compassionate words and gestures on the part of "Aryan" Germans.

Both diarists refer to the state-ordained assault on the Jews as the attempt to "excruciate" them from German society, using the same German word, *Austreibung*. They both differentiate between genuinely "evil" Nazis and people who seem only "touched by" (*angehaucht*) National Socialist ideology but not "mean-spirited."[29] And both convey a sense that German society seemed to have been hijacked by a vicious minority, more unable than unwilling to stand up against it. Cohn very likely recorded every single "proof of human loyalty [*Treue*]" he noticed in his daily encounters, always hoping for the regime's immanent implosion. "In general, one often experiences decency and loyalty even if there is a lot of smearing [*Verhetzung*]," he wrote in July of 1940, "some people try to blame the Jews for everything, but there are also people, who already think differently and who blame the leadership for the wounding [*Verwundung*]."[30] Only the profiteers (*Nutznießer*) remained loyal. As late as 1941, he lived in the expectation that an "awakening" and a "revolution" would soon erupt from within German society and end it all.[31] Becoming ever more aware of the murderous nature of the anti-Jewish measures, Cohn concluded that the group of perpetrators still was very limited—the "blood of the ... dead Jews stains the name of Himmler, the leader of the SS and head of the German police."[32]

Behrend-Rosenfeld wrote much less detailed about her views of German society but shared Cohn's basic outlook. Being closely embedded in a network of prewar friendships and collegial relationships, she believed that the regime actually had a hard time separating Jews from non-Jews. With the steady growth of the initially "invisible walls of the ghetto, we are being forced to take care of us all by ourselves ... and it is clear that they therefore are able to control and prevent contacts between 'Aryans' and Jews," Behrend-Rosenfeld noted after Jews were being moved into *Judenhäuser* in the fall of 1939 (she always put "Aryans" in quotation marks).[33] In September 1941, when Jews were forced to wear the Star of David, Behrend-Rosenfeld paused to reflect on this latest "blow to our faces" and added a detailed analysis of German bystanders:

How is the population reacting to this? Most people pretend that they don't see the Star; very rarely someone on the tram expresses his satisfaction that finally one can recognize the Jewish scum [*Judenpack*]. However, we also experienced and experience many expressions of disgust [*Abscheu*] with this measure and many words of sympathy for us, the affected. Schoolchildren, who have to wear the Star from the age of six, are being hit the hardest. Two boys, about seven years old, were terribly beaten by "Aryans" of the same age. One of them, though, was stopped by an older gentleman just passing by, who scolded and chased the boys away and accompanied the crying, little victim all the way to his front door. A soldier gave one of the elder [Jewish] women in our home his coupons worth a weeklong supply of bread, [and] on the tram a man made a deep bow and ostentatiously offered his seat to another one on her way to work. Our butcher and the butter tradesman declared to me that now they would deliver to us better than ever; they ranted about the humiliation that was inflicted on us... It seems to me that, at least in Munich, the rulers will not succeed in achieving what they intend with this order: that the majority [*Menge*] of the people will completely ostracize the Jews [*vollkommene Verfemung der Juden*]. Still, after only three days one cannot pass a final verdict on this.[34]

It seems unlikely that Behrend-Rosenfeld severely brushed over her account to reach a reluctant postwar bystander audience, as Mark Roseman suggests, because she originally kept her diary for her husband and later felt that she was also documenting the deeds of those who helped her survive.[35] It would thus be unwise to discount her—however tentative—sense of solidarity among non-Jewish Germans and the limited enthusiasm for Nazi policies.[36] Notably, she recorded here a few situations in which bystanders acted defiantly. Yet, however widespread that collective refusal to "ostracize the Jews" was, Behrend-Rosenfeld's account also underlines that courage was a scarce sentiment.

Cohn mused in a similar way about the depth of the commitment to the regime's antisemitic program among the population after hearing about the sudden deportation of the Berlin Jews in the fall of 1941. Apparently, he concluded, all "contact" (*Berührung*) between the two *Volksgruppen* was to be prevented to avoid mutual "spiritual encouragement" (*seelische Beeinflussung*).[37] Cohn distinguished between "old," "decent," "valuable," "correct" and "new," "small," "brutal" Gestapo officials who treated Jews accordingly, and he would always add the behavior of the Jews to the equation. He blamed spitting and cussing attacks against himself, his children, and friends on the street on seduced and blinded members of the League of German Girls (BDM) and rude youngsters (*Bengels*) without manners whom he would have slapped in the face in "normal times."[38] Unlike the non-Jewish elder man who intervened on behalf of the Jewish boy in Behrend-Rosenfeld's account, Cohn did not dare to act. Yet, he also encountered meanness and hate. After a shopkeeper was denounced for selling food to his wife in November 1940, Cohn called this "awful" Frau Belit one of "too many *Untermenschen*," revealing with this word choice his deeply ambivalent "sense of loyalty to Germany."[39]

Nonetheless, both diaries reflect an unremitting sense of non-Jews sympathizing whenever they interacted in a safe or familiar space—in the nearby church, the apartment building, the neighborhood, the *Dombibliothek*, or the barbershop of Paul Duscha, whom Cohn describes as a "Nazi *Hurrapatriot*" and his "direct line" to popular opinion. When Duscha was condemned by local party officials for accepting Jews as customers, he parted ways with Cohn in an agitated state, and, ironically, Cohn felt sorry for the old man who now had to realize "where all the denunciations lead."[40] Or, talking to an inspector he had known for a long time at the local police station, Cohn noted in November 1939:

> He remembered me, too. He did not even want to see my ID card... I told him, we were alone, how painful all this was for me, how gladly I still would have served Germany, how humiliating it was to have my fingerprints taken, how terrible it was to be separated from the children. One saw it in the man, how he felt all this, too. At the end, he also shook my hand. How decent the Germans are, if you deal with them individually, and how they condemn so much that has happened![41]

Very often, conversations with "Aryans" carefully charted the entire spectrum of shared grievances in the ongoing war: food and energy shortages, children sent off and unheard of at the front or in exile, or fear of another nightly air raid. With the *Blitzsieg* euphoria dwindling, Cohn noted in February 1941 that, increasingly, "Aryan people have the desire to relieve themselves when they speak with us and to express their true views of the situation." Thus, the milkman drew him into a conversation about "the overall situation"—"as Aryans currently very much like to do"—hoping somehow to hear "from us how it really is."[42] A friend assured him how bad the mood was among the population and that "many say it would have been better not to have started the *Judengeschichte* in the first place"—clearly a conclusion inspired not by compassion but by self-pity.[43]

Repeatedly, the notion is voiced that the lot of non-Jews was intricately connected to the treatment of Jews and that the fate that befell the Jews would ultimately hit all Germans—either as a result of an ever more fiercely fought war of revenge or of an ever more expanding Nazi terror state. Likewise, in conversations with Professor Theodor Goerlitz at the *Domarchiv*, Cohn discussed the ramifications of the bombing of German cities and grew convinced that there was "awakening everywhere ... people wonder about the outcome of the war."[44] Thus, the hardships of daily life had become a regular topic of small talk and everyday conversations, and Cohn took every word of sympathy for the Jews' lot as a sign of growing estrangement between the regime and the people.

Likewise, Behrend-Rosenfeld recorded instances of perceived unity in suffering between her community and the "Aryans" outside, notably the nuns in the nearby monastery who provided food and vegetables without compensation in "sisterly affection." As late as 1941, she considered most of her neighbors in her Icking apartment as being trustworthy friends.[45] Clearly, diaries do not reflect the full breadth of experience but instead document impressions selectively. Even so, they suggest that within a relatively stable interpersonal discourse of shared grievances, the fragile connectedness to one's *Mitbürger* (fellow citizens, as Cohn put it) remained intact for some time. Most of the diarists' immediate neighbors took an interest in their families' fates, helped with food stamps, gave advice, or uttered a few words of encouragement—contacts Cohn occasionally even evaded in order to spare himself the nagging question of "why he was still here," and the others the feeling of risking their safety. Behrend-Rosenfeld expressed a similar sense, for example, when she noted that while she can recognize other Jews on the street by the "stony look on their face," she actually preferred not to look at all at others in an effort not to be seen herself. We find evidence for both, the unease connected to the question of why they were "still here" and for the measured sympathy of non-Jewish Germans, in other diaries as well. One striking passage from Victor Klemperer's diary reads as follows:

> Yesterday afternoon at the library the clerk, Striege or Striegel, a man of medium position and age, *Stahlhelmer* ... [said to me]: I should come with him into a back room. In the same way he had informed me a year ago about the ban from the reading room, he now told me about the complete ban from the library, thus the ultimate shutdown [*Mattsetzung*]. It was still different from a year ago. The man was filled with disbelieving desperation; I had to calm him down. He stroked my hand incessantly, he could not suppress the tears, he stumbled: ... Whether I could store my manuscript at some consulate ... Whether I could get out ... Whether I would drop him a line. Even before (when I did not know yet about the ban) in the catalog room, the [clerk] Rothin shook my hand with a bleak face: whether I could not get away, things are coming to an end here, "with us too—before the synagogue the Marcus Church went up in flames and the Zions Church was threatened with the same unless they changed their name ..." She spoke to me as to a dying man, she said goodbye to me for good.[46]

Yet, stronger than Cohn's and Behrend-Rosenfeld's accounts relay, Klemperer felt that "these compassionate and desperate ones are few, however, and they too are afraid."

In fact, both seem to have been reluctant to record instances of hostile bystander behavior because it depressed them too much. In Behrend-Rosenfeld's case, this side of her experience often looms in between the lines of her account. A few weeks after the outbreak of the war, she thought about "how our people" coped with the worsening conditions, as the "still invisible walls of the Ghetto" rose steadily. Many, she pondered, at least on the outside, took it with patience and quietly succumbed to their fate, convinced that there was nothing they could do to change it. Others, depending on the "sensibility of the individual, not only register all the mortifications [and] exclusions internally," but these experiences were also causing "festering wounds that slowly poison the soul and the mind of most people."[47]

Another example for this reluctance stems from the time when Behrend-Rosenfeld realized that she could not think of a single friend or acquaintance in Berlin to whom she could turn for a place to hide after she had escaped deportation ("My Berlin friends passed by me in my mind. Whom was I allowed to burden that much?").[48] Instead, comforting herself, she would make broad observations such as, "In general, people are only able to be compassionate about things they or their loved ones experience firsthand."[49] Such soothing sentiments about universally human behavioral patterns surface in other accounts as well, for instance, in Ruth Friedrich's Berlin diary: "Man has no imagination for injustice. What he does not see with his own eyes, he is unable to imagine."[50]

Likewise, Cohn probably underrepresented disturbing experiences and overrepresented compassionate contacts to comfort himself. He repeated the statement that "today, for the first time," he was attacked as a Jew personally several times throughout the years, as if he had forgotten over and over again that it had happened before. It is crucial to acknowledge that victims' accounts of bystander (as well as perpetrator) behavior are not tainted and thus somehow "unreliable" but dented because of the diarists' need to make sense and, by delineating the interior and exterior landscapes of their real-life existences, to create and preserve a last zone of comfort.

Conclusion: In Search of (Subjunctive) Solidarity

Analyzing genocide as a social process is an immensely complex undertaking for historians. Yet, contemporary accounts in diaries and letters of the victims offer valuable clues for such an analysis. Unlike postwar accounts of survivors and bystanders, which relay history as a series of cumulative episodes with a known outcome, diaries reflect the experience of history as an open-ended stream. They offer chronological, linear narratives even if the life stories they tell are full of ruptures. The reflections they contain routinely travel to experiences in the past, compare and weigh the changing social climate in the course of time, so that recordings of events unfolding in their present often contain astute analyses from *within* the process historians seek to understand. Moreover, many victims' accounts display an—in view of their own predicaments—astounding ability to empathize with the dilemmas of their non-Jewish contemporaries. Diaries are thus relevant not because they can be treated as recovered black boxes filled with what people "actually knew" of the Holocaust and as template for mind games on how "we" might have or should have felt and reacted. Rather, they convey how humans described and understood their often painful experiences at particular moments in time; in that sense, diaries "form a mirror held up not only to the horror but also to the reader."[51]

What arises from such a reading is that even under a system of systemic violence, for bystanders there *was* room for maneuvering. This room was ever evolving and changing. Unlike the victims, so often left only with "choiceless choices," lesser- or nontargeted contemporaries could make real, meaningful choices.[52] The degree to which they were "implicated" as subjects by the events unfolding was determined by the changing degree to which the systemic violence encroached their immediate *Lebenswelt* and social relations.[53] The resultant spectrum of reflexive and deliberate choices of action changed over time, and through them, every single bystander directly influenced the broader system of structural violence, enhancing or impeding its effectiveness.

Jews observed these dynamics with astuteness and sensibility, learning over time to accept that, in the worst case, their *Mitmenschen* could turn into *Gegenmenschen*, who would question, undermine, and ultimately deny them the very right to exist.[54] Reflecting on the changes in interpersonal relations within their communities, as well as in the social fabric of German society at large, they clung to a sense of connectedness—first to cope with the spiraling effects of social exclusion, later to defy a war that seemed to take an equal toll on non-Jewish Germans, turning the bystanders into victims. This longing prompted Else Behrend-Rosenfeld in January 1944 to confine a remarkable analogy to her diary:

Everything repeats itself exactly. Their wealth, their houses are being taken away and shattered, they are hurdled together in ever-poorer emergency shelters ... Their men, brothers, sons are fighting and falling on foreign soil, the women, sisters, and daughters have to work eleven, twelve hours a day just as we had to... Women and children are being exposed to mass extermination [*Massenvernichtung*] in a previously unimaginable way.[55]

The diary analysis thus illustrates what the notion of the Holocaust as "social process" actually meant in the everyday lives of Jewish families. It suggests that we add to considerations about the dynamics of exclusion the dimension of "social reactivity," a concept Jacques Semelin has introduced with an eye on the history of wartime France and based exclusively on postwar Jewish testimony.[56] While we have come to view bystanders as passive and indifferent at best and as complicit and guilty at worst, Semelin identifies a thin but cohesive social net of spontaneous, minor gestures of solidarity and underlines the importance of the many undocumented acts of quiet refusal to give in to the demands of the surrounding structural violence. Clearly, as far as German society is concerned, Semelin's notion of "social reactivity" has little bearing; there was no broad, sustained sense of solidarity inspiring a concerted societal effort to help the Jews evade their fate. Instead, the relatively regular encounters of sympathy the two diaries document suggest something like a *subjunctive solidarity*—manifold expressions of an *intention* to help, an expressed willingness to assist *if only* circumstances were not as dire and dangerous.[57]

Very often, these sympathetic encounters were framed by and depended on a sense of shared fate—not surprisingly perhaps, as the notion of *Schicksalsgemeinschaft* is an enduring aspect of German political culture. Hannah Arendt has vividly described the coldhearted self-pity and "cheap sentimentality" inherent in this notion in her conversations with ordinary Germans in 1949, and connected it to their political apathy and indifference both before and after 1945.[58] From the perspective of victim diaries observing bystanders during the war, it seems that if non-Jewish Germans felt that a Jewish person understood their hardship, they were more likely to respond with empathy toward the plight of a Jewish individual. As Cohn's and Behrend's diaries illustrate, a sense of shared hardship functioned as the basis for a mutual albeit often ephemeral, even "cheap" solidarity that rendered much hope on the part of the victims and very little actual assistance on the part of bystanders. By appealing, particularly after 1939, to a common *Erfahrungsgemeinschaft* (a society at war), Jews and non-Jews, wherever they were still able to interact, continuously negotiated a sense of connectedness. With the war worsening, the particularly fragile existence of the Jews as a social group was more and more neglected by bystanders, while the victims sought to retain it in an increasingly futile effort to stay connected as long as ever possible.

Christina Morina is DAAD Visiting Assistant Professor at the Amsterdam Institute for German Studies. Her research focuses on major themes in nineteenth- and twentieth-century German and European history, political and memory culture, the history of Marxism, and the history of historiography. She received a PhD from the University of Maryland in 2007. Her dissertation was published as *Legacies of Stalingrad: Remembering the Eastern Front War in Germany since 1945* (Cambridge University Press, 2011). Her second monograph is a group portrait of the first generation of European Marxists, entitled *Die Erfindung des Marxismus: Wie eine Idee die Welt eroberte* (Siedler Verlag, 2017). She is also co-editor of *Das 20. Jahrhundert erzählen: Zeiterfahrung und Zeiterforschung im geteilten Deutschland* (Wallstein, 2016, with Franka Maubach).

Notes

1. Joachim Prinz, "Das Leben ohne Nachbarn: Versuch einer ersten Analyse," *Jüdische Rundschau* 40, nos. 31–32 (17 April 1935): 3, emphasis added. All translations are my own unless otherwise noted.
2. Frank Bajohr, "The 'Folk Community' and the Persecution of the Jews: German Society under National Socialist Dictatorship, 1933–1945," *Holocaust and Genocide Studies* 20, no. 2 (2006): 183. Examples of recent works in this field are Susanna Schrafstetter and Alan E. Steinweis, *The Germans and the Holocaust: Popular Responses to the Persecution and Murder of the Jews* (New York, 2015); Froukje Demant, "Verre buren: samenleven in de schaduw van de Holocaust" (PhD diss., University of Amsterdam, 2015); Mary Fulbrook, *Dissonant Lives: Generations and Violence through the German Dictatorships* (Oxford, 2011); Peter A. Fritzsche, *Life and Death in the Third Reich* (Cambridge, MA, 2008); Doris Bergen, *The Holocaust: A New History* (Stroud, 2008); Saul Friedländer, *Nazi Germany and the Jews: The Years of Extermination, 1939–1945* (New York, 2007); Michael Wildt, *Volksgemeinschaft als Selbstermächtigung: Gewalt gegen Juden in der deutschen Provinz 1919 bis 1939* (Hamburg, 2007); Frank Bajohr, *"Aryanisation" in Hamburg: The Economic Exclusion of Jews and the Confiscation of Their Property in Nazi Germany* (Hamburg, 2002); Saul Friedländer, *Nazi Germany and the Jews: The Years of Persecution, 1933–1939* (New York, 1997).
3. See, e.g., Friedländer, *Nazi Germany and the Jews*; Alexandra Garbarini, *Numbered Days: Diaries and the Holocaust* (New Haven, CT, 2006); Nicholas Stargardt, *Witnesses of War: Children's Lives under the Nazis* (New York, 2007).

4. Mark Roseman, "Holocaust Perpetrators in Victims' Eyes," in *Years of Persecution, Years of Extermination: Saul Friedländer and the Future of Holocaust Studies*, ed. Paul Betts and Christian Wiese (London, 2010), 97; see also Mark Roseman, *Barbarians from Our "Kulturkreis": German-Jewish Perceptions of Nazi Perpetrators* (Göttingen, 2017); Amy Simon, "The Modern Haman: Ghetto Diary Writers' Understanding of Holocaust Perpetrators," *Holocaust Studies* 17, nos. 2–3 (2011): 123–144. On the historiographical treatment of diaries, see Amos Goldberg, "Jews' Diaries and Chronicles," in *The Oxford Handbook of Holocaust*, ed. Peter Hayes and John K. Roth (Oxford, 2010), 1–12; Frank Bajohr, "Das 'Zeitalter des Tagebuchs'? Subjektive Zeugnisse aus der NS-Zeit: Einführung," in *"... Zeugnis ablegen bis zum letzten": Tagebücher und persönliche Zeugnisse aus der Zeit des Nationalsozialismus und des Holocaust*, ed. Frank Bajohr and Sybille Steinbacher (Göttingen, 2015), 7–21. On the issue of Holocaust "knowledge" based on diary research, see Bart van der Boom, *"Wij weten niets van hun lot": Gewone Nederlanders en de Holocaust* (Amsterdam, 2012). For a critique of this approach, see Christina Morina, "The 'Bystander' in Recent Dutch Historiography," *German History* 32, no. 1 (2014): 101–111; Krijn Thijs, this volume.
5. Bajohr, "Das 'Zeitalter des Tagebuchs'?" 18.
6. Alain Girard, *Le Journal Intime* (Paris, 1963), xvi, cited in David Patterson, "Through the Eyes of Those Who Were There," *Holocaust and Genocide Studies* 18, no. 2 (2004): 276.
7. Alfred Schütz and Thomas Luckmann, *The Structures of the Life-World*, vol. 1, trans. Richard M. Zaner and H. Tristam Engelhardt Jr. (Evanston, IL, 1973).
8. Willy Cohn, diary entry 13 April 1933. All entries are quoted from Willy Cohn, *Kein Recht, nirgends. Tagebuch vom Untergang des Breslauer Judentums 1933–1941*, 2 vols. (Köln, 2007).
9. Cohn, entries 12 and 24 October 1939. Cohn recorded events and impressions of both political and private nature as the basis for the second part of his memoirs; he finished the first part running until 1933 in the fall of 1941, shortly before he was deported. The manuscript, along with most of his diaries, survived the war, and the memoir was published in 1995 under the title *Verwehte Spuren*. See Willy Cohn, *Verwehte Spuren: Erinnerungen an das Breslauer Judentum vor seinem Untergang* (Cologne, 1995). On Cohn's diary (compared to Victor Klemperer's account), see recently Guy Miron, "'Lately, Almost Constantly, Everything Seems Small to Me': The Lived Space of German Jews under the Nazi Regime," *Jewish Social Studies* 20, no. 1 (2013): 121–149.
10. Else Behrend-Rosenfeld diary entry, 28 August 1939. All entries are quoted from Else R. Behrend-Rosenfeld and Siegfried Rosenfeld, *Leben in zwei Welten: Tagebücher eines jüdischen Paares in Deutschland und im Exil* (Munich, 2011).
11. Wildt, *Volksgemeinschaft als Selbstermächtigung*.
12. Behrend-Rosenfeld, entry 6 September 1939.
13. Ibid.
14. Marion A. Kaplan, *Between Dignity and Despair: Jewish Life in Nazi Germany* (New York, 1998), 150.
15. Andrea Löw ed., *Die Verfolgung und Ermordung der europäischen Juden durch das nationalsozialistische Deutschland, Bd. 3: Deutsches Reich und Protektorat Böhmen und Mähren September 1939–September 1941* (Munich, 2012), 47.
16. Jeffrey Herf, *The Jewish Enemy: Nazi Propaganda during World War II and the Holocaust* (Cambridge, MA, 2008), 1; Stargardt, *Witnesses of War*.
17. Kaplan, *Between Dignity and Despair*, 145–169.
18. Herf, *The Jewish Enemy*, 209.

19. Cohn, entries 11 September 1939, 30 November 1939, 7 October 1939, and 19 December 1940.
20. Cohn, entry 24 October 1939.
21. Cohn, entries 18 May 1940, 23 May 1940, and 17 June 1940.
22. Cohn, entry 8 September 1941.
23. Cohn, entries 20 June 1940, 29 July 1940, 10 and 22 September 1940, and 16 October 1941.
24. Cohn, entry 19 October 1940.
25. Behrend-Rosenfeld, entry 14 December 1942.
26. Behrend-Rosenfeld, entry 24 September 1939.
27. Letter to Eva Schmidt (Weimar), 5 November 1939, cited in Behrend-Rosenfeld and Rosenfeld, *Leben in zwei Welten*, 104.
28. Götz Aly, *Hitler's Beneficiaries: Plunder, Racial War, and the Nazi Welfare State* (New York, 2007).
29. Behrend-Rosenfeld, entry 17 August 1941.
30. Cohn, entry 30 July 1940.
31. Cohn, entry 14 February 1941.
32. Cohn, entry 7 October 1940.
33. Behrend-Rosenfeld, entry 5 November 1939.
34. Behrend-Rosenfeld, entry 21 September 1941.
35. The character of the diary is contested, as Behrend-Rosenfeld edited it into a book and first published it in 1945 as *Verfemt und verfolgt: Erlebnisse einer Jüdin in Nazideutschland* (Zürich, 1945). See the details in Marita Krauss, "Zur Einführung," in Behrend-Rosenfeld and Rosenfeld, *Leben in zwei Welten*, 39–44. Roseman argues that her account was all along "tailored for a postwar audience" and that she seems to have consciously recorded a text to reach a public "that would have been alienated had there been more explicit evidence offered of its own behavior." Roseman, *Barbarians from Our "Kulturkreis,"* 61–62.
36. To that point see also the findings in Anna Ullrich, "Fading Friendships and the 'Decent German': Reflecting, Explaining and Enduring Estrangement in Nazi Germany, 1933–1938", in *Holocaust and European Societies: Social Processes and Social Dynamics*, edited by Frank Bajohr and Andrea Löw (London, 2016), 17–31.
37. Cohn, entry 21 October 1941.
38. Entry 3 May 1940.
39. Cohn, entries 7 November 1940 and 11 September 1939.
40. Cohn, entry 16 May 1941.
41. Cohn, entry 7 November 1939.
42. Cohn, entries 1 and 3 February 1941.
43. Cohn, entry 27 January 1941.
44. Cohn, entry 14 February 1941.
45. Behrend-Rosenfeld, entries 17 August 1941 and 4 May 1941.
46. Victor Klemperer, *Ich will Zeugnis ablegen bis zum letzten, Bd. 3: Tagebücher 1937–1939* (Berlin, 1999), 114–115 (entry 3 December 1938).
47. Behrend-Rosenfeld, entry 5 November 1939.
48. Behrend-Rosenfeld, entry 7 August 1942.
49. Behrend-Rosenfeld, entry 14 April 1940.
50. Ruth Andreas-Friedrich and Jörg Drews, *Der Schattenmann: Schauplatz Berlin: Tagebuchaufzeichnungen, 1938–1948* (Frankfurt, 2006), 25.
51. Patterson, "Through the Eyes," 276. On reading diaries, see also James E. Young, "Interpreting Literary Testimony: A Preface to Rereading Holocaust Diaries and Memoirs," *New Literary History* 18, no. 2 (1987): 403–423.

52. On the notion of "choiceless choices," see Lawrence L. Langer, *Versions of Survival: The Holocaust and the Human Spirit* (Albany, 1982), 72.
53. On the "implicated" subjectivity as a malleable "mode of historical relations," see Michael Rothberg, "Multidirectional Memory and the Implicated Subject: On Sebald and Kentridge," in *Performing Memory in Art and Popular Culture*, ed. Liedeke Plate and Anneke Smelik (New York, 2013), 40, 46.
54. Jean Améry, *Jenseits von Schuld und Sühne: Bewältigungsversuche eines Überwältigten* (Munich, 1966), 70.
55. Behrend-Rosenfeld, entry 8 January 1944.
56. See Jacques Semelin, this volume.
57. In a similar way, echoing Jaspers's notion of nominal going along, Nicholas Stargardt has recently suggested to rethink Martin Broszat's concept of *Resistenz* as "that state of moral and political alienation from Nazism which found its expression, not in any outward show of resistance, but in a degree of non-conformity and inner withdrawal from the regime's exhortations and demands." See Nicholas Stargardt, "The Troubled Patriot: German Innerlichkeit in World War II," *German History* 28, no. 3 (2010): 327; Nicholas Stargardt, *The German War: A Nation under Arms, 1939–1945: Citizens and Soldiers* (New York, 2015).
58. Hannah Arendt, "The Aftermath of Nazi Rule: Report from Germany," *Commentary* 10 (1950): 342. On the *Schicksalsgemeinschaft*, see Franziska Rehlinghaus, *Die Semantik des Schicksals: Zur Relevanz des Unverfügbaren zwischen Aufklärung und Erstem Weltkrieg* (Göttingen, 2015).

Bibliography

Aly, Götz. *Hitler's Beneficiaries: Plunder, Racial War, and the Nazi Welfare State*. New York: Metropolitan, 2007.
Améry, Jean. *Jenseits von Schuld und Sühne: Bewältigungsversuche eines Überwältigten*. Munich: Szczesny, 1966.
Andreas-Friedrich, Ruth, and Jörg Drews. *Der Schattenmann: Schauplatz Berlin—Tagebuchaufzeichnungen, 1938–1948*. Frankfurt: Suhrkamp, 2000.
Arendt, Hannah. "The Aftermath of Nazi Rule: Report from Germany." *Commentary* 10 (1950): 342–353.
Bajohr, Frank. *"Aryanisation" in Hamburg: The Economic Exclusion of Jews and the Confiscation of Their Property in Nazi Germany*. New York: Berghahn Books, 2002.
———. "Das 'Zeitalter des Tagebuchs'? Subjektive Zeugnisse aus der NS-Zeit: Einführung." In *"... Zeugnis ablegen bis zum letzten": Tagebücher und persönliche Zeugnisse aus der Zeit des Nationalsozialismus und des Holocaust*, edited by Frank Bajohr and Sybille Steinbacher, 7–21. Göttingen: Wallstein, 2015.
———. "The 'Folk Community' and the Persecution of the Jews: German Society under National Socialist Dictatorship, 1933–1945." *Holocaust and Genocide Studies* 20, no. 2 (2006): 183–206.
Behrend, Rahel. *Verfemt und verfolgt: Erlebnisse einer Jüdin in Nazideutschland*. Zürich: Büchergilde Gutenberg, 1945.
Behrend-Rosenfeld, Else R., and Siegfried Rosenfeld. *Leben in zwei Welten: Tagebücher eines jüdischen Paares in Deutschland und im Exil*. Edited by Erich Kasberger and Marita Krauss. Munich: Volk Verlag, 2011.
Bergen, Doris. *The Holocaust: A New History*. Stroud: History Press, 2008.

Boom, Bart van der. *"Wij weten niets van hun lot": Gewone Nederlanders en de Holocaust*. Amsterdam: Boom, 2012.

Cohn, Willy. *Verwehte Spuren: Erinnerungen an das Breslauer Judentum vor seinem Untergang*. Cologne: Böhlau, 1995.

———. *Kein Recht, nirgends. Tagebuch vom Untergang des Breslauer Judentums 1933-1941*, 2 vols. Köln: Böhlau, 2007.

Demant, Froukje. "Verre buren: Samenleven in de schaduw van de Holocaust." PhD diss., University of Amsterdam, 2015.

Friedländer, Saul. *Nazi Germany and the Jews: The Years of Extermination, 1939-1945*. New York: HarperCollins, 2007.

———. *Nazi Germany and the Jews: The Years of Persecution, 1933-1939*. New York: HarperCollins, 1997.

Fritzsche, Peter A. *Life and Death in the Third Reich*. Cambridge, MA: Belknap Press, 2008.

Fulbrook, Mary. *Dissonant Lives: Generations and Violence through the German Dictatorships*. Oxford: Oxford University Press, 2011.

Garbarini, Alexandra. *Numbered Days: Diaries and the Holocaust*. New Haven, CT: Yale University Press, 2006.

Goldberg, Amos. "'Jews' Diaries and Chronicles." In *The Oxford Handbook of Holocaust Studies*, edited by Peter Hayes and John K. Roth, 1-12. Oxford: Oxford University Press, 2010.

Herf, Jeffrey. *The Jewish Enemy: Nazi Propaganda during World War II and the Holocaust*. Cambridge, MA: Belknap Press, 2008.

Kaplan, Marion A. *Between Dignity and Despair: Jewish Life in Nazi Germany*. New York: Oxford University Press, 1998.

Klemperer, Victor. *Ich will Zeugnis ablegen bis zum letzten, Bd. 3: Tagebücher 1937-1939*. Berlin: Aufbau-Taschenbuch-Verlag, 1999.

Langer, Lawrence L. *Versions of Survival: The Holocaust and the Human Spirit*. Albany: State University of New York Press, 1982.

Löw, Andrea, ed. *Die Verfolgung und Ermordung der europäischen Juden durch das nationalsozialistische Deutschland, Bd. 3: Deutsches Reich und Protektorat Böhmen und Mähren September 1939-September 1941*. Munich: Oldenbourg, 2012.

Miron, Guy. "'Lately, Almost Constantly, Everything Seems Small to Me': The Lived Space of German Jews under the Nazi Regime." *Jewish Social Studies* 20, no. 1 (2013): 121-149.

Morina, Christina. "The 'Bystander' in Recent Dutch Historiography." *German History* 32, no. 1 (2014): 101-111.

Patterson, David. "Through the Eyes of Those Who Were There." *Holocaust and Genocide Studies* 18, no. 2 (2004): 274-290.

Prinz, Joachim. "Das Leben ohne Nachbarn: Versuch einer ersten Analyse." *Jüdische Rundschau* 40, nos. 31-32 (17 April 1935): 3.

Rehlinghaus, Franziska. *Die Semantik des Schicksals: Zur Relevanz des Unverfügbaren zwischen Aufklärung und Erstem Weltkrieg*. Göttingen: Vandenhoeck & Ruprecht, 2015.

Roseman, Mark. *Barbarians from our "Kulturkreis": German-Jewish Perceptions of Nazi Perpetrators*. Göttingen: Wallstein, 2017.

———. "Holocaust Perpetrators in Victims' Eyes." In *Years of Persecution, Years of Extermination: Saul Friedländer and the Future of Holocaust Studies*, edited by Paul Betts und Christian Wiese, 81-97. London: Continuum, 2010.

Rothberg, Michael. "Multidirectional Memory and the Implicated Subject: On Sebald and Kentridge." In *Performing Memory in Art and Popular Culture*, edited by Liedeke Plate and Anneke Smelik, 39-58. New York: Routledge, 2013.

Schrafstetter, Susanna, and Alan E. Steinweis. *The Germans and the Holocaust: Popular Responses to the Persecution and Murder of the Jews*. New York: Berghahn Books, 2015.
Schütz, Alfred, and Thomas Luckmann. *The Structures of the Life-World*. Vol. 1. Translated by Richard M. Zaner and H. Tristam Engelhardt Jr. Evanston, IL: Northwestern University Press, 1973.
Simon, Amy. "The Modern Haman: Ghetto Diary Writers' Understanding of Holocaust Perpetrators." *Holocaust Studies* 17, nos. 2–3 (2011): 123–144.
Stargardt, Nicholas. *The German War: A Nation Under Arms, 1939–1945: Citizens and Soldiers*. New York: Basic Books, 2015.
———. "The Troubled Patriot: German Innerlichkeit in World War II." *German History* 28, no. 3 (2010): 326–342.
———. *Witnesses of War: Children's Lives under the Nazis*. New York: Vintage Books, 2007.
Ullrich, Anna. "Fading Friendships and the 'Decent German.' Reflecting, Explaining and Enduring Estrangement in Nazi Germany, 1933–1938." In *Holocaust and European Societies: Social processes and Social Dynamics*, edited by Frank Bajohr and Andrea Löw, 17–31. London: Palgrave Macmillan, 2016.
Wildt, Michael. *Volksgemeinschaft als Selbstermächtigung: Gewalt gegen Juden in der deutschen Provinz 1919 bis 1939*. Hamburg: Hamburger Edition, 2007.
Young, James E. "Interpreting Literary Testimony: A Preface to Rereading Holocaust Diaries and Memoirs." *New Literary History* 18, no. 2 (1987): 403–423.

Chapter 9

Martin Heidegger's Nazi Conscience

Adam Knowles

In the history of National Socialism, few individual cases of complicity have garnered as much interest as that of the philosopher Martin Heidegger. This is because the "Heidegger case" is saturated with lurid details and puzzling contradictions. It is the story of the son of a Catholic sexton from the Swabian provinces casting aside his pious upbringing, rising to philosophical fame with the publication of his pathbreaking 1927 magnum opus *Being and Time*, and eventually ascending to become the Rector of the University of Freiburg in 1933 under National Socialism. As Rector, Heidegger took out his grudges against Jewish and non-Jewish scholars, all while unsuccessfully courting proximity to Hitler. During this time, Heidegger betrayed his mentor Edmund Husserl in an act of Freudian patricide, unceremoniously removing the elder philosopher from service in April 1933. Meanwhile, Hannah Arendt, one of the twentieth century's greatest political theorists, and Heidegger's former lover, spurned him while in exile in New York, only to return to reconcile with him in 1952. After the war, Theodor Adorno and Jürgen Habermas, two of Germany's most venerable thinkers, publicly berated Heidegger for his Nazi crimes, and he responded by uttering hardly a single public word until the 2013 publication of his *Black Notebooks*.

In the *Black Notebooks*, Heidegger characterizes what he calls his "error of 1933" as the refusal to be a bystander, which he describes dismissively as a position attributable only to those with a "lack of will."[1] Judged a fellow traveler (*Mitläufer*) by the University of Freiburg's independent denazification commission in 1946, Heidegger was punished with a teaching ban that barred him from the university premises and from contact with students until 1952. This judgment, however, is deeply misleading and has allowed Heidegger to occlude effectively many aspects of his involvement in National Socialism. First, it has distracted from his administrative role in implementing the "Aryanization" of the University of Freiburg. Second, it distracts from Heidegger's own perception of himself after 1934 as the self-proclaimed guardian of a pure vision of "spiritual National Socialism," who proclaims, "we will remain at the invisible front of the secret spiritual Germany."[2] Heidegger portrays himself as being pushed into the position of the bystander by a movement that no longer stood by him as National Socialist cultural, and pedagogical politics failed to align itself with Heidegger's ambition of creating "the metapolitics of 'the' historical people."[3] This "metapolitics" would require a renewed return to the essence of the German people through a cultural and political revolution with universities at the center of a movement to radicalize the youth of Germany.

This chapter will argue that, while Heidegger was by no means a bystander due to his administrative complicity from 1933 to 1934, he also harbored a deep intellectual complicity that he carried with him into the postwar era, even while manipulating the concept of the bystander to receive a relatively favorable judgment from the denazification commission. Common representations of his relationship with National Socialism, including by both his defenders and detractors, tend to follow Heidegger's own narrative and underestimate the depth of his complicity as Rector from April 1933 to April 1934 by overlooking his administrative activities as Rector.[4] As this chapter will show, the *Black Notebooks*, combined with documentary evidence from the archives of University of Freiburg and the German Federal Archives, refute any notion that Heidegger, as stated in his denazification report, had "devoted himself exclusively to his philosophical studies" after 1934.[5] Instead, I demonstrate that Heidegger was still actively negotiating with the Ministry of Science, Education, and Culture in Berlin until 1935. Meanwhile, as a thinker purportedly standing by on "the invisible front of the secret spiritual Germany," he conceived of himself as preserving a politics so pure that it could not be uttered in words. By

1936, Heidegger depicted himself in the *Black Notebooks* as a thinker in a world that had betrayed his kind, as a prophet in a world that could not listen to his prophecies. Yet, even despite these grand delusions, he never failed to be highly attentive to his concrete position within the cultural politics of National Socialism. As a result, he managed to carve out an advantageous position within a regime that valued the affiliation with, though not necessarily the input of, philosophers. After 1936, Heidegger remained politically reliable in the eyes of the regime by maintaining a research and teaching agenda aligned with the Nazi promotion of *Heimatkunde* (Germanic studies) while avoiding topics that would have provoked undue political suspicion.

In order to use the Heidegger case to contribute to this volume's critical rethinking of the category of the bystander, I argue that Claudia Koonz's concept of the "Nazi conscience" offers the best theoretical framework for dealing with Heidegger's thinking and actions both during his public political life and in the years thereafter. Koonz identifies four attributes of the Nazi conscience: (1) the *Volk* is an "organism marked by stages of birth, growth, expansion, decline and death"; (2) the rootedness of a people to a place in which it "develops the values appropriate to its nature and to the environment within which it evolved"; (3) the justification of the use of violence against people in conquered lands to benefit the *Volk*; (4) the cancellation of rights and citizenship "of assimilated citizens on the basis of what the government defined as their ethnicity."[6] As a perpetrator, Heidegger was primarily guilty of the fourth of these attributes during his Rectorate. As a thinker, there is little evidence that he supported violent expansion in accordance with the third principle. However, Heidegger's philosophy was deeply rooted within the kind of Volkish thought analyzed in George L. Mosse's *The Crisis of German Ideology*, and his most influential works rejuvenated a thinking of place, belonging, and rootedness while celebrating the language of the Swabian provinces.[7] Heidegger thus had a robust vision of the *Volk* as an organism bound to its particular essential place. In this vision, the *Volk* was taken away from this place and thus from its "historical destiny" by turning to calculative rationality as the primary means of understanding itself and the world. However, in his peculiar political vision developed in the *Black Notebooks*, because of the extent to which Nazism had embraced technology and employed calculative rationality, it was, according to Heidegger, in fact contributing to the death and not the flourishing of the German people. This "betrayal," in Heidegger's words, was the "most vile action devised by Germans against Germans"[8] and constituted a crime "the magnitude of which could not be measured against the atrocities of the 'gas chambers..'"[9] In other words, the peculiarity of the Heidegger case is that he regarded himself as maintaining a Nazi conscience purer than the conscience of the Nazi regime itself. For this reason, he regarded himself as being forced into the position of a bystander who remained alone on "the invisible front of secret spiritual German." As a result, if he assumed a less active role in National Socialism after 1935, it is because—as disturbing as it might seem—he did not regard the regime as radical enough.

Heidegger wrote the *Black Notebooks* ostensibly in the form of diaries. Kept secret until 2013, the volumes of the *Black Notebooks* published thus far cover the period from 1932 to 1948.[10] Unlike other famous diaries from the Nazi era, the style of the *Notebooks* is unique.[11] They consist not of traditional entries but instead of flowing passages of text. Rarely does Heidegger note a specific date, and, whenever possible, I have indicated such an estimated date for the entries used in this chapter.

Heidegger as a Nazi Bureaucrat

Since it would be impossible to give a full recounting of Heidegger's Rectorate or of his relation to National Socialism in such a brief essay, I would instead like to focus on a few moments reflected in the archival record of Heidegger's year as Rector in order to characterize his bureaucratic activities during this time. Despite the significant body of literature devoted to Heidegger, his activities as a Nazi bureaucrat have often been overlooked.[12] In fact, I would argue that the author of some of philosophy's most impenetrable prose was a far more effective bureaucrat than he was an ideologue, despite all attempts by interpreters to cast him as the latter.[13] Heidegger's postwar self-mythologizing indeed has been very effective at distracting from his bureaucratic activities, and, no less crucially, some of the major works analyzing Heidegger's Rectorate, which were written in the 1980s, did not have access to the full archival record available now.

Heidegger joined the Nazi Party on 1 May 1933 and remained a member until the end of World War II.[14] However, Heidegger's overt ties to radical right-wing politics date back to at least March 1933 when he served as a founding member of the Cultural-Political Working Group of German University Professors (Kulturpolitische Arbeitsgemeinschaft deutscher Hochschullehrer), a group that defined itself as a "community of conviction, work, and struggle," according to its founding document. This document is of particular importance because, aside from Heidegger's repeated pledges of loyalty to Hitler, it constitutes the most detailed political platform that he not only endorsed but also helped craft. Although the group disavowed affiliation with any particular party, it nonetheless called for, among other things, "German universities to wear a German face," "for the renewal of an ethnic [*völkisch*] consciousness," and for the leading role of the German university as a "site of national-political education." While the group limited its numbers to "ethnically German university professors," it did not overtly call for the outright dismissal of any non-ethnic Germans from the university. It did, however, declare that those who do not recognize the "ethnic bounds of all genuine culture ... have no place among us."[15] Given how prominently fellow signatories such as Erich Jaensch of Marburg and Ernst Krieck of Frankfurt would figure in Aryanizing their respective universities in the months thereafter, one could perhaps interpret the phrase "among us" in the broadest possible sense.

With the passage of the Law for the Restoration of the Professional Civil Service on 7 April 1933, the then Rector of the University of Freiburg, Wilhelm von Möllendorf, a man described derisively as "an avowed democrat" in an anonymous report written by a member of the Kulturpolitische Arbeitsgemeinschaft, was no longer regarded as suitable for the task of Aryanizing the university. Although Heidegger would later claim to the denazification commission that he assumed the Rectorate because he was "persuaded to accept by friends and admirers," the same report from the *Arbeitsgemeinschaft* contradicts this. The report, dated 9 April 1933, states:

> To take the first point raised at our recent discussion, concerning the alliance of National Socialist university teachers, we have ascertained that Professor Heidegger has already entered into negotiations with the Prussian Ministry of Education. He enjoys our full confidence, and we would therefore ask you to regard him for the present as our spokesman here at the University of Freiburg.[16]

The report is important because it documents not only Heidegger's ambitions within the University of Freiburg, but also his early ambitions to move beyond Freiburg to Berlin. In what Hugo Ott describes as a coup that "removed the last obstacle to *Gleichschaltung* at the University of Freiburg," Möllendorf resigned on 20 April and called a special election, which resulted in Heidegger being selected as his successor.[17] In the words of the economist Adolf Lampe, an Auschwitz survivor and former colleague at Freiburg who later served on Heidegger's denazification commission, Rector Heidegger "defended his positions with fanatical and terroristic intolerance and summoned the political force of the party to his defense."[18]

Heidegger adapted with incredible alacrity to his role as a Nazi bureaucrat. Documents signed by Heidegger on 19 April 1933, one day even before his election, show that his first order of business was to implement the anti-Jewish measures across the university.[19] Heidegger's work toward the *Gleichschaltung* of the University of Freiburg was exemplary, and he proved to be a conscientious and detail-oriented bureaucrat. Both Heidegger and Möllendorf faced a great amount of resistance against the implementation of the Aryanization measures, including pragmatic objections from the faculties of law, medicine, and the natural sciences, though there was little or no resistance from the humanities. Thus, for example, several directors of institutes and clinics requested a more precise "definition" of a Jew, including clarification on the status of converted Jews, half-Jews, and quarter-Jews. The dermatology clinic claimed that releasing its X-ray technician would result in the danger of radiation exposure, while the director of the pediatric clinic objected that he would not release his "only decent, fully trained pediatrician present in house."[20] It was not Heidegger's style of leadership to respond to these individual complaints, and he did not seem to be particularly troubled by either manner of objection. Indeed, as we will see in more detail later, Heidegger's style of leadership was based on the use of silence as a tool of power. By 28 April 1933, the day on which Heidegger issued a decree "requesting a complete and clear implementation of measures from 7 April" to all deans of the university, all Jewish professors had been released from service.[21] Heidegger allowed his own former academic assistant Werner Brock, who was Jewish, to stay behind to "rearrange the library of the seminar" until August 1933.[22]

Two further incidents from Heidegger's Rectorate serve to illustrate the nature of what I would like to call Heidegger's bureaucratic Nazi conscience. First, the case of Husserl's release is instructive for understanding the nature of Heidegger's bureaucratic power. As the luminary figure in the school of philosophy known as phenomenology and one of the most innovative philosophers of the early twentieth century, Husserl had generously helped place Heidegger in positions in Marburg in 1923 and eventually as his successor in Freiburg in 1928. While a rumor ran through the German-Jewish émigré community in the United States that Heidegger had barred Husserl, then an emeritus at Freiburg, from the library in a dramatic confrontation, the reality is far more anonymous and indifferent.[23] Husserl was simply another name listed among all the other professors and academic assistants who were to be released from service. Unfortunately, Husserl's personnel file is missing, but the documents from the university archives indicate that Heidegger handled Husserl with the same bureaucratic efficiency as any other case. Indeed, there was nothing personalized about the treatment of any professor. The sole personal touch was a letter that Heidegger's wife, Elfriede, sent to Malvine Husserl in late April 1933, along with flowers. Husserl was simply released, unceremoniously, although Heidegger does note in passing to the Ministry of Culture of Baden in June 1933 that he "would have no objection to" Husserl continuing to hold lectures.[24] This suggestion did not come to fruition and from then on Husserl was obligated to apply to the Ministry of Culture for permission (which was often denied) to travel, publish, or present his work until his death in 1938.

A second incident from the archival record involves violence against members of the Jewish fraternity Neo-Friburgia and ransacking of the fraternity's house by the members of the Nazi-led German Student Union (Deutsche Studentenschaft) and the National Socialist German Students' League (Nationalsozialistischer Deutscher Studentenbund, NSDStB) in May and June 1933. The fraternity was formed in 1925 on the "basis of an orientation toward the German fatherland" with the goal of "combating antisemitism among the student body."[25] In a letter to the university secretariat dated 21 April 1933, Neo-Friburgia declared that it had been dissolved because of a ban on Jewish student organizations. Separate accounts from the Nazi student groups and from Neo-Friburgia's lawyer largely agree about the details of the incidents but obviously disagree about their legality. The May 1933 monthly report of the Freiburg chapter of the NSDStB provides a detailed account of the students' motivations. It describes how the students, angered by rumors that the fraternity was still operating despite the ban on Jewish student groups stormed the house, physically removed its members and took possession of the house for nearly three weeks with the tacit approval of the police. The report from the following month goes on to state that Neo-Friburgia's lawyer persuaded a certain Constable Dold to order the guard to leave and to return the house to the custody of the fraternity members.[26] This angered the students and led to a significant escalation in violence following an anti-Versailles rally on 28 June. The June 1933 monthly report of the NSDStB narrates the events as follows:

> As the German Student Union became aware of [the return of the house] on Wednesday after the anti-Versailles protest, a mob of thousands of highly agitated students stormed toward Baslerstrasse after the volte-face of the parade, stormed the house, and turned the inhabitants over to the police, who, incomprehensibly, immediately released them. Incriminating material was found once again in the house. On Thursday evening, the guard formed by the National Socialist German Students' League was withdrawn and the house again sealed by the police. The police commanders behaved quite

peculiarly and spoke of disturbing the peace; a complaint against their behavior has already been filed with the Interior Minister Pflaumer.²⁷

The report reflects an atmosphere of physical violence by student organizations that felt entitled to intimidate even the police, who at this time seemed to have been less nazified than the student organizations.

On 11 July 1933, the state attorney's office wrote to the Rector requesting his support in an investigation against the student organizations, and neither Heidegger nor any other university official responded to the request. On 25 July, the state attorney's office reiterated its request to the Rector, and on 1 August, Heidegger finally responded with the following explanation:

> Our own inquiries have determined that nonstudents participated in the events at the Neo-Friburgia house and that the leader of the German Student Union immediately appeared at the site to restore order and peace once he had become aware of the occurrence, and that he did indeed restore peace. The attack commando he called to his assistance did not appear. It is not possible for me to take make individual students responsible, nor to name them, nor to take any further steps in this matter.²⁸

Heidegger's response is remarkable first for its resolute silence over a period of three weeks but also for its outright fabrication of events, for his account contradicts the student groups' own depiction, as well as the accounts of the police and Neo-Friburgia's lawyer. The moment is exemplary of Heidegger's skillful navigation of Nazi bureaucratic structures and of his leadership style, buttressed by close alliances with violent Nazi student groups who created a sense of terror in the city. Moreover, the event is not singular, for Heidegger responded similarly to accusations that students dressed in Nazi regalia beat a local communist sympathizer during a university-sponsored work camp in the nearby village of Löffingen.²⁹ As a Nazi bureaucrat, Heidegger helped to transform "ordinary citizens who happened to have Jewish ancestors into alien beings."³⁰

As Rector Heidegger sought to find a place for him and the discipline of philosophy within what Per Leo has recently called the ideological "space of possibility" that emerged during the period of *Gleichschaltung*.³¹ If Heidegger's rise within Nazi circles was meteoric, so too was his fall. By April 1934, he was pushed out of the Rectorate. Heidegger's attempts to endear himself to the party were always at odds with his peculiarly erudite speeches. In his public utterances as Rector, Heidegger blended his philosophy with National Socialist buzzwords to propagate a politics of spiritual renewal that would have the university and youth of Germany as its central force of revitalization, forming a "community of struggle [*Kampfgemeinschaft*] of teachers and students."[32] Heidegger adhered to what he called "spiritual National Socialism," a program that he continued to defend even after he had declared himself at odds with "vulgar National Socialism."[33] Heidegger's "spiritual National Socialism" called for a "return" to the supposed essence of the German people as the people of the thinkers and poets. His *Black Notebooks* from the time of the Rectorate illustrate this political vision:

> The basic defect of today's "political education"—a tautology—is not that too little is done and is done only hesitantly and unsurely, but that too much is done and everything is supposed to be made anew hastily in the blink of an eye. As if National Socialism were merely a veneer that could quickly be applied over everything. *When will we grasp something of the simplicity of the essence and the deliberate steadiness of its unfolding into races* [Geschlechtern]?

Already we can see Heidegger at odds with actually existing National Socialism. While it required the type of rapid exclusion of "alien" forces that he fostered as Rector, that did not mean that the Nazis themselves were yet National Socialist enough. The development of Heidegger's vision of National Socialism would be a slow, deliberate process of education by gradually returning to an alleged German essence through thinking. Heidegger then goes onto underscore the importance of philosophy in the following entry: "A popular remark: National Socialism was not first developed as '*theory*' but instead began with praxis. Fine. But does it follow that 'theory' is superfluous? Does it follow even that we merely 'otherwise,' 'for the rest,' deck ourselves out with bad theories and 'philosophies'?"[34] Heidegger did not merely theorize the place of philosophy and political education within National Socialism, but instead negotiated for a place of intellectual influence within the regime.

Throughout 1934, Heidegger engaged in seemingly fruitful negotiations with the Ministry of Science, Education, and Culture in Berlin under Bernhard Rust about becoming the leader of a *Dozentenakademie* for academics at the postdoctoral level (*Habilitanden*). This ideological training academy was to be erected in the countryside near Kiel and would consist primarily of "SA-style" physical training, including labor and communal singing, to teach the participants that "the fundamental elements of the National Socialist worldview were also to be realized through science."[35] However, the negotiations turned against Heidegger as the result of an unsolicited character assassination by the philosophers Ernst Krieck and Erich Jaensch sent to the Ministry of Science, Education, and Culture. In a detailed analysis of Heidegger's work and personality, Jaensch described his work as "Talmudic-Kabbalist" and repeatedly noted that it was held in suspiciously high esteem by "Jews, half-Jews, and representatives of a neo-scholastic, distinctly Catholic worldview." Moreover, Jaensch went so far as to say it would be an "offense against reason" to appoint Heidegger, whom he called "one of the greatest scatterbrains and most prominent eccentrics whom we have in the realm of higher education" and a man who might fall on the "other side" of the line between "mental health and illness."[36] While this characterization was extreme and might have been motivated by personal rivalries between ambitious philosophers under National Socialism, it is representative of the extent to which Heidegger had made significant enemies during his time as Rector.[37]

This assessment is also echoed from contemporaries in Freiburg. In 1935, Minster Rust made one last attempt to install Heidegger as Dean of the Faculty of Arts (*Philosophische Fakultät*) in Freiburg. His successor, Rector Eduard Kern, responded that Heidegger had "by and large lost the trust of his Freiburg colleagues" and that "there is no possibility of working in a relationship of trust with Prof. Heidegger."[38] By this time, Heidegger's political capital was spent, and from then on, according to the legend he produced during denazification in 1946, he "devoted himself exclusively to his philosophical studies."[39]

Given his activities as both a public figure and bureaucrat before 1935, and specifically his role in the nazification of the University of Freiburg, Heidegger occupied a clear perpetrator position. However, after 1935 his case is much murkier, and it raises fundamental questions about academic complicity in general and the complicity of philosophical practice specifically. Although Heidegger's denazification report would declare that he had been "fiercely opposed to [the party] in private"[40] after 1935, the next section will demonstrate that Heidegger in fact retained an unwavering Nazi conscience or, if you will, remained a sympathetic bystander, even until after the regime's downfall in 1945.

"Politically Reliable" Professor in the Third Reich

The *Black Notebooks* are significant because they demonstrate that Heidegger never renounced the political ideals that had drawn him to National Socialism but instead ceased to regard the Nazi Party as capable of fulfilling his vision of "spiritual National Socialism." While the earliest literature on the *Black Notebooks* has primarily focused on the vehement antisemitism that Heidegger expressed after 1938, I shift the focus to what they reveal about Heidegger's continued attachment to his "Nazi conscience" even beyond 1945. The Nazi conscience allowed Heidegger to carve out a peculiar place of "freedom" for himself as a philosopher within National Socialism.

The Nazis may have been "'men of action' who did not tend toward contemplation or even critical reflection,"[41] but as Wolfgang Bialas and Anson Rabinbach point out, philosophers nonetheless held a place of influence within the regime: "Precisely because the Nazi worldview played at best a symbolic function, indeterminate, yet at the same time in constant need of refinement and reinterpretation, philosophers found themselves in a unique position to give shape and substance to a new political reality.[42] Despite his own ambitions, Heidegger failed to be the kind of thinker who would "give shape and substance to a new political reality." Yet, after 1935 he keenly recognized that the regime, which was eager to perpetuate the German reputation of philosophical greatness, also desired to ally itself with reputable philosophers who maintained a purportedly nonpolitical research agenda.

A document from 1942 helps us understand Heidegger's renegotiated place within the regime after 1935.[43] The "Assessment of the Worldview and Political Attitudes of Philosophy Professors at German Universities" commissioned by the Ministry of Science, Education, and Culture in Berlin classified all professors according to five categories: those affiliated to a particular confession, liberal, indifferent, politically reliable, and National Socialist. The report categorized Heidegger among twenty-one "politically reliable" professors. He thus fell a rung below the eleven professors characterized as "attempting to create a National Socialist philosophy." The individual report on Heidegger doubts whether his "radical form of questioning is capable of supporting National Socialist science" and—reflecting the assessment by Jaensch and Krieck—deems "questionable" his "earlier relationships to Catholic and Jewish circles."[44] Yet, it is important to note that these questionable relationships are not treated with outright suspicion, and, even more importantly, the archival record provides no evidence to corroborate Heidegger's claim that his lecture courses were under surveillance by the SS Security Service.[45]

Following his withdrawal from politics, Heidegger occupied a unique position distinct from philosophers whom the report categorized as "National Socialist philosophers," including Krieck, Jaensch, and Alfred Baeumler. As Heidegger recognized, the goal of the regime was not necessarily to radicalize the "politically reliable" professors into full Nazi philosophers but instead to cultivate actively a roster of "moderate" professors who would uphold the legitimacy and prestige of German philosophy abroad with a certain degree of independence from Nazi ideology.

This became official policy for the Ministry of Science, Education, and Culture after the delegation of philosophers approved by the party was shamed publicly by other national delegations for defending the philosophical merit of Hitler and National Socialist racial ideology in 1934 at the International Congress of Philosophy in Prague. Thus in 1936, the Ministry of Science, Education, and Culture courted Heidegger to lead a delegation to the 1937 International Congress of Philosophy in Paris.[46] Far from raising suspicions, Heidegger's lecture courses on Hölderlin, Schelling, and Nietzsche during these years would have been perfectly attuned with the kind of *Heimatkunde* fostered by the regime. Moreover, Heidegger's return to pre-Socratic philosophers such as Heraclitus and Parmenides in the early 1940s would have fit perfectly well within the Greek revivalist tendencies of Nazi mythologizing. Described as one of the "most important thinkers of the present domestically and abroad" in the aforementioned 1942 report, it is evident that Heidegger's international notoriety always afforded him a place of relative privilege within the regime.

After the end of the war, this aura of respectability evaporated as Heidegger was judged a *Mitläufer—Keine Sühnemassnahmen* by the University of Freiburg's independent denazification commission in 1946, reversing the milder recommendation a French denazification commission had given in September 1945. The reversal was based in part on an evaluation with the philosopher Karl Jaspers, Heidegger's former friend and academic collaborator, wrote in December of 1945 to the denazification commission at Heidegger's request.[47] In his evaluation, Jaspers praised the merits of Heidegger's work and "urgently" recommended that Heidegger be given the freedom to continue this thinking in solitude. Yet, Jaspers likewise dissuaded the commission from allowing Heidegger to have contact with students because of his manner of thinking, which he judged to be "unfree, dictatorial, uncommunicative." Heidegger's thinking was "dangerous," Jaspers wrote, and contained an "aggressiveness which can easily change directions." It is worth noting that it is this aggressiveness—this dangerous dictatorial style and lack of pluralistic communicative skills—that concerned Jaspers, and not Heidegger's complicity in 1933 and 1934.

In the concurrent diary entries, clearly aware of Jaspers's evaluation,[48] Heidegger addresses Jaspers's concern with this "dangerous" element and reflects on the denazification process that was being carried out, Heidegger seems to believe, by those who had been too cowardly to act in a moment in which the "historical destiny of the German people"[49] was on the line. In these postwar reflections, Heidegger portrays 1933 as a moment when it was impossible to merely stand by (*danebenstehen*) and depicts his removal from office in 1934 as a moment when *Nazism no longer stood by him*. For Heidegger, Nazism itself had "betrayed" the "historical destiny of the German people," and the Allied victory and occupation of Germany was continuing this "betrayal ... by different means." Moreover, for Heidegger, responsibility for this "betrayal" rested overwhelmingly with the "self-professed know-it-all bystanders," those who did not embrace the National Socialist movement in all its "massive brutality"[50]: "How despicable is the helpless groveling under the shadowing carried out by the planetary terror of the global public sphere, in comparison with which the massive brutality of 'National Socialism' is entirely harmless, even despite the undeniable palpability of the devastation that it *participated* in wreaking."[51] According to Heidegger's peculiar historical vision, the bystanders were most responsible for failing to seize the possibility of returning to the history of the German people; at least the active participants in the movement, readily accepting the "devastation" it unleashed, had tried to take on the challenge. Indeed, as disturbing as it might sound, Heidegger's central disappointment with National Socialism was seemingly that it had not been radical enough. Since it failed to address the ills of the German essence at a metaphysical level, National Socialism for Heidegger was ultimately only a superficial movement.

This assessment is corroborated by a passage, written in 1945, in which Heidegger makes one of his few direct statements about the Holocaust, a passage that illustrates most clearly Heidegger's Nazi conscience:

> Is it not the case that the *misrecognition* of this destiny... would be, when thought from the perspective of the destiny, a more essential "guilt" and a "collective guilt," the magnitude of which could not be measured against the atrocities of the "gas chambers"? Would this not be a guilt that is more disturbing than any "crime" that can be publicly "decried," a guilt from which no one in the future could forgive? Do "they" sense that the German people and land are already a single "*concentration camp*"—of a sort that "the world" has not yet "seen" and "the world" does not want to see? And do "they" not see that this not wanting to see is an *even stronger will* than our *lack of will* against the barbarization of National Socialism? What could be the result of this? That on the one side they fall back into the time *before* 1932 and on the other side they take up National Socialism anew with the opinion that "it was in fact right."[52]

As the will to the "lack of will," standing by according to Heidegger represents an even stronger will than the will of Nazi supporters. Standing by and not contributing to the Nazi cause was an active form of doing nothing, and it led to Germany being turned over to the forces of global capitalism under the guise of what Heidegger calls "Americanism." For Heidegger, the guilty bystanders were those who were allowing this crime—the "misrecognition" of the historical moment for a "return" to German greatness—to unfold unabated. Americanism is robbing the German people of its place, forcing an alien set of values on it in the same manner in which "world Jewry" had done before.[53] For Heidegger's Nazi conscience, this "betrayal" of the German people is the true crime, the "essential" guilt, of National Socialism, not the Holocaust.

In the *Notebooks*, Heidegger critiques the public discourse about collective and individual guilt in several oblique references to Jaspers's 1946 work *The Question of German Guilt*. These scattered passages reveal that the Holocaust was not a phenomenon of significant ethical concern for Heidegger but instead only a matter of numbers, and hence of calculative rationality. Accordingly, the Holocaust was simply a matter of ethical indifference to him. Heidegger underscores this in a passage from 1946 in which he diminishes the importance of the Holocaust by comparing it to a lack of philosophical attention to the work of Leibniz:

> And if it is "guilt" we are talking about—is there no "guilt" when one pushes *Leibniz*, even today on his 300th birthday, into oblivion as if nothing had happened there? ... And yet *this* entire outcry about the perishing of the masses that one does not know and does not want to know. This is not to say that it should somehow be justified—for it is only a matter of standard and rank—but only to raise the question, whether at an essential level (for it is not easily graspable and cannot be shown on the public display boards and with bellowing posters) there is not any rigor or responsibility—whether "one" can then simply speak about everything according to one's taste and mood and desire for confirmation, whether one can simply walk on by, and whether or not the inability to think is an omission regarded with the greatest indifference. Or will one recognize someday that one is here the slave of a forgetfulness and the fellow traveler [*Mitläufer*] of a lack of responsibility that long ago trumped all morality, whether public or otherwise?[54]

Heidegger's position here is one of astounding moral obtuseness, for he defends the stance that actual acts of genocide are a matter of no moral importance until we can engage philosophically with the metaphysical problems that make that act of genocide possible in the first place. In other words, a world that is no longer able to recognize the greatness of Leibniz because of its reduction of everything to a calculative rationality is a world predisposed to commit and repeat acts of genocide. Hence, according to Heidegger, we are all bystanders and onlookers to a far more fundamental destruction of thinking that he alone, standing by on the "invisible front of the secret spiritual Germany," resists. Yet, attention to the precise philosophical content of this stance should not distract from the expedient nature of this position as a way of evading guilt, for it allows Heidegger to distance himself from actual support for the Holocaust, even while fostering the structures that made it possible. With the sovereign distance of an ambivalent attention to metaphysics, Heidegger fostered the actual enactment of the Holocaust, even while shielding himself with convenient forms of legal deniability.

Conclusion

Given Heidegger's activities as Rector, he followed a pattern of behavior common to many professors who enthusiastically embraced the rise of National Socialism during *Gleichschaltung*. In his activities both as Rector and as a professor during the Nazi era, Heidegger exhibited a relatively typical Nazi conscience, though one marked by a peculiar extremism expressed in his unpublished writings. These writings cast Heidegger's activities after the Rectorate into a new light, raising questions about what it meant to be a professor in an ideologically critical discipline such as philosophy under National Socialism. As a professor, Heidegger was occasionally even mildly critical of certain aspects of Nazi ideology in his lecture courses. Such nuanced ideological disagreements, however, fell well within the bounds of the kind of behavior tolerated from a politically reliable professor. The politically reliable philosophy professor, as opposed to overtly National Socialist philosophy professor, was expected not to espouse Nazi ideology but instead to pursue a research agenda that complemented that ideology. While Heidegger maintained a level of academic legitimacy well above that of such doctrinaire philosophers as Jaensch, Krieck, and Baeumler, this "legitimacy" was actively fostered by the party. In slipping into the role of the apparent bystander after 1935, Heidegger took on a position granted to him by the Ministry of Education. This role secured for Heidegger a relative distance from the regime and likewise set him up to position himself, like many other professors, to be regarded as little more than a bystander during denazification. The independent denazification commission of the University of Freiburg was more than willing to sanction this narrative, for it was deeply concerned with protecting the academic and administrative independence of the university by downplaying the complicity of the professoriate in the crimes of National Socialism. In other words, Heidegger was *produced* as a purported bystander in a flawed process of denazification that relied on a relatively restricted definition of complicity.

Far from actually being a bystander, Heidegger was first an active perpetrator and later a deeply complicit thinker who forged a space for himself within a regime that he did not consider radical enough. He felt sidelined, condemned to "stand by the invisible front," as Germans failed to seize their historical moment of greatness. At the same time, in his own postwar self-representation, Heidegger crudely spun the category of the bystander to diminish his own complicity—and he coldly hijacked the notion of German guilt to obfuscate the truly historic monstrosity of German crimes.

Adam Knowles is Assistant Teaching Professor in the Department of Philosophy at Drexel University. His book *Heidegger's Fascist Affinities*, which documents Heidegger's ties to Weimar-era *völkisch* movements, is forthcoming with Stanford University Press. He is a former fellow of the US Holocaust Memorial Museum and the European Holocaust Research Infrastructure.

Notes

I would like to thank the Holocaust Educational Foundation of Northwestern University for generously funding the archival research for this chapter with the 2016 Sharon Abramson Research Grant.

1. Martin Heidegger, *Anmerkungen I–V (Schwarze Hefte 1942–48)*, ed. Peter Trawny (Frankfurt, 2015), 100; Heidegger refers to his "error" at 98, 143, 147.
2. Martin Heidegger, *Ponderings II–VI: Black Notebooks 1931–1938*, trans. Richard Rojcewicz (Bloomington, IN, 2016), 99, 114.
3. Ibid., 91.
4. The strongest defensive version of this narrative can be found in Rüdiger Safranski, *Martin Heidegger: Between Good and Evil* (Cambridge, MA, 1998). Victor Farías, *Heidegger and Nazism* (Philadelphia, 1991) is remarkable for its archival detail, but fails to persuade in its attempt to cast Heidegger as a Nazi ideologue.
5. Quoted in Hugo Ott, *Martin Heidegger: A Political Life* (London, 1993), 326.
6. Claudia Koonz, *The Nazi Conscience* (Cambridge, MA, 2003), 6–8.
7. George L. Mosse, *The Crisis of German Ideology: Intellectual Origins of the Third Reich* (New York, 1981).
8. Heidegger, *Anmerkungen I–V*, 80.
9. Ibid., 99.
10. For a detailed reconstruction of the events surrounding Heidegger's denazification process, see Ott, *Political Life*, esp. part 5, "The Post-War Years: Heidegger under Scrutiny"; for Heidegger's concurrent reflections on the process see Heidegger, *Anmerkungen I–V*, 80–102.
11. On the importance of diaries for our evolving understanding of both victims and perpetrators of National Socialism, see Frank Bajohr and Jürgen Matthäus, "Einleitung," in *Alfred Rosenberg: Die Tagebücher von 1934 bis 1944* (Frankfurt, 2011), 16–19.

12. In the standard literature on Heidegger, Ott and Farías offer the most detailed analysis of his bureaucratic activities, though with limited access to the archival material now open in the University of Freiburg archives. Bernd Grün, *Der Rektor als Führer: Die Universität Freiburg i. Br. von 1933 bis 1945* (Freiburg, 2010) provides the most significant analysis based on the currently available archival record.
13. Emmanuel Faye, *Heidegger: The Introduction of Nazism Into Philosophy in Light of the Unpublished Seminars of 1933–1935* (New Haven, CT, 2009) presents the strongest attempt to cast Heidegger as a Nazi ideologue.
14. See Heidegger's membership card from the Zentralkartei der NSDAP, printed in Alfred Denker and Holger Zaborowski, eds. *Heidegger-Jahrbuch 4: Heidegger und der Nationalsozialismus I—Dokumente* (Freiburg, 2009), 245.
15. Bundesarchiv Berlin-Lichterfelde, BArch R8088/1155.
16. Quoted in Ott, *Political Life*, 325.
17. Ibid., 146.
18. Letter to the Rector of the University of Freiburg, 6 October 1945, Universitätsarchiv Freiburg, file C67/2817.
19. Heidegger augmented in his own handwriting a list of "non-Aryan" civil servants dated and stamped 19 April 1933, Universitätsarchiv Freiburg, file B1/3986.
20. These and other complaint letters can be found in Universitätsarchiv Freiburg, file B1/3986.
21. Decree Nr. 4012, Universitätsarchiv Freiburg, file B1/3986.
22. Heidegger to the Minister des Kultus, des Unterrichts und der Justiz, 14 February 1934, Universitätsarchiv Freiburg, file B1/3349.
23. Hannah Arendt, "What Is Existential Philosophy?" in *Essays in Understanding, 1930–1954: Formation, Exile, and Totalitarianism* (New York, 1987), 187.
24. Heidegger to the Minister des Kultus, des Unterrichts und der Justiz, 20 July 1933, Universitätsarchiv Freiburg, file B3/789.
25. Satzungen der Verbindung im K.C. "Neo-Friburgia" zu Freiburg i. Br., 20 May 1925, Universitätsarchiv Freiburg, file B1/2555.
26. Letter from the Altherrenverband Friburgo-Ghibellinia to the Rector of the University of Freiburg, 26 May 1933, Universitätsarchiv Freiburg, file B1/2555.
27. Monatsbericht über den Nationalsozialistischen Studentenbund Freiburg, July 1933, Bundesarchiv Berlin-Lichterfelde, BArch NS38/3738.
28. Letter from the Rector of the University of Freiburg to the Staatsanwaltschaft in Freiburg, 1 August 1933, Universitätsarchiv Freiburg, file B1/2555.
29. Wehrsportanlage Löffingen, Universitätsarchiv Freiburg B1/2023.
30. Koonz, *Nazi Conscience*, 9.
31. Per Leo, "Über Nationalsozialismus sprechen: Ein Verkomplizierungsversuch," *Merkur* 70, no. 804 (2016): 40. The occasion for Leo's reflections was a conference held on the *Black Notebooks* at the University of Siegen, 22–25 April 2015.
32. Martin Heidegger, "Die Selbstbehauptung der deutschen Universität," in *Reden und andere Zeugnisse eines Lebensweges, 1910-1976* (Frankfurt, 2000), 116.
33. Heidegger, *Ponderings II–VI*, 99, 104.
34. Ibid., 98 (this and the previous excerpt), emphasis added.
35. Geheimes Staatsarchiv Preußischer Kulturbesitz, HA, Rep. 76 IVa, Nr. 71.
36. The most important speeches are published in Heidegger, *Reden und andere Zeugnisse eines Lebensweges*.
37. Jeffrey Herf, *Reactionary Modernism: Technology, Culture, and Politics in Weimar and the Third Reich* (Cambridge, 1983), 109–115, documents the extent to which Heidegger was held in suspicion by many of his contemporaries.

38. Letter from Eduard Kern to the Reichs- und Preußische Kulturminister für Wissenschaft, Erziehung und Volksbildung, 18 May 1935, Bundesarchiv Berlin-Lichterfelde, BArch NS21/824.
39. Quoted in Ott, *Political Life*, 326.
40. Quoted in ibid., 324.
41. Bajohr and Matthäus, "Einleitung," 16.
42. Wolfgang Bialas and Anson Rabinbach, "Introduction: The Humanities in Nazi Germany," in *Nazi Germany and the Humanities: How German Academics Embraced Nazism*, ed. Wolfgang Bialas and Anson Rabinbach (Oxford, 2007), xxviii.
43. Bundesarchiv Berlin-Lichterfelde, BArch R4901/12444. Portions of this report have been translated and published in George Leaman and Gerd Simon, "Deutsche Philosophen aus der Sicht des Sicherheitsdienstes des Reichsführers SS," in *Jahrbuch für Soziologiegeschichte*, ed. Carsten Klingemann, Michael Neumann, Karl-Siegbert Rehberg, Ilja Srubar, and Erhard Stöling (Opladen, 1992), 261–292.
44. Bundesarchiv Berlin-Lichterfelde, BArch R4901/12444.
45. Martin Heidegger, "Das Rektorat 1933/34: Tatsachen und Gedanken," in *Reden und andere Zeugnisse eines Lebensweges*, 293.
46. Bundesarchiv Berlin-Lichterfelde, BArch R4901/2940.
47. The report is in the form of a letter written to Friedrich Oehlkers on 22 December 1945. The letter is translated in Ott, *Political Life*, 336–341. A copy of the original letter can be found in the Universitätsarchiv Freiburg, file B254/32.
48. Ott, *Political Life*, 343: "It is clear that Heidegger learned of the gist of the report, and in particular the concrete proposals put forward by Jaspers, sometime between Christmas and New Year." Heidegger comments directly on Jaspers throughout the *Black Notebooks* and he specifically addresses this concern for the "dangerous element [*das Gefährliche*]" in a deeply embittered tone at Heidegger, *Anmerkungen I–V*, 83–85.
49. Heidegger, *Anmerkungen I–V*, 83.
50. Ibid., 88.
51. Ibid., 87.
52. Ibid., 99–100.
53. On Heidegger's references to "world Jewry," see Peter Trawny, *Heidegger and the Myth of the Jewish World Conspiracy* (Chicago, 2015); see also Andrew J. Mitchell and Peter Trawny, eds., *Heidegger's Black Notebooks: Responses to Anti-Semitism* (New York, 2017).
54. Heidegger, *Anmerkungen I–V*, 129.

Bibliography

Arendt, Hannah. "What Is Existential Philosophy?" In *Essays in Understanding, 1930–1954: Formation, Exile, and Totalitarianism*, 163–188. New York: Harcourt, Brace & Co., 1987.
Bajohr, Frank, and Jürgen Matthäus. "Einleitung." In *Alfred Rosenberg: Die Tagebücher von 1934 bis 1944*, edited by Frank Bajohr and Jürgen Matthäus, 9–116. Frankfurt: S. Fischer Verlag, 2011.
Bialas, Wolfgang, and Anson Rabinbach. "Introduction: The Humanities in Nazi Germany." In *Nazi Germany and the Humanities: How German Academics Embraced Nazism*, edited by Wolfgang Bialas and Anson Rabinbach, viii–lii. Oxford: Oneworld, 2007.

Denker, Alfred, and Holger Zaborowski, eds. *Heidegger-Jahrbuch 4: Heidegger und der Nationalsozialismus I—Dokumente*. Freiburg: Verlag Karl Alber, 2009.

Farías, Victor. *Heidegger and Nazism*. Philadelphia: Temple Press, 1991.

Faye, Emmanuel. *Heidegger: The Introduction of Nazism Into Philosophy in Light of the Unpublished Seminars of 1933–1935*. New Haven, CT: Yale University Press, 2009.

Friedländer, Saul. *Nazi Germany and the Jews: the Years of Persecution, 1933–1939*. New York: HarperCollins, 1998.

Grün, Bernd. *Der Rektor als Führer: Die Universität Freiburg i. Br. von 1933 bis 1945*. Freiburg: Verlag Karl Alber, 2010.

Heidegger, Martin. *Anmerkungen I–V (Schwarze Hefte 1942–1948)*. Edited by Peter Trawny. Frankfurt: Vittorio Klostermann, 2015.

———. *Ponderings II–VI: Black Notebooks 1931–1938*. Translated by Richard Rojcewicz. Bloomington: Indiana University Press, 2016.

———. *Reden und andere Zeugnisse eines Lebensweges, 1910–1976*. Frankfurt: Vittorio Klostermann, 2000.

Herf, Jeffrey. *Reactionary Modernism: Technology, Culture, and Politics in Weimar and the Third Reich*. Cambridge: Cambridge University Press, 1983.

Koonz, Claudia. *The Nazi Conscience*. Cambridge, MA: Belknap Press, 2003.

Leaman, George and Gerd Simon. "Deutsche Philosophen aus der Sicht des Sicherheitsdienstes des Reichsführers SS." In *Jahrbuch für Soziologiegeschichte*, edited by Carsten Klingemann, Michael Neumann, Karl-Siegbert Rehberg, Ilja Srubar, and Erhard Stöling, 261–292. Opladen: Leske & Budrich, 1992.

Leo, Per. "Über Nationalsozialismus sprechen: Ein Verkomplizierungsversuch." *Merkur* 70, no. 804 (2016): 29–41.

Mitchell, Andrew J., and Peter Trawny, eds., *Heidegger's Black Notebooks: Responses to Anti-Semitism*. New York: Columbia University Press, 2017.

Mosse, George L. *The Crisis of German Ideology: Intellectual Origins of the Third Reich*. New York: Schocken Books, 1981.

Ott, Hugo. *Martin Heidegger: A Political Life*. London: Basic Books, 1993.

Safranski, Rüdiger. *Martin Heidegger: Between Good and Evil*. Cambridge, MA: Harvard University Press, 1998.

Trawny, Peter. *Heidegger and the Myth of the Jewish World Conspiracy*. Chicago: Chicago University Press, 2015.

Chapter 10

Natura Abhorret Vacuum
Polish "Bystanders" and the Implementation of the "Final Solution"

Jan Grabowski

The focus of this chapter is on those people who found themselves—usually without any conscious choice or decision on their part—faced with one of the most difficult moral challenges: how to respond to mass murder that, quite literally, was going on right in front of their eyes. This aspect of the history of the Holocaust—which occurred in those unfortunate geographic locations where the Germans decided to implement the "final solution" and where Jewish victims encountered not only the perpetrators but also other witnesses to their fate—is quite likely one of the most contentious and hotly debated fields of contemporary historical research. Moreover, because the archives in Eastern Europe have quite recently yielded an unprecedented volume of new historical evidence, the discussions in the near future are most likely to reach new levels of emotional fervor and engagement.

Raul Hilberg divided the human spectrum of the Holocaust into three categories: the victims, the perpetrators, and the bystanders.[1] Hilberg was not the first historian to inquire into the nature of relationships between the "onlookers"—as "bystanders"[2] have also been sometimes called—and the Jews at the time of the Holocaust. His concept of "triad" was linked to earlier research undertaken in the 1970s by several other scholars who studied the phenomenon of rescue and the lack of rescue.[3] During the following decade, the term "bystanders" was also selectively applied to the Allied and neutral nations but excluded the societies of occupied Europe.[4] While the clearly defined perpetrators and victims became objects of intense historical scrutiny, the third category has been perceived as difficult to pinpoint and describe, as ambiguous and potentially less rewarding to study; consequently, it has attracted much less attention on the part of Holocaust scholars.

For Hilberg, who was most familiar with the Western European context of the genocide, the bystanders constituted a heterogeneous mass of largely uninvolved people—Belgians, French, Czechs, Danes, or Dutch—who could neither help nor hurt the persecuted Jews. With time, however, historians began to ask questions about the limits of the "bystanding phenomenon." First came the reassessment of the issue of direct involvement of certain non-German organizations and institutions in the destruction of the European Jews. During the late 1970s and early 1980s, several important studies have detailed the sinister role played by French politicians, bureaucrats, and police in furthering the German designs. Bankers, lawyers, and petty bureaucrats in nearby Holland and Belgium were also involved in the policies of the *Endlösung*.[5] Although painful at times, the public debates that ensued helped reshape our understanding of the true meaning of collaboration, complicity, and the extent of alleged ignorance among the "bystanders" of the real fate of Jews "deported to the East," to use the contemporary euphemism. It is altogether unsurprising that, after years of critical historical analysis, the pendulum has swung back. Nowadays, some historians seek to counter the "myth" of Western wartime societies that in recent years came to be seen increasingly as nations of "guilty bystanders."[6]

While various institutions (and governments) had to come to terms with their corporate culpability, and some have been forced to make amends, the historical analysis of the "bystanding" phenomenon on the general, social level proved to be a much more challenging proposition. This second, much more difficult and painful glimpse in the historical mirror brought people face to face with individual choices made day after day, year after year, by Europeans who found themselves living under German rule. As Saul Friedländer has stated in his seminal work on the Holocaust as a European crime, "many social constituencies, many power groups were directly involved in the expropriation of the Jews and eager, be it out of greed, for their wholesale disappearance. Thus, Nazi and related anti-Jewish policies could unfold to their most extreme levels without the interference of any major countervailing interests."[7] Even if there were some exceptions of institutional dissent, as, for example, by the Bulgarian Orthodox Church, Friedländer's verdict a fair description of the prevailing attitudes in Europe at the time.

The West seems to have come to terms with the Nazi past—with various degrees of success and, as the Dutch controversy shows, still open to contestation—but in Eastern Europe, similar questions were initially sidestepped. Later, having touched a raw nerve, it triggered a strong and very negative reaction. In these countries, the period of occupation is still seen through the lens of personal suffering, which leaves little or no room for serious reexamination of the many more problematic aspects of the national past. Moreover, the historical analysis in the East must begin at a more critical stage than the investigations conducted in the occupied countries of Western Europe. In Poland, Ukraine, or the Baltics, there is no question, for instance, about the extent of knowledge about the Holocaust among the local "bystanders"; nearly everyone was aware of the genocide happening next door. Moreover, "next door" in this context is not a figure of speech: in many cases, the Holocaust literally visited the rooms and houses of "bystanders."

Not that this statement finds unanimity among scholars. The American historian Timothy Snyder wrote: "In occupied Poland, the Holocaust began more than two years after the German invasion and was largely isolated from the local population. In the occupied Soviet Union, the killing of Jews took place in the open air, in front of the population, with the help of young male Soviet citizens.[8] Snyder is wrong. The few closed ghettos (such as Warsaw or Kraków) were exceptions—and even in these cases, the contacts with the "Aryan" side were frequent and multiple. The majority of Polish Jews, however, were removed into half-open or open ghettos where the only real physical barrier separating them from the non-Jewish population consisted of wooden fences or barbed wire, both easily breached. The real borders of the ghettos were in the minds of the gentiles, who enforced (with great efficiency) and helped to enforce the restrictions placed by the Germans on Jews. To makes Snyder's assertion even more implausible, hundreds of thousands of Polish Jews were resettled into the ghettos only in the spring and summer of 1942, on the eve of the implementation of the "final solution." For these reasons, there can be no question about the isolation of the Jews from the rest of the society. What is more important, the liquidations of hundreds of ghettos across Poland (Germans referred to them as *Aktionen*) occurred in the midst of Polish towns, and cities and millions of Poles witnessed the destruction of Jewish communities.

To restate the obvious: in the *Generalgouvernement*, the extermination of the Jews was a public, terrifying spectacle, with millions of more or less engaged and fully aware spectators. Both Jews and non-Jews knew what was happening at the death sites of Treblinka, Sobibór, Chełmno, Bełżec, and Auschwitz. Very soon—already in the early summer of 1942—the news of gas chambers and the crematoria had reached the general populace. Nevertheless, very few people—only a tiny minority, undeterred by the threat of German reprisals and the hostile disapproval of their peers, neighbors, and sometimes families—expressed any interest or willingness in helping the desperate Jews on the run. However, helping was just one and the most courageous reactions on a spectrum of possible responses. Some would actually inflict harm on the Jewish refugees; others would refuse to help and shut the door; still others would offer momentary, small gestures of help; and the "paid helpers" would make fortunes from hiding Jews who were able to pay for it, yet, from time to time, seeking another monetary reward, they would then turn them over to the German authorities. In short, there was a significant range of options, but the extremely brutal context in general instantaneously transformed "bystanders" into active participants. As Jan Tomasz Gross, commenting on Polish society during the Holocaust, has noted, an "attitude of 'doing nothing,' 'un-involvement,' or 'disinterest' was simply not among the possible options because of the sheer scale of terror instituted in the public sphere by the process of the extermination of the Jews."[9]

In Eastern Europe, the subsequent political developments, the communist repression, but also the will of the people living there conspired to limit the examination of these painful questions. Decades of censorship and ideologically charged historiography blended together with a triumphant nationalist ethos—a rare, if not unique, alliance—helped keep studies about local non-Jews' attitudes to the Holocaust (except for unabashed and unapologetic hagiographies) to an absolute strict minimum. Moreover, the implementation of the "final solution" in Poland, Ukraine, Belorussia, or the occupied parts of the Soviet Union differed fundamentally from the persecution unfolding in the West for several reasons. First, Eastern Europe is where the vast majority of European Jews actually lived. Second, the extraordinary level of terror instituted by the Germans in the conquered Eastern territories was incomparable with its Western equivalent. And third, this is where the physical extermination of European Jews actually took place. All three factors made "bystanding" in the East a very different—and, until now, little-studied—phenomenon. In these areas, the Germans created a system governed by temptation, greed, fear, and impunity. It was a system within which—at least as far as the victimization of the Jews was concerned—no good deed went unpunished and evil found its reward.[10] Before we move on to fear and impunity, let us begin with temptation and greed.

Temptation and Greed

The universality of the mechanisms used in the destruction of European Jewry can be shown through the prism of robbery and theft. The extent of this phenomenon found its way into European vocabularies and resulted in the creation of new terms—terms that acquired a life of their own and, in the East, some that outlived Hitler and the Third Reich. In German, the term *Arisierung* (Aryanization; in Polish: *arianizacja*, i.e., turning over Jewish property to the Germans) appeared early in the public discourse, and *Entjudung*, or de-Judification (in Polish: *odżydzenie*) soon followed.

Franz Stangl, the longest-serving commander of the Treblinka extermination camp, when asked in the 1960s, while awaiting trial, about the reasons for the "final solution" of the "Jewish question" in Europe, answered: "They wanted their money, of course! Have you any idea of the fantastic sums that were involved?"[11] Stangl's self-serving reply was incorrect, but it provides at least a small part of the answer. For many, getting a hand on Jewish wealth was a deep and burning desire. And the feeling was universal—whether we look at the good citizens of Amsterdam, Parisian lawyers, or Ukrainian and Polish peasants. It was the German state, however, that led the charge: seizures and theft started with large companies and with banks and firms with "Jewish capital." Later came Jewish real estate: houses and apartments were expropriated and sold, or rented to "Aryan" buyers and tenants. Then Jews' personal property became an object of closer bureaucratic scrutiny.

The time frame varied from one country to another, but the pattern remained the same: Jews were ordered to report their personal valuables to the authorities. In Poland, the forms issued on 24 January 1940 stipulated the registration of jewelry, clothing, paintings, cash, loans, and transfers made to third parties; bank accounts were frozen and later seized; and "Aryan" business executives were offered a chance to avail themselves of Jewish slave labor. At each stage of this process, the German authorities made a conscious decision to expand the circle of beneficiaries.[12] In his study of Aryanization in Hamburg, Frank Bajohr describes auctions that drew thousands of otherwise upright Germans.

They purchased the belongings of their former neighbors, Jews who were deported to be killed in 1942 and 1943.[13] Likewise, thousands of Frenchmen embraced the role of *Administrateurs provisoires* (trustees) of the seized Jewish property.[14] Indeed, their justification was a lofty one: to protect French "national heritage" and, at the same time, to thwart the plans of the occupying power.

How quickly Jewish property became "national heritage" depended on the area, but here again, the pattern was clear and repeated. In Poland in 1940, thousands of people from different walks of life and from various strata of Polish society decided to participate in the process of expropriating Jews. Regularly, lawyers and judges took part in the Aryanization of Jewish real estate in Warsaw in the spring and summer of 1940 or in Kraków, where local lawyers and magistrates were involved as early as October 1939. Business executives and industrialists, using the proviso of absent lenders, started to cancel their prewar letters of debt held by Jews, who now were conveniently incarcerated in the ghettos and thus unable to dispute their losses.[15] Others looked with growing hope at the emerging housing opportunities in the liquidated ghettos. A thriving commercial exchange (illegal, for the most part) between the ghettos and the "Aryan side" helped thousands of Poles improve their lot, and, even after the destruction of the ghettos, smuggling wares, merchandise, and other movables continued unabated. It comes, therefore, as no surprise that the appeal of "Jewish fortune" attracted intense interest, and very few "bystanders" did actually stand by this massive assault on Jewish legal and property rights.

The second stage of Aryanization began as soon as the Jews were killed, immediately after the liquidation of the ghettos. Sometimes this stage began even while the ghettos were in the process of being liquidated. Across the occupied East, tens of thousands of houses, cabins, apartments, and other dwellings now stood empty. It has been said that *natura abhorret vacuum*, nature abhors void, vacuum, emptiness, and that life soon fills in the empty spaces. Indeed, new lives quickly moved into Jewish homes; sometimes, the new residents took over the still-warm beds and cooking pots. Stanisław Żemiński, a teacher from Łuków, a small town east of Warsaw, who observed the liquidation of the local ghetto, made the following note in his diary:

> They surrounded the village and the hunt began. They pulled out the Jews from the houses; they caught them in the fields, in the meadows. The shots are still ringing, but our hyenas already set their sights on the Jewish riches. The [Jewish] bodies are still warm, but people already start to write letters, asking for Jewish houses, Jewish stores, workshops, or parcels of land.[16]

However, this "infusion of new life" came at a price, and extracted consequences for the new owners. Some experienced immediate guilt feelings; others were of longer duration—lingering uneasiness, or aggression, not infrequently directed at the victims, or the memory of the victims, whose phantoms lurked in the newly reclaimed spaces, depriving the living of psychological comforts. Thus, what essentially happened in the case of Jewish property, after the extermination of 90 percent of its legitimate owners in Eastern Europe, was a straightforward continuation and expansion of the previous policies of expropriation and theft. The lion's share went, as it usually does, to the lion. Better houses, new furniture, and seized valuables all became property of the German state or fell into the hands of its greedy and unscrupulous representatives of various stripes. The rest went to smaller predators, and, finally, whatever was left became available to the larger public.

Yet, German willingness to share the loot with the Ukrainians, Poles, Byelorussians, or Balts was by no means prompted by a sense of compassion, generosity, or even the willingness to foster cooperation. What happened was that the German system of theft, however ingenious and efficient, first was strained and later collapsed under the weight of the task. In order to avoid complete chaos—in other words, wild robbery of the emptied ghettos, which was already occurring—the local German "custodians of ex-Jewish property"[17] authorized mayors, *wójts* (local rural leaders), and village elders to sell the "post-Jewish" goods at public auctions. In Kraków, for instance, these "ex-Jewish goods" included furniture. The better pieces went to ethnic Germans; pieces of lesser value were sold off to Poles.[18] In Radomyśl, a shtetl some fifty miles away, 150 Jewish wooden houses were simply torn down and the lumber sold off at auctions.[19] Close to Warsaw, in the town of Łosice, Germans started to sell off Jewish clothing after the liquidation of the local ghetto. According to one eyewitness:

> People from villages nearby came to Łosice in the early morning and formed a queue that snaked for hundreds of yards. Some spent the previous night in town to assure themselves a good spot in the next day's line. There were sales every few days. The first objects sold were berets and hats. A few days later, it was the turn of shirts, trousers, undergarments, bedding, or other items... Occasionally the shoppers got into fights.[20]

Greed was further fueled by the tales of "Jewish gold." This universal conviction about Jewish riches just waiting for new owners was a phenomenon reported by many witnesses. Associating Jews with gold was one of the most common antisemitic clichés. According to the deep conviction of ordinary people, Jews had gold—*all* Jews. From today's perspective, the strength of this conviction may seem surprising.[21] After all, before the war, the local Jews were often just as poor as their non-Jewish neighbors were. The deep and absolute belief in the universality of "Jewish gold" is, therefore, a powerful testament to the influence of prewar nationalist and church-led antisemitic propaganda and the German efforts undertaken in the same direction during the war. Again, *natura abhorret vacuum*—not only in taking possession of objects but also in a variety of other, more elusive ways.

According to the Polish sociologist Andrzej Leder, the spaces "vacated" by the murdered Jews offered chances for rapid—and until then unthinkable—advancement of impoverished peasants.[22] Now they could migrate from their poverty-ridden villages to the relative comforts associated with urban living. However, migration from rural to urban areas went hand in hand with a dramatic shift on the socio-professional ladder. First, the ghettoization and later the extermination of Polish Jewry meant new work opportunities for those non-Jews who were willing to seize the moment and undertake the necessary effort to retool themselves for the new careers suddenly opening up for them. Businesses had to reopen; merchants were needed to facilitate the transfer of goods to the hungry urban population. In some areas of Poland in 1942, construction halted because of a lack of skilled roofers. Elsewhere, the prices of clothing skyrocketed, owing to a lack of tailors. Lawyers, jewelers, and doctors all found themselves facing more traffic than they could handle. Therefore, to fill these lacunae, new doctors were trained, new roofers learned the trade, new lawyers hung out their shingles, and new merchants moved into empty stores. Contemporaries did not consider this massive transfer of people and skills a fleeting, reversible phenomenon. It was an *acquis communautaire*, acquired social capital, that, if the need arose, had to be defended tooth and nail. Already in January 1941, a member of the nationalist underground wrote:

> Polish public opinion does not condone [German] violence against the Jews, but we have to stress it strongly that the same public opinion would never accept the Jews returning to their previous influence and careers. Jews lost their privileged position in economic life and Polish society will never agree to return to the status quo.[23]

In February 1944, the underground newspaper *Szaniec* (Rampart) elaborated further on the same topic, arguing that businesses, "taken over by the Poles during the war, have to remain at all cost in Polish hands. Polish society has to forcefully counter all attempts at returning these businesses to their former Jewish owners, or their heirs."[24]

Among official circles, one encounters the same kind of narrative and the same set of arguments. In a July 1943 report sent to London by the foreign affairs section of the Delegatura Rządu (the political underground leadership in Poland), Polish officials wrote:

> Throughout the country, the state of things is such that the return of Jews, even in much reduced numbers, to their settlements and workshops is to be absolutely ruled out. Non-Jews have filled Jews' places in towns and townships and this is a fundamental change of a final nature. A massive return of Jews would be perceived by the population more in the light of an invasion to be thwarted—even physically—than of restitution.[25]

The actual scale of the socio-professional change in the wake of the extermination of the Polish Jews is still unknown. No exhausting studies have been done to ascertain the size of wartime migration from rural to urban areas, and no comprehensive historical research has been done on the transfer of goods and services from the ghettos to the non-Jewish side. What is certain, however, is the relentless pressure that forced Polish "bystanders" to make constant choices dictated by the policies of extermination.

Fear and Impunity

The phenomenon of "bystanding" implies a degree of impartiality and detachment that is difficult to imagine in more ordinary times and impossible to contemplate under the extreme conditions prevailing at the time. In her discussion of Dutch bystanders, Christina Morina observed, "The way that Gentiles acted during the German occupation, both those in authority and ordinary non-Jewish men and women, was at least partially responsible for the fact that so many Dutch Jews were deported and killed by the Germans."[26] Some 25 percent of Dutch Jews survived the Holocaust; this made Holland one of the most deadly places for Jews in occupied Europe, and definitely the most deadly place in Western Europe. However, when we look at the Dutch numbers from an Eastern European perspective, the situation changes: in occupied Poland, home to the largest Jewish population in prewar Europe, the chances of survival for Jews were about 1.5 percent to 2 percent.[27] Only thirty thousand to forty thousand of the three million who found themselves under German rule survived—many in the still-operating labor camps. The destruction of the nation of Polish Jews was so extensive and so complete that a thousand-year-old culture disappeared along with 98 percent of its members.

Inevitably, in the occupied East, in the areas where the vast majority of European Jews dwelled, the process of destruction, starting with the liquidation of the ghettos, was always a public display of horror. A German official from Tarnów noted that during the day of the liquidation, the city resonated with gunfire, and "dead bodies littered the streets."[28] Even in Warsaw, despite the walls that isolated the ghetto from the rest of the city, "bystanders" would have to make a very determined effort not to notice and not to acknowledge the liquidation of the ghetto.

During the "Great Deportation," which began on 22 July 1942, when some three hundred thousand Jews were shipped off from the Warsaw Ghetto to the extermination camp in Treblinka, the Warsaw-based retired engineer Franciszek Wyszyński noted in his diary: "Horrible things are happening over there in the ghetto... People saw a Jew being thrown down from the fourth floor. The Germans will have a grave sin on their conscience, but after the war the power of our Jewry will be broken to a great extent and life will be easier."[29] A nineteen-year-old Polish woman from Tarnów wrote after the war:

> I could hear shots being fired. From behind the window, I could see Germans in uniforms. In front of my window, I could see the body of a dead Jew and a Jewess who was still moving. I looked through the window, and I could see Jews running away and Germans shooting in their direction. To me, it looked like a hunt. The shooting lasted until 2 p.m. I went to the main square as soon as the shooting tapered off. I saw the Jews on their knees and holding their arms high in the air. They were arranged in groups, young people, old people, women with children. I was there for a very short while. Terrified, I fled.[30]

Shraga Feivel Bielawski, in hiding in the attic of his house, witnessed the liquidation of the ghetto in Węgrów, a small city northeast of Warsaw. He noted in his haunting memoirs:

> I heard the screams of women and children from the town square just below our attic hideaway. The SS hurried their victims yelling: "Faster!" Faster!" The screams of Jews mingled with the shouting of Germans and the laughter of Poles. Children wailed to their mothers: "Mama, I don't want to die! I don't want to die!" Everyone knew where they were going and what would happen when they got there. All day the SS with the enthusiastic help of the Poles loaded Jews onto open trucks that sped toward Treblinka.[31]

A historian can bring multiple descriptions of this kind, but all of them convey the same message: the extraction of Jews from their hometowns, from the liquidated ghettos, was a brutal, horrifying affair, and countless Polish bystanders were witnessing and well aware of what happened. Consequently, they were faced with choices for which they were ill prepared.

As time went on, the value of Jewish life meant progressively less and less, until, finally, in the eyes of the many it became utterly worthless. The existentially important question touches on the issue of time and scale of this phenomenon: *when* did Jewish life become worthless, and *how many* people shared the notion of its worthlessness? The timing depended, of course, on the area. The mass shootings of Jewish civilians began at the Eastern Front in the summer and autumn of 1941, inaugurating "the Holocaust by bullets." However, the dramatically deteriorating position of Jews in Poland became clear even earlier among the starving ghetto populations in the *Generalgouvernement*. Once the ghettos were liquidated, the Jews no longer had the right to live.

Even in the absence of survivors' testimonies (and there were often no survivors to tell the story), a historian today can catch a glimpse of the past through the often-opaque window formed by the "documents of destruction." These are pieces of archival evidence that, while insignificant by themselves, acquire a critical informative mass when taken together. Among these documents of destruction, we can find a short bill submitted by a construction company to the Municipality of Tarnów requesting a payment of 200 zlotys to cover the cost of removing bloodstains from the city sidewalks following the liquidation of the local ghetto. Or an unsentimental, formal request sent by a commander of the Polish "Blue" police detachment to his German superiors asking for additional bullets (these were required to replenish the dwindling stock of ammunition that his police officers had expended by shooting Jews during the recent "liquidation" of the ghetto). Or a request for payment submitted by Polish voluntary firefighters who had to move from one area to another in order to help the German authorities seal the local ghettos before their liquidation.[32]

Nevertheless, in order to achieve a true "final solution" of the "Jewish question," the Germans needed more than just the support of the local police forces and other uniformed collaborators. They needed the active involvement of "bystanders." When the Polish police officers received their orders, civilians had to take part, too. In some areas, the *Landräte* (local rural German administrators) and *Kreishauptmänner* (county heads), as well as the local commanders of the gendarmerie, offered modest rewards to those who took part in the "struggle with the racial enemy," to quote the language used by German propagandists. The rewards for delivering the Jews to the authorities or for providing information about their whereabouts would include, for example, four pounds of sugar or two bottles of vodka per person. Sometimes the informers would collect as much as one-third of the value of the personal goods and clothes seized on the victim. However, the German authorities also coerced the non-Jewish population into cooperation by means of ruthless terror. In late 1941, the death penalty was introduced for aiding and abetting Jews on the run, and the Polish administration was instructed to convey this message forcefully to the locals.

One such order was preserved in the dossiers of the Kraków Appellate Court. On 28 August 1942, Franciszek Rusina, the *wójt* from Kośmice Wielkie, sent a letter to the elder in Janowice (a village close to Kraków) saying:

> Regarding the regulation issued by the county authorities on 14 August 1942 and concerning the deportation of the Jews from our area, I hasten to inform you that the matter is very serious. You are to make absolutely sure that not even one single Jew, Jewess, or Jewish child is left on the territory of your commune. You have to immediately order the people to search the entire area, back alleys, bushes, and so on, in order to make certain that no [Jews] are left. Whenever caught, Jews are to be delivered to the nearest station of the Polish Police. I repeat that the penalty for hiding Jews is death. Village elders are also responsible for Jews hidden on the territory of their commune, and—in case of negligence—can face the death penalty. I remind you to make certain that these orders are being followed; you are responsible under the penalty of death. —Kośmice Wielkie, 28 August 1942.[33]

The policy of rewards on the one hand and terror on the other produced results. Few "Aryans" in the occupied East could remain aloof, distant, and indifferent. For the local population, it was a lesson in obedience: the Germans were the masters over life and death, and Jewish life had no value at all. Even as the value of Jewish life declined, the rewards for Jewish death rose steadily. According to one Jewish witness, the hunts for Jews in the rural areas became so common that close to the liquidated ghettos "even dogs got used to the sound of gunfire, and stopped howling."[34]

Seeking to grasp the historical significance of innumerable incidents of neighbors killing neighbors, Omer Bartov has coined the concept of "communal genocide" or "communal massacre." The social, cultural, and psychological consequences of this, he rightly argues, reach far beyond the war and far deeper than the victims' experiences:

> Communal massacre devastates lives and warps psyches. It belies the very notion of passive bystanders: everyone becomes a protagonist, hunter and prey, resister and facilitator, loser and profiteer. Often, in the course of events, people come to play several roles. And the resulting sorrow and

shame, self-deception and denial, still infuse the way in which people remember, speak, and write about that past.[35]

Before the war, antisemitic feelings ran strong and were on the rise. The late 1930s were a period of growing tension, and the boycott of Jewish commerce (sanctioned by the state) started to erode the foundations of the Jewish community's economic life. After the war, the situation did not change at all. The returning survivors were met with deep apprehension, distrust, and often hatred, which frequently exploded in deadly violence, as in the July 1946 Kielce pogrom that claimed the lives of forty-two Holocaust survivors. Kielce, because of the sheer scale of the murder, became the most notorious example of the postwar anti-Jewish violence in Poland, but smaller locations did not fare any better. The reports sent from the provinces to the Central Committee of the Polish Jews from 1944 to 1947 provide ample proof of this depressing phenomenon.[36]

This prevailing attitude comes across strongly in the account of a Jewish soldier of the First Polish Army (a Soviet-led formation) who found himself in freshly liberated Lublin in the summer of 1944. There, from a member of the local elite he heard:

"Dear compatriots, we are thrilled that you have chased away the Hitlerite monster, but why in hell did you bring back with you all these Jews?! The only thing that Hitler did right was to cleanse Poland of the Jews!" It was my first encounter in postwar Poland with open anti-Semitism, which became, as I learned soon enough, much more pronounced than it was in prewar Poland.[37]

Once again, the examples of the prevailing anti-Jewish sentiments are abundant and their meaning impossible to dismiss. It is, therefore, highly unlikely that the prewar hostility and postwar hatred could somehow accommodate the wartime "interlude" of the alleged indifference, as recently suggested by some historians.[38]

Conclusions

What is the meaning of this mounting evidence? In Poland—and a very similar, horrible dynamic played out in the rest of Eastern Europe—police, firefighters, peasants, concerned citizens, cowards, and ideologues—people of various walks of life—took part, in one way or another, in making the Holocaust as complete and as inescapable as possible.[39] Nevertheless, the German system, although deadly efficient, did have its weaknesses. And here the role of "bystanders" in reinforcing the system and thus making Jewish survival much more unlikely, proved to be crucial. Further studies are needed to establish, or at least to discuss, the proportion of those who helped the Jews versus those who harmed them and those who remained aloof and indifferent to their plight. Quite often, as we now know, these categories overlapped or mutated one into another.

In order to explain the attitude of non-Jews at the time of the Holocaust, some authors used the Gaussian distribution, commonly referred to as the "bell curve." The bell curve, when used in discussion of social responses to the Holocaust, would indicate equally insignificant numbers of people both helping and hurting the victims while keeping the overwhelming majority in the "bystanding" or "indifferent" category. The problem, of course, is that the Gaussian distribution represents "normal distribution, under mild conditions," to cite the scientific definition of this function. As we know, in Eastern Europe, during the *anni horribili*, conditions were all but normal and mild. In fact, according to many Jewish survivors, if the majority of the non-Jewish population had indeed at least remained as "indifferent," this would have been a blessing in disguise. *Primum non nocere* (first, do not harm) is the age-old principle of the adepts of the medical profession. Unfortunately, the problem here was not an abundance of indifference; it was a distinct deficit of indifference.[40]

Marc Bloch once wrote, "Historians are no 'judges in Hades, charged with meting out praise or blame to dead heroes.'"[41] While abstaining from judgment, the historian's task is to put in place all pieces of evidence, occasionally to generalize, enabling us to come closer to understanding the tragic choices and the complexity of the not-too-distant past. In order to meet this challenge, however, historians need basic categories of description, and here we end up wanting. The growing body of historical evidence suggests that the term "bystander" no longer holds the necessary explanatory value. Indeed, it obscures and obfuscates the dilemmas of people caught between the German killing machine and the desperate Jewish victims. How can we describe them? What new terms do we have to coin? How do we describe people who, fearful of German reprisals, shut their door in front of the fleeing Jews, knowing full well that their gesture would seal the fate of innocent people? And what do we call children who were often first to point out the fleeing or hiding Jews to the clueless gendarmes? What about all those who turned away their eyes from the unfortunates? Are they all bystanders? Fellow travelers? Enablers? Facilitators? Associates? The absence of adequate nomenclature and terminology is in itself a reflection of the social malaise surrounding this topic. Christopher Browning, writing about the middle-echelon bureaucrats' path to complicity in mass murder, remarked that this path "was not marked by a single decisive and dramatic turning point. Instead the path was a gradual, almost imperceptible, descent past the point of no return."[42] In the case of Polish "bystanders," this "descent" was swifter and much more personal.

The decisions about the fate of the European Jews were made, as we well know, on the various levels of the German bureaucracy. Once put in motion, however, the machinery of destruction acquired a momentum of its own, bringing to the fore, as Zygmunt Bauman suggested, "the old tensions which modernity ignored, slighted or failed to resolve—and the powerful instruments of rational and effective action that modern development itself brought into being."[43] A combination of these underlying "old tensions" with the mechanisms of the German genocidal project created a horrible mix, which, in the occupied East, made bystanding an impossible proposition.

Jan Grabowski is Professor in the Department of History at the University of Ottawa, Canada. He is an eminent scholar of the Holocaust in Poland and Eastern Europe, with a focus on relations between the Jewish and non-Jewish populations in context of the German occupation. He has published wildly on this subject. In 2014, he received the Yad Vashem International Book Prize for Holocaust Research for his book *Hunt for the Jews: Betrayal and Murder in German-Occupied Poland* (2013).

Notes

An earlier version of this chapter was published in *Yad Vashem Studies* 43, no. 1 (2015): 113–133.

1. Raul Hilberg, *Perpetrators Victims Bystanders: The Jewish Catastrophe, 1933–1945* (New York, 1992), xi.
2. Given the massive involvement (or the lack of indifference and the direct exposure) of the local populations to the extermination of the Jews, I will—whenever dealing with the realities of Eastern Europe—refer to "bystanders" rather than bystanders.
3. See Yisrael Gutman and Efraim Zuroff, eds., *Rescue Attempts during the Holocaust* (Jerusalem, 1977). One needs to stress in this context the importance of the book by Yisrael Gutman and Shmuel Krakowski, *Unequal Victims: Poles and Jews during World War Two*, trans. Ted Gorelick and Witold Jedlicki (New York, 1986).
4. Michael R. Marrus, *The Holocaust in History* (New York, 1987); David Cesarani and Paul A. Levine, *"Bystanders" to the Holocaust: A Re-evaluation* (London, 2002).
5. Michael R. Marrus and Robert O. Paxton, *Vichy France and the Jews* (New York, 1981); Maxime Steinberg, "The *Judenpolitik* in Belgium within the West European Context: Comparative Observations," in *Belgium and the Holocaust: Jews, Belgians, Germans*, ed. Dan Michman (Jerusalem, 1998), 199–221.

6. See, e.g., on the Dutch case, Bart van der Boom, *"Wij weten niets van hun lot": Gewone Nederlanders en de Holocaust* (Amsterdam, 2012); Bart van der Boom, "Ordinary Dutchmen and the Holocaust: A Summary of Findings," in *The Persecution of the Jews in the Netherlands, 1940-1945: New Perspectives*, ed. Peter Romijn and Bart van der Boom, (Amsterdam, 2012), 29–54. On the debate, see Christina Morina, "The 'Bystander' in Recent Dutch Historiography," *German History* 32, no. 1 (2014): 101–111; Krijn Thijs, this volume.
7. Saul Friedländer, *The Years of Extermination: Nazi Germany and the Jews* (London, 2008), xxi.
8. Timothy Snyder, *Black Earth: The Holocaust as History and Warning* (New York, 2015), 150.
9. Jan T. Gross, "Sprawcy, ofiary i inni" [Perpetrators, victims and others], *Zagłada Żydów* 10, no. 1 (2014): 885–888. All translations are my own unless otherwise indicated.
10. Interview with Barbara Engelking, *Newsweek* (Polish edition, supplement *Historia*), 4 September 2014.
11. Gitta Sereny, *Into That Darkness: An Examination of Conscience* (New York, 1983), 101.
12. See, e.g., Götz Aly, *Hitler's Beneficiaries: Plunder, Racial War, and the Nazi Welfare State* (New York, 2007).
13. Frank Bajohr, *"Aryanisation" in Hamburg: The Economic Exclusion of Jews and the Confiscation of Their Property in Nazi Germany* (New York, 2002).
14. Marrus and Paxton, *Vichy France and the Jews*, 152–159.
15. Jan Grabowski, "Zarząd Powierniczy i nieruchomości żydowskie w Generalnym Gubernatorstwie: 'Co można skonfiskować? W zasadzie wszystko'" [The trustee administration and Jewish property in the *Generalgouvernement*: "What can be confiscated? Basically everything"], in *Klucze i Kasa: O Mieniu żydowskim w Polsce podczas okupacji*, ed. Jan Grabowski and Dariusz Libionka, (Warsaw, 2014), 73–113.
16. Archive of the Jewish Historical Institute, Warsaw (AŻIH), 302/30, Diary of Stanisław Żemiński. Żemiński was a rural teacher and before the war a member of the Polish Socialist Party. His diary was found in a heap of garbage in the Majdanek concentration camp where, most probably, he died in 1943.
17. Representatives of *Zentralverwaltung der Herrenlosen u. jüdischen Hauser u. Grundstücke*.
18. Dagmara Swałtek-Niewińska, "'Gospodarowanie' żydowskimi meblami w Krakowie w latach 1939–1945: Działalność Möbelbeschaffungsamt" [The "administration" of Jewish furniture in Krakow, 1939–1945: The activities of the *Möbelbeschaffungsamt*], in Grabowski and Libionka, *Klucze i Kasa*, 255–299.
19. Visual History Archive (University of Southern California); see the testimony of Harold Brand (b. 1927), index no. 43549, and the testimony of Antoni Balaryn, index no. 48515.
20. Eddie Weinstein, *17 Days in Treblinka: Daring to Resist, and Refusing to Die* (Jerusalem, 2008), 89–90.
21. For more on this topic, see Jan T. Gross and Irena Grudzinska-Gross, *Golden Harvest: Events on the Periphery of the Holocaust* (New York, 2012).
22. Andrzej Leder, *Prześniona rewolucja: Cwiczenie z logiki historycznej* (Warsaw, 2013), 80–95. For more on the same topic, see Jan T. Gross, *Fear: Anti-Semitism in Poland after Auschwitz—An Essay in Historical Interpretation* (New York, 2006), 302.
23. The report by Count Janusz Radziwiłł, quoted in Janusz Gmitruk, Zygmunt Hemmerling, and Jan Sałkowski, eds., *W kraju i na emigracji: Materiały z londyńskiego archiwum ministra prof. Stanisława Kota* (Warsaw, 1989), 216.

24. "Sprawa majątków pożydowskich," *Wielka Polska*, no. 7 (11 May 1944), 4–5, cited in Dariusz Libionka, "'Kwestia żydowska' i problemy własnościowe w ująciu wydawnictw konspiracyjnych ugrupowań nacjonalistycznych," in Grabowski and Libionka, *Klucze i Kasa*, 198.
25. Sebastian Rejak and Elżbieta Frister, eds., *Inferno of Choices: Poles and the Holocaust* (Warsaw, 2012), 52.
26. Morina, "The 'Bystander' in Recent Dutch Historiography," 103.
27. Excluding, of course, those who fled the Nazis to the Soviet Union and survived the war there.
28. Jan Grabowski, *Hunt for the Jews: Betrayal and Murder in German-Occupied Poland* (Bloomington and Indianapolis, 2013), 124–125; Bundesarchiv Ludwigsburg (BAL), B 162/2151, 1153, testimony of Heinrich Anlauf.
29. Franciszek Wyszyński, *Dzienniki 1941–1944* (Warsaw, 2007).
30. BAL, dossier B 162/8940, 27–29 (19 June 1969), testimony of Janina Jadwiga Starzyk.
31. Shraga Feivel Bielawski, *The Last Jew from Wegrow: The Memoirs of a Survivor of the Step-by-Step Genocide in Poland*, ed. Louis W. Liebovich (New York, 1991), 68.
32. Archive of the Institute of National Remembrance, Warsaw (AIPN), Main Commission (GK), 652, dossier 148, vol. 1.
33. AIPN, GK 255/319, 4.
34. Grabowski, *Hunt for the Jews*, 54. The quote is taken from the testimony of Chaja Rosenblatt, AŻIH, 302/318.
35. Omer Bartov, "Wartime Lies and Other Testimonies: Jewish-Christian Relations in Buczacz, 1939–1944," *East European Politics and Societies* 25, no. 3 (2011), 492.
36. A recent study of postwar attempts by the Polish Jews to resist this wave of antisemitic aggression sheds light on the scope of this phenomenon. See Alina Cała, *Ochrona bezpieczeństwa fizycznego Żydów w Polsce powojennej: Komisje Specjalne przy Centralnym Komitecie Żydów w Polsce* [The protection of physical safety of Jews in post-war Poland: The special commissions of the Central Committee of Polish Jews] (Warsaw, 2014).
37. Testimony of Józef Konskowolski, YVA, O.33/109.
38. Marcin Zaremba, *Wielka Trwoga: Polaska 1944–1947* [Great fear: Poland, 1944–1947] (Kraków, 2012); Barbara Engelking, *Such a Beautiful Sunny Day... Jews Seeking Refuge in the Polish Countryside, 1942–1945* (Jerusalem, 2017), 160–162. For critical discussion, see Elżbieta Janicka, "Mord rytualny z aryjskiego paragrafu" [Ritual murder based on an "Aryan" paragraph], *Kultura i Społeczeństwo* 52, no. 2 (2008): 248.
39. A different dynamic of "communal genocide" played itself out in the Lithuanian and Belorussian borderlands. There, the large forested areas allowed the Jewish refugees to form family camps (sometimes with the help of the Soviet partisans) and to resist attacks from their Lithuanian neighbors. For the Polish Jews in the densely populated *Generalgouvernement*, this survival strategy was a highly unlikely scenario. See Christopher R. Browning, "The Holocaust in Marcinkance in the Light of Two Unusual Documents," in *The Holocaust: The Unique and the Universal—Essays Presented in Honor of Yehuda Bauer*, ed. Shmuel Almog, David Bankier, Daniel Blatman, and Dalia Ofer, (Jerusalem, 2001), 66–83.
40. The term "deficit of indifference" was first introduced by Janicka, "Mord rytualny z aryjskiego paragrafu," 229–252.
41. Marc Bloch, *The Historian's Craft: Reflections on the Nature and Uses of History and the Techniques and Methods of Those Who Write It* (Manchester, 2004), 139.

42. Christopher R. Browning, "Bureaucracy and Mass Murder," in *The Path to Genocide: Essays on Launching the Final Solution*, ed. Christopher R. Browning (Cambridge, 1992), 144.
43. Zygmunt Bauman, *Modernity and the Holocaust* (Cambridge, 1989), 2–3.

Bibliography

Aly, Götz. *Hitler's Beneficiaries: Plunder, Racial War, and the Nazi Welfare State*. New York: Metropolitan, 2007.

Bajohr, Frank. *"Aryanisation" in Hamburg: The Economic Exclusion of Jews and the Confiscation of Their Property in Nazi Germany*. New York: Berghahn Books, 2002.

Bartov, Omer. "Wartime Lies and Other Testimonies: Jewish-Christian Relations in Buczacz, 1939–1944." *East European Politics and Societies* 25, no. 3 (2011): 486–511.

Bauman, Zygmunt. *Modernity and the Holocaust*. Cambridge: Polity, 1989.

Bielawski, Shraga Feivel. *The Last Jew from Wegrow: The Memoirs of a Survivor of the Step-by-Step Genocide in Poland*. Edited by Louis W. Liebovich. New York: Praeger, 1991.

Bloch, Marc. *The Historian's Craft: Reflections on the Nature and Uses of History and the Techniques and Methods of Those Who Write It*. Manchester: Manchester University Press, 2004.

Boom, Bart van der. "Ordinary Dutchmen and the Holocaust: A Summary of Findings." In *The Persecution of the Jews in the Netherlands, 1940–1945: New Perspectives*, edited by Peter Romijn and Bart van der Boom, 29–54. Amsterdam: Vossiuspers, 2012.

———. *"Wij weten niets van hun lot": Gewone Nederlanders en de Holocaust*. Amsterdam: Boom, 2012.

Browning, Christopher R. "Bureaucracy and Mass Murder." In *The Path to Genocide: Essays on Launching the Final Solution*, edited by Christopher R. Browning, 125–144. Cambridge: Cambridge University Press, 1992.

———. "The Holocaust in Marcinkance in the Light of Two Unusual Documents." In *The Holocaust: The Unique and the Universal, Essays Presented in Honor of Yehuda Bauer*, edited by Shmuel Almog, David Bankier, Daniel Blatman, and Dalia Ofer, 66–83. Jerusalem: Yad Vashem, 2001.

Cała, Alina. *Ochrona bezpieczeństwa fizycznego Żydów w Polsce powojennej: Komisje Specjalne przy Centralnym Komitecie Żydów w Polsce*. Warsaw: ŻIH, 2014.

Cesarani, David, and Paul A. Levine. *"Bystanders" to the Holocaust: A Re-evaluation*. London: Frank Cass, 2002.

Engelking, Barbara. *Such a Beautiful Sunny Day ... Jews Seeking Refuge in the Polish Countryside, 1942–1945*. Jerusalem: Yad Vashem, 2017.

Friedländer, Saul. *The Years of Extermination: Nazi Germany and the Jews*. London: Phoenix, 2008.

Gmitruk, Janusz, Zygmunt Hemmerling, and Jan Sałkowski, eds. *W kraju i na emigracji: Materiały z londyńskiego archiwum ministra prof. Stanisława Kota*. Warsaw: Ludowa Spółdzielnia Wydawnicza, 1989.

Grabowski, Jan. *Hunt for the Jews: Betrayal and Murder in German-Occupied Poland*. Bloomington: Indiana University Press, 2013.

———. "Zarząd Powierniczy i nieruchomości żydowskie w Generalnym Gubernatorstwie: 'Co można skonfiskować? W zasadzie wszystko.'" In Grabowski and Libionka, *Klucze i Kasa*, 73–113.

Grabowski, Jan, and Dariusz Libionka, eds. *Klucze i Kasa: O Mieniu żydowskim w Polsce podczas okupacji*. Warsaw: Polish Center for Holocaust Research, 2014.
Gross, Jan T. *Fear: Anti-Semitism in Poland after Auschwitz—An Essay in Historical Interpretation*. New York: Random House, 2006.
———. "Sprawcy, ofiary i inni." *Zagłada Żydów* 10, no. 1 (2014): 885–888.
Gross, Jan T., and Irena Grudzinska-Gross. *Golden Harvest: Events on the Periphery of the Holocaust*. New York: Oxford University Press, 2012.
Gutman, Yisrael, and Efraim Zuroff, eds. *Rescue Attempts during the Holocaust*. Jerusalem: Yad Vashem, 1977.
Gutman, Yisrael, and Shmuel Krakowski. *Unequal Victims: Poles and Jews during World War Two*. Translated by Ted Gorelick and Witold Jedlicki. New York: Holocaust Library, 1986.
Hilberg, Raul. *Perpetrators Victims Bystanders: The Jewish Catastrophe, 1933–1945*. New York: HarperCollins, 1992.
Janicka, Elżbieta. "Mord rytualny z aryjskiego paragrafu." *Kultura i Społeczeństwo* 52, no. 2 (2008): 229–252.
Leder, Andrzej. *Prześniona rewolucja: Ćwiczenie z logiki historycznej*. Warsaw: Krytyka Polityczna, 2013.
Libionka, Dariusz. "'Kwestia żydowska' i problemy własnościowe w ujęciu wydawnictw konspiracyjnych ugrupowań nacjonalistycznych." In Grabowski and Libionka, *Klucze i Kasa*, 181–254.
Marrus, Michael R. *The Holocaust in History*. New York: Meridian, 1987.
Marrus, Michael R., and Robert O. Paxton. *Vichy France and the Jews*. New York: Basic Books, 1981.
Morina, Christina. "The 'Bystander' in Recent Dutch historiography." *German History* 32, no. 1 (2014): 101–111.
Rejak, Sebastian, and Elżbieta Frister, eds. *Inferno of Choices: Poles and the Holocaust*. Warsaw: Rytm, 2012.
Sereny, Gitta. *Into That Darkness: An Examination of Conscience*. New York: Vintage Books, 1983.
Snyder, Timothy. *Black Earth: The Holocaust as History and Warning*. New York: Tim Duggan Books, 2015.
Steinberg, Maxime. "The *Judenpolitik* in Belgium within the West European Context: Comparative Observations." In *Belgium and the Holocaust: Jews, Belgians, Germans*, edited by Dan Michman, 199–221. Jerusalem: Yad Vashem, 1998.
Swałtek-Niewińska, Dagmara. "'Gospodarowanie" żydowskimi meblami w Krakowie w latach 1939–1945: Działalność Möbelbeschaffungsamt." In Grabowski and Libionka, *Klucze i Kasa*, 255–299.
Weinstein, Eddie. *17 Days in Treblinka: Daring to Resist, and Refusing to Die*. Jerusalem: Yad Vashem, 2008.
Wyszyński, Franciszek. *Dzienniki 1941–1944*. Warsaw: Mowią Wieki-Bellona, 2007.
Zaremba, Marcin. *Wielka Trwoga: Polaska 1944–1947*. Kraków: Znak, 2012.

Chapter 11

Defiant Danes and Indifferent Dutch?

Popular Convictions and Deportation Rates in the Netherlands and Denmark, 1940–1945

Bart van der Boom

Less than 25 percent of the Jews in the Netherlands survived World War II, the lowest percentage of all occupied Western European countries. In Denmark, 99 percent of the Jews survived, the highest percentage anywhere. It is thus not surprising to find dramatic differences in the Dutch and Danish collective memory of the Holocaust.

The fact that the large majority of Dutch Jews was deported and killed is understandably regarded as an indictment of Dutch society. Opinion leaders routinely remind the country that Dutch bystanders "subtly at first, crassly later on, distanced themselves from their Jewish fellow citizens," that "to many, tolerance turned out to be indifference," that "most Dutchmen" "looked away," "indifferently, or driven by morbid curiosity, but in any case passively, gawked at the Jews collected in their streets." The numbers are taken to prove that "the country that had long succeeded in posing as the nation of resistance-fighters and Anne Frank's helpers" in reality was "the best pupil of the Germanic class," in "the same league as traditionally antisemitic countries like Poland, Hungary, and Slovakia," or, in a phrase that came to encapsulate modern collective memory, *"Holland deportatieland"*—the Netherlands, deportation country.¹

The fact that the large majority of Danish Jews survived—they were rescued by fellow Danes who surreptitiously ferried them to Sweden—is equally understandably regarded as proof of their solidarity and courage. Danes were inspired, Bo Lidegaard writes in his well-received history of the rescue, by a notion of "societal inclusiveness" and knew "that the intimidation of one individual is a threat to the entire society."² They "refused to remain passive at a moment when their Jewish fellow citizens were in deadly danger," to quote a typical phrase from a 1983 exhibition catalogue.³ "No matter what contextual complexities scholarly research may ascribe to it," reads the introduction to a collection of essays on the Danish rescue, "the deed speaks for itself."⁴

The deed, or lack of it, indeed seems to speak for itself. While deportation rates obviously depended on many factors, such as, importantly, the eagerness of the persecutors, Jews could survive only with gentile help. While it has been widely recognized that Danish circumstances were highly unusual—as will be explained later—the conclusion seems inescapable that survival rates so dramatically apart as the Dutch and Danish ones indicate differences in bystander sympathy and courage. This, however, is a circular argument, by which survival rate is both explained by, and taken as proof of, a particular bystander mind-set. In fact, there are strong indications that Dutch and Danish popular convictions regarding the persecution of the Jews and the merits of resistance were strikingly similar.⁵

Denmark: Jews and Gentiles

The historical trajectory of Danish attitudes toward Jews seems unremarkable. During the eighteenth century, rich Jews were welcome in Denmark, but poor Jews were expelled. The government was generally well disposed toward Jews, but the guilds and the church were not. As elsewhere, Jews were excluded from certain professions and academic pursuits. In 1819, there were mob attacks against Jews in Copenhagen. By that time, Jews had been granted full citizenship, however, and during the nineteenth century they assimilated and were accepted into society. Assimilation, in fact, shrunk Jewish numbers, and around 1900, most communities outside Copenhagen had disappeared. Immigration from Eastern Europe briefly replenished the Jewish community, until the authorities put an end to it in 1917. Danish refugee policy in the 1930s was unwelcoming even by the standards of the time, limiting the number of Jewish refugees from Germany to 1,200. The Jewish community in Denmark thus remained very small at around 7,800 when World War II broke out, or 0.2 percent of the population.[6]

A detailed study of Danish antisemitism in the 1930s by Sofie Lene Bak concludes that political antisemitism was marginal, but cultural antisemitism was common—common enough, in fact, for the progressive political establishment to fight it by consistently linking antisemitism to Nazi-Germany. This strategy worked: increasingly, and definitively after the German occupation of the country in April 1940, antisemitism was regarded as "un-Danish." In Bak's assessment, this was as much a nationalist sentiment as an antidiscriminatory conviction.[7]

It thus seems likely that the Danish would have disapproved of anti-Jewish measures if the German occupiers had introduced them. However, they did not, until early October 1943, when they tried to round up all Jews for deportation. The Danes responded with outrage. Dozens of institutions and organizations, from the king and the permanent secretaries to farmers and student unions, raised their voices in protest. After initial hesitation, leading politicians joined in, insisting that Jews were "a vital part of our people" whose persecution flew in the face of "the Danish consciousness of law."[8] The bishop of Copenhagen had a message read in all churches that "the understanding of justice rooted in the Danish people and settled through centuries in our Danish Christian culture" was incompatible with persecution of the Jews, who as Danish citizens "have an equal right and responsibility under the law."[9] Ordinary Danes, Lidegaard writes, "were completely alienated by the idea of separating Jews from the rest of society, seeing them as an explicit part of the 'us,' as a part of the nation."[10] And they acted on this conviction. In October 1943, thousands of Danes spontaneously helped Jews to flee to the coast, where fishermen ferried them over the Sunt to Sweden. It was, one rescuer later said, the "national" thing to do. "Having a national attitude implied helping other nationals," Lidegaard adds, "including as a matter of course Jewish citizens. That was the whole point."[11] More than seven thousand Danish Jews safely reached Sweden, and fewer than five hundred were apprehended and sent to Theresienstadt, where the large majority survived.

Denmark: Accommodation

In apparent contradiction to this dramatic turn of events, Danish society had, up to the summer of 1943, almost unanimously supported a policy of collaboration. As a small country bordering and economically depending on Germany, Denmark was widely believed to have little choice. Thus, after the Danish surrender, the highly respected King Christian X. called for "loyal behavior to everyone exercising authority."[12] Minister of Foreign Affairs (and later Prime Minister) Erik Scavenius forcefully pushed for a policy of "active collaboration," by which he meant making it worth the Germans' while to leave Denmark a significant degree of independence.[13]

The German authorities were interested in such a deal, settling on "a pragmatic occupation policy that was more geared to short-term gains than to longer term ideological goals."[14] In return for a compliant foreign policy, a strict maintenance of domestic law and order and uninterrupted exports of foodstuffs—amounting to up to 15 percent of German needs[15]—they agreed on a "peaceful occupation" and the semblance of Danish sovereignty. One of the implications was that no antisemitic measures would be imposed. The Danish authorities argued that these measures, being alien to Danish law, tradition, and political culture, would antagonize the population and undermine government legitimacy and its moderating influence. The Germans accepted the argument—for the time being.

Despite the general rule of noninterference in domestic affairs, the Danes had to accept some infringement on democracy and due process. Criticizing the occupation or the occupier was outlawed. After the German invasion of the Soviet Union in June 1941, hundreds of communists—many more than the Germans had demanded—were rounded up by Danish police. Foreign Jews were expelled at German request. Danish Jews, too, suffered some discrimination. Under German economic pressure, they were shunted out of industrial leadership positions. State radio stopped playing Jewish composers and sidelined Jewish announcers. Government agencies consciously tried to keep Jews out of the spotlight and out of prominent positions. Danish police forces were expanded to fight the resistance. Leading politicians and the king forcefully denounced all resistance as unpatriotic and even treasonous.[16]

The population at large agreed. The parliamentary elections of March 1943 excluded the communists but included left-wing and right-wing parties opposing the policy of collaboration. With a 90 percent turnout, they received only 5 percent of the votes. Until the summer of 1943, Nathaniel Hong concludes, "active resistance against the German occupiers was the furthest thing from most Danes' minds." The resistance movement indeed remained very small and dominated by communists, until a conservative-nationalist resistance organization was founded in April 1943.[17] Sabotage did increase over the next months, however, prompting German countermeasures, which in turn triggered protests and strikes. The Danish government tried to quell the unrest but ultimately rejected German demands for harsh repression, including imposing the death penalty. At the end of August 1943, the cabinet resigned and handed over power to the secretaries-general, while the German authorities declared a state of emergency and disbanded the Danish armed forces. With the need to placate the Danes much reduced, Berlin finally ordered the deportation of Danish Jews.

The deportation of Danish Jews thus commenced relatively late. This could be relevant to our case, because willingness to collaborate in general is likely to have decreased with dwindling chances of a German victory and growing repression, and willingness to collaborate with the persecution of the Jews specifically is likely to have decreased with growing awareness of the fate of the deported. Denmark, however, seems to have lagged behind other occupied territories in both respects. Despite the resounding German defeat at Stalingrad, the Danish electorate in March 1943 still massively supported its collaborating government. In addition, there is no indication that the Danes had a better understanding of the fate of the deported in the fall of 1943 than the Dutch did a year earlier.[18]

The fact that the collaborationist reflex was still very much alive in October 1943—and that awareness of German intentions was limited—is vividly illustrated by the immediate reaction to the deportation order on the part of the Danish permanent secretaries, who now made up the Danish government. Instead of resigning, as they had earlier threatened to do, they moved to mitigate the harm. With the consent of both the cabinet that had just resigned and the leadership of the Jewish community, they proposed to Werner Best, the Reich plenipotentiary, to intern the Danish Jews themselves, in Denmark, if need be with the aid of Danish police—that is, using force.[19] Apparently, they believed that the Germans essentially wanted to *imprison* the Jews and would be content if this task was taken from their hands. The plan was never executed, because Best rejected it, but it is hard to argue with Gunnar Paulsson's terse remark that "only an accident of history prevented the Danish camp of Horserød from becoming another Westerbork"—the transit camp in the Netherlands.[20]

The fact that government involvement in the persecution of the Jews was actually negotiable is also illustrated by the transport of the few hundred Jews who were caught in October 1943 and sent to Theresienstadt. While most were carried off by ship, Danish police officers forced many them on cattle wagons, provided by the Danish railways, driven by Danish personnel. There was no protest or sabotage.[21]

It is Paulsson who again asks the uncomfortable question: "If a few thousand instead of a few hundred Jews had been hauled off to Theresienstadt, would the Danish response have been qualitatively different? It seems unlikely."[22]

The Netherlands: Jews and Gentiles

The Jews in the Netherlands in 1940 counted about 1.5 percent of the population. That population was not religiously homogeneous, like the Danes, but divided into strongly integrated subcultures ("pillars") of Catholics, Orthodox Protestants, and social democrats. While this "pillarization" in some respects isolated the Jewish community, which was too small and too divided to form its own pillar, it also embodied the recognition that divergent, even hostile ideological groups could together form a coherent nation. This tolerance of diversity had in fact become a dominant part of the national self-image: the Netherlands, having sprung from a rebellion against Habsburg religious persecution in the sixteenth century and subsequently serving as a refuge for persecuted minorities and freethinking intellectuals, were seen as a quintessentially tolerant nation by most of its citizens. That included its Jewish citizens, many of whom saw themselves as Dutchmen first and Jews second. On the eve of World War II, Bernard Wasserstein concludes, no Jewish community in Europe was as firmly anchored in its city as the Jewish community of Amsterdam.[23]

Antisemitism in the Netherlands was comparatively mild and moderate but might also have been more surreptitious. Politically, it was insignificant. The notion that discriminating against Jews was mediaeval and un-Dutch was reinforced, as it was in Denmark, by its association with Nazism, certainly after the country was occupied in May 1940.[24] In marked difference to Denmark, however, the occupier in the Netherlands quickly introduced anti-Jewish measures. Because of the backlash this created, we are unusually well informed about Dutch feelings toward this persecution: they can be deduced from public protests, from small acts of solidarity, from public opinion reports drawn up by the authorities, and, most vividly, from the abundance of wartime diaries kept by both Jews and gentiles.

The first instance of widespread protest against anti-Jewish measures was sparked by the "declaration of Aryan descent" that all civil servants had to sign in October 1940 and by the dismissal of Jews the next month. The permanent secretaries, to whom the cabinet had entrusted authority upon fleeing in May 1940, objected (just like the

Danish cabinet) that antisemitic measures were incompatible with both the Dutch constitution and Dutch tradition and that it would undermine their own standing with the population, which would not take kindly to it.[25]

Indeed, it did not. Protestant denominations collectively lodged a protest with Arthur Seyss-Inquart, which was read from the pulpits, reminding him of his promise "to respect our national character."[26] Professors protested and students went on strike in Leiden and Delft, showing, as a young Jewish accountant from Amsterdam noted with satisfaction in his diary, whose side young intellectuals were on.[27] The anti-Jewish regulations, the *Reichskommissariat* reported to Berlin in January 1941, were "widely discussed" and "almost universally criticized sharply.[28] A month later, a massive strike broke out in Amsterdam in protest against the apprehension of more than four hundred young male Jews in retaliation for several violent clashes between German police, Dutch Nazis, and Jews. As the shutdown of the city's public transport signaled the strike, employees walked out of offices and factories in a spontaneous show of solidarity. The strike was violently suppressed on the second day; three strikers were executed a few weeks later, while death notices of the young Jews who had been rounded up soon came pouring in from Mauthausen.

This repression had a cautioning effect when in May of 1942 the occupiers ordered all Jews to wear the Star of David. Ordinary people were aghast that this could happen in Holland. Some gentiles donned the Star in protest, but many did not dare to. They found another way of showing their solidarity, however, by demonstrative friendliness to those who wore the Star.[29] A Jewish sociologist wrote in his diary that he did not know of a single instance of spiteful reactions. Even Dutch Nazis, he wrote, did not dare look him in the eye, "apparently aware of the fact that this was simply too un-Dutch."[30] A SiPo informer ruefully reported that the reaction to the Star once again showed the *Judenfreundlichkeit* of the Dutch.[31]

Barely two months later, in early July 1942, the news was out that Dutch Jews would be deported to "labor camps" in Germany or, some thought, Poland. The churches, both Protestant denominations and the Catholic Church, sent Seyss-Inquart a joint protest, claiming the deportation of the Jews went against "the most profound moral consciousness of the Dutch people."[32] Wartime diaries show that this was no idle claim: many were profoundly shocked, while some felt the occupation had hit rock bottom.[33] In its overview of 1942, the *Reichskommissariat* complained to Berlin of the "generally uncomprehending and pro-Jewish attitude of the average Dutchman."[34]

The Netherlands: Accommodation

This "pro-Jewish attitude," however, did not translate into active resistance. In general, the Netherlands reacted to the German occupation much like Denmark did: willing to cooperate, despite the widespread and unmistakable dislike of the occupier and his ideology, to maintain some level of influence to the benefit of the country. While the government in exile did not pull its punches in excoriating the occupier and promising his swift demise, it notably did not call for active resistance, for fear of brutal repercussions.[35]

This accommodating stance did wear off much earlier, but also more gradually, than it did in Denmark. The February Strike of 1941 both demonstrated anti-German feeling among the population and moved the occupier to present it with an explicit choice: either with us or against us. Nazification efforts turned more coercive, before being abandoned as hopeless. The first resistance fighters were executed in February 1941, and more than 1,200 hostages were taken in May and July 1942, five of whom were executed in August. Labor conscription started in earnest in April 1942 and was stepped up a year later, coinciding with the announcement that the former Dutch army would be sent to POW camps, sparking another massive strike. By the summer of 1943, the occupier had squandered all remaining goodwill and a serious resistance movement had emerged, producing hundreds of illegal newspapers and ultimately providing hiding for hundreds of thousands unwilling labor conscripts.

As in Denmark, however, the residual Dutch civil administration did continue to cooperate, until the country descended into chaos in the "hunger winter" of 1944–1945. Thus, many Dutch institutions were involved in the isolation, despoliation, and, ultimately, deportation of Dutch Jews. Municipalities, for instance, registered Jews and stamped their IDs with a "J," the state telephone company disconnected Jewish subscribers, employment agencies organized labor camps for Jewish unemployed, and the Supreme Court of the Netherlands accepted the dismissal of its Jewish president.

The deportations, commencing in July 1942, did not fundamentally alter this accommodating stance. The permanent secretaries, who had earlier threatened to resign should the Jews be deported, did not do so (just like their Danish counterparts) but did remind the German authorities of their strict disapproval and refused to issue orders relating to the deportation process themselves. The Germans were happy to go along with this "strategy of shrinking competence,"[36] cutting Dutch authorities out of the loop and issuing orders directly to crucial institutions like the police. While very few police officers actually refused to cooperate in the roundups of Jews, their manifest reluctance forced the Germans to commit SiPo men, specially trained police battalions or Dutch Nazi volunteers to the task.[37]

The fact that a serious resistance movement was sparked not by the deportation of the Jews but by the escalation of labor conscription obviously shows that people are more protective of relatives and friends than of strangers. This, however, is unlikely to be a Dutch idiosyncrasy, while the integration of Jews does not seem to differ significantly between Denmark and the Netherlands. Likewise, Dutch society undoubtedly was no more averse to risk and disobedience and thus eager for accommodation than Danish society. For the purposes of the Danish-Dutch comparison, another factor explaining accommodation regarding the persecution of the Jews seems more relevant: its apparent rationality. The Dutch quickly found out that the occupation regime in the Netherlands, in marked contrast to that in Denmark, was determined to carry out anti-Jewish policies regardless of the obvious political drawbacks. All sorts of measures were negotiable, but not those targeting Jews.[38] This left the bystanders in a quandary: protests and resistance were unlikely to achieve much, while there would be a price to pay.

The February Strike, for instance, in no way mitigated the persecutors' anti-Jewish campaign, but it did reveal their ruthlessness: the young men whose roundup had ignited the strike were sent to Mauthausen, where almost all died. The same fate befell another five hundred young Jews rounded up in retaliation measures in the summer and fall of 1941. To press the point, the German authorities made sure families were duly notified of the death of their loved ones, often within weeks. Essentially, all Jews were treated like hostages. This explains why many Dutch bystanders felt unable to prevent a persecution that they also abhorred. In a large sample of wartime diarists, one in five explicitly calls themselves powerless. "However you turn it, the Jews will be the ones who suffer," a student, who felt terrible about the fate that befell some of her Jewish friends, wrote in her diary: "If we resist or revolt—it will be avenged on the Jews."[39] While a cynic can discount this conviction as a self-serving cover for cowardice, it nevertheless seemed to be a realistic estimate.

Moreover, many of the victims shared this sentiment. Virtually all Jews showed up for registration in January 1941. No more than a handful of Jews refused to wear the Star. The Jewish Council, consisting of a host of well-respected community leaders, essentially cooperated fully with the authorities, hoping to exert some influence in the victims' interests. The tenability of this strategy was fundamentally questioned within the council more than once, but every time the unheroic but pragmatic choice for the lesser evil prevailed.[40]

Even when deportations to "the East" commenced in the summer of 1942, it was imaginable that this choice made sense. While nobody knew what deportation entailed, one did not need to know anything to suspect that the deported would be treated harshly and some, perhaps many, would die over time. Some Jews, like Anne Frank's family, decided that averting this horror was worth the risk of punishment. Many others, however, were less sure. The Jewish neighborhoods of Amsterdam were "boiling," a young Jewish diarist wrote of the summer of 1942: "Groups of people everywhere. With one topic of conversation only: to go or not to go." He also discussed the options with many of his Jewish and gentile friends but had to conclude that, with so many unknown factors, there was no way to make a well-informed choice.[41]

When one tries to view the situation through the eyes of the contemporaries, one sees how complicated indeed this choice was. However awful deportation would be, punishment, it was understandably assumed, would be worse. By expecting the war to be over within months, if not weeks, it was possible that deportation to a harsh labor camp offered better chances of survival than going into hiding and risk punishment, that is, a quick death in Mauthausen. That explains why many Jews who had the option of going into hiding, hesitated. Many sincerely believed that resistance would hurt, not help, them.[42]

That obviously complicated the position of the bystanders, too. Some were convinced that offering hiding was worth the risk and were willing to take it; at least twenty-eight thousands Jews in fact went into hiding, requiring the help of many more gentiles. Many gentiles, no doubt, were too scared or too indifferent to offer hiding. Others, however, simply thought it a reckless move, for themselves and the victims alike. Determined to deport all Jews regardless of the political damage, the perpetrators thus made sure the costs of resistance seemed so high—to both bystanders and victims—that obedience could be construed as the lesser evil. Lacking any reliable information on the fate of the deported and unable to imagine the reality of the death camps, few understood that *any* course of action was preferable to obedience.

The Danish Exception

This is where the Danish case is exceptional: the Danes were faced with the choice between obedience and resistance under circumstances that were uniquely conducive to the latter. These circumstances were created not by the bystanders but by the perpetrators, more specifically, by Werner Best. The Reich plenipotentiary essentially played a double game. He proposed the deportation of Danish Jews to Berlin in an attempt to burnish his hardline credentials there after his policy of cooperation had floundered. He did not actually want deportation to happen, however, hoping to revive cooperation, and thus not wanting to antagonize Danish leading circles. Confronted with this dilemma, he hit on a "solution" to the "Jewish question" that would more or less satisfy Berlin without irking Copenhagen: a mass flight to Sweden.[43]

Lidegaard, following Hannah Arendt, claims that Danish distaste for antisemitism actually forced Best's hand. The Nazis could not carry out their policy of extermination, he writes, without the "sounding board" or "fig leaf" of local indifference.[44] This is untenable: the Dutch case shows no fig leaf or sounding board was necessary. Best *chose* to humor his indigenous counterparts, just as Seyss-Inquart chose to ignore them. Had it served their purposes, Paulsson rightly notes, the Germans could and would have brushed aside Danish opposition to antisemitism, "as they did in Holland and elsewhere."[45]

The first step in Best's plan was to scare the Jews into fleeing. Through one of his close collaborators, he warned leading Danish politicians that German police officers would conduct a raid on the night of 1 October 1943. The news spread quickly, and when the raid came, many Jews had fled their homes. When they had not, all they needed to do to evade the German grasp was not answer the door; Best had forbidden his men to force their way in. He also stipulated that the entire action was to last no more than three hours, after which all police officers returned to their barracks. Fewer than three hundred Jews were caught that night, mostly people who had not been warned.[46]

The next step was to ensure that the Jews could make it to Sweden, which, as Best had anticipated, issued an open invitation to flee on the day after the raid.[47] The 1,800 German police officers who had been sent to Copenhagen were ordered to stand aside. When inadvertently encountering fleeing Jews, they often looked away. A declaration threatening those who helped Jews with repercussions remained unpublished. Trains overflowing with Jews heading for the coast were not searched, let alone stopped—extra trains were put on. While the embarkation all along the coast was a "practically overt operation,"[48] it was very seldom interfered with. Surveillance of the Sunt, which had been performed by the now disbanded Danish navy, was not resumed until November, when all Jews had safely arrived in Sweden. The oft-described Gestapo raid on the church of the coastal town of Gilleleje, where eighty Jews who were awaiting their flight were arrested, was the exception to the rule of noninterference. Fewer than two hundred Jews were apprehended in the weeks following the first roundup. Likewise, not one of the hundreds of fishing vessels that ferried the refugees to Sweden was stopped at sea. The few rescuers who were caught during those weeks were handed over to Danish police and Danish courts, which imposed minimal, if any, punishment.[49] The attempted deportation of Danish Jews was "essentially a charade, no doubt answering some devious political purpose, but never seriously meant to succeed," Paulsson rightly concludes: what to Danes and Jews looked like a daring rescue, to the Germans consisted of "the entirely successful expulsion of the Danish Jews."[50]

The effect of this highly unusual state of affairs was that it was not particularly difficult or dangerous for Jews to flee or for Danes to save them. Without effective German hindrance, the seven thousand or so Danish Jews could have been ferried to Sweden in a matter of days. In practice, it took several weeks, because it proved difficult to find fishermen willing to make the short trip. Many hesitated, some refused, and those who agreed demanded considerable sums of money. On average 1,000 kroner was paid per person, the equivalent of three months' earnings of a skilled laborer. The price of the crossing has been shown to fluctuate with supply and demand, suggesting that to the fishermen the rescue was a commercial undertaking. During the first days, Jews without funds in fact had to hide and wait until they found someone to pay their fare. Ultimately, the money was found for everyone, and, by the middle of October 1943, 90 percent of all fleeing Jews had arrived safely in Sweden.[51]

The fact that many thousands of Danes spontaneously participated in the rescue seems remarkable, considering the fact that up to the summer of 1943 most Danes had been averse to any active resistance. To many helpers, however, the rescue of the Jews was not so much an act of resistance as an act of civil disobedience. Many remained opposed to any violence or sabotage, and in some cases, saboteurs wanting to flee were denied a place on board. It has been suggested that the participation of so many in what was essentially an overt operation produced a feeling of invulnerability—as happened, perhaps, during the February Strike in the Netherlands.[52]

The crucial question is to what extent the rescuers *knew* they ran little risk. Hans Kirchhoff argues they must have been intimidated by the few occasions when authorities did try to hinder the rescue and shots were fired. The more recent literature counters, more convincingly, that the *paucity* of such violent reactions must actually have *reassured* them. Moreover, the Danes had witnessed none of the draconian punishments the German occupier meted out in other occupied territories. Many helpers probably realized they did not run particularly large risks.[53] The same applies to the victims. Up to the turn of events of September 1943, the Jewish leadership had urged Jews *not* to flee, for fear of repercussions, and very few had. Community leaders had even threatened to report Jews participating in illegal activities.[54] Now, however, most seem to have quickly overcome their qualms about acting illegally. Apparently, few of the victims doubted that fleeing was in their own best interest.

Conclusion

The dramatically different deportation rates in Denmark and the Netherlands cannot be explained from the mind-set of the bystanders, which was very similar. Both the Dutch and Danes considered the Jews bona fide fellow citizens, even more so once a hostile regime singled them out for persecution. Both populations cherished an inclusive national identity. Moreover, both populations—and administrations—tended to believe in the logic of accommodation, the strategy of the lesser evil. If most Danish Jews had been deported, we would have no trouble explaining this from the Danes' willingness to collaborate. If Dutch Jews had almost all been saved, we would have no trouble explaining that from the widespread indignation toward their persecution.

But indignation at injustice in itself does not produce resistance. There also needs to be a seemingly viable way of opposing that injustice, a course of action that is certain to help the victims, at acceptable risks. In Denmark, such a course of action was manifestly clear; in the Netherlands, much less so. The Danish circumstances were in fact so bizarrely favorable, Gunnar Paulsson points out, that it did not take a particularly brave or sympathetic population to save the Jews; the relatively small number of helpers needed could have been found anywhere in occupied Europe.[55] His merciless rationality, however, seems unusual among his colleagues, many of whom try to have it both ways: accepting that the rescue was entirely dependent on German connivance yet claiming Danish courage made the difference—turning a necessary precondition into a sufficient explanation.[56] Lidegaard even maintains that "of course" "the rejection of the logic of the Jewish extermination [could] have stopped the project in other occupied countries—even in Germany itself."[57] However seductive, such a belief in the power of bystander convictions seems unwarranted.

Bart van der Boom is Assistant Professor of modern Dutch history at the University of Leiden. His Dutch publications include a short biography of the National Socialist Kees van Geelkerken, a history of Dutch civil defense during the Cold War, and three books dealing with the German occupation of the Netherlands: on the city of The Hague, on Dutch popular opinion generally, and on popular opinion and knowledge regarding the Holocaust specifically. His English language publications include "'The Auschwitz Reservation': Dutch Victims and Bystanders and Their Knowledge of the Holocaust," *Holocaust and Genocide Studies* 31, no. 3 (2017); and "Indifference? Dutch Bystanders and the Persecution of the Jews in the Netherlands," *Yad Vashem Studies* 45, no. 1 (2017).

Notes

1. These quotations from various Dutch press and media sources between 1992 and 2011 are documented in Bart van der Boom, *"Wij Weten Niets van hun Lot": Gewone Nederlanders en de Holocaust* (Amsterdam, 2012), 11–12.
2. Bo Lidegaard, *Countrymen: The Untold Story of how Denmark's Jews Escaped the Nazis, of the Courage of their Fellow Danes—and of the Extraordinary Role of the SS* (New York, 2013), 363, 366.
3. Hanne Trautner-Kromann, "The History of the Jews in Denmark 1622–1940," in *Kings and Citizens: The History of the Jews in Denmark 1622–1983*, vol. 1, ed. Jørgen H. Barfod, Norman L. Kleeblatt, Vivian B. Mann, and Susan L. Braunstein (New York, 1983), 91.
4. Leo Goldberger, "Editor's Preface," in *The Rescue of the Danish Jews: Moral Courage under Stress*, ed. Leo Goldberger (New York, 1987), xviii.
5. The comparison has been made before. See Leni Yahil, "Methods of Persecution: A Comparison of the 'Final Solution' in Holland and Denmark," in *Studies in History*, vol. 18, ed. David Asheri and Israel Schatzman (Jerusalem, 1972), 279–300; Gunnar S. Paulsson, "The Bridge over the Øresund: The Historiography of the Expulsion of the Danish Jews from Nazi-Occupied Denmark," *Journal of Contemporary History* 30, no. 3 (1995): 459–460.
6. Trautner-Kromann, "The History of the Jews in Denmark," 13–22; Hans Kirchhoff, "The Rescue of Danish Jews in October 1943," in *Nazi Europe and the Final Solution*, ed. David Bankier and Israel Gutman (New York, 2009), 551.
7. Sofie Lene Bak, "Studier i Dansk Antisemitisme 1930–1945" (PhD diss., University of Copenhagen, 2003), summary.
8. Kirchhoff, "The Rescue of Danish Jews," 552.
9. Michael Mogensen, "October 1943: The Rescue of the Danish Jews," in *Denmark and the Holocaust*, ed. Mette Bastholm Jensen and Steven L. B. Jensen (Copenhagen, 2003), 46, 44–45.
10. Lidegaard, *Countrymen*, 352.
11. Ibid., 307.
12. Nathaniel Hong, *Occupied: Denmark's Adaptation and Resistance to German Occupation 1940–1945* (Copenhagen, 2012), 30.
13. Ibid., 38.

14. Kirchhoff, "The Rescue of Danish Jews," 546.
15. Hong, *Occupied*, 42.
16. Kirchhoff, "The Rescue of Danish Jews," 550, 551; Hong, *Occupied*, 50–51, 76, 127–129, 187, 191–192.
17. Hong, *Occupied*, 117, 154, 162.
18. Ibid., 196, 198; Mogensen, "October 1943," 39; Lidegaard, *Countrymen*, 228; Bart van der Boom, "Ordinary Dutchmen and the Holocaust: A Summary of Findings," in *The Persecution of the Jews in the Netherlands, 1940–1945: New Perspectives*, ed. Wichert ten Have (Amsterdam, 2012), 42–45.
19. Sofie Lene Bak, "Between Tradition and New Departure: The Dilemmas of Collaboration in Denmark," in *Collaboration with the Nazis: Public Discourse after the Holocaust*, ed. Roni Stauber (London, 2011), 118; Lidegaard, *Countrymen*, 130–134.
20. Paulsson, "The Bridge over the Øresund," 460.
21. Bak, "Between Tradition and New Departure," 121–122; Kirchhoff, "The Rescue of Danish Jews," 550.
22. Paulsson, "The Bridge over the Øresund," 456.
23. Rena G. Fuks-Mansfeld, "Verlichting en Emancipatie omstreeks 1750–1814: Religieus, Cultureel en Sociaal Leven," in *Geschiedenis van de Joden in Nederland*, ed. J. C. H. Blom, Rena G. Fuks-Mansfeld, and Ivo Schöffer (Amsterdam, 1995), 181, 197; Rena G. Fuks-Mansfeld, "Moeizame Aanpassing (1840-1870)," in Blom et al., *Geschiedenis van de Joden in Nederland*, 224; Bernard Wasserstein, *On the Eve: The Jews of Europe before the Second World War* (New York, 2015), 104–105; Ivo Schöffer, "Nederland en de Joden in de Jaren Dertig in Historisch Perspectief," in *Nederland en het Duitse Exil 1933–1940*, ed. Kathinka Dittrich and Hans Würzner (Amsterdam, 1982), 89; Karin Hofmeester, "Antisemitismus in den Niederlanden im 19. und 20. Jahrhundert," in *Ablehnung—Duldung—Anerkennung: Toleranze in den Niederlanden und in Deutschland—Ein historischer und aktueller Vergleich*, ed. Horst Lademacher, Renate Loos, and Simon Groenveld (Münster, 2004), 607–609; Van der Boom, *"Wij Weten Niets van hun Lot,"* 182–185.
24. Hofmeester, "Antisemitismus in den Niederlanden," 604–605; Van der Boom, *"Wij Weten Niets van hun Lot,"* 179–186.
25. Loe de Jong, *Het Koninkrijk der Nederlanden in de Tweede Wereldoorlog*, 14 vols., academic edition, (The Hague, 1969–1991), 4:762; Pim Griffioen and Ron Zeller, *Jodenvervolging in Nederland, Frankrijk en België 1940–1945: Overeenkomsten, Verschillen, Oorzaken* (Amsterdam, 2011), 312.
26. De Jong, *Koninkrijk*, 4:775.
27. Van der Boom, *"Wij Weten Niets van hun Lot,"* 156.
28. "… in weiten Kreisen der Bevölkerung lebhaft diskutiert und fast durchweg scharf abgelehnt." Meldungen aus den Niederlanden, 29, 21 January 1941, NIOD Institute for War, Holocaust and Genocide Studies (NIOD), 077, 354.
29. On the relevance and substance of such gestures of solidarity in France and Germany, see Jacques Semelin and Christina Morina, this volume.
30. Van der Boom, *"Wij Weten Niets van hun Lot,"* 173.
31. Lageberichte D. Hatenboer, 7 May 1942, NIOD, HSSPF 26 a, filmnr. 300.
32. De Jong, *Koninkrijk*, 6:13.
33. Van der Boom, *"Wij Weten Niets van hun Lot,"* 213–216.
34. "…die allgemein verständnislose und judenfreundliche Haltung der Durchschnittsniederländer." Meldungen aus den Niederlanden, Sonderbericht Jahresbericht 1942, NIOD, 077, 358.
35. Onno Sinke, *Verzet vanuit de verte: De behoedzame koers van Radio Oranje* (Amsterdam, 2009), 230.

36. Peter Romijn, *Burgemeesters in Oorlogstijd: Besturen onder Duitse Bezetting* (Amsterdam, 2006), 453–455.
37. De Jong, *Koninkrijk*, 5:1042; Griffioen and Zeller, *Jodenvervolging in Nederland*, 324, 545, 555–560; Guus Meershoek, *Dienaren van het Gezag: De Amsterdamse Politie tijdens de Bezetting* (Amsterdam, 1999), 249.
38. Griffioen and Zeller, *Jodenvervolgin in Nederland g*, 545.
39. Van der Boom, "Wij Weten Niets van hun Lot," 404.
40. Bob Moore, *Victims and Survivors: The Nazi Persecution of the Jews in the Netherlands* (London, 1997), 64, 109; De Jong, *Koninkrijk* , 5:550.
41. Van der Boom, "Wij Weten Niets van hun Lot," 389.
42. Ibid., 387–401.
43. Hong, *Occupied*, 194–196, 207; Paulsson, "The Bridge over the Øresund," 455; Kirchhoff, "The Rescue of Danish Jews," 546–547.
44. Lidegaard, *Countrymen*, 58, 348, 353, 355.
45. Paulsson, "The Bridge over the Øresund," 458.
46. Ibid., 446; Kirchhoff, "The Rescue of Danish Jews," 548–549; Mogensen, "October 1943," 56–57.
47. Lidegaard, *Countrymen*, 66–67.
48. Leni Yahil, *The Holocaust: The Fate of European Jewry, 1932–1945* (New York, 1990), 576.
49. Hong, *Occupied*, 204; Kirchhoff, "The Rescue of Danish Jews," 548–549; Hans Kirchhoff, "Denmark: A Light in the Darkness of the Holocaust? A Reply to Gunnar S. Paulsson," *Journal of Contemporary History* 30, no. 3 (1995): 468; Mogensen, "October 1943," 38, 49–55; Lidegaard, *Countrymen*, 158, 252.
50. Paulsson, "The Bridge over the Øresund," 435, 441.
51. Mogensen, "October 1943," 39, 48; Hong, *Occupied*, 200; Kirchhoff, "The Rescue of Danish Jews," 550; Sofie Lene Bak, "Copenhagen: Bright Hope and Deep Gloom—A New View of the 1943 Rescue Operation in Denmark," in *Civil Society and the Holocaust: International Perspectives on Resistance and Rescue*, ed. Anders Jerichow and Cecilie Felicia Stokholm Banke (New York, 2013), 22; Lidegaard, *Countrymen*, 335–336
52. Mogensen, "October 1943," 46; Sofie Lene Bak, "From Rescue to Escape in 1943: On a Path to De-victimizing the Danish Jews," in *The Holocaust as Active Memory: The Past in the Present*, ed. Claudia Lenz, Marie Louise Seeberg, and Irene Levin (Farnham, 2013), 145; Kirchhoff, "The Rescue of Danish Jews," 553–554; Bak, "Copenhagen," 25.
53. Hong, *Occupied*, 198, 206; Lidegaard, *Countrymen*, 349; Bak, "Copenhagen," 24–25; Kirchhoff, "The Rescue of Danish Jews," 554; Kirchhoff, "Denmark," 476.
54. Mogensen, "October 1943," 39; Kirchhoff, "The Rescue of Danish Jews," 544.
55. Paulsson, "The Bridge over the Øresund," 458.
56. Mogensen, "October 1943," 60; Cecilie Felicia Stokholm Banke, "Copenhagen: Refugees and Rescue—The Ambivalence of Danish Holocaust History," in Jerichow and Stokholm Banke, *Civil Society and the Holocaust*, 183; Yahil, "Methods of Persecution," 299; Yahil, *The Holocaust*, 576; Kirchhoff, "The Rescue of Danish Jews," 555; Lidegaard, *Countrymen*, 353.
57. Lidegaard, *Countrymen*, 348.

Bibliography

Bak, Sofie Lene. "Between Tradition and New Departure: The Dilemmas of Collaboration in Denmark." In *Collaboration with the Nazis: Public Discourse after the Holocaust*, edited by Roni Stauber, 110–124. London: Routledge, 2011.
———. "Copenhagen: Bright Hope and Deep Gloom—A New View of the 1943 Rescue Operation in Denmark." In Jerichow and Stokholm Banke, *Civil Society and the Holocaust*, 18–39.
———. "From Rescue to Escape in 1943: On a Path to De-victimizing the Danish Jews." In *The Holocaust as Active Memory: The Past in the Present*, edited by Claudia Lenz, Marie Louise Seeberg, and Irene Levin, 139–152. Farnham: Ashgate, 2013.
———. "Studier i Dansk Antisemitisme 1930–1945." PhD diss., University of Copenhagen, 2003.
Blom, J. C. H., Rena G. Fuk-Mansfeld, and Ivo Schöffer. *Geschiedenis van de Joden in Nederland*. Amsterdam: Balans, 1995.
Boom, Bart van der. "Ordinary Dutchmen and the Holocaust: A Summary of Findings." In *The Persecution of the Jews in the Netherlands, 1940–1945: New Perspectives,* edited by Wichert ten Have, 29–52. Amsterdam: Amsterdam University Press, 2012.
———. *"Wij Weten Niets van hun Lot": Gewone Nederlanders en de Holocaust*. Amsterdam: Boom, 2012.
Fuks-Mansfeld, R. G. "Moeizame Aanpassing (1840–1870)." In Blom et al., *Geschiedenis van de Joden in Nederland*, 207–246.
———. "Verlichting en Emancipatie omstreeks 1750–1814: Religieus, Cultureel en Sociaal Leven." In Blom et al., *Geschiedenis van de Joden in Nederland*, 129–176.
Goldberger, Leo. "Editor's Preface." In *The Rescue of the Danish Jews: Moral Courage under Stress*, edited by Leo Goldberger. New York: New York University Press, 1987.
Griffioen, Pim, and Ron Zeller. *Jodenvervolging in Nederland, Frankrijk en België 1940–1945: Overeenkomsten, Verschillen, Oorzaken*. Amsterdam: Boom, 2011.
Hofmeester, Karin. "Antisemitismus in den Niederlanden im 19. und 20. Jahrhundert." In *Ablehnung—Duldung—Anerkennung: Toleranze in den Niederlanden und in Deutschland—Ein historischer und aktueller Vergleich*, edited by Horst Lademacher, Renate Loos, and Simon Groenveld, 604–630. Münster: Waxmann, 2004.
Hong, Nathaniel. *Occupied: Denmark's Adaptation and Resistance to German Occupation 1940–1945*. Copenhagen: Danish Resistance Museum, 2012.
Jerichow, Anders, and Cecilie Felicia Stokholm Banke, eds. *Civil Society and the Holocaust: International Perspectives on Resistance and Rescue*. New York: Humanity in Action Press, 2013.
Jong, Loe de. *Het Koninkrijk der Nederlanden in de Tweede Wereldoorlog*. 14 vols. Academic edition. The Hague: Sdu, 1969–1991.
Kirchhoff, Hans. "Denmark: A Light in the Darkness of the Holocaust? A Reply to Gunnar S. Paulsson." *Journal of Contemporary History* 30, no. 3 (1995): 465–479.
———. "The Rescue of Danish Jews in October 1943." In *Nazi Europe and the Final Solution*, edited by David Bankier and Israel Gutman, 539–555. New York: Berghahn Books, 2009.
Lidegaard, Bo. *Countrymen: The Untold Story of how Denmark's Jews Escaped the Nazis, of the Courage of their Fellow Danes—and of the Extraordinary Role of the SS*. New York: Knopf, 2013.
Meershoek, Guus. *Dienaren van het Gezag: De Amsterdamse Politie tijdens de Bezetting*. Amsterdam: Van Gennep, 1999.

Mogensen, Michael. "October 1943: The Rescue of the Danish Jews." In *Denmark and the Holocaust*, edited by Mette Bastholm Jensen and Steven L. B. Jensen, 33–61. Copenhagen: Institute for International Studies, Department for Holocaust and Genocide Studies, 2003.

Moore, Bob. *Victims and Survivors: The Nazi Persecution of the Jews in the Netherlands*. London: Arnold, 1997.

Paulsson, Gunnar S. "The Bridge over the Øresund: The Historiography of the Expulsion of the Danish Jews from Nazi-Occupied Denmark." *Journal of Contemporary History* 30, no. 3 (1995): 431–464.

Romijn, Peter. *Burgemeesters in Oorlogstijd: Besturen onder Duitse Bezetting*. Amsterdam: Balans, 2006.

Schöffer, Ivo. "Nederland en de Joden in de Jaren Dertig in Historisch Perspectief." In *Nederland en het Duitse Exil 1933–1940*, edited by Kathinka Dittrich and Hans Würzner, 79–92. Amsterdam: Van Gennep, 1982.

Sinke, Onno. *Verzet vanuit de verte: De behoedzame koers van Radio Oranje*. Amsterdam: Augustus, 2009.

Stokholm Banke, Cecilie Felicia. "Copenhagen: Refugees and Rescue—The Ambivalence of Danish Holocaust History." In Jerichow and Stokholm Banke, *Civil Society and the Holocaust*, 176–187.

Trautner-Kromann, Hanne. "The History of the Jews in Denmark 1622–1940." In *Kings and Citizens: The History of the Jews in Denmark 1622–1983*, vol. 1, edited by Jørgen H. Barfod, Norman L. Kleeblatt, Vivian B. Mann, and Susan L. Braunstein, 12–24. New York: Jewish Museum, 1983.

Wasserstein, Bernard. *On the Eve: The Jews of Europe before the Second World War*. New York: Simon & Schuster, 2015.

Yahil, Leni. *The Holocaust: The Fate of European Jewry, 1932–1945*. New York: Oxford University Press, 1990.

———. "Methods of Persecution: A Comparison of the 'Final Solution' in Holland and Denmark." In *Studies in History*, vol. 18, edited by David Asheri and Israel Schatzman, 279–300. Jerusalem: Magnes Press, 1972.

Chapter 12

The Notion of Social Reactivity
The French Case, 1942–1944

Jacques Semelin

In some countries, France has a strong reputation for antisemitism. This stems from the Dreyfus Affair and even more so from the Vichy government's role in the deportation of Jews during World War II. In their pathbreaking study *Vichy France and the Jews* (1981), Michael Marrus and Robert Paxton reconstructed the stages of the French state's collaboration with the Nazis.[1] Eighty thousand Jews, French and foreign, were killed in the Holocaust, 25 percent of the Jewish population identified as such in 1940. This therefore means that 75 percent of the Jews in France escaped this fate, as Serge Klarsfeld, the most prominent Jewish public figure regarding the remembrance of the Holocaust in France, has regularly reminded us.[2] Michael Marrus and Robert Paxton did not take into account this reality—the fact that a vast proportion of the Jewish population of France did survive, giving the country one of the highest survival rates in Nazi-occupied Europe. It is a blind spot in the general historiography of the Holocaust in France.

How can this "French paradox"[3] be explained, since it is generally assumed that the French were strongly antisemitic? I have recently addressed this question thoroughly, and this chapter draws heavily on these findings.⁴ There is no forgetting of all those Jews who were deported from France and who perished in Auschwitz. However, as researchers, we must also take into account the other side of the statistics, as Suzanne Zuccotti suggests in her pioneering work.⁵ Without forgetting the dead, what is at stake today is an investigation into why 25 percent of the Jewish population in this country perished while 75 percent survived. This result is particularly striking since in the other countries in Western Europe, the proportion of Jews exterminated is far higher: 75 percent in the Netherlands and 45 percent in Belgium. Yet, the Wehrmacht invaded these three countries at the same time (May and June 1940), and the "final solution" was enacted at the same time (June 1942). So how can we explain the French case?

We already have the important comparative work done by Pim Griffioen and Ron Zeller.⁶ In this chapter, I will propose a new paradigm as a complement to their own findings, based on a multifactorial analysis. I shall begin with a schematic presentation of the multiple factors that contributed to the survival of Jews in France. Then I shall outline the notion of *social reactivity* to highlight why it is necessary to view the "bystander" no longer merely as a historical actor whose actions were potentially harmful but as one whose actions and inactions in many instances could and did have a positive effect on the victims of persecution, at least in the French context.

A Plurality of Factors

Serge Klarsfeld has estimated that 330,000 Jews were in France in the fall of 1940 and that 80,000 were dead by the end of the war.⁷ Consequently, this means that 250,000 were still alive in 1944. However, from 1940 to 1944, some of them managed to cross the Swiss or Spanish border. Ruth Fivaz-Silbermann has estimated that 13,500 Jews succeeded in reaching Switzerland.⁸ I am not aware of a comparably comprehensive study for Spain. Certainly, significantly fewer people crossed this border since it was more difficult to do so than to get through the one in the Geneva region. Consequently, approximately 220,000 Jewish people were in France in 1944. How can we explain this figure? I suggest at least seven complementary reasons.

The high survival rate of Jews in France is partly because of external factors and primarily to the success of the Allied landings in June 1944. This liberation of France from the Nazi domination, which happened later in Belgium and the Netherlands, had positive consequences, not least for the Jews. Their lives nonetheless remained in peril until the

Germans were chased out of France. Yet, the decisive influence of this military operation should not prevent us from acknowledging the other factors particular to France that restricted the Holocaust in this country.

The second factor is geographical. The territory of France is much larger than that of Belgium or Holland, and the country was occupied only partially. As early as 1940, many Jews fled the occupied zone for the "free zone," and from there, a small number managed to cross into Switzerland or Spain. The vast majority, however, stayed in France. While some remained at home, or nearby, a large number spread out into rural areas reaching even the most remote regions.[9] Yet, we must also take into account the attitude of the inhabitants of the regions where the Jews arrived. In the countryside, almost everything comes out eventually; "strangers" to a region do not go unnoticed. If the French population had indeed been very antisemitic, the worst could have been feared: tens of thousands of Jews would have been denounced and deported. Nevertheless, and crucially, this large-scale denunciation did not occur.

A third issue is the history and the severity of French antisemitism. The hypothesis of virulent antisemitism in France is challenged by the fact that three-quarters of the Jews there survived. Nevertheless, there is no doubt that antisemitism was a reality in France from the nineteenth century onward. Yet, it is hard to distinguish between antisemitism and xenophobia, especially in the 1930s, as Julian Jackson pointed out.[10] After all, France had one of the highest, if not the highest, rates of immigration in the world during the 1930s. In any event, the formation of the Vichy government in 1940 was the political incarnation of this hostile attitude toward the Jews at the worst moment: under German eyes.

However, it is questionable whether the French population largely shared this state-generated antisemitism. Marrus and Paxton are convinced that this was indeed the case, and they based their argument on reports coming from the French prefects.[11] Nevertheless, research done by other historians such as Asher Cohen[12] and Pierre Laborie[13] (the most prominent French historian on public opinion under Vichy), whose work is also based on the Vichy archives, has strongly contested their views. Whatever the importance of antisemitism, the key issue is chronology. When mass arrests occurred in the summer of 1942, people were moved, even shocked, when the police picked up women, children, and elderly people. There is now a consensus among historians, including Marrus and Paxton, that these dramatic events marked a turning point in the population, as expressed by the archbishop of Toulouse, Jules Saliège, who found the courage to say openly in his cathedral, on 23 August 1942: "These Jews are men, these Jewesses are women; these aliens are men and women. Not all is permissible against them ... , against these fathers and mothers. They belong to mankind."[14]

From 1942 until 1944, the most horrific period with mass deportations and mass murders, ordinary people helped Jews through innumerous, often inconspicuous, small gestures of protection: the concierge, the police officer, the teacher, the farmer, the priest or the pastor. Had antisemitic prejudices disappeared? Not necessarily. Denunciation or indifference to persecution continued to exist until the end of the German occupation, yet it might not always have determined people's actions. Thus, a Catholic priest, Christian de Chaunac, said to a Polish Jewish woman, Marthe Hoffnung, who wanted to cross the demarcation line with her children in 1942, "I don't trust Jews, but I am going to help you."[15] In this instance, as in many others, compassion prevailed over stigmatization.

We can distinguish four types of compassionate "bystanders" offering such ephemeral aid: the one who gives shelter, the guardian angel, the forger, and the *passeur* (someone smuggling people across the border into another country). This mutual aid was not always disinterested: if you had more money, you had more chances of pulling through. Yet, the notion of social reactivity to be discussed later can be useful in describing the large variety of small gestures that emerged particularly during the critical years of 1942 to 1944. It does not presuppose a unanimity of the social fabric; other elements remained indifferent to the fate of the Jews or even approved of what was happening to them. Such small gestures were of course demonstrated beyond France as well (and comparative research is much needed here), but my hypothesis is that they took on a particular breadth given the country's history.

Fourth, looking at the percentage of Jews who survived in France, two numbers are really striking: almost 90 percent of French Jews survived the Holocaust, compared with 60 percent of the foreign Jews.[16] It is striking that so many French Jews survived. In addition, the rate of survival among foreign Jews is relatively high compared to the terrible losses in other countries. How can we explain the difference between the survival rates of French and foreign Jews? First, we certainly need to look back at French history. In 1791, in the wake of the French Revolution, France was the first country in Europe to emancipate the Jewish people. Jews in France were eventually assimilated, and some moved up to become part of the nation's elite. Especially in view of their extraordinary commitment and their contributions to the nation, they perceived the Vichy Jewish Statute (3 October 1940), as a political betrayal. Nevertheless, to evade persecution, many French Jews could rely on social resources. Because of their cultural assimilation, many non-Jewish French citizens might not even have perceived of them as Jews. In general, French Jews had much wider networks of friends and acquaintances than foreign Jews. They spoke French and were more likely to be able to rally both professional and other contacts as persecution intensified. Some succeeded better than others. Bob Moore and Ben Braber have come to the same conclusion when looking at the role social ties played and to what extent the Jewish people could take advantage of them to avoid anti-Jewish laws.[17] To the contrary, foreign Jews, recently arrived in France, did not speak French very well and rarely had social networks. They were much more vulnerable and indeed became the first target of the Nazis and the Vichy regime.

Most of the efforts of rescue organizations, Jewish as well as Christian ones, concentrated on protecting and saving these foreign Jews, starting with their children. Vivette Samuel, a Jewish volunteer social worker in the Rivesaltes internment camp in 1941 who became president of the Children's Welfare Agency in 1979, wrote in her memoirs after the war that "8,000 to 10,000 children, in general of foreign origin, were able to be put in safety thanks to Jewish organizations that allowed them to emigrate abroad, to cross into Switzerland or Spain, or via clandestine networks to be put in the care of families or non-Jewish institutions (convents, lay institutions)." It must be acknowledged, she adds, that:

> Although we have no statistics on this point, that French Jewish families or families with French cultural backgrounds had an easier time placing their children in safety, so long as they realized in time the danger of being "born Jewish." It was mainly the children of foreign families whom the Children's Welfare Agency had to take charge of and hide.[18]

Consequently, the citizenship parameter is highly significant regarding the rate of survival.[19] This difference between national and foreign Jews can be noticed in other countries as well. In this regard, there is no French exceptionalism.

The sixth factor pertains to the structural nature of the occupier-occupied relationship. After the French military defeat in June 1940, Hitler had a strategic interest in keeping a national government in France in place. The offer of state "collaboration" proposed by Marshal Philippe Pétain to Berlin thus perfectly suited Hitler's goals. As a result, the Vichy regime was established in the southern part of France, on one-third of its territory, the poorest part of the country, quickly called the "free zone." It turned out that the existence of this "free zone" had a favorable effect on the fate of the Jews in France. It belongs to what

I call the "structural factors" of Jewish survival. Of course, the "free zone" was not established to save Jews, but Jewish people used it as an opportunity to escape their Nazi persecutors. One piece of evidence supporting this claim is that all Jewish organizations left Paris in 1940 to move to the "free zone." In the "free zone," Vichy certainly issued antisemitic laws, like those implemented by the Germans in the occupied part of the country.

However, many personal accounts indicate that living conditions for the Jews there were less severe than in the northern zone under German military rule, even after the German invasion (apart from the Vichy camps, such as Gurs or Rivesaltes, where the living conditions were extremely harsh). To give an example, the yellow star was never imposed in the "free zone" because the Vichy regime refused to introduce it. However, in December 1942 the obligation to have a "J" on one's identity card was issued but did not trigger the same stigmatizing effect. Furthermore, the upholding of a national government offered the Vichy regime some latitude, especially regarding the Jewish question. This can be observed in other countries as well, keeping in mind the political configuration of Nazi Europe in general. As I have argued in *Unarmed against Hitler*,[20] a comparative analysis highlights at least two major trends: (a) In countries where the national state was almost destroyed (such as Poland or Ukraine) or where national administrations were directly under German control (such as the Netherlands or Belgium), the rate of Holocaust losses are in general very high; and (b) In countries that maintained a national government either as allies of Berlin (such as Italy, Romania after 1942, Hungary until 1944, and Bulgaria), or as states that collaborated (such as Denmark or France), the Germans put pressure on these governments to convince them to do the "dirty work" in order to resolve the "Jewish question." Sometimes these governments were cooperative, and sometimes not. Thus, this explains why in these countries the rate of Holocaust losses was much lower.[21]

What are the consequences of this general approach to explaining Vichy policy? During the two first years of the occupation, the Vichy regime was truly cooperative with the Germans. The Bousquet-Oberg agreement of early July 1942 was proof of this, as it involved the arrest of forty thousand Jews by the French police. However, it should be remembered that Vichy arranged for Jews with French citizenship to be excluded from this mass arrest. Thus, the Vel d' Hiv roundup of July 1942 only targeted foreign Jews, even if some of the captured and deported children had been born in France. Yet, after several bishops' protested in the summer of 1942, the Vichy regime was more reluctant to arrest Jews. This moral protest had the effect of thwarting Vichy's part in the "final solution," as Wolfgang Seible has demonstrated.[22]

We indeed have some evidence for such a shift. Serge Klarsfeld has found a German report of a meeting on 2 September 1942, between the SS officers Carl Oberg and Helmut Knochen with Pierre Laval that states:

> Regarding this opposition of the clergy, President Laval has requested that, if possible, we do not make new demands on the Jewish question. In particular, we must not impose a priori numbers of Jews to be deported. We had, for example, demanded that 50,000 Jews be delivered for the 50 trains at our disposal. He asks us to believe in his total honesty when he promises to settle the Jewish question, but he says he is not going to deliver Jews as though they were merchandise at a *Prisunic* [supermarket] where you can get whatever products you want, all for the same price.[23]

Consequently, the number of Jews arrested and deported from France decreased significantly thereafter. In 1942, the most terrible year, 41,951 Jews were deported from France. Yet, in 1943, this number fell to 17,069, not least because of a less intense involvement of the Vichy police in arresting Jews. In that regard, a significant change occurred in 1943 after Petain's refusal at the last minute, on 1 September, to rescind the French citizenship of Jews who had obtained it starting in 1927. If this new Vichy law, pushed by the Germans, had been adopted, thousands of Jews would have been immediately arrested and deported. In 1944, however, the figures increased again: 16,025 Jews who had arrived from France perished in Auschwitz during the first six months of the year. Nevertheless, the Vichy regime at that time was almost dying: It had evolved into a militia state, fully under German control.

To sum up, the latitude that Vichy had because of its structural position as a collaborative government, nonexistent in the Netherlands and in Belgium, is certainly part of the reason why 75 percent of the Jews in France survived. I share here Griffioen and Zeller's analysis with regard to the evolution of the Vichy government on the "Jewish question." This government at first provided efficient support for Nazi measures but also, to some extent and for a limited time, hampered the deportation process.[24] In 1943, this same government functioned as somewhat of a passive shield because of a less cooperative stance toward the Nazis and their anti-Jewish policies. However, Vichy lost all autonomy in 1944 when Joseph Darnand was appointed Secretary of State for Law Enforcement at the request of the Germans. Consequently, arrests and deportations of Jews—both French and foreign—increased once again.

Discussing factors and structural determinants, one can easily forget, as a seventh factor, the human beings at the center of this drama: those men, women, and children persecuted as Jews. Concretely, what did they do to circumvent the Vichy and Nazi persecutions? How did they react when the first anti-Jewish German and French laws were issued? If they lost their job, how did they manage to survive? How did they react when the yellow star was introduced? And when the mass arrests started, what did they do to protect their children? Many clichés prevail regarding the living conditions of the Jews in France during World War II, such as that Jews in this country survived only when they stayed in hiding places, cellars, attics, or secret apartments (such as Anne Frank's family did in Amsterdam). However, this was not the general situation in France. We certainly know of some cases like this, such Albert Grunberg, a Jewish hairdresser in Paris who spent twenty-two months hidden in a maid's room.[25] Yet, most Jewish people in France did not hide like this over months or even years. They often went out, sometimes with forged identity documents. Others lived legally wearing their yellow star in Paris, passing by German soldiers in the streets without being arrested or shot immediately.[26]

Jews in France were nevertheless in grave danger, since some were indeed arrested and deported as late as July and August 1944, including children. Yet, thanks to the diverse daily survival tactics of the Jewish people, many were able to survive. As stated earlier, this would not have been possible without the various acts of solidarity and complicity on the part of the French non-Jewish population. If the survivors' accounts, on which my argument is based partly, frequently testify to the indifference or even hostility they had to endure, they also underline the importance of those small gestures of support that they could take advantage of to assure their survival. Let us now try to grasp the nature and evolution of these acts.

Small Gestures: Social Reactivity and Civil Resistance

By "small gestures," I mean a word or an act, often from a stranger expressing a sign of solidarity with someone who is persecuted, a stranger who, in certain situations, can save you from the worst, starting with arrests. The ephemeral nature of these small gestures frequently crops up in witness accounts. One example is the journalist Jacques Biélinky, who wrote regular reports about the life of Jews in Paris from the summer of 1940 to December 1942, the date of his deportation to Auschwitz.[27] They also can be noticed in personal diaries, such as the one written by Hélène Berr from June 1942 to 1944, when she was arrested and deported.[28] Postwar Jewish memoirs also refer to these small gestures, for instance, in those of the historian Annie Kriegel[29] or of Arlette Scali,[30] in which she seeks, after the war, to understand how she and her family were able to escape the Holocaust.

While each witness relates distinct anecdotes specific to their personal experience, the points of convergence in the stories are often striking. These small gestures of help coming from strangers seem less frequent at the beginning of the occupation, although Biélinky notes a discrete kindness of Parisians toward Jews as early as autumn 1940.[31] However, from the summer of 1942 on, these individual demonstrations are more noticeable and unambiguous. Following the German-imposed obligation to wear the yellow star in the occupied zone, some people expressed their sympathy and support for passersby in the street wearing the yellow star In Paris in particular, some students wore a fake yellow star with the inscription "Swing" or "Negro" or put a sort of yellow star around their dog's neck.[32] Subsequently, the mass arrests during the summer of 1942 diversified and radicalized these attitudes of support, partly transforming them into illegal acts. In short, the whole period from the summer of 1942 to the end of the war favored the evolution of these small gestures of protection for the Jews, and not only them. Let us illustrate a variety of them and discuss their meaning according to the different contexts.

The most elementary, the most "microscopic" dimension of the small gesture is not even a gesture, but a sign, an expression on the face, a smile, a glance. The tales of witnesses attest to this, whether they are recalled fifty years later or written about at the time. Take, for example, Hélène Berr, a young student in Paris, using similar words to talk of the glance from a passerby who sees her with her yellow star. She writes: "Another woman in the street smiled at me. That brought tears to my eyes, I do not know why."[33] Such signs of sympathy in no way protect the individual wearing the star, but they serve to reassure them of their human condition. In a way, the friendly expression of a stranger helps them live by reassuring those stigmatized of their own dignity, to prevent them from slipping into the precipice of their exclusion. There are also the more obvious small gestures that attract attention, such as the incident in the Paris Métro in 1942 described by Annie Becker in company of her friend Roger:

> I still remember the scene where Roger and I are alone in the last carriage of the train because I was wearing the yellow star. Roger, his cap of a future college student ostentatiously worn on his head, wrapped his arm round my

shoulders. He did it with such an air of defiance that, in the face of this young Christian wildly protecting his very small, very young Jewish fiancée, the travelers, far from being shocked, were touched and smiled. Into this last carriage stepped deliberately, among the rest, travelers who meant to demonstrate their silent sympathy for those persecuted.[34]

Another example is the case of Guy and Simon Benayoun, who remember their teachers reprimanding the other students for hectoring them and trying to pick a fight. A classmate of Simon's had greeted him the first day he wore his star by saying, "So you're a Jew, are you?" and slapping him in the face, prompting the teacher to stand up for the Benayoun brothers. Or we could point to the women from the Catholic order Little Sisters of the Poor who took care of young Adrien Borstein and his sister without charge while their family was hiding in Figeac.[35]

In certain critical situations, small gestures uttered at the right, life-saving moment offered crucial advice: "Don't go home!" or "Turn right whatever you do!"—spontaneous instructions that, if they were followed, saved Jews from being arrested. Arlette Scali remembers such an episode. One day in October 1942, she went to Toulouse with her children's governess, Miss Jeanne, to do some shopping. At midday, they lunched in a café, and Arlette left the main room to go to the toilet, which was in the basement.

> I had locked myself in and I suddenly heard a noise, shouts and chairs being turned upside down. Someone knocked on the door, "Don't move; don't open." I heard a lot of commotion. I didn't move and stayed where I was for half an hour. After a while, someone came and said, "It's over. They're gone." There had just been a round up and people had been arrested. They'd taken away all those they thought were Jews.[36]

Arlette Scali and Miss Jeanne did not return to Toulouse for the rest of the occupation. In other cases, lies were used to warn of or ward off danger. Several accounts report that adults sometimes spontaneously protected children who were alone. For example, in the train that was taking Joseph and Maurice Joffo, two Jewish children fleeing to Dax, the Germans carried out a raid. As they did not carry a passport, the two children asked a priest traveling in the same compartment to help them. The priest protected them by telling the Germans that the two children were traveling with him. Then he took them to have breakfast at the station buffet, gave them his name and address, and, when Maurice thanked him for lying in order to help them, said, "I wasn't lying; you were with me the same as all children in the world are. That's one of the reasons why I'm a priest—to be with them."[37]

We could continue the list of these instances of small gestures, which no longer appear small when we consider their positive effects on the lives of individuals. Thus, from the most spontaneous to the most determined, there were a thousand and one ways for bystanders to be of assistance to individuals persecuted for being Jews. Of course, these small gestures can also occur between people who already know each other more or less well. In such a case, the help rendered appears more "normal," even though it was not, since it was given to persecuted individuals at a time of constant intimidation. An example in point is neighbors who agree to keep the belongings of families forced to leave, as was the case for the Benayouns, a Sephardic Jewish family, who hid their furniture at their upstairs neighbors' in case further confiscation of property took place. Similarly, the Beckers, who left Paris just after the Vel d'Hiv roundup, entrusted their belongings to neighbors and then recovered them with no difficulty at the end of the war.[38] Unfortunately, there are other examples showing just the opposite reaction.[39]

Francine Weiller was already well known to the Paris shopkeepers in her district. When Jews only had the right to do their shopping between 3 and 4 p.m. in the shops and from noon on in the markets, a time when there was little left to buy, she explains that the shopkeepers she was used to buying from asked her every day what she needed for the following day and kept aside the food she asked for.[40] Or take the case of Albert Grunberg, the aforementioned Jewish hairdresser who hid in a maid's room in the Rue des Écoles in Paris for twenty-two months (until the liberation at the end of August 1944). He was lucky enough to receive a visit from a neighbor, Mr. Chabanaud, who dropped by from time to time to have a chat and break his isolation. Another neighbor, Mr. Bon, before leaving for the "free zone," gave his flat keys to Grunberg so that he could go and get warm and listen to the radio from time to time.[41]

The most remarkable is the variety of small gestures coming from strangers during coincidental encounters. Their interventions in the lives of Jews who were fleeing seem largely to have been a matter of chance. In fact, these people only made a brief appearance in their lives; they appeared and then they vanished. Joseph Joffo's book about his childhood in occupied France is full of such episodes.[42] Did the people they met always know they were Jews? Most likely not. Joseph and his brother Maurice looked to them like children left to their own devices. For example, at a moment when they were particularly tired, the two young boys met an aristocrat, Count de V, who took them in his carriage to Aire-sur-l'Ardour. In another incident, a fellow traveler on a train gave them some bread, slices of veal, eggs, and biscuits. At one point, Joseph worked for a farmer in Saint-Agnès and Maurice for a butcher in

Menton. Meanwhile, the Joffo children traded all sorts of goods on the black market with Italian soldiers. This book reads like the adventures of two kids lost in the war, always at risk because they were Jews. Still, they managed to survive from day to day, since they turned out to be resourceful and managed to get out of tricky situations, often thanks to the help of strangers. This book displays the main characters of assistance: the guardian angel, the one who gives shelter, the forger and the *passeur*, as well as those anonymous contemporaries who played secondary but nonetheless crucial roles, coming to give them a helping hand at the right moment and free of charge as they boys were always short on money. Those who helped very rarely asked to be paid, except for the smugglers.

This help without payment, considered by the one helping as a "normal" gift, a natural gesture that cannot and should not be bargained, is also mentioned in several other accounts. When Marthe Hoffnung, a young Polish Jew, decided to organize her family's escape to the "free zone," a former colleague at the Poitiers town hall, Mr. Charpentier, spontaneously offered to provide her with forged identity documents. Yet, when she wanted to compensate him, he burst into tears:

> "Miss Hoffnung," he eventually said in a voice shaken with emotion, "I don't want your money. That isn't why I offered you my services ... I'm acting at my level and within my means," he carried on. "You can't stay with your arms crossed. If I've got the chance to help a family escape from the Germans, I must seize it. If I stayed indifferent, I couldn't look myself in the mirror.'[43]

At the same time, the prevalence of such incidents of benevolent help must not be exaggerated, since some people did indeed ask to be paid. Hospitality beyond a brief period was by no means always free of charge. You sometimes had to pay a high price to have credible forged documents. And whoever had the position or influence to act as a potential guardian angel was definitely open to money. Police officers or officials could be bribed to show less vigilance at the right moment. Thus, if you had the means to pay, you stood a far higher chance of pulling through until the end of the war. Moreover, we can understand why Jewish organizations, which sought to help the poorest immigrant Jews, starting with their children, needed substantial amounts of money, if only to defray the cost of accommodations. Yet, to reduce the issue of help and protection in occupied France to a question of financial resources means shifting the focus away from what is essential here. Sooner or later, rich and poor were faced with persecution. Thus, to stand a chance of pulling through, Jews needed to seek the help of others, known to them or not. Thus, networks of informal solidarity emerged, always fragile but nevertheless offering spaces of relative peace and quiet in the turmoil.

Elie and Arlette Scali's story, as recounted by the latter, is a significant example of this. The family certainly did not lack financial resources, and they had good social ties, even within the Vichy government. Still, as persecution intensified, the Scalis had to break up and sometimes rely on the help of strangers. At the end of her memoirs, Arlette Scali reckons that between 1940 and 1944, no fewer than thirty-nine people contributed to saving their lives.[44] These included her husband's colleagues and workmates, prewar friends, people they met at Graulhet near Albi, where the Scalis settled, servants, particularly the nurses, as well as the inhabitants of the little village of Murat where she sought refuge with her children in December 1943. Among the people mentioned, some worked for the Vichy regime; others were resistance fighters or people without political commitment. One might have expected her to point out one name in particular that she recognized as one of "the Righteous." Yet, such is not her frame of mind. It all appears as if she wanted to express her gratitude to a multitude of unknown people who, from her point of view, enabled them to avoid the worst.

Since these gestures of solidarity, both active and passive, occurred between people who did not necessarily know each other, how can the survival of this family be explained? Observing the evolution of the population's state of mind can help us understand why and how they multiplied and spread. Pioneering studies have affirmed that "saviors" were characterized by an altruistic personality that developed because of their upbringing during childhood. Research on the saviors and later on "the Righteous" also attempted to elucidate their motives, Christian in majority, humanist in general.[45] Such psychological explorations have marked a first stage in the investigation of this matter but appear too limited and can even be considered problematic if we neglect the factors and contexts shaping these situations; without them, we are unable to fully understand the culture of helping gestures. There is hesitation over appropriate vocabulary to describe this individual behavior, which at the same time had a collective dimension.

The particular sociopolitical context can help us understand the variety of gestures of help coming from individuals who were very different one from the other. I believe that the notion of social reactivity is relevant here, inspired by my earlier research on civil resistance. I speak of *reactivity* because individuals spontaneously "did something" without liaising with each other, hence their multifarious small gestures, and I speak of *social* because the simultaneous occurrence of such conducts cannot be explained by merely pointing to individual stories. In my view,

France experienced an important movement of social reactivity between 1942 and 1944, in the sense that many individuals, without necessarily knowing each other, brought help to other individuals whom they mostly did not know but whose situation of distress, or at least great vulnerability, they nonetheless realized. This phenomenon is in itself a remarkable event of this historical period. However, as stated earlier, this is not to argue for a French exceptionalism, since we can observe similar moments of social reactivity in countries such as Belgium, Denmark, or Bulgaria as well.

These gestures of mutual help, small or large, are not, strictly speaking, acts of resistance in the accepted sense of the word. They do not derive from a political, organized will to struggle, with or without arms, against the occupier and the Vichy regime. Is it still legitimate to refer to them as acts of "resistance"? When, in one and the same country and period, farmers start increasingly putting up Jewish children, priests and vicars taking care of fleeing refugees, young women taking children into foster care, work inspectors closing their eyes to the origin of certain workers, social workers falsifying records, school headmasters enrolling pupils under false names, doctors taking Jewish staff into their services, municipal employees producing forged French identity documents for foreigners, police officers warning those they are supposed to arrest, *passeurs* taking risks to transport their little groups to their destination across the border—did not all these anonymous actors in a broader sense work together and, without concertation, in the same direction? Did they not, every one of them, testify to the mind-set of a civil society in resistance, of a state of civil resistance?

I have previously introduced the notion of civil resistance to qualify this sociohistorical pattern.[46] In light of the relevant historiography on resistance, however, such an approach appears too broad: it ultimately dilutes the notion of "resistance" strictly speaking, for which it is necessary to retain the dimension of a deliberate, organized practice. It is indeed more appropriate to speak of civil resistance when referring to organized, deliberate, and premeditated mutual help to assure safety through the actions of Jewish and non-Jewish organizations. Thus, to account for the vague phenomenon of spontaneous gestures of mutual help, by definition not coordinated, I suggest the notion of social reactivity. Of course, social reactivity and civil resistance are interrelated; people often moved from spontaneous help to organized help. Once it is set up, civil resistance can and must benefit from the occasional "helping hand" to make a success of its actions and to develop.

Thus, it is "small gestures" that make up the vague sphere, the living matter, of social reactivity. They are not the results of a central command, and their number cannot be counted like soldiers in an army. Social reactivity is both spontaneous and volatile. The small gestures of help toward the persecuted can come from very different people, including individuals belonging to the sphere of collaboration. These gestures are discreet in two senses: they are more often than not silent and inconspicuous. Still, social reactivity was sufficiently widespread in French society all across the country that, from the summer of 1942 onward, front doors and schools opened to take in persecuted Jews. These scattered helper groups or individuals operated as a protective, nourishing "cloak" over people designated as pariahs. A multitude of people played a minor or decisive, but never negligible, role to enable this supportive "social cover" to stand firm despite the adversity and risk of denunciation. Whether or not we know them as "Righteous among the Nations," we should pay homage to all of those, whose names, motives, and actions history will never fully tell.

In all regimes, even the most terrifying, there are individuals offering such humane gestures toward those who are stigmatized and threatened. They certainly occurred in all Nazi-occupied countries of Europe. Yet, their importance naturally depended on the ferocity of the local regime toward the persecuted Jews. In Poland, these gestures of help toward the Jews were very rare. Whoever was caught hiding a Jew was executed on the spot, often along with the other members of the family, and the house often burned down. This was not true in France (and Western Europe as a whole), where there was no German instruction to punish those assisting Jews. In the occupied zone, a decree of 10 December 1941 issued by the Paris Prefecture of Police required "Jewish or non-Jewish persons accommodating Jews" to declare this at the police station "within twenty-four hours." This repressive measure could have justified reprisals against residents who ignored it, but such was not the case. On the other hand, German repression was ruthless against those who helped an Allied pilot, this behavior being considered an act of war; it was generally punished by deportation. In the eyes of the Germans, protecting a Jew was not equivalent to rescuing an Anglo-American soldier (or a member of the Allied intelligence network).

The final months of the war in France, however, resulted in operations of extreme violence against civilians, notably in Corrèze and Périgord. These reprisals were carried out by SS divisions (particularly the *Das Reich* and *Brehmer* divisions) in the wake of their ruthless hunt for resistance fighters deemed "terrorists." Their operations indiscriminately targeted civilians as well, including Jews and those who accommodated them.[47] For its part, during the summer of 1942, the Vichy regime expressed its will to take repressive measures against whoever sought to help Jews. An instruction issued by René Bousquet on 10 August 1942 repressed "the escape of administrative internees and complicity as regards escape," and provided for three months to one year imprisonment for hiding escapees from camps. Yet, this text does not seem to have been applied. In fact, the Vichy regime, apart from a few exceptions, did not show any strong determination to repress those who brought help to the Jews. This does not diminish the value of the gesture or of the act of the one who helped, for they still felt they were doing something forbidden and were haunted by the fear of reprisals. But usually there were none.

So, is it appropriate to speak of a French singularity? Can it be explained by the majority rejection in public opinion of open antisemitic persecution by the summer of 1942? Did the multiplication of small gestures of help and disobedience in favor of the Jews, particularly from this date on, prevent both the occupier and the Vichy authorities from "going too far" in the persecutions and arrests? Even if there were other seemingly indiscernible factors preventing, for example, the Germans from deporting the fifty thousand Jews who still lived in Paris in 1944 while at the same time deporting all Jews from Warsaw or Amsterdam, the notion of social reactivity adds significantly to our understanding of the "French paradox."

The Bystander versus the Social Reactivity Approach

Based on these considerations, I am not comfortable with Hilberg's notion of the bystander. The term is too vague and general. His trilogy "perpetrators, victims, and bystanders" is too limited, even with the fourth category of rescuers. It implies that the behavior of almost the entire non-Jewish population of Europe was mainly characterized by passivity and indifference. In the French case, we have seen that the historical and social context is much more complex. Certainly, a part of the population was indifferent to the Jews or even hostile to them. However, another part tried to help them, mainly from the summer of 1942 onward. Thus, we need a different approach to describe this evolution and the notion of social reactivity as an informal, unorganized reaction of some people to help the Jews seems useful.

This is not, however, an alternative notion to Hilberg's categorization but rather a complementary one adding sophistication and nuance. It does not mean that these non-Jewish helpers were ready to help Jews because they loved them. I have not found any proof that people helped Jews in France because they knew that their final destination was

Auschwitz. This is an unrealistic hypothesis. Consequently, Bart van der Boom's argument, which holds that the willingness of the non-Jewish Dutchmen to help "would have been larger, much larger perhaps," had they known that the "Jews were killed upon arrival" and that, thus, "ignorance of Auschwitz" is not a "sufficient" but a "necessary" explanation for bystander behavior is not convincing.[48] The French case (among others) demonstrates that some non-Jews were prepared to do something to help Jews while remaining unaware of the specifics of mass murder.

Looking back at their lives, many surviving Jews came to the following conclusion: "I was lucky." Obviously, they have in mind the fate of those who perished in the gas chambers. In comparison, they think that their survival was a miracle. Even though such a statement is perfectly understandable from a psychological point of view, it must be questioned and discussed from an historical perspective. In a given moment, in a given situation, they might simply have been lucky because they could have been arrested and then deported. However, it was not only a matter of luck. These survivors benefitted from the emergence of an informal social network of informal support, to ease the fate of the persecuted and hunted people in occupied France, mainly between the summer of 1942 and the summer of 1944. This network was sustained by a spirit of non-collaboration and disobedience. However, from the perspective of the victims, this network providing ephemeral moments of relative security was fragile. Nobody was entirely safe from the risk of denunciation or a French or German police raid. That is why Jewish lives remained fundamentally threatened until the last German soldier had left the country.

Jacques Semelin is Professor of History and Political Sciences at Sciences Po, Paris and Senior Researcher at the Centre de Recherches Internationales. A leading scholar in the field of genocide studies, he has received a transdisciplinary education in contemporary history, social psychology, and political science. His research focuses on Holocaust, genocide, and mass violence in a comparative perspective (*Purify and Destroy*, 2007), as well as on forms of civil resistance in contexts of extreme violence (*Unarmed against Hitler*, 1994). Forthcoming: *The Survival of Jews in France (1940–1944)* (Oxford University Press/ Hurst, 2018).

Notes

1. Michael R. Marrus and Robert O. Paxton, *Vichy France and the Jews* (New York, 1981).
2. Serge Klarsfeld, *La Shoah en France, tome 1: Vichy-Auschwitz* (Paris, 2001).
3. Maxime Steinberg, "Le paradoxe français dans la solution finale à l'Ouest," *Annales* 48, no. 3 (1993): 583–594; Jacques Semelin, "Le paradoxe français," *Le Débat* 183, no. 1 (2015): 186–192.
4. Jacques Semelin, *Persécutions et entraides dans la France occupée, comment 75% des Juifs de France ont échappé à la mort* (Paris, 2013).
5. Suzanne Zuccotti, *The Holocaust, the French, and the Jews* (New York, 1993).
6. Pim Griffioen and Ron Zeller, "Comparing the Persecution of the Jews in the Netherlands, France and Belgium, 1940–1945: Similarities, Differences, Causes," in *The Persecution of the Jews in the Netherlands, 1940–1945: New Perspectives*, ed. Wichert ten Have (Amsterdam 2012) 55–92.
7. Klarsfeld, *La Shoah en France*, 359–360.
8. Ruth Fivaz-Silbermann, " The Swiss Reaction to the Nazi Genocide: Active Refusal, Passive Help," in *Resisting Genocide: The Multiple Forms of Rescue*, ed. Jacques Semelin, Claire Andrieu, and Sarah Gensburger (New York/London, 2011), 247–258.
9. See for the diversity of these internal migrations between 1940 and 1944 and two unpublished maps showing their dispersal in the Southern zone (based on the Vichy archives): Semelin, *Persécutions et entraides*, 121, 140.
10. Julian Jackson, *France: The Dark Years, 1940–1944* (Oxford, 2001).
11. Marrus and Paxton, *Vichy France and the Jews*, 181–182. This position is shared by Renée Poznanski; see *Jews in France during World War II*, trans. Nathan Bracher (Hanover, 2001).
12. Asher Cohen, *Persécutions et sauvetages: Juifs et Français sous l'Occupation et sous Vichy* (Paris, 1993).
13. Pierre Laborie, *L'opinion française sous Vichy: Les Français et la crise d'identité nationale— 1936–1944* (Paris, 2001).
14. See his biography, Jean-Louis Clément, *Monseigneur Saliège, archevêque de Toulouse, 1929–1956* (Paris, 1994), 215. On the evolution of the Catholic church about the 'Jewish Question" see also: Sylvie Bernay, *L'Église catholique et la persécution des Juifs en France (1940–1944): entre incompréhension et sauvetages*. PhD diss., Pantheon-Sorbonne University, 2010. All translations are my own unless otherwise indicated.
15. Marthe Cohn and Wendy Holden, *Derrière les lignes ennemies: Une espionne juive dans l'Allemagne nazie* (Paris, 2009), 101–102.
16. Klarsfeld, *La Shoah en France*.
17. Bob Moore, *Survivors: Jewish Self-Help and Rescue in Nazi-Occupied Western Europe* (Oxford, 2010); Ben Braber, *This Cannot Happen Here: Integration and Jewish Resistance in the Netherlands, 1940–1945* (Amsterdam, 2013).
18. Vivette Samuel, *Sauver les enfants* (Paris, 1995), 162.
19. For more evidence, see Semelin, *Persécutions et entraides*.
20. Jacques Semelin, *Unarmed against Hitler: Civilian Resistance in Europe, 1939–1943* (Westport, CT, 1993).
21. With similar conclusions, see recently Timothy Snyder, *Black Earth: The Holocaust as History and Warning* (London, 2015).
22. Wolfgang Seibel, *Macht und Moral: Die Endlösung der Judenfrage in Frankreich, 1940–1944* (Konstanz, 2010).

23. Cited in Klarsfeld, *La Shoah en France*, 179–180.
24. Griffioen and Zeller, "Comparing the Persecution of the Jews," 77.
25. Albert Grunberg, *Journal d'un coiffeur juif à Paris sous l'Occupation* (Paris, 2001).
26. On these living conditions of the Jews in Paris in 1944, we especially have the Maurice Brenner report of the *American Jewish Joint Distribution Committee* (available at the Ghetto Fighters'House—Israel: Z.1064.FC.106).
27. Jacques Biélinky, *Un journaliste juif à Paris sous l'Occupation: Journal, 1940–1942* (Paris, 2011).
28. Hélène Berr, *Journal: 1942–1944* (Paris, 2008), 254.
29. Annie Kriegel, *Ce que j'ai cru comprendre* (Paris, 1991).
30. Arlette Scali, *Les justes de Graulhet* (Paris, 2007).
31. Biélinky, *Un journaliste juif*, 77.
32. These students were arrested, brought to Drancy, and liberated a few weeks after. See Cédric Gruat and Céline Leblanc, *Ami des juifs, résistants aux étoiles* (Paris, 2005).
33. Berr, *Journal*, 58.
34. Kriegel, *Ce que j'ai cru comprendre*, 50.
35. Semelin, *Persécutions et entraides*, 586.
36. Scali, *Les Justes de Graulhet*, 115.
37. Joseph Joffo, *Un sac de billes* (Paris, 1973; Paris, 1998), 115–117. Citations refer to the 1998 edition.
38. Jean-Jacques Becker, *Un soir de l'été 1942: Souvenirs d'un historien* (Paris, 2009), 78.
39. Shannon L. Fogg, *Stealing Home, Looting, Restitution, and Reconstructing Jewish Lives in France, 1942–1947* (Oxford, 2017).
40. Semelin, *Persécutions et entraides*, 590.
41. Grunberg, *Journal d'un coiffeur*, 352.
42. Joseph Joffo, *A Bag of Marbles* (Chicago, 2000).
43. Cited by Marthe Hoffnung in Cohn and Holden, *Derrière les lignes ennemies*, 101–102.
44. Scali, *Les justes de Graulhet*; Semelin, *Persécutions et entraides*, 594.
45. Samuel P. Oliner and Pearl M. Oliner, *The Altruistic Personality: Rescuers of Jews in Nazi Europe* (New York, 1988).
46. See Semelin, *Unarmed against Hitler*.
47. See, e.g., Guy Penaud, *Les Crimes de la division Brehmer* (Périgueux, 2004).
48. Bart van der Boom, "Ordinary Dutchmen and the Holocaust: a summary of findings," in Have, *The Persecution of the Jews in the Netherlands*, 48. On this Dutch debate, see Thijs, this volume.

Bibliography

Becker, Jean-Jacques. *Un soir de l'été 1942: Souvenirs d'un historien*. Paris: Larousse, 2009.

Bernay, Sylvie. *L'Église catholique et la persécution des Juifs en France (1940–1944): entre incompréhension et sauvetages*. PhD diss., Pantheon-Sorbonne University, 2010.

Berr, Hélène. *Journal: 1942–1944*. Paris: Tallandier, 2008.

Biélinky, Jacques. *Un journaliste juif à Paris sous l'Occupation: Journal, 1940–1942*. Paris: Éditions du Cerf, 2011.

Boom, Bart van der. "Ordinary Dutchmen and the Holocaust: A Summary of Findings." In Have, *The Persecution of the Jews in the Netherlands*, 29–52.

Braber, Ben. *This Cannot Happen Here: Integration and Jewish Resistance in the Netherlands, 1940–1945*. Amsterdam: Amsterdam University Press, 2013.

Clément, Jean-Louis. *Monseigneur Saliège, archevêque de Toulouse, 1929–1956*. Paris: Beauchesne, 1994.

Cohen, Asher. *Persécutions et sauvetages: Juifs et Français sous l'Occupation et sous Vichy*. Paris: Éditions du Cerf, 1993.

Cohn, Marthe, and Wendy Holden. *Derrière les lignes ennemies: Une espionne juive dans l'Allemagne nazie*. Paris: Tallandier, 2009.

Fivaz-Silbermann, Ruth. "The Swiss Reaction to the Nazi Genocide: Active Refusal, Passive Help." In *Resisting Genocide: The Multiple Forms of Rescue*, edited by Jacques Semelin, Claire Andrieu, and Sarah Gensburger, 231–243. New York/London: Columbia University Press, 2008.

Fogg, Shannon L. *Stealing Home, Looting, Restitution, and Reconstructing Jewish Lives in France, 1942–1947*. Oxford: Oxford University Press, 2017.

Griffioen, Pim, and Ron Zeller. "Comparing the Persecution of the Jews in the Netherlands, France and Belgium, 1940–1945: Similarities, Differences, Causes." In Have, *The Persecution of the Jews in the Netherlands*, 55–92.

Grossman, Vasily. *Life and Fate*. New York: New York Review Books, 2006.

Gruat, Cédric, and Céline Leblanc. *Ami des juifs, résistants aux étoiles*. Paris: Edition Tirésias, 2005.

Grunberg, Albert. *Journal d'un coiffeur juif à Paris sous l'Occupation*. Paris: Les Éditions de l'Atelier, 2001.

Have, Wichert ten. *The Persecution of the Jews in the Netherlands, 1940–1945: New Perspectives*. Amsterdam, 2012.

Jackson, Julian. *France: The Dark Years, 1940–1944*. Oxford: Oxford University Press, 2001.

Joffo, Joseph. *A Bag of Marbles*. Chicago: University of Chicago Press, 2000.

———. *Un sac de billes*. Paris: Hachette, 1998. First published 1973 by J.-C. Lattès (Paris).

Klarsfeld, Serge, ed. *La Shoah en France, tome 1: Vichy-Auschwitz*. Paris: Fayard, 2001.

Kriegel, Annie. *Ce que j'ai cru comprendre*. Paris: R. Laffont, 1991.

Laborie, Pierre. *L'opinion française sous Vichy: Les Français et la crise d'identité nationale—1936–1944*. Paris: Editions du Seuil, 2001.

Marrus, Michael R., and Robert O. Paxton. *Vichy France and the Jews*. New York: Schocken Books, 1981.

Moore, Bob. *Survivors: Jewish Self-Help and Rescue in Nazi-Occupied Western Europe*. Oxford: Oxford University Press, 2010.

Oliner, Samuel P., and Pearl M. Oliner. *The Altruistic Personality: Rescuers of Jews in Nazi Europe*. New York: Free Press, 1988.

Penaud, Guy. *Les Crimes de la division Brehmer*. Périgueux: La Lauze, 2004.

Poznanski, Renée. *Jews in France during World War II*. Translated by Nathan Bracher. Hanover: Brandeis University Press, 2001.

Samuel, Vivette. *Sauver les enfants*. Paris: Liana Levi, 1995.

Scali, Arlette. *Les justes de Graulhet*. Paris: Editions Scali, 2007.

Seibel, Wolfgang. *Macht und Moral: Die Endlösung der Judenfrage in Frankreich, 1940–1944*. Konstanz: University Press, 2010.

Semelin, Jacques. "Le paradoxe français." *Le Débat* 183, no. 1 (2015): 186–192.

———. *Persécutions et entraides dans la France occupée, comment 75% des Juifs de France ont échappé à la mort*. Paris: Seuil & Les Arènes, 2013.

———. *Unarmed against Hitler: Civilian Resistance in Europe, 1939–1943*. Westport, CT: Praeger, 1993.

Snyder, Timothy. *Black Earth: The Holocaust as History and Warning*. London: Bodley Head, 2015.
Steinberg, Maxime. "Le paradoxe français dans la solution finale à l'Ouest." *Annales* 48, no. 3 (1993): 583–594.
Zuccotti, Suzanne. *The Holocaust, the French, and the Jews*. New York: Basic Books, 1993.

Part III
Memory

CHAPTER 13

ORDINARY, IGNORANT, AND NONINVOLVED?
THE FIGURE OF THE BYSTANDER IN DUTCH RESEARCH AND CONTROVERSY

Krijn Thijs

In the past two decades, the Netherlands have witnessed some fierce debates about the interpretation of "ordinary Dutchmen" during the Holocaust. What was the level of involvement of the broader Dutch society in the genocidal conflict between the (German) Nazis and the (Dutch) Jews? How important was the social context for the high deportation rates from the occupied Netherlands? The zone of "the bystander" thus has become a major battlefield in Dutch historiography.[1] This chapter discusses a recent episode in this debate: the controversy surrounding the 2012 book *"Wij weten niets van hun lot": Gewone Nederlanders en de Holocaust* ("We don't know anything about their fate": Ordinary Dutchmen and the Holocaust). Author Bart van der Boom polemically directs his study against the "myth of the guilty bystander," which he ascribes to the Dutch memorial culture. Resisting the impression that the Dutchmen were "a nation of indifferent bystanders" because they had not been able to save the Jews, Van der Boom sets out to reconstruct these bystanders' point of view.[2] Extensive analysis of diaries leads him to conclude that to contemporaries, resistance to the deportations often seemed unwise and the unprecedented killing methods of the Holocaust were unknown. Initially, the book was praised for its rich material and "brave" conclusions. It was awarded the prestigious Dutch Libris History Prize for the best public history book of 2012. Then, a critical wind started to blow within and outside academia, ultimately leading to a series of bitter public clashes between professional colleagues.[3]

The controversy reveals much of the explosive potential of giving central voice to the people in history we usually call "bystanders." This concerns issues both of methodology and of cultural memory. Methodological questions arise because bystanders build an inherently instable category, tending to dissolve as soon as studied more closely. While the bystander's basic characteristic is that they seem to not be involved in the violence between perpetrators and victims, it is still only in the genocidal process that bystanders become bystanders. The group is therefore constituted by a paradoxical non-relation, and by focusing on them specifically, their manifold manners of involvement result in dissolving the category altogether. Furthermore, by asking why bystanders did not become rescuers, historians set out to write histories of things that did not happen, spawning counterfactuals and the semantics of "missed opportunities." As the Dutch case demonstrates, problems of definition and demarcation arise everywhere: Where does genocide begin? Who are "ordinary people?" What is "normal" behavior?

Of course, such conceptual questions are intricately linked to questions of morality and memorial culture. This is not just about the analytical identification *of* the bystander. Fundamental to this are also different ways of identification *with* the bystander. What does their story mean to present-day readers, scholars, and students? How do "they" in the past relate to "us" in the present? Why are we still blaming or defending, or even just studying them? Answers of course not only depend on "them" but also on "us." Thus, the debate recaptured here serves as a case in point to observe underlying dynamics and possibly some fundamental shifts in Holocaust historiography and culture at the beginning of the twenty-first century. Who are "we"? A nation of Dutchmen? A community based on values? A series of different subgroups, each tied to different pasts? These are, of course, open political questions. They directly transgress historiography, whether scholars like it or not. Moreover, the figure of the bystander still is a powerful emblem in present political discourse. Therefore, debating diaries of "ordinary Dutchmen" and their "knowledge" of the Holocaust is ultimately also a proxy discussion for talking about challenges of the present world.

Diaries and Knowledge

It is a commonplace claim that most contemporaries in the West did not know but *could have* known about the killings in the East, often implying that they *should* have known.[4] While it is one thing to reconstruct what knowledge was available in occupied Europe, it is quite another to explore its reception: how were different sources and rumors about the mass murder actually judged and adapted in different local settings? For the Dutch case, there happens to be an unusually rich empirical base for questions of this nature, since a large body of wartime diaries has been collected from 1945 onward. This enables historians to study how both attitudes and imaginations about the ongoing murder in Poland were actually recorded by very different Dutch people. This is the way in which Bart van der Boom (Leiden University), a leading expert on wartime diaries in the Netherlands, proceeded. From more than two thousand available diaries, he created a sample of 164 to study what "ordinary Dutchmen" imagined to be "the fate" of the deported Jews. Among the diarists are 53 Jewish and 111 non-Jewish Dutchmen. Van der Boom does not claim his sample of diaries to be representative in a strict sense. In case of convergence, however, he likes to generalize from them and to conclude about overall "popular opinion."

Discussing a rich spectrum of examples, Van der Boom demonstrates how most of the non-Jew diarists felt compassion with the persecuted Jews. The influence of antisemitism on these sentiments was limited, the study argues, although "antisemitic stereotypes show up in 24 of 111 diaries written by gentiles." Yet, the self-consciousness of a tolerant nation created distance to the German racial policy and methods. Thus, "antisemitism as it existed in the Netherlands during the occupation did not imply support for German antisemitic measures. There can be no doubt that Dutch bystanders were not indifferent to the fate of the victims. Very few people ignored the persecution, virtually nobody supported it."[5] Indeed, Van der Boom presents much empirical support for this conclusion, sketching general feelings of indignation, fear, and powerlessness in the Netherlands. Moreover, the diary entries offer an innovative and previously unknown bystander perspective on the persecution of the Jews, "in a way," as Christina Morina writes, "that can until now only rarely be found in scholarly literature."[6]

Turning to the question of knowledge, Van der Boom's material also shows that most of the diarists, Jews and non-Jews alike, "did not at all feel certain about the fate of the Jews." The destination of the deportation trains was described consistently "as unknown and mysterious."

Referring to victims of earlier roundups and punishments, people had learned that being sent to concentration camps in the Nazi empire as a prisoner usually was fatal. Everybody also knew about the murderous plans to exterminate the Jewish people. To be sure, in speculating what was happening in Poland, many Dutch diarists use terms such as "mass murder," "extermination," or "destruction" of the Jews. However, Van der Boom maintains that these words meant different things to the contemporaries than to our present world, since most of these diarists "also imagined the Jews would be put to work and housed in camps."[7] Therefore, he sets out to reconstruct in more detail what people knew, hoped, and feared about the East, collecting all sorts of rumors, illusions, and reassurances—including reports about gas, medical experiments, reserves, work programs, and resettlements. From the overall inconsistencies in the diary entries, he concludes that their authors apparently didn't realize that "extermination" meant being killed in Poland immediately.

In the course of his argument, Van der Boom portrays most of the diary authors as uncertain and often helpless. He tends to downplay their knowledge and instead stresses contradictions and doubts. In his words, most Dutchmen did understand that the Jews were bound to die, but "they could not imagine the unprecedented speed and efficiency with which the Germans set to realize their aim."[8] This aspect of time and tempo is probably the most relevant new factor presented here. Since people imagined "the East" in terms of deadly working camps and were unaware about the gas chambers, Van der Boom reasons, they supposed there would be time left in the East. Jews invested in their preparations for deportation, following the illusion that one ought to be strong, healthy, and well equipped to survive until the end of the war. These are important aspects for any assessment of the situation of the contemporaries—albeit more with regard to the victims than to the bystanders.

Up to this point, this is a new and relevant account, and one based on original sources. However, the conclusions that Van der Boom draws from his analysis are surprising—and highly controversial. After dozens of pages depicting people deliberating, hinting, understanding, fearing, and erring about what happened in the East, the conclusion he offers is that the Dutch population in fact had "no knowledge" at all:

> To sum up: there was no knowledge regarding the fate of the Jews, there were only rumors and suspicions and fears. The dominant expectation was not determined by concrete information, which was scarce, diffuse and inconsistent, but by plausibility and the limits of imagination. It was taken

for granted that the Germans were committing a serious and sinister crime; obvious these virulent antisemites did not transport an entire people to Poland to treat them well there. One did not need to know anything concrete to assume that the intention was to "exterminate" the Jews—that is what the Germans themselves boasted. What did not seem plausible, however, what most contemporaries did not even consider, was the reality of industrial genocide.[9]

While the larger argument of this summary is hardly disputable, the one-sided label "no knowledge" leaves many readers puzzled, myself included. It ignores all differentiations in the diaries themselves, dismissing beliefs, fears, and rumors as unreliable to the contemporaries, subsuming everything under the bulk category of "ignorance." At the end of his book, Van der Boom even adopts the highly problematic German phrase *nicht gewusst* to the Dutch situation, along with its suggestive echo: had they known, they would have acted differently. This apologetic framing potentially has discredited his entire research project and, unfortunately, a younger research field studying experiences of "bystanders" in general.

Criticism and Controversy

It is no surprise, therefore, that the study caused a lot of debate. Directing his conclusions against the supposed "myth of the guilty bystander," and against the "holy indignation" surrounding Holocaust research,[10] the author himself expected "to get controversy. They will say I am defending indefensible behavior."[11] Indeed, the debate has been fierce, multilayered, and complex; I shall distinguish four basic topics of discussion. A first type of criticism was put forward by Dutch ego-document specialists, claiming it is simply impossible to study knowledge through diaries or to study diaries in series.[12] Diaries usually are studied in a micro-historical way to reconstruct the biographies of their individual authors. However, research on social knowledge based on series of ego-documents has been quite fruitful in other cases, for example, regarding German *Feldpost* letters.[13] It is hard to argue that certain sources would principally block certain questions—rather, it is up to historiography to find proper methods using them.

Yet, this type of criticism is reinforced by Van der Boom's own rejection of sophisticated methodic reflections. Abstaining from thorough theoretical analysis about the relationship between the thoughts and feelings of an author and the text of the diary itself, he just assumes basic coherence between the two. Van der Boom prefers to deal with his diary material in a "casual and conformable way," based on empathy with every author.[14] Such statements ignore (and in fact even dismiss) large parts of scholarly diary research, which invests a great deal of energy reaching for the deeper layers of texts.[15] Accordingly, Van der Boom's outspoken preference for what might be called no-nonsense approaches and common-sense reasoning account for many of the reservations precisely among ego-document scholars.

In the result, however, Van der Boom has demonstrated most of these principal objections to his sources as groundless. From his diary sample, he has collected a large amount of highly relevant entries on the persecution and deportation of the Dutch Jews. The study proves it is indeed possible to pursue questions about knowledge based on serial (not quantitative or schematic) diary research. Refraining from building typologies among his diarists, he conducts individual analyses—initially sticking close to the material and then reaching for generalizations.

A second point of discussion concerns the definitions that Van der Boom employs. Portraying "the average Dutchman" as ignorant, the study unsurprisingly uses a very limited definition of knowing about the Holocaust, namely "subjective certainty" of "murder upon arrival." Such an approach reduces the Holocaust to the gas chambers in Poland—far away from the Netherlands—and does not allow for alternative wordings, inconsistencies, and beliefs as ways of contributing to "knowledge." This is so narrow a definition that indeed nobody knew: not a single Dutch diary reflects this kind of knowledge of the Holocaust, neither non-Jewish nor Jewish. Therefore, his conclusion is very strong, Van der Boom argues. On the contrary, critics such as Remco Ensel, Evelien Gans, and Christina Morina hold that this shows that such a definition of knowledge is flawed in the first place.[16] Indeed, the fact that there is not a single knower left in the entire study should make one wary: This definition is apparently defining things not present in the historical reality. After all, for most Europeans, certainty about the existence of the gas chambers is a postwar novelty, as is, by the way, the term "Holocaust" itself. For that matter, Van der Boom succeeds in confirming the truism that contemporaries did not know what we know today. Yet, so wide a gap between the central working category and the empirical material is rather problematic—for any kind of historical research.

If framed in such a way, definitions fully dictate research outcome. Van der Boom forced his results into an unsatisfactory yes/no game, replacing one popular generalization ("everybody knew") with another ("nobody knew"). The real challenge would of course be to develop definitions that allow for differentiations *within* the body of source material—not outside it. Consequently, the author employs term "ignorance" in an unusually broad sense. In fact, it serves as a bulk category encompassing all "normal" people in the Netherlands, or at least every single one of his 164 diarists. Yet many diary entries actually suggest that some contemporaries built an uncertain, instable, and inconsistent body of knowledge about what happened in "the East," partly accurate and partly erroneous. Only in the world of Van der Boom's narrow definitions do these people become people who did *not* know about the Holocaust.[17] Not knowing about the gas chambers, however, is one thing, being "ignorant about the Holocaust" is quite another.

A third type of criticism directly concerns the category of the bystander. It has been formulated most clearly by Guus Meershoek: "Who are ordinary Dutchmen?"[18] There is no proper discussion of the category in the book, except that the author also includes Jews as "ordinary Dutchmen" until the onset of deportations in 1942. Yet we do not know very much about the specific behavior of the "ordinary" diarists, nor how "ordinary" this was in historical reality, as Meershoek pointed out. We only know that Van der Boom did not discuss diaries from active Dutch Nazis as such, who, because of their behavior, might have been better informed and more involved in this history. It might be for this reason that people who consciously and radically *act* in this history—be it on the side of perpetrators or of resistance—seem to be underrepresented in this bystander study. All this tends to create a confusing and tautological overlap between normality, ordinariness, noninvolvement, not acting, and not knowing.[19]

Among the diarists, we encounter never any "average" person but instead only specific individuals. All of them, just by their writings, contribute to Van der Boom's schematic body of supposedly ignorant people, whereas their individual behavior and position becomes a matter of secondary importance. This leads to abstractions from the historical context and makes the entire argument elusive, as Meershoek stressed. In this case, "average" remains an artificial and obfuscating category, a category beyond control, one present only in the work of the historian, not in history. This is a central challenge for the study of bystander populations.

A fourth point of controversy, developed by Jaap Cohen among others, concerns the supposed importance of knowledge for behavior.[20] To Van der Boom, the case is clear. "Understanding that deportation would lead to an *immediate* death was crucial to an adequate response," he states.[21] Therefore, "people didn't know enough to be able to act adequately."[22] Thus, he offers the overall "ignorance" about the gas chambers as "explanation" for the passiveness and obedience among Dutch Jews and non-Jews alike. The argument even goes so far as to spell out its counterfactual variant, suggesting that more action would have been taken and more hiding places would have been offered if more knowledge had been available. "With a full grasp of the seriousness of the situation," he writes, "the willingness of non-Jews to take risks for the Jews" would not have been unlimited, yet "higher—much higher perhaps." And: "If the fate of the Jews would have been clear, more non-Jews would have taken the risk of resistance."[23]

Of course, this is highly speculative—and to some readers, it is an offensive whitewashing of the passive bystander. Yet counterfactuals in themselves are not objectionable, as they are a common instrument in historiography.[24] The present case nevertheless is not convincing, as a closer look at the argument might demonstrate. To trace the impact of lacking knowledge, Van der Boom turns to the situation of the Dutch Jews, from the summer of 1942 onward, as the deportations from the Netherlands started. He zooms in on their decisions whether to hide, and observes in their diaries a panic-ridden uncertainty about how to react to the fatal call for deportation. Should one obey and follow the order to the deportation train and hope for the best? Or should one try to find a hiding place and hope not to be detected or betrayed? Van der Boom now finds it "fascinating" that "this choice was hard to take."[25] He points at the rather low information level in the occupied Netherlands: Dutch Jews were unaware that deportation almost certainly meant death. Indeed, some of them explicitly complained about the lack of certainty and clarity of their situation. Judging from their diaries, some of the victims (the exact number remains contested) even did have opportunities to hide but found the risks too high: they thought that they might be more likely to survive in "the East" until liberation. "On the assumption that 'extermination' was a time-consuming affair, it was imaginable that obedience was safer than resistance, that deportation offered better chances of survival than hiding."[26] At this point, the lack of precise knowledge about the extermination camps is painfully striking, indeed. Here, the counterfactual reasoning ("had they known ...") seems to lend support for the argument. It is unclear how many Jews actually took the "wrong" decision. Yet many critics generally are troubled by the discussion of the Jews' trapped position in terms of "choices," "options," and "risk calculations"—I will come back to that.

More importantly, however, all these considerations apply to the victims, not to the non-Jewish population. The situation of Dutch non-Jews of course was entirely different. To them, the question was whether to take personal risks by helping their Jewish neighbors, or to not intervene and remain a safe and passive bystander. However, about these decisions and about the impact of knowledge or the lack thereof on their decisions, the 111 non-Jewish diaries are far less informative than the 53 Jewish ones. Therefore, Van der Boom is forced to substitute reasoning with conjecture: "If Jews could decide that resistance was an unwise choice, gentiles could, too—not out of indifference or antisemitism, but out of a faulty appraisal of the risks; out of ignorance of the true nature of deportation."[27] This extension of Jewish dilemmas to the non-Jewish bystanders proves to be both unconvincing and highly controversial.[28] To me, it is rather telling that barely any non-Jewish diary deliberates about whether to give hiding places. Apparently, this choice was not as pressing as it was for the victims themselves, who were forced to choose between two evils. Many non-Jews were compassionate, but they had other sorrows as well, as Van der Boom documents extensively. A comparative look at the victims cannot provide evidence for the argument that more knowledge would have turned more bystanders into rescuers; any transfer of conclusions needs support by empirical proof and cannot come instead of it. According to his staunchest critics, Van der Boom at this point "uses the Jewish diarists to fill up a crucial hiatus in his knowledge and employs the Jews as legitimation for the bystanders' behavior."[29]

On a closer look, the entire study in fact lacks positive examples of the supposed correlation between knowledge and behavior. To those "rescuers" helping the Jews on behalf of their "firm conviction," knowledge about the gas chambers apparently did not play any role.[30] Here, other factors and considerations were decisive. People who offered hiding places did so for all sorts of different reasons, including earning some extra money. Yet it remains fully unclear how "sure knowledge" (if available) would have played into these deliberations, since none of the diaries discussed displays the supposed mechanism.[31] As for the victims themselves, diary analysis shows that the vital decisions whether to search for hiding places were often painstaking deliberations over long periods of time. The factual impact of knowledge on the outcome, however, remains empirically undocumented. There are no examples of Jews first getting new information about "the East" and then deciding to go in hiding. Rather, the diaries suggest that the "behavior" of the victims depended on many other things and factors, such as the attitude of friends and family, the availability of hiding places, and personal character. Van der Boom would have a case in point if he just could offer a single diary where the supposed knowledge-action-connection is actively working. Apparently, there is not.

Since knowledge about the Holocaust in Van der Boom's definition is entirely absent in the occupied Netherlands, and since there were nevertheless all forms of behavior, ranging from passivity to hiding and active resistance, it seems rather hard to claim some sort of correlation between the two. Therefore, the explanatory power of knowledge in this definition for actual bystander behavior seems to be rather limited.

To summarize the discussion up to this point: the study doubtless has much to say about Dutch bystander experiences under occupation. It is hard to claim after Van der Boom's analysis that people in the occupied Netherlands were aware that most of the deported Jews were going to be killed immediately. Additionally, the charge that "the Dutch people" did not care about, or even secretly welcomed, the persecution of the Jews seems to be untenable. Van der Boom's material and arguments in these cases are dense and convincing, and I see a heavy onus of proof with those historians still sticking to them. The study indeed demonstrated that many Dutch bystanders did not look away but instead consciously registered what was happening to the Jews—and that many of them felt dazed, angry, and powerless and unable to act.

However, it remains heavily disputed to what extent lacking certainty about the nature of the direct killings can account for this passivity. The interpretation Van der Boom proposes—that "ignorance" is "crucial," something like the missing link in Dutch Holocaust historiography—turns out to be unconvincing. On the contrary, for many readers *"Wij weten niets van hun lot"* still leads to the conclusion that Dutch people actually knew quite a lot about the Holocaust. In such a reading, contrary to the author's argument, the detailed diary analysis might indeed affirm popular unease about the topic: Why did no more resistance and help for the Jews occur in the Netherlands given the level of all available observations, rumors, and beliefs about "the East?" Consequently, even the supportive reviewers of the book end up posing troubling questions—to most of his colleagues, Van der Boom has pushed his case too hard. A reader's letter posed the question very bluntly: "This is the core question: If witnessing serious injustice, when are you going to throw yourself into it? Only when the victims are being gassed?"[32]

Moralism, Worldview, and Identification

In course of the discussion about *"Wij weten niets van hun lot,"* issues of moral judgments have repeatedly fueled new responses. One critic rejected the concluding bystander apology as "implausible," "irresponsible," and even "demagogic."[33] Van der Boom proved to be highly sensitive to such assessments, immediately dismissing them as an "almost moral disqualification of my argument."[34] The most radical critique came from the historians Evelien Gans (who passed away in 2018) and Remco Ensel, specialists in Jewish history and antisemitism. After the book had been awarded the Libris History Prize, they launched a review in the weekly *De Groene Amsterdammer*, with a scathing critique of both Van der Boom's approach and its success among Dutch readers. They regarded the author as downplaying differences between Jewish victims and Dutch bystanders and neglecting the role of antisemitism in Dutch history. Gans and Ensel added a broad range of targeted conceptual criticisms. The central one was the accusation that this book had violated the "Jewish perspective." By confusing victims' and bystanders' experiences, it manifested an apologetic "tendency" in Dutch historiography. The piece was an overall disqualification of the prize-winning book and its author.[35]

Van der Boom likewise responded with indignation, in turn attacking the alleged moralism of his opponents. In their anger, he wrote, the critics had failed to evaluate his empirical analysis and instead directly scandalized the "uncomfortable" results, "acting not like critical colleagues, but as political-moral executioners. That is ... way beyond the scholarly order."[36] Moral criticism he finds "academically irrelevant. Gans rejects conclusions as unwelcome, without considering whether they are true." Gans "is interested not in the past but only in present memory," he claimed. "She fights not my results but my supposed agenda," and "her anathema poisons the discussion."[37] Sticking to his sources and repeating his results, he called most of the criticism ideologically motivated and refused to discuss the moral and conceptual underpinnings of his study. The clash proceeded in a series of articles, not without dwindling into personal disqualifications.[38]

This attitude, trying to separate "true" and "professional" historiography from an "activist" memory discourse, was hardly consistent. Van der Boom himself did not hesitate to delegitimize his critics and their agendas, accusing them of unprofessionalism and thus keeping the discussion at the ad hominem level. More importantly, his own analytical operations are not at all free of affects relating to Dutch memory cultures. To identify and debunk a "myth of the guilty bystander" in a scholarly study (and to blame a range of historians and opinion leaders for working on that myth) of course is itself an act of memory politics. Since the impulse for the project came from outside academia, *"Wij weten niets van hun lot"* indeed even demonstrates how close and how fruitful the relations between memory and history often are. Fair reflection on this entanglement seems all the more urgent, since it is precisely in the translation of the scholarly research back to public audiences that Van der Boom's analysis loses plausibility, for example, by summarizing rich and manifold diary entries under the heavily loaded German wording *nicht gewusst*. In turn, it is not credible to play deaf when the provoked moral outrage indeed comes up. Contemporary history is public history *per definitionem*—and the integrity of our profession would be served by a serious consideration of its context.[39] In the following, I propose some avenues of interpretation.

In the Dutch controversy, the implicit key question is why so many people remained bystanders and did not act on behalf of the victims.[40] In other words, scholars set out to explain something that did *not* happen, which tells a lot about their frames of expectation. These frames of course differ: Historians do not necessarily agree about the standards of human behavior—about what "normal" events in the past pass unquestioned and which "deviances" needs to be explained. What is regular behavior? Is humanity principally "good" or "bad?" To what degree is a discrepancy between acting and knowledge "normal?" How do emotions and reason interact? Such questions are the reason why, recently, the a priori worldview of historians has become an explicit issue in Dutch debates. A newcomer to the field in 2001 was the first, by opening his "gray history" of occupation with a reference to his own "dark vision of humanity" in order to explain to the reader both his deviant moral framework and new narrative of the past.[41] Today, Dutch historians regularly appeal to their own or their opponents' human convictions—as to Bart van der Boom, he confesses to being an "optimist" and in turn finds his critics "misanthropic."[42]

Seen from this angle, one of the fundamental particularities of *"Wij weten niets van hun lot"* is the very rational universe of consistency and cost-benefit balances, which the author evokes. Many readers do not feel comfortable in this kind of setting—translating the predicament of the Dutch Jews into a position of binary "choices," "calculations," and "risk management." By just allowing rational behavior in his analysis, Van der Boom might be neglecting some essential aspects of human life—especially in emergencies. "Because the information base was so small," he writes, "similar people in similar situations could take very different decisions."[43] In other words, the expectation somehow seems to be that with enough knowledge, there would be no discussion, no doubt, and no differences possible: Jews would risk everything to resist deadly deportation and non-Jews would more generously offer hiding places. This, apparently, is the implicit "normal" standard that Van der Boom employs, expecting homogeneity among human beings on rational grounds. Some critics principally find this naive. To me, the long period of postponement and doubting of many Jews, rather than being an indication of cognitive uncertainty, also indicates a high level of emotional complexity, feelings of belonging, and even the irrationality of acting when one's life is in danger.

Such an emphatic perspective on the victims is exactly what many critics regard as lacking in the work of Van der Boom, where the Dutch bystander, and not the Jewish victim, is the central protagonist. This shift in perspective has major consequences for debates on remembering. After all, by adopting the everyday life experiences of bystanders and "ordinary people" as vantage points to tell Holocaust history, the genocide itself paradoxically might cease to be its narrative core. Critics refuse to allow "ordinary Dutchmen" a conceptual position outside the genocidal conflict. All this directly touches on the basic questions that Saul Friedländer and Martin Broszat discussed in 1987 and 1988: How normal can "normal" history be in relation to genocide? Not coincidentally, there are many references to their correspondence in present Dutch writings. Gans and Ensel often replayed the famous correspondence with a Dutch cast, voicing Friedländer and framing respective opponents in the role of Broszat and his poorly reflected historicization program.[44] When Van der Boom called for "a milder judgment" about the ignorant bystanders and encourages his readers to "complicate the guilt question," to "neglect taboos," and to "discuss with arguments,"[45] Gans and Ensel encountered him with fundamental distrust, defending the priority of the victim's points of view. While acknowledging the debate to be about "the centrality of the Holocaust in broader Dutch memory culture," their frame of reference still seemed to be the German *Historikerstreit*.[46] Such a paralleling of Dutch and German histories (and historiographies) has its own pitfalls, however, since it might blur differences between German occupiers and Dutch social majorities, losing sight of the Nazi perpetrators themselves. Still, the main question is: How legitimate is a narrativization of occupation history focused on the majority of non-Jewish Dutchmen? Is the historian bound to have empathy with the victims only or with "ordinary Dutchmen" as well? Or even with everybody? Questions such as these irrefutably will go on to cause further controversy in the future.

And they are hardly to be solved through academic methodology alone. Apart from moral orientations, these questions directly concern implicit identifications with the category of "ordinary Dutchmen." That is why the subject positions of historians on this field of research are discussed much more directly than usual. Bart van der Boom, like many others, does understand the Dutch bystander as someone belonging to himself. Therefore, critical readers immediately started to speculate about his family history, asking the author how his own grandfather behaved during occupation.[47] But the question of connectedness and historical voicing also acts on more sophisticated levels. While Van der Boom stated in an interview, "it's quite something to say that our grandparents found it all right that their Jewish neighbors were killed," Gans and Ensel posed questions about the "we" guiding that phrase: "Whose grandparents does he mean?"[48] Following Friedländer and Dominick LaCapra, they display a preoccupation with Van der Boom's "transgenerational" involvement with this history. That he denies any personal involvement makes them wary.[49] In this way, historians personally become entangled in the controversy, enhancing the likelihood of troublesome ad hominem arguments and biographical speculations.

Yet, rather than family ties, identification with "ordinary" bystanders usually runs along national lines. The explicit "we" in the present debate suggests a continuing community of (ordinary) Dutchmen then and now, culminating in his diachronic relief: "We didn't know."[50] Accordingly, it's the historiographical framework of the nation that is most hotly contested here. Some critics discard the affirmative self-evidence in which the subtext of the "tolerant nation" operates in this case. Apart from the urgent question of whether (and until/from when) the Dutch Jews belong to this "we," many of Van der Boom's opponents fundamentally reject any national preoccupation for the twenty-first century. Rather, they refer to other master narratives, such as human rights, civil responsibility, and emancipation. They also take the memory of the Holocaust as a central point of reference, deriving lessons about the dangers of passivity, discrimination, and exclusion.[51] In this type of narrative, the traditional Dutch values of tolerance shamefully turned into indifference towards the Jews during the Holocaust—and hence, self-criticism rather than national affirmation guides historical orientation here. Van der Boom sets out to challenge such an interpretation, both investing a great deal of effort into falsifying the indifference thesis and arguing that the self-imagination of the tolerant nation had real impact in favor of the victims. All this directly touches on the sensitive questions of whether "Dutch tolerance" is (or ever has been) a real thing, and whether anything of it is left today, to be mobilized in present debates about such issues as democracy, religious minorities, refugee policy, or social diversity.[52] Here, past and present come together, time and again fueling controversy, reflection, and new scholarship.

Conclusion

This chapter identified the troubled figure of "the bystander" as the categorical *enfant terrible* of recent Dutch historical debates. All discussants agree that Dutch resistance to the deportations of the Jews was relatively low. The basic tension is between historians stressing the co-responsibility of "ordinary Dutchmen" during the Holocaust, observing a regrettable lack of civil courage, engagement, and braveness to stand up more strongly in favor of their Jewish neighbors. Their opponents defend Dutchmen in the past by rehabilitating the powerless but not indifferent bystanders and by attacking the critics for their high level of moralism. In primarily focusing on the "ordinary Dutchmen," the German occupiers as perpetrators of the first order often seem to be pushed out of sight.

In this context, *"Wij weten niets van hun lot"* has successfully demonstrated that most people in the occupied Netherlands did not have a clear imagination of the gas chambers. Whether this "ignorance" is "crucial" to understanding their relatively passive behavior has been shown to be fundamentally disputable. Hence, it is quite unlikely that the book managed to bust the "myth of the guilty bystander." In writing history, let alone contemporary history, there is no "objective," "normal," or amoral stance delivering apologies for the bystander. In the end, questions of guilt and blame are directed to present society and its memoryscapes, rather than being issues of empirical, academic verification alone. Historians with their academic research serve and feed into these debates, and their work is pervaded by the social and cultural issues of their own world—especially when taking up such sensitive topics as bystander narratives of the Holocaust.

Krijn Thijs is Senior Researcher at the Amsterdam Institute for German Studies and Lecturer at the University of Amsterdam. He has published on political history, memory cultures, and historiography in Germany and the Netherlands. In 2006, he received his PhD from Amsterdam Free University. His dissertation about Berlin master narratives in the twentieth century was published as *Drei Geschichten, eine Stadt: Die Berliner Stadtjubiläen 1937 und 1987* (Böhlau Verlag, 2008). Currently, he is working on a book on professional and biographical upheavals in East German historiography after 1989. He also publishes on the experiences of Wehrmacht soldiers in the occupied Netherlands and on controversies in Dutch historiography. He is cofounder of a Dutch-German history workshop.

Notes

1. For introductions, see Wichert ten Have, ed., *The Persecution of the Jews in the Netherlands, 1940–1945: New Perspectives* (Amsterdam, 2012); Krijn Thijs,

1. "Niederlande—Schwarz, Weiß, Grau: Zeithistorische Debatten seit 2000, Version: 1.0", *Docupedia-Zeitgeschichte*, 3 June 2011, https://www.docupedia.de/zg/Niederlande_-_Schwarz_Weiss_Grau; Ido de Haan, "Imperialism, Colonialism and Genocide: The Dutch Case for an International History of the Holocaust," *BMGN-LCHR* 135, nos. 2–3 (2010): 301–327.
2. Bart van der Boom, *"Wij weten niets van hun lot": Gewone Nederlanders en de Holocaust* (Amsterdam, 2012), 15, 416, 428. Cf. Bart van der Boom, "Ordinary Dutchmen and the Holocaust: A Summary of Findings," in Have, *The Persecution of the Jews in the Netherlands*, 29–52; Bart van der Boom, "'Wij weten niets van hun lot': Gewone Nederlanders en de Holocaust," blog, http://wijwetennietsvanhunlot.blogspot.nl.
3. About the controversy, see also, Christina Morina, "The 'Bystander' in Recent Dutch Historiography," *German History* 32, no. 1 (2014): 101–111; Remco Ensel and Evelien Gans, "Historikerstreit: The Stereotypical Jew in Recent Dutch Holocaust Studies," in *The Holocaust, Israel and "The Jew": Histories of Antisemitism in Postwar Dutch Society*, ed. Remco Ensel and Evelien Gans (Amsterdam, 2016), 341–373.
4. Recently, for the Dutch case, see Frits Boterman, *Duitse daders: De Jodenvervolging en de nazificatie van Nederland (1940–1945)* (Amsterdam, 2015), 352–353. For Germany most clearly, see Bernward Dörner, *Die deutschen und der Holocaust: Was niemand wissen wollte, aber jeder wissen konnte* (Berlin, 2007).
5. Van der Boom, "Ordinary Dutchmen," 41–42.
6. Morina, "The 'Bystander,'" 108
7. Van der Boom, "Ordinary Dutchmen," 43.
8. Ibid., 44.
9. Ibid., 45.
10. Van der Boom, *"Wij weten niets,"* 15, 428 All translations are my own unless otherwise indicated.
11. Bart Funnekotter, "We wisten het niet," *NRC Handelsblad*, 24 April 2012.
12. Cf. Morina, "The 'Bystander,'" 105 ("there should be a plausible nexus between a historical question and the sources used to answer it."); Arianne Baggermand and Rudolf Dekker, "Egodocument als bron," *De Groene Amsterdammer*, 24 January 2013 ("tunnelvision"); Remco Ensel and Evelien Gans, "We weten iets van hun lot: Nivellering in de Geschiedenis," *De Groene Amsterdammer*, 12 December 2012 (diaries "cover up as much as they uncover").
13. Klaus Latzel, *Deutsche Soldaten: Nationalsozialistischer Krieg? Kriegserlebnis, Kriegserfahrung 1939–1945* (Paderborn, 1999).
14. Van der Boom, *"Wij weten niets,"* 116.
15. Marijke Huisman, Anneke Ribberink, Monica Soeting, and Alfred Hornung, eds., *Life Writing Matters in Europe* (Heidelberg, 2012); Thomas Etzemüller, *Biographien. Lesen—Erforschen—Erzählen* (Frankfurt, 2012).
16. Remco Ensel and Evelien Gans, "Wij weten iets van hun lot II," *De Groene Amsterdammer*, 6 February 2013; Morina, "The 'Bystander',"105.
17. Examples would be the diaries of Jewish Mirjam Levie, who even is writing in Bergen-Belsen, Jewish Etty Hillesum, or non-Jewish Willem van Rede, as discussed by Van der Boom, *"Wij weten niets,"* 264–270, 322–326, 332–334. See also Bart van der Boom, "Een antwoord aan mijn critici," *De Groene Amsterdammer*, 6 February 2013.
18. Guus Meershoek, "Een aangekondigde massamoord," *De Groene Amsterdammer*, 30 January 2013.
19. See also Remco Ensel and Evelien Gans, "De inzet van Joden als 'controlegroep,'" *Tijdschrift voor Geschiedenis* 126, no. 3 (2013): 388–396.

20. Jaap Cohen, "Hoe cruciaal is onwetendheid?" *NRC Next*, 3 April 2013. See the ongoing discussion at Van der Boom's blog, http://wijwetennietsvanhunlot.blogspot.nl.
21. Van der Boom, "Ordinary Dutchmen," 43.
22. Van der Boom, "Stap over het ongemak heen," *New Israelitisch Weekblad*, 8 November 2012.
23. Van der Boom, *"Wij weten niets,"* 415.
24. Nearly all predecessors of Van der Boom, writing history of the deportation of the Dutch Jews, posed the counter factual question: "Could it also have been different"? See the discussion by Conny Kristel, *Geschiedschrijving als opdracht: Abel Herzberg, Jacques Presser en Loe de Jong over de jodenvervolging* (Amsterdam, 1998), esp. 116.
25. Van der Boom, *"Wij weten niets,"* 388.
26. Van der Boom, "Ordinary Dutchmen," 47.
27. Ibid.
28. It also conflicts most clearly with research for the German case; see, e.g., Lars Fischer, "Public Knowledge of the Shoah in Nazi Germany," *Holocaust Studies* 14, no. 3 (2008): 159.
29. Ensel and Gans, "De inzet van Joden," 392. Van der Boom admits his analysis is limited here while sticking to his claim. Bart van der Boom, "Een opvallend gebrek aan argumentatie," *Tijdschrift voor Geschiedenis* 126, no. 4 (2013): 565, 567.
30. Van der Boom, *"Wij weten niets,"* 406–407.
31. Ibid., 387–406.
32. Reader's letters to *NRC Handelsblad*, 19 July 2013 (Peter R. Hein).
33. Anet Bleich, "Onwetend?" *Nieuw Israelitisch Weekblad*, 5 November 2012.
34. Van der Boom, "Stap over het ongemak."
35. Ensel and Gans, "Wij weten iets van hun lot II."
36. Quoted in Ensel and Gans, "De inzet van Joden," 389.
37. Bart van der Boom, "Ook die Joodse verraders zijn interessant," *De Groene Amsterdammer*, 9 January 2013.
38. Ibid.; Van der Boom, "Een antwoord aan mijn critici" ; Ensel and Gans, "Wij weten iets van hun lot II," ; Ensel and Gans, "De inzet van Joden"; Van der Boom, "Een opvallend gebrek."
39. See Gabriele Metzler, "Zeitgeschichte: Begriff—Disziplin—Problem, Version: 1.0" *Docupedia-Zeitgeschichte*, 7 April 2014, https://www.docupedia.de/zg/Zeitgeschichte.
40. See Mary Fulbrook, this volume.
41. Chris van der Heijden, *Grijs Verleden: Nederland en de Tweede Wereldoorlog* (Kampen, 2001), 15.
42. Bernard Hulsman, "Doe het niet, zou je willen schreeuwen," *NRC Handelsblad*, 12 July 2013.
43. Van der Boom, *"Wij weten niets,"* 401.
44. Ensel and Gans, "Wij weten iets van hun lot II." For earlier examples, see Thijs, "Niederlande—schwarz, weiss, grau." Similar references to Friedländer and Broszat guide are in Martijn Eickhoff, Barbara Henkes, and Frank van Vree, "De verleiding van een grijze geschiedschrijving: Morele waarden in historische voorstellingen," *Tijdschrift voor Geschiedenis* 123, no. 3 (2010): 322–339.
45. Van der Boom, "Stap over het ongemak heen."
46. Ensel and Gans, "Wij weten iets van hun lot II"; Evelien Gans, "Iedereen een beetje slachtoffer, iedereen een beetje dader," *De Groene Amsterdammer*, 28 January 2010; Ensel and Gans, "Historikerstreit."
47. Van der Boom, "Ook die joodse verraders."
48. Bas Kromhout, "Nederlanders hebben het nicht gewusst," *Historisch Nieuwsblad*, 24 April 2012; Ensel and Gans, "We weten iets van hun lot."

49. See Ensel and Gans, this volume.
50. Funnekotter, "We wisten het niet,"; Ensel and Gans, "Historikerstreit."
51. Eickhoff et al., "De Verleiding van een grijze geschiedschrijving"; Barbara Henkes, "De Bezetting revisited: Hoe van De Oorlog een "normale" geschiedenis werd gemaakt die eindigt in vrede," *BMGN-LCHR* 125, no. 1 (2010): 73–99. On pedagogics, see Henrik Edgren, ed., *Looking at the Onlookers and Bystanders: Interdisciplinary to the Causes and Consequences of Passivity* (Stockholm, 2012).
52. Nicole Colin, Matthias N. Lorenz, and Joachim Umlauf, eds., *Täter und Tabu. Grenzen der Toleranz in deutschen und niederländischen Geschichtsdebatten* (Essen, 2011); Bart van der Boom and Bas Kromhout, "PVV wil islam vervolgen en iedereen zwijgt," *De Volkskrant*, 23 November 2016.

Bibliography

Boom, Bart van der. "Een opvallend gebrek aan argumentatie." *Tijdschrift voor Geschiedenis* 126, no. 4 (2013): 564–570.

———. "Ordinary Dutchmen and the Holocaust: A Summary of Findings." In Have, *The Persecution of the Jews in the Netherlands*, 29–52.

———. *"Wij weten niets van hun lot": Gewone Nederlanders en de Holocaust*. Amsterdam: Boom, 2012.

Boterman, Frits. *Duitse daders: De Jodenvervolging en de nazificatie van Nederland (1940–1945)*. Amsterdam: De Arbeiderspers, 2015

Colin, Nicole, Matthias N. Lorenz, and Joachim Umlauf, eds. *Täter und Tabu: Grenzen der Toleranz in deutschen und niederländischen Geschichtsdebatten*. Essen: Klartext, 2011.

Dörner, Bernward. *Die Deutschen und der Holocaust: Was niemand wissen wollte, aber jeder wissen konnte*. Berlin: Propyläen, 2007.

Edgren, Henrik, ed. *Looking at the Onlookers and Bystanders: Interdisciplinary to the Causes and Consequences of Passivity*. Stockholm: Living History Forum, 2012.

Eickhoff, Martijn, Barbara Henkes, and Frank van Vree. "De verleiding van een grijze geschiedschrijving: Morele waarden in historische voorstellingen." *Tijdschrift voor Geschiedenis* 123, no. 3 (2010): 322–339.

Ensel, Remco, and Evelien Gans. "De inzet van Joden als 'controlegroep.'" *Tijdschrift voor Geschiedenis* 126, no. 3 (2013): 388–396.

———. "Historikerstreit: The Stereotypical Jew in Recent Dutch Holocaust Studies." In *The Holocaust, Israel and "The Jew": Histories of Antisemitism in Postwar Dutch society*, edited by Remco Ensel and Evelien Gans, 341–373. Amsterdam: Amsterdam University Press, 2016.

Etzemüller, Thomas. *Biographien: Lesen—Erforschen—Erzählen*. Frankfurt: Campus, 2012.

Fischer, Lars. "Public Knowledge of the Shoah in Nazi Germany." *Holocaust Studies* 14, no. 3 (2008): 142–162.

Haan, Ido de. "Imperialism, Colonialism and Genocide: The Dutch Case for an International History of the Holocaust." *BMGN-LCHR* 135, nos. 2–3 (2010): 301–327.

Have, Wichert ten, ed. *The Persecution of the Jews in the Netherlands, 1940–1945: New Perspectives*. Amsterdam: Vossiuspers, 2012.

Heijden, Chris van der. *Grijs Verleden: Nederland en de Tweede Wereldoorlog*. Kampen: Contact, 2001.

Henkes, Barbara. "De Bezetting revisited: Hoe van De Oorlog een 'normale' geschiedenis werd gemaakt die eindigt in vrede." *BMGN-LCHR* 125, no. 1 (2010): 73–99.

Huisman, Marijke, Anneke Ribberink, Monica Soeting, and Alfred Hornung, eds. *Life Writing Matters in Europe*. Heidelberg: Winter, 2012

Kristel, Conny. *Geschiedschrijving als opdracht: Abel Herzberg, Jacques Presser en Loe de Jong over de jodenvervolging*. Amsterdam: Meulenhoff, 1998.

Latzel, Klaus. *Deutsche Soldaten: Nationalsozialistischer Krieg? Kriegserlebnis, Kriegserfahrung 1939–1945*. Paderborn: Schöningh, 1999.

Metzler, Gabriele. "Zeitgeschichte: Begriff—Disziplin—Problem, Version: 1.0." *Docupedia-Zeitgeschichte*, 7 April 2014. https://www.docupedia.de/zg/Zeitgeschichte.

Morina, Christina. "The Bystander in Recent Dutch Historiography." *German History* 32, no. 1 (2014): 101–111.

Thijs, Krijn. "Niederlande: Schwarz, Weiß, Grau. Zeithistorische Debatten seit 2000, Version: 1.0." *Docupedia-Zeitgeschichte*, 3 June 2011. https://www.docupedia.de/zg/Niederlande_-_Schwarz_Weiss_Grau.

CHAPTER 14

HIDDEN IN PLAIN VIEW
REMEMBERING AND FORGETTING THE BYSTANDERS OF THE HOLOCAUST ON (WEST) GERMAN TELEVISION

Wulf Kansteiner

Media technologies are not neutral containers of historical content. Each technology has particular strengths, blind spots, and biases. The history of Holocaust memory would have evolved differently if historical novels or video games had been the new popular communication tool of the day in the middle of the twentieth century. As it was, from the beginning of public broadcasting in postwar Europe to the proliferation of cable networks at the onset of the new millennium, TV and Swastika enjoyed a close, symbiotic relationship based on compatible strategies of making sense of the world. In particular, during the heyday of TV culture in the late twentieth century, television was the quintessential vehicle for the exploration of fascism, war, and genocide, especially in Germany.[1] In part, the affinities on display between television and Nazi memory result from simple timing. TV became a key theater of cultural reflection at the very moment when European societies belatedly engaged in discussions about their communicative memories of World War II and shortly thereafter began crafting enduring transnational cultural memories of the war for future generations.[2] In addition, there were other, more sinister affinities at work that explain the intimate relationship between TV culture and NS memory. Throughout formerly occupied Europe and especially in Germany, viewers fascinated by the violent histories unfolding on their TV screens eerily resembled the citizens of a Nazi-dominated continent similarly enthralled by the violence erupting outside their homes. Television technology was an extraordinarily suitable communication apparatus for addressing memories of Nazism, because the little screen in the living room offered similar vantage points of noninvolvement as the living room window during the Nazi era. Window and screen neatly separated private from public sphere, "normal" citizens from Nazis and Jews and thus fostered seemingly clear-cut categories of belonging that rendered violence manageable. TV worked beautifully for the process of coming to terms with the past because it doubled and helped sidestep the key moral challenge of the Nazi years providing, yet again, a position of comfortable voyeurism and channeling a myth of *Heimat* as a safe and nonpolitical space. With critical distance, the problem of the bystander thus emerges as a key concern of televisual remembrance equipped with an uncanny ability to naturalize and validate the bystanders' point of view after the fact through specific structures of television consumption. At the same time, the exploration of relevant parallels between the social construction of passivity in different historical and media settings should not give rise to the misconception of TV viewing as a homogenous and essentially passive activity. TV has historically engendered a wide range of subject positions and memory practices including lending support to memory activism.[3] The close relationship between TV and Swastika was based on elective as well as structural affinities.

Identifying the vantage point of the NS bystander as a key gravitational force of postwar memory culture does not mean that the term was clearly defined. Quite the contrary: as memory politics became an increasingly important arena of public debate, the demarcation of the vast and amorphous terrain of Nazi bystanding became subject to intense negotiations. Key memory events in postwar West Germany first served the strategic objective of generously extending the exculpatory category of "fellow travelers" to include almost the entire population of the Third Reich. Then, in later decades, memory disputes exposed former NS perpetrators who had been enjoying postwar prosperity seemingly safely tucked away in the memory comfort zone of NS bystanding. In this fashion, the memory politics of the 1950s championed large-scale amnesties, whereas social movements of the 1960s and 1970s targeted specific individuals and issued sweeping indictments against entire generations.[4] Exposing the fascist leanings of the contemporaries of the Third Reich and, by extension, turning them into present-day political liabilities worked wonders as a political weapon precisely because the vast majority of the former *Volksgemeinschaft* considered themselves passive spectators of the German catastrophe. Incidentally, similar generational rebranding efforts destroyed self-serving fantasies of communal resistance in countries across Europe.[5]

The intense negotiations about where to draw the line between historical valor, innocence, shame, and guilt fueled political battles across a diversified print media landscape and, in less explicit and incendiary terms, set the agenda for historical coverage in the elite-controlled, consensus-driven media environment of public television. Decades of historical programming provided viewers with an opportunity to investigate repeatedly and at times obsessively the four central, regularly readjusted historical subject positions of NS perpetrator, NS bystander, NS victim, and Nazi era hero. These four emblematic figures constitute a robust narrative machine reminiscent of Greimas's semiotic square,[6] spewing forth a seemingly endless series of documentaries, docudramas, TV plays, and feature films (the latter hijacked from the big screen). Each broadcast derived its communicative value from exploring one or more of the four thematic segments of the square. Stringing together different subject positions by way of more of less plausible narrative arcs resulted in entertaining television, and nearly all theoretically possible options have been produced at one point or another. The TV screen, for instance, regularly revealed NS bystanders and even NS perpetrators as heroes or victims. Thus, following the logic of the semiotic square and given the nature of public broadcasting, one might assume that defensive plot lines outnumbered decidedly self-critical narrative arcs. That hypothesis deserves to be tested by identifying narrative trajectories, which have been particularly frequently pursued on the screen, by checking how TV media events have contributed to the realignment of the symbolic square of NS memory and by paying particular attention to the task of historicizing the contours of TV bystander memory.

The bystander section of the square has proved to be a special zone of collective media memory both subdued and, on second glance, extraordinarily busy. The classical bystander figure, removed, noninvolved, perhaps fearful or opportunistic, has only occasionally been the primary focus of historical TV fare. Passivity simply does not make for good television. Yet, in memory politics off and on the screen, bystanding nevertheless constituted an important imaginary space. In the constant reshuffling of victims, heroes, and perpetrators, the bystander figure has occupied the all-important narrative parking space at the margins of the brightly lit arenas of historical reckoning. The bystanders are the silent majority, the reserve army, the storage memory of unsung heroes, forgotten victims, and undetected criminals with excellent narrative potential. Moreover, the bystander zone, both in real life and according to TV's narrative rationale, constituted a realm of extraordinary attraction. During the Nazi years, the victims of the regime would have loved nothing more than remaining uninvolved bystanders of the rise and fall of the Third Reich. Likewise, after its collapse, the few exposed perpetrators would have loved nothing more than disappearing into the anonymity of the bystander category, a label indeed generously handed out by postwar Allied and German denazification courts.[7]

The topic of bystanding thus gives rise to stories of movement from the bystander segment of the square toward its other three segments on the levels of both history and memory. In the narrative universe of the Third Reich, television tends to turn initial bystanders of Nazism into perpetrators, victims, or resisters. In the narrative world of postwar memory, the anonymity of political bystanding turns into heroic practices of memory activism and reconciliation. Thus, with few exceptions, the bystanding position features prominently in many stories on the screen but disappears more or less quickly in the course of the broadcast. TV renders bystanding omnipresent and normal yet also relatively invisible and unproblematic. Moreover and probably not coincidentally, TV producers rarely deliberately and critically explored bystanding in history and memory because, over many years, the NS bystanders comprised the vast majority of the audience and the creative TV staff. Instead, producers time and again paraded around the relatively small collectives of perpetrators, victims, and heroes for the amusement of these very same history and memory bystanders. That is the disturbing complicity of television in misrepresenting the history and legacy of the Third Reich.[8]

The few available quantitative analyses and a more extensive set of case studies suggest that Holocaust memory on (West) German television developed in four overlapping phases: (1) an unfocused, distanced, at times apologetically structured, but with hindsight nevertheless remarkable exploration of the moral depravity of Nazi anti-Jewish policies, primarily in the 1960s and 1970s, often conducted by way of foreign productions and delivered from a memory angle, that is, engaging with postwar efforts of coming to terms with the past;[9] (2) a self-critical, emotionally challenging realization of the enormity of the Holocaust communicated through a string of foreign and West German productions broadcast in the 1970s and 1980s often focused on everyday life during Nazism;[10] (3) an even more extensive, less self-reflexive succession of professionally produced documentaries and docudramas screened around the turn of the century and conveying intriguing, highly entertaining, ambivalent, and immersive visions of Nazi culture often highlighting themes of German victimhood;[11] and (4) a possible fourth phase, as yet insufficiently documented and analyzed, featuring narratively and ethically complex and ambitious inquiries into the experiences of the "normal" perpetrators of the Third Reich and probably even more subject to re- and pre-mediation processes than the previous phases.[12]

The first phase was a niche phenomenon with limited viewership, although some of the programs were screened in prime time because the networks still lacked sufficient off-primetime programming slots. The second and third phase had important prime time components, not least of all media events like the TV series *Holocaust* and Knopp TV. During the last phase, nonfiction history returned to late-night and was screened on history cable channels while high-profile fiction remained prime time fare. In the course of these four phases and five decades, a process of professionalization changed the way in which TV communicated with its viewers about the past. In the first decades of its existence, television addressed questions that also dominated other spheres of West German historical culture. Like many intellectuals, academics, and artists—with whom they often communicated—TV journalists and producers tried to grasp why the Nazis had come to power and wreaked havoc across Europe. Since the second phase, TV professionals shifted gradually to a different set of guiding questions trying to figure out how it felt like to suffer from Nazi persecution or partake in Nazi crimes. The shift from why to how, from causality to reenactment, corresponded to a shift from primarily discursively to primarily visually constituted programming and probably resulted in different kinds of collective memories of the Nazi past. Over the decades, television constructed and conveyed different feelings about the Nazi past moving from a concern with a sense of intellectual control supported by discursive aesthetics of why to a persistent curiosity about sensing facets of trauma through simulative aesthetics of how. The shift toward new modes of perception and entertainment also aimed at enhancing the bystander experience because TV focused now specifically on offering viewers an opportunity to experience vicariously the Nazi past and acquire a sense of memory advocacy.[13]

In October 1963, six months after ZDF went on the air, the station already broadcast its first TV play about the persecution and mass murder of German Jews in the Third Reich.[14] The author of the script for *Sadowski Comes at Eight O'clock* was none other than Herbert Reinecker, (West) Germany's most prolific TV screenwriter and creator of memorable crime series like *Der Kommissar* and *Derrick*. Unlike some of his peers, Reinecker never made a secret of the fact that he had worked as a Nazi journalist in the Third Reich, although he only revealed in the 1990s that he had been a member of a Waffen-SS propaganda unit.[15] In that capacity, he egged on members of Hitler Youth to sacrifice themselves for Fatherland and *Führer*. As a crime fiction author after the war, he incessantly crafted narrative worlds about average people committing violent crimes as a result of seemingly uncontrollable urges and drives, resulting in guilt without responsibility.[16] It is tempting to relate Reinecker's proclivity for hapless criminals to personal feelings of responsibility for Nazi crimes he might have experienced after the collapse of the Third Reich. On first sight, however, *Sadowski Comes at Eight O'clock* does not follow this apologetic logic. Quite the contrary: the play speaks plainly about the base motives of the Nazi generation, put on display, as so often on West German television, as a drama of memory not history.

Sadowski features a successful West German business executive celebrating his fiftieth birthday who is accused by his adult son of having betrayed a Jewish business partner during the war. Rather than buying out his partner, Sadowski, at the severely discounted Aryanization rate, the father reported him to the Gestapo, thus assuring his deportation to a death camp. The father's despicable behavior now becomes an issue because Sadowski's daughter has filed a lawsuit seeking financial redress and the executive's son has promised to help her by turning over key documents during her next visit—at eight o'clock on this very evening. In a dramatic finale, Sadowski shows up, her shadow clearly visible behind the front door, but nobody in the family dares to let her in. The father does not find the courage to admit to his guilt or to bribe her with a settlement, as his lawyer recommends, and the son, emotionally overtaxed and pressured by family members, does not find the courage to act on his principles and turn over the documents. In the showdown between the mover and shaker of a father and his introvert, insecure son, the older generation keeps the upper hand. The father retains tentative control over his dirty secret and a sense of integrity because he treats his son respectfully throughout their discussions. He explains his behavior with remarkable restraint, highlighting Gestapo pressure, the complexity of the situation, his son's lack of experience and comfortable ex post hoc perspective, and invoking the need for family solidarity. In the end, the play leaves no doubt that the father committed a serious mistake, but by maintaining the status quo Reinecker also seems to suggest that Nazis with similar track records do not deserve to be publically humiliated.

Sadowski Comes at Eight O'clock reflects a prominent storyline in postwar German culture featuring survivors of Nazi terror and a handful of upright citizens or law enforcement personnel struggling to identify former Nazis and seeking some sort of just punishment for them. In the courts and on the screen, Nazi criminals are thus moved from the bystander to the perpetrator segment of the narrative square. Depending on the author's point of view, the stories thus separate a large group of more or less innocent fellow travelers from a small group of committed killers, or they invoke the specter of a sizeable army of recalcitrant Nazis lurking in the shadows of the West German economic miracle.[17] Reinecker supports the first story type. Having exposed the businessman's secret, the *Sadowski* script comes to rest in a scene of twofold passivity. According to Reinecker, the members of the postwar generation simply do not have the gumption to pursue their facile, armchair antifascism to its logical conclusion and turn in their parents, whereas the members of the Nazi generation, who failed spectacularly in their efforts to make history, turn out to be less callous and conniving as the youngsters claim. Bystanding in history and memory comes in many different flavors, but Reinecker, as many of his colleagues at the time, works with readily available stereotypes and rules in favor of his allegedly sufficiently wizened and chastened peers.[18] There is no indication that he changed his mind once the generational relationship assumed a much more confrontational and overtly political character in the late 1960s and 1970s.

The script of *Sadowski* is an interesting document of television historiography. A few months before the beginning of the Auschwitz trial in Frankfurt in December 1963, Reinecker already presents the viewer with a succinct list of Nazi crime iconography clearly linked to the genocide of European Jewry.[19] Reinecker has the son explicitly mention Auschwitz and the many books about concentration camps he has read. As a result, the son is haunted by succinct visions of camps, train stations, barracks, mud, snow, forest clearings, floodlights, selections, screaming people, and poison gas capsules inserted through ventilation ducts.[20] These text passages constitute a highly standardized inventory of NS crime images and story elements connected to the memory site Auschwitz and, more specifically, to the Jewish victims of Nazi persecution. Since Reinecker mobilizes the stories and images in a compact and condensed format, we can safely assume that he invoked narratives and an iconography that were already well established in the viewer's imagination, above all through extensive postwar media coverage.[21] Moreover, television had already started to connect the narrative worlds of Nazi terror to the suffering of European Jewry, although the link was often crafted hesitatingly and indirectly.[22] In this sense, *Sadowski* and similarly structured media texts offer key insights into the profile of mass media memory of the "final solution" before the development of a full-scale Holocaust paradigm in the late 1970s and 1980s. Broadcasts like *Sadowski* provided the foundation for the success of *Holocaust* because the NBC miniseries could tap into a well-established and sophisticated interpretive frame of reference. At the same time, *Holocaust* transgressed and even revolutionized the previous narrative worlds as a more comprehensive look at relevant programming illustrates.

Sadowski was an exceptional broadcast in the context of the 1960s while also reflecting key characteristics of Holocaust TV avant la lettre. The TV play's detour through memory and its self-defensive conclusion corresponded to West German TV executives' predilection for uplifting rescue and resistance stories, especially stories featuring Germans saving Jews, and a strange genre of philo-Semitic TV that acknowledged the "final solution" in passing but primarily celebrated Jewish culture, thus symbolically and counterfactually circumventing the very destruction of European Jewry.[23] At the same time, *Sadowski* addressed the Nazi anti-Jewish crimes fairly straightforwardly and in that respect can be compared to a series of impressively self-reflexive Eastern European feature films about the "final solution" broadcast by ARD and especially ZDF in the 1960s and 1970s. These films were often of exceptional cinematic quality representing prime products of sophisticated movie industries trying to escape the control of Communist party censorship.[24] They delved into the history of German occupation, invariably highlighting civilian suffering and, in the minds of West German TV executives, sending an important didactic message to German viewers. But the impact of the films on collective memory is difficult to ascertain based on available reception data. Critics reacted generally enthusiastic, but many viewers seemed to have remained deeply skeptical about what they perceived as Communist propaganda purchased with viewer fees in the midst of a Cold War against the Soviet Union.

The Eastern European films often had a self-critical edge in that they did not focus on German perpetrators and instead relentlessly probed to what extent Eastern Europeans could have done a better job protecting the groups who fell victim to Nazi terror. The films thus advocated for a memory of World War II in Eastern Europe that was victim and bystander centered and decidedly self-reflexive. They focused on complex stories of reluctant resistance, hesitant collaboration, and fearful accommodation with camera and narrative focus directed at the bystander segment of local societies.[25] Unfortunately, however, that strategy of Eastern European self-reflexivity seems not to have worked in West Germany's television landscape. Rather than feeling encouraged to reflect about their own failings as terror bystanders, the relatively few German viewers appeared to have walked away feeling vindicated about their lack of resistance in the Third Reich. They construed symbolic parallels between Eastern European impotent responses to Nazi terror and their own inability to prevent what they perceived as the Nazi occupation of German society. Cold War borders notwithstanding, they apparently imagined a transnational coalition of bystander-victims unable to stop the Nazi juggernaut.

Moreover, these films reflected prevailing ambivalence about the status of Jews in Eastern European memories. Some filmmakers courageously emphasized the exceptional suffering of Jews in Nazi occupied Eastern Europe; others followed the Communist party line that had written Jews out of the official histories of World War II.[26] Thus, the films provided a contradictory contribution to nascent Holocaust memory in the West. It was all too easy to dismiss wholeheartedly or develop little curiosity about the dubbed, foreign-made movies presenting narrative worlds of limited intrinsic interest to German viewers.

In November 1966, ZDF broadcast the Czechoslovak movie *The Shop on Main Street*, which had won the 1965 Academy Award for Best Foreign Film.[27] The movie's directors, Jan Kadar and Elmar Klos, had already crafted several noteworthy films including *The Accused* highlighting the contradictions between the ideals of Communism and its less than perfect postwar Czechoslovakian rendition.[28] In *The Shop on Main Street*, Kadar and Klos trained their self-reflexive eyes on the essential contributions to genocide of average Slovaks who implemented the Aryanization of Jewish property and the deportation of their Jewish fellow citizens with various degrees of enthusiasm. Driven by pedestrian motives such as greed and fear rather than antisemitic zeal, these normal collaborators proved very helpful to their German overlords even if they developed qualms about their actions. In *The Shop on Main Street*, the middle-aged Tono is such an ambivalent figure. Spurred on by his wife, he accepts an offer to become the Aryan supervisor of a little fabric shop owned by Rosalie Lautmann, an old Jewish woman. Mrs. Lautmann does not understand the political situation and Tono's presence. She gratefully assumes that Tono is a distant cousin come to help her run her business. Tono quickly finds himself in a difficult situation because he likes the old lady and tries to hide her from the authorities when the deportations begin. In the end, they have a fateful misunderstanding. Being unaware of any threat, the old lady becomes suspicious of Tono's motives when he aggressively pressures her to go into hiding. The stress causes her to suffer a fatal heart attack, and Tono commits suicide.

Had it been broadcast twenty years later, *The Shop on Main Street* might have helped shape popular Holocaust memory because it appears perfectly compatible with the narrative strategies of the 1980s and 1990s that established the Holocaust at the center of German and global history. Kadar and Klos's film is well suited to generate empathy with the victims of Nazi genocide and offers an innovative bottom-up inquiry into the motives of ordinary men who facilitated the Holocaust. Despite its slow pace and a few problematic dream sequences, *The Shop on Main Street* provides an entertaining mix of comic and tragic story elements following Tono vacillating between the bystander, perpetrator, and resister segments of the narrative world of Nazi occupation. Consequently, most reviewers praised the film's self-critical exposure of Slovak collaboration. Some called for similarly self-reflexive explorations from a German point of view, noting that efforts in this direction were all too often dismissed as *Nestbeschmutzung*, while others advised against addressing the topic of Nazism on German TV and reported with noticeable relief that the film did not feature a single German Nazi perpetrator.[29] The film also found a significant audience. Almost half the people watching television that night tuned in to watch *The Shop on Main Street* rather than the entertainment programs offered by ARD (28 percent vs. 32 percent).[30] Yet, there is no indication that *The Shop on Main Street* touched viewers emotionally in significant numbers—or at least not in the way in which TV executives had hoped it would. In fact, consumer responses channeled yet another kind of multidirectional memory likely to represent the feelings of many viewers in front of the ZDF screen that night. Two passionate letters reached the station explaining to ZDF executives that the movie simply addressed the wrong topic. The Czechoslovakian people had plenty of reasons to apologize—not for the "final solution" but for the expulsion of ethnic Germans after 1945.[31]

In Cold War West Germany, *The Shop of Main Street* was variably perceived as a piece of Communist propaganda, a reminder of how little anybody could have done against the Nazis, including Germans themselves, or a as praiseworthy or misplaced effort of Slovak self-reproach. Few of the responses indicate that the film made viewers think seriously about their own responsibilities for Nazi genocide. West German historical culture of the 1960s simply pursued other priorities. People were still trying to understand how the Nazis could have come to power and how to make sense of their personal fates and failures in the Third Reich. For the latter purpose, they were busily fitting contradictory life trajectories into neat story categories, which, often also by way of television, divvied up Nazi society into a few devilish Nazis, many heroic resisters, some nondescript bystanders, and generously apportioned groups of victims comprising first and foremost German soldiers, POWs, expellees, and victims of Allied bombing raids and denazification efforts.[32] Jewish victims did not gain exceptional visibility because they were not perceived as an important part of West German society and the role of Nazi victim—as opposed to martyred resister—had not yet attained special prestige. *The Shop on Main Street* simply proved to be the wrong story in the wrong place at the wrong time—sharing that fate with countless memory products across the world.

Incidentally, East German cinema produced a few similarly self-reflexive films about Nazi anti-Jewish crimes, most prominently Konrad Wolf's *Sterne* released in 1959. Now considered an important early Holocaust movie, *Sterne* features a veteran soldier turned reluctant resister as a result of his encounter with Jewish deportees en route to Auschwitz. But, unlike *The Shop on Main Street*, the impressive bystander drama became a victim of Cold War politics. It was released in West German cinemas in 1960 in a truncated version, pulled from ZDF broadcasting schedules after the Soviet invasion of Czechoslovakia in 1968, and aired for the first time by ZDF only in 1983, now in a fully restored version. *Sterne* remained an unusual site of memory in East German historical culture where the "final solution" only became a relevant topic for TV in the late 1980s, after decades of anti-Zionist neglect and antifascist resistance stories.[33]

Despite their ambivalent reception, Eastern European feature films made an important contribution to German historical culture. In the context of 1960s and 1970s German TV, they represent a sizeable, coherent body of work that delved directly into the dark universe of Nazi crimes seeking to reconstruct for the audience the dynamics of victimization and bystanding. West German screenwriters, directors, and journalists also touched on the topic, similarly stressing its terrifying scope and emphasizing German responsibility for genocide and racial warfare. But with few exceptions, they preferred to take a detour through memory. West German TV plays, documentaries, and features about the "final solution" approached the topic by way of an explicit present-day narrative frame focused on the process of coming to terms with the past. Some programs pursued a philo-Semitic angle documenting Jewish culture in Europe before and after the Holocaust and presenting present-day remnants of that culture as resources worthy of careful preservation.[34] Other programs already crafted a small but narratively robust inventory of survivor stories that would become a key staple of the Holocaust paradigm.[35] Yet another set of nonfiction programs focused on the West German legal, administrative, and symbolic efforts of making amends.[36] In this way, television documented West German restitution efforts directed at Israel and individual Jewish survivors and criticized the belated, morally and legally flawed efforts of bringing NS criminals to justice. The programs in the latter thematic category assume particular relevance with hindsight because they belong to just a handful of West German programs that focus squarely on NS perpetrators.[37]

In the first decades of history programming, an intriguing separation of labor thus emerged on West German television. Foreign and especially Eastern European feature films provided potentially taxing simulations of the Nazi onslaught. In contrast to these narrative worlds of destruction and doom, West German nonfiction and fiction programs, with their present-day focus, always included a silver lining. They acknowledged crimes and responsibilities but also highlighted efforts of making amends along with the praise these efforts received from abroad. In this way, the programs stressed Germans' duty to remember with the best of didactical intentions, but in their discussion of postwar criminal justice and restitution efforts, they also provided a modest counterweight to the extraordinary criminal energy of Nazi society. The programs constructed an implicit German viewership who regained a measure of control over their problematic history. Even if the restitution and law enforcement efforts were found wanting—and they were often criticized on television—there nevertheless always existed the options of improving them. In that sense, the West German programs focusing on memory contained a modicum of structural optimism that the Eastern European narrative worlds of persecution could not offer its viewers. As *Sadowski* and *The Shop on Main Street* powerfully illustrate, the dividing lines between historical victims, perpetrators, and bystanders could always be reimagined, but, on the level of history, the devastating outcome of the story was (as yet) difficult to circumnavigate. In contrast, on the level of Nazi memory, the utopia of rigorously self-critical memory work, especially on the part of the many bystanders past and present, remained a real possibility.

When West German collective memory shifted decisively in January 1979 after the broadcast of the NBC miniseries *Holocaust*, the cultural elites of the German Federal Republic found themselves in a tricky situation. They had to explain to the public why they had paid relatively little attention to the history of the Holocaust, now unequivocally considered the key event of modern German history. From today's perspective, that criticism seems both reasonable and problematic. Reasonable because Holocaust memory remains a key anchoring point for collective identities in the West, and, judged by its standards, postwar European memory culture appears to have lacked moral integrity for failing to recognize the extraordinary historical and ethical-political relevance of Nazi genocide. But the ex post factum indictment of postwar memory culture also seems problematic from today's perspective because more than seventy years after the collapse of the Third Reich and more than thirty-five years after the conception of popular Holocaust memory the potential ethical shortcomings of Holocaust memory, including its ethnocentrism and political opportunism, are more vigorously discussed than ever.[38] As a result, the invention of the Holocaust paradigm in the 1970s no longer qualifies as unequivocal memory progress, and the pre-Holocaust memory culture of the 1950s and 1960s no longer appears as a bleak memory scape of denial.[39]

Notwithstanding the different conceptual perspectives for the assessment of postwar memory culture, *Holocaust* remains a pivot point in the history of modern memory. In an exceptional feat of mass communication, *Holocaust* succeeded in solidifying a specific moral perspective that previously had only limited social-political reach. Once established as a moral certainty, that perspective proved highly efficient for the purpose of criticizing postwar Nazi apologetics and turning Nazi genocide into a popular site of memory. The media event *Holocaust* was both a reflection and an important catalyst of the popular turn to memory that swept Western societies a quarter of a century after World War II.[40] The series helped usher in the kind of cultural externalization of memory in memorials, museums, and visual culture whose existence is largely taken for granted today. *Holocaust* thus represents a first highlight of the politics of regret that became official (West) German and European memory in the 1980s and 1990s.[41]

Holocaust was a scandal before it became a cause célèbre. Many critics on both sides of the Atlantic initially vigorously rejected its fast-cut, relentlessly entertaining, emotionally manipulative, profit-mongering aesthetics.[42] Consequently, in internal discussions before the acquisition of *Holocaust*, ARD leaders did not highlight the series' aesthetic qualities or likely success with German audiences when speaking in favor of broadcasting it. Instead, they pointed out that it would be perceived as hypocritical if ARD now took a pass on *Holocaust* after having just broadcast *Roots*, which used the very same problematic aesthetics to highlight the history and legacy of slavery in the United States.[43] It seems that these multidirectional memory considerations won the day. *Holocaust* came to Germany because German TV executives did not want to look foolish to their peers in Western Europe and the US. There are worse reasons for good memory politics.

Holocaust set an unprecedented and never again reached benchmark for self-critical memory politics. Before *Holocaust*, prime time historical programming that elicited 100 to 150 viewer responses, including factual questions, script requests, or detailed commentary, counted as successful history television. Thus, nobody was prepared for tens of thousands of Germans pouring out their hearts in phone calls and letters expressing deep felt regret, confusion, and resentment.[44] A combination of emotion-centered, innovative, and expensive color TV aesthetics (especially innovative in the German context), excellent scriptwriting and acting featuring attractive victim and non-stereotypical perpetrator figures, unparalleled PR efforts, and a historical culture already sensitized to self-reflexive Nazi memory (especially through television)—all these factors combined turned *Holocaust* into a perfect storm of a media event nobody had considered possible. Thirty-four years after the liberation of Auschwitz, significant segments of the society that had launched genocide understood the scale of their crimes, felt empathy for the victims, and experienced a sense of loss at their own moral depravity. *Holocaust* thus inadvertently set a high bar for history culture past and present. A mass media product could apparently play a decisive role in crafting new paradigms of historical self-criticism. Ever since, the representation of historical violence in popular culture can be held to higher standards. Television, films, and video games dealing with past crimes may entertain and make money, but they should ideally also serve an ethical function. Writers and producers can and should ask the question of what ethical-political purpose media violence serves and how a production can trigger self-critical reflections about past and present human rights violations. Put bluntly, mediations of trauma should contribute to the important task of preventing people from becoming perpetrators (again). The Holocaust memory paradigm ushered in by *Holocaust* might be dated, but the high expectations directed at mass culture that the TV series raised are worth retaining.

The media event *Holocaust* reconfigured popular memories of Nazi genocide without decisively changing perceptions of NS bystanding. At the beginning of the miniseries, all main characters are busy bystanders, uninvolved in the political process and focused on their personal lives. From their positions in the margins of the Nazi state they advance at different speeds to the center of Holocaust history, that is, the power hub of the SS elite; key sites of Nazi persecution including Buchenwald, Hadamar, Theresienstadt, and Sobibór; and important locations of Jewish resistance and survival like partisan camps, the Warsaw Ghetto, and the DP route to Palestine. The different narrative trajectories of *Holocaust* thus reflect a picture-perfect transformation of bystanders into victims, perpetrators, and resisters. This act of creative emplotment inadvertently turns Holocaust bystanding yet again into an underexplored narrative terrain. It is important to note, however, that the Western popular Holocaust paradigm differs from the TV product *Holocaust* it was named after in important respects. The paradigm, first developed in the process of Americanization of the Holocaust, tends to highlight the extent of Jewish victimhood and the triumph of survival at the expense of any similarly sustained inquiry into the motives of bystanders *and* perpetrators.[45] In comparison, the TV series also neglects the bystanders but develops impressive curiosity about the normal perpetrators of genocide and remains rather subdued in its celebration of survival.

After *Holocaust*, visual culture in the West has continued over decades to produce consciously crafted responses to the NBC miniseries including such memorable media events as *Shoah* (1985), *Heimat* (1984) *Schindler's List* (1993), *Holokaust* (2000), and *Generation War* (2013). In the course of these responses, the topic of bystanding came better into focus—as one would expect following the logic of Greimas's semiotic square.[46] In a testament to the relative diversity of emerging Holocaust memory, cultural elites, ever skeptical of popular TV in general and *Holocaust* in particular, chose their own sites of Holocaust memory, most prominently Claude Lanzman's more than nine-hour-long documentary *Shoah*. *Shoah*, like *Holocaust*, was broadcast on West Germany's regional TV channels but unlike *Holocaust* only found a miniscule audience. While an average of 4 percent of TV households tuned in to *Shoah*, *Holocaust* had attracted up to 40 percent under similarly unfavorable broadcasting conditions.[47] To this date, however, *Shoah* remains an important reference point for academic memory culture enthralled by a narrative universe in which the narrator figure of Lanzman pulls the strings alternately duplicitously cuddling up to real Nazis in an undercover sting operation, relentlessly seducing survivors into restaging their humiliating past or obsessing about Polish callousness and merriment in the face of Judeocide. The Polish figures, rendered unforgettable on the covers of *Shoah* products, effectively export the figure of the Holocaust bystander out of Western Europe. *Shoah* has not had the same important self-critical effects as one of its predecessors, Marcel Ophuls's documentary media event *The Sorrow and the Pity* (1969), which almost single-handedly established the figure of the French collaborator as an icon of Vichy memory.[48] *Shoah* lacks self-critical depth and amounts to Western academic memory kitsch exploring the abyss of genocide from the superior point of view of a peculiar anti-intellectual intellectualism, which takes great pride in unflinchingly confronting victims, perpetrators, and bystanders of genocide without realizing that this attitude of cold aloofness is a significant part of the problem and implicated in the crimes.⁴⁹ Thus, both *Holocaust* and *Shoah*, representing the center of popular and intellectual Holocaust memory, systematically avoid raising challenging questions about the implied viewer figures, the media event bystanders, inscribed in their respective narrative worlds. *Holocaust* remains mostly silent about the average people watching ostracization, deportation, and genocide unfold in real life and on screen, and *Shoah* fails to scrutinize its own fascination with the extremity and consistency of Nazi violence. Considering genre, production context, and narrator self-stylization, the shortcomings of *Shoah* weigh heavier than the shortcomings of *Holocaust*.

Among all the answers to *Holocaust*, *Schindler's List* is the most conventionally structured product showcasing the time-tested metamorphosis of a bystander into a hero and concluding the Americanization of the Holocaust with a carefully planned and highly entertaining act of simulative commodification with limited self-critical potential.⁵⁰ In contrast, Edgar Reitz's *Heimat*, the first answer to *Holocaust*, constituted a courageous, self-conscious challenge of the emerging Holocaust paradigm daring to highlight the relative innocence of the bystander subject position in a complex yet ultimately romantic exploration of provincial life in twentieth-century Germany in which the Holocaust is simply not an event of great significance.⁵¹ Through his intervention, Reitz hoped to take control again of German history that, he felt, "the Americans have stolen ... through *Holocaust*."⁵² As different as they are, *Heimat*, *Shoah*, and *Schindler's List* are all auteur films, highly wrought, self-reflexive confrontations with the powerful interpretive framework of Holocaust history. They all try to insert explicit reflections on the bystander perspective as if the auteurs had perceived of the previous lack of engagement with that perspective and perhaps also had a sense of the implication of the cinema and television spectator in the social construction of political bystanding.

Heimat, *Shoah*, and *Schindler's List*—like *Holocaust*—are transnational sites of memory that played an important role in the evolution of NS memory in Germany. However, in terms of popular resonance, the auteur films have been overshadowed by a series of stunningly successful and morally disappointing documentaries and docudramas broadcast by German public television since the turn of the century and screened on cable channels in many countries. The programs elegantly circumnavigated and subverted the Holocaust paradigm by paying lip service to Holocaust memory, emphasizing the depravity of the Nazi elite but embracing the bystanders of war and genocide as the true measure of normal behavior in times of crisis. The docudramas and documentaries—the latter are often linked to the name of the ZDF TV executive Guido Knopp—amounted to a third wave of history TV. They lacked the self-consciousness of auteur cinema and settled on predictable transformations of German bystanders into German victims. Yet the millennium wave also self-confidently accomplished what German memory culture had rarely dared previously. It gave voice and image to the figure of the somber German bystander, emotionally shaken by seeing so much violence but nevertheless bravely fulfilling the duty of (Holocaust) bystanding by relating the lessons of actual or belated Holocaust proximity—observe, lament, and testify—to a transnational public. As we have seen, the subject position of the bystander played an important role in many TV productions, often through its thoughtless or deliberate absence. But now, at an advanced age, its lined face exuding authenticity, wisdom, and the innocence of physical incapacity, the figure of the bystander stepped into the limelight and went on a great farewell tour through living rooms across the West celebrating its own passivity. In signature documentaries like *Holokaust* (2000) and countless similar productions, the Holocaust bystander figure came into its own generously borrowing character traits from other better known figures (especially the survivor) while establishing an independent, innocent presence on the screen. The bystander-hero of Knopp TV was an attractive emotional sounding board for exploring the now distant Nazi past precisely because it lacked any capacity for sustained self-criticism.[53]

The hitherto last response to *Holocaust*, *Generation War*, deserves credit as a high-profile program focusing squarely on average NS perpetrators.[54] The series belongs to a sustained, internationally traded wave of entertaining, high-quality docudramas dealing with historical topics and settings.[55] *Generation War* also seems to be part of a more extensive, belated televisual inquiry into "normal" Nazi perpetrators, although we lack comprehensive TV data to assess the volume and the social relevance of these programs.[56] *Generation War* builds up viewer identification with a group of five young, attractive NS bystanders and then carefully and compellingly depicts their descent into the moral quagmire of World War II. All but the token Jewish member of the group become embroiled in Nazi crimes, but in the end, the script remains too protective of its main characters. The production falls into a generation trap because the friends are simply too young to carry political responsibility for the rise of Nazism. In addition, the protagonists are morally redeemed by premature deaths, attempts at desertion, and experiences of rape resulting in the three most innocent characters surviving the war. Eventually, the production team behind *Generation War* pushed the characters too far into the victim segment of their NS universe, making it difficult for viewers to retain ambivalent, self-critical feelings about the figures' participation in NS crimes.[57]

The narrative square seems to have come full circle. Before and after *Holocaust*, ARD and ZDF only sporadically confronted their viewers with the most painful legacy of Nazism, that is, the deeds and continued presence of hundreds of thousands of perpetrators and many more bystanders in the midst of German society. Belatedly, the networks acknowledged the crimes and the suffering of the victims with impressive detail, candor, and frequency, but they also often let average perpetrators and bystanders linger in the shadows—nameless, faceless stereotypes devoid of stories worth exploring. The aesthetic construction of these lacunae changed substantially over time. In the 1960s and 1970s, the perpetrators and bystanders of the "final solution" did not become primetime protagonists because West Germany's historical culture had not yet conceived of Nazi genocide as the primary focus of its efforts at coming to terms with the past. In the 1980s, a consciousness of the extraordinary relevance of the Holocaust quickly permeated all layers of West Germany's historical culture, but now the perpetrators and bystanders took a back seat, visually and narratively, to the survivors of the "final solution" who came to play a decisive role in the narrative worlds of television. Finally, since the 1990s, the average perpetrators were overshadowed by the figures of the *Führer* and his henchmen who conveniently absorbed all responsibility for the Holocaust. At the same time, TV embraced the aged figure of the bystander as the measure of appropriate moral conduct in times of war and genocide. Television only seems to have developed a more persistent curiosity about ordinary men's complicity in genocide more than six decades after the crimes at a point in time when the vast majority of murderers and bystanders were already dead and when historical coverage had lost social relevance and thematic focus in a highly diversified TV market. It seems unlikely that the exploration of NS narrative worlds will pick up speed any time soon in the dated setting of television. The next narrative history frontiers are video games and AI settings whose immersive, simulative, and counterfactual environments offer fabulous opportunities to explore the moral conundrum of Holocaust bystanding and complicity—if Holocaust memory institutions can muster the courage to develop truly interactive digital memoryscapes.[58]

Wulf Kansteiner is Professor of History at Aarhus University and holds a PhD from the University of California, Los Angeles. He is a cultural historian, historical theorist, and memory studies expert whose research focuses on representations of history in visual culture, especially in regard to Nazism and the Holocaust; the narrative structures of historical writing; and the methods and theories of memory studies. He is the author of *In Pursuit of German Memory: History, Television, and Politics after Auschwitz* (2006) and coeditor of *The Politics of Memory in Postwar Europe* (2006), *Historical Representation and Historical Truth* (2009), *Den Holocaust erzählen: Historiographie zwischen wissenschaftlicher Empirie und narrativer Kreativität* (2013), and *Probing the Ethics of Holocaust Culture* (2016). He is also cofounder and coeditor of the journal *Memory Studies*.

Notes

1. The abundance of Nazi-related TV fare is often invoked anecdotally (see, e.g., Lukas Gedziorowski, "Nazi TV," Fragmenteum: Blog für Comics und Popkultur, 18 July 2014, https://fragmenteum.wordpress.com/2014/07/18/nazi-tv), but reliable data have actually only been assembled relatively rarely; see esp. Edgar Lersch and Reinhold Viehoff, *Geschichte im Fernsehen: Eine Untersuchung zur Entwicklung des Genres und der Gattungsästhetik geschichtlicher Darstellungen im Fernsehen 1995 bis 2003* (Düsseldorf, 2007), 160; see also Christoph Classen, *Bilder der Vergangenheit: Die Zeit des Nationalsozialismus im Fernsehen der Bundesrepublik Deutschland 1955–1965* (Cologne, 1999), 28; Wulf Kansteiner, *Television and the Historicization of National Socialism in the Federal Republic of Germany: The Programs of the Zweite Deutsche Fernsehen between 1963 and 1993* (Ann Arbor, MI, 1997), 115, 117.
2. Jonathan Bignell and Andreas Fickers, eds., *A European Television History* (Malden, MA, 2008).
3. See the classic deconstruction of TV viewing as mere bystanding in Henry Jenkins, *Textual Poachers: Television Fans and Participatory Culture* (New York, 2013), 54–60.
4. Norbert Frei, *Vergangenheitspolitik: Die Anfänge der Bundesrepublik und die NS-Vergangenheit* (Munich, 1996); Klaus Wernecke, "1968," in *Lexikon der Vergangenheitsbewältigung in Deutschland*, ed. Torben Fischer and Matthias Lorenz (Bielefeld, 2015), 188–193.
5. Richard Lebow, Wulf Kansteiner, and Claudio Fogu, eds., *The Politics of Memory in Postwar Europe* (Durham, NC, 2006).
6. Algirdas Greimas, *Structural Semantics: An Attempt at Method* (Lincoln, NE, 1983).
7. Lutz Niethammer, *Die Mitläuferfabrik: Die Entnazifizierung am Beispiel Bayerns* (Berlin, 1972).
8. On this dynamic, see esp. Leif Kramp, *Gedächtnismaschine Fernsehen*, 2 vols. (Berlin, 2011).
9. Georg Feil, *Zeitgeschichte im Deutschen Fernsehen: Analyse von Fernsehsendungen mit historischen Themen (1957–1967)* (Osnabrück 1974); Classen, *Bilder der Vergangenheit*.
10. Judith Keilbach, *Geschichtsbilder und Zeitzeugen: Zur Darstellung des Nationalsozialismus im Bundesdeutschen Fernsehen* (Münster, 2008), 166–189; Michael Geisler, "The Disposal of Memory: Fascism and the Holocaust on West German Television," in *Framing the Past: The Historiography of German Cinema*

and Television, ed. Bruce Murray and Christopher Wigham (Carbondale, 1992), 220–260; Wulf Kansteiner, *In Pursuit of German Memory: History, Television, and Politics after Auschwitz* (Athens, OH, 2006), 115–130.

11. Axel Bangert, *The Nazi Past in Contemporary German Film: Viewing Experiences of Intimacy and Immersion* (Rochester, NY, 2014); Tobias Ebbrecht-Hartmann, "German Docudrama: Aligning the Fragments and Accessing the Past," in *Docudrama on European Television: A Selective Survey*, ed. Ebbrecht-Hartmann and Derek Paget (London, 2016), 27–51; Keilbach, *Geschichtsbilder*, 224–236; Kansteiner, *In Pursuit of German Memory*, 154–180.

12. The fourth phase features media events like *Generation War* (ZDF, 17, 18, 20 March 2013) and *Das radikal Böse* (ZDF, 1 May 2015); see Bernd Graff, "Bestien wie du und ich," *Süddeutsche Zeitung*, 30 April 2015; Christoph Classen, "Unsere Nazis, unser Fernsehen," *Zeitgeschichte Online*, April 2013, http://www.zeitgeschichte-online.de/film/unsere-nazis-unser-fernsehen.

13. On collective moods, see Ben Highmore, *Cultural Feelings: Mood, Mediation and Cultural Politics* (New York, 2017); on reenactments of NS trauma, see Stella Bruzzi, "Re-enacting Trauma in Film and Television: Restaging History, Revisiting Pain," in *Therapy and Emotions in Film and Television: The Pulse of Our Times*, ed. Claudia Wassmann (London, 2015), 89–98; Thomas Elsaesser, *German Cinema-Terror and Trauma: Cultural Memory since 1945* (New York, 2014).

14. *Um acht Uhr kommt Sadowski* (ZDF, 16 October 1963).

15. My thanks to Haydée Mareike Haass for information on Reinecker's postwar public persona.

16. Rolf Aurich, Niels Beckenbach, and Wolfgang Jacobsen, *Reineckerland: Der Schriftsteller Herbert Reinecker* (Munich, 2010).

17. See, e.g., *Kennwort Gewalt: Jahrmarkt des Todes*, ARD, 9 June 1965; *Der Tod eines Mitbürgers*, ZDF, 8 March 1967; *Mord in Frankfurt*, ARD, 30 January 1968; *Rosen fur den Staatsanwalt* (German movie 1959), ZDF, 2 December 1968; *Die Beichte*, ZDF, 11 November 1970; *Revolution auf dem Papier*, ARD, 16 May 1971; *Zwei Briefe an Pospischiel*, ZDF, 13 October 1971; *"Sondergerichtsakte 86/43": Rechtsprechung im Namen des deutschen Volkes*, ARD, 22 February 1972; *Die Mörder sind unter uns* (German movie, 1946), ARD 18 December 1971; *Herrenpartie* (German movie, 1963), ARD, 11 July 1973.

18. "Kolportage," *Der Abend*, 18 October 1963; "Die Schnulze unserer Schuld," *Hamburger Echo*, 17 October 1963; "Zeitkritik als Schablone," *Tagesspiegel*, 18 October 1963.

19. See Jürgen Wilke, Birgit Schenk, Akiba A. Cohen, and Tamar Zemach, *Holocaust und NS-Prozesse: Die Berichterstattung in Israel und Deutschland zwischen Aneignung und Abwehr* (Cologne, 1995); Sabine Horn, *Erinnerungsbilder: Auschwitz-Prozess und Majdanek-Prozess im westdeutschen Fernsehen* (Essen, 2009).

20. Herbert Reinecker, *Um 8 Uhr kommt Sadowski*, film script without date, 62, 89–91.

21. Ulrike Weckel, *Beschämende Bilder: Deutsche Reaktionen auf alliierte Dokumentarfilme über befreite Konzentrationslager* (Stuttgart, 2012); Habbo Knoch, *Die Tat als Bild: Fotografien des Holocaust in der deutschen Erinnerungskultur* (Hamburg, 2001).

22. Classen, *Bilder der Vergangenheit*, 86–92; see, e.g., *Schluf der Gerechten*, ARD, 21 November 1962, broadcast a year before *Sadowski*.

23. Kansteiner, *In Pursuit of German Memory*, 112–115; Wulf Kansteiner, "What Is the Opposite of Genocide? Philosemitic Television in Germany, 1963–1995," *Philosemitism in History*, ed. Jonathan Karp and Adam Sutcliffe (Cambridge, 2011), 289–313.

24. Aniko Imre, ed., *Companion to Eastern European Cinemas* (Malden, MA, 2012).

25. *Der Neunte Kreis* (Yugoslav movie, 1960), ZDF, 20 November 1963; *Zwei Halbzeiten in der Hölle* (Hungarian movie, 1961), ZDF, 21 June 1965; *Romeo, Julia und die Finsternis* (Czech movie, 1959), ZDF, 15 November 1965; *Die Passagierin* (Polish movie, 1963), ZDF, 24 November 1966; *Der erste Tag der Freiheit* (Polish movie, 1964), ARD, 3 November 1971; see also Adam Bingham, "War," in, *Directory of World Cinema: Eastern Europe*, ed. Adam Bingham (Bristol, 2011), 36–40.
26. See, e.g., Marek Haltof, *Polish Film and the Holocaust* (New York, 2012).
27. ZDF, 21 December 1966.
28. ZDF, 25 October 1965.
29. "Das Geschäft an der Hauptstrasse," *Der Vorwärts*, 30 November 1966; "Das Geschäft an der Hauptstrasse," *Badische Neuste Nachrichten*, 26 November 1966; Norman Gephardt, "Das Geschäft an der Hauptstrasse," *Recklinghauser Zeitung*, 23 November 1966.
30. Infratest-Index, 21 November 1966.
31. Letter by Josef D. addressed to ZDF and dated 20 December 1966; letter by Erwin S. addressed to ZDF and dated 27 November 1966.
32. Frei, *Vergangenheitspolitik*; Peter Reichel, *Politik mit der Erinnerung: Gedächtnisorte im Streit um die nationalsozialistische Vergangenheit* (Munich, 1995); Kansteiner, *In Pursuit of German Memory*.
33. Rüdiger Steinmetz and Reinhold Viehoff, eds., *Deutsches Fernsehen Ost: Eine Programmgeschichte des DDR-Fernsehens* (Berlin, 2008), 468–469; see also Thomas Beutelschmidt and Rüdiger Steinlein, eds., *Realitätskonstruktion: Faschismus und Antifaschismus in den Literaturverfilmungen des DDR-Fernsehens* (Leipzig, 2004), 45; Ulrike Schwab, ed., *Fiktionale Geschichtssendungen im DDR-Fernsehen* (Leipzig, 2007).
34. To name just two examples: *Die goldene Stadt des Rabbi Löw: Ein Film über die Judengemeinde Prags*, ARD, 28 September 1963; *Die Juden von Prag*, ZDF, 11 October 1968.
35. E.g., *Wiedersehen mit Laupheim: Ein jüdischer Emigrant besucht seine Heimatstadt*, ZDF, 12 April 1968; *Denk ich an Deutschland: Schicksale von Menschen, die Deutschland vertrieb*, ARD, 25 April 1965.
36. E.g., *Stellvertreter ihrer Väter: Aktion Sühnezeichen in sechs Ländern*, ARD, 15 September 1963; *Die unbezahlbare Schuld: Ist die Wiedergutmachung abgeschlossen?* ZDF, 8 November 1964.
37. *Der Himbeerpflücker*, ARD, 24 June 1965; *Dr. W.: Ein SS-Arzt in Auschwitz*, ZDF, 12 September 1976.
38. Claudio Fogu, Wulf Kansteiner, and Todd Presner, eds., *Probing the Ethics of Holocaust Culture* (Cambridge, MA, 2016).
39. From the vantage point of Michael Rothberg's concept of multidirectional memory, the postwar decades of economic success and decolonization assume an aura of intriguing memory ambivalence. Michael Rothberg, *Multidirectional Memory: Remembering the Holocaust in the Age of Decolonization* (Stanford, CA, 2009).
40. Astrid Erll, *Memory in Culture* (New York, 2011).
41. Jeffrey Olick, *The Sins of the Fathers* (Chicago, 2016).
42. Jeffrey Shandler, *While America Watches: Televising the Holocaust* (Oxford, 1999); Jürgen Wilke, "Die Fernsehserie 'Holocaust' als Medienereignis," *Zeitgeschichte Online*, March 2004, http://zeitgeschichte-online.de/thema/die-fernsehserie-holocaust-als-medienereignis.
43. On the intersection of the two media events in West Germany, see Timothy Havens, *Black Television Travels: African American Television around the Globe* (New York, 2013), 47–50.

44. Raul Jordan, *Konfrontation mit der Vergangenheit: Das Medienereignis Holocaust und die politische Kultur der Bundesrepublik Deutschland* (Frankfurt, 2008).
45. For a definition and critique of the Holocaust paradigm from different scholarly points of view, see Alvin Rosenfeld, "The Americanization of the Holocaust," in *Thinking about the Holocaust*, ed. Alvin Rosenfeld (Bloomington, 1997), 119–150; Peter Novick, *The Holocaust in American Life* (Chicago, 1999); Anne Rothe, *Popular Trauma Culture: Selling the Pain of Others in the Mass Media* (New Brunswick, NJ, 2011), 36–41; Rebecca Jinks, *Representing Genocide: The Holocaust as Paradigm?* (London, 2016).
46. Frederic Jameson, "Foreword," in *On Meaning: Selected Writings in Semiotic Theory*, by Algirdas Julien Greimas (Minneapolis, 1987), xvi.
47. Thiele, *Publizistische Kontroversen*, 311, 397.
48. Pauline Kael, *Hooked* (New York, 1989), 84–88; Henri Rousso, *The Vichy Syndrome: History and Memory in France since 1944* (Cambridge, MA, 1994), 100–114.
49. Dominick LaCapra, *History and Memory after Auschwitz* (Ithaca, NY, 1998), 95–138; Tzvetan Todorov, *Facing the Extreme: Moral Life in the Concentration Camp* (New York, 1996), 277.
50. Yosefa Loshitzky, ed., *Spielberg's Holocaust: Critical Perspectives on* Schindler's List (Bloomington, IN, 1997).
51. Anton Kaes, *From Hitler to Heimat: The Return of History as Film* (Cambridge, MA, 1989), 163–192.
52. Edgar Reitz, *Liebe zum Kino: Utopien und Gedanken zum Autorenfilm 1962–1983* (Cologne, 1984), 102.
53. Thomas Fischer and Rainer Wirtz, eds., *Alles authentisch? Popularisierung der Geschichte im Fernsehen* (Konstanz, 2008); Keilbach, *Geschichtsbilder*; Kansteiner, *In Pursuit of German Memory*; Wulf Kansteiner, "Aufstieg und Abschied der NS-Zeitzeugen in den Geschichtsdokumentationen des ZDF," in *Die Geburt des Zeitzeugen nach 1945*, ed. Martin Sabrow and Norbert Frei (Göttingen, 2012), 320–353; Ebbrecht-Hartmann, "German Docudrama."
54. *Unsere Mütter, unsere Väter: Eine andere Zeit*, ZDF, 17 March 2013; *Unsere Mütter, unsere Väter: Ein anderer Krieg*, ZDF, 18 March 2013; *Unsere Mütter, unsere Väter: Ein anderes Land*, ZDF, 20 March 2013.
55. Ebbrecht-Hartmann and Paget, *Docudrama on European Television*.
56. See, e.g., *Das radikal Böse*, ZDF, 1 May 2015, which finally provides the kind of compelling analysis of average NS perpetrators on TV already presented in scholarly form by Christopher Browning, *Ordinary Men: Reserve Police Battalion 101 and the Final Solution in Poland* (New York, 1992).
57. Ulrich Herbert, "Die Nazis sind immer die anderen," *die tageszeitung*, 21 March 2013; Classen, "Unsere Nazis, unser Fernsehen."
58. Wulf Kansteiner, "The Holocaust in the 21st Century: Digital Anxiety, Transnational Cosmopolitanism, and Never Again Genocide without Memory," in *Digital Memory Studies: Media Pasts in Transition*, ed. Andrew Hoskins (New York, 2017), 110–140.

Bibliography

Aurich, Rolf, Niels Beckenbach, and Wolfgang Jacobsen. *Reineckerland: Der Schriftsteller Herbert Reinecker*. Munich: Text & Kritik, 2010.
Bangert, Axel. *The Nazi Past in Contemporary German Film: Viewing Experiences of Intimacy and Immersion*. Rochester, NY: Camden House, 2014.

Beutelschmidt, Thomas, and Rüdiger Steinlein, eds. *Realitätskonstruktion: Faschismus und Antifaschismus in den Literaturverfilmungen des DDR-Fernsehens*. Leipzig: Leipziger Universitätsverlag, 2004.
Bignell, Jonathan, and Andreas Fickers, eds. *A European Television History*. Malden, MA: Wiley, 2008.
Bingham, Adam. "War." In *Directory of World Cinema: Eastern Europe*, edited by Adam Bingham, 36–40. Bristol: The Mill, 2011.
Browning, Christopher. *Ordinary Men: Reserve Police Battalion 101 and the Final Solution in Poland*. New York: HarperCollins, 1992.
Bruzzi, Stella. "Re-enacting Trauma in Film and Television: Restaging History, Revisiting Pain." In *Therapy and Emotions in Film and Television: The Pulse of Our Times*, edited by Claudia Wassmann, 89–98. London: Palgrave Macmillan, 2015.
Classen, Christoph. *Bilder der Vergangenheit: Die Zeit des Nationalsozialismus im Fernsehen der Bundesrepublik Deutschland 1955–1965*. Cologne: Böhlau, 1999.
———. "Unsere Nazis, unser Fernsehen." *Zeitgeschichte Online*, April 2013. http://www.zeitgeschichte-online.de/film/unsere-nazis-unser-fernsehen.
Ebbrecht-Hartmann, Tobias. "German Docudrama: Aligning the Fragments and Accessing the Past." In *Docudrama on European Television: A Selective Survey*, edited by Tobias Ebbrecht-Hartmann and Derek Paget, 224–236. London: Palgrave Macmillan, 2016.
Elsaesser, Thomas. *German Cinema-Terror and Trauma: Cultural Memory since 1945*. New York: Routledge, 2014.
Erll, Astrid. *Memory in Culture*. New York: Palgrave Macmillan, 2011.
Feil, Georg. *Zeitgeschichte im Deutschen Fernsehen: Analyse von Fernsehsendungen mit historischen Themen (1957–1967)*. Osnabrück: Fromm, 1974.
Fischer, Thomas, and Rainer Wirtz, eds. *Alles authentisch? Popularisierung der Geschichte im Fernsehen*. Konstanz: UVK, 2008.
Fogu, Claudio, Wulf Kansteiner, and Todd Presner, eds. *Probing the Ethics of Holocaust Culture*. Cambridge, MA: Harvard University Press, 2016.
Frei, Norbert. *Vergangenheitspolitik: Die Anfänge der Bundesrepublik und die NS-Vergangenheit*. Munich: Beck, 1996.
Gedziorowski, Lukas. "Nazi TV." Fragmenteum: Blog für Comics und Popkultur, 18 July 2014. https://fragmenteum.wordpress.com/2014/07/18/nazi-tv.
Geisler, Michael. "The Disposal of Memory: Fascism and the Holocaust on West German Television." In *Framing the Past: The Historiography of German Cinema and Television*, edited by Bruce Murray and Christopher Wigham, 220–260. Carbondale: Southern Illinois University Press, 1992.
Greimas, Algirdas Julien. *Structural Semantics: An Attempt at Method*. Lincoln: University of Nebraska Press, 1983.
Haltof, Marek. *Polish Film and the Holocaust*. New York: Berghahn Books, 2012.
Havens, Timothy. *Black Television Travels: African American Television around the Globe*. New York: New York University Press, 2013.
Highmore, Ben. *Cultural Feelings: Mood, Mediation and Cultural Politics*. New York: Routledge, 2017.
Horn, Sabine. *Erinnerungsbilder: Auschwitz-Prozess und Majdanek-Prozess im westdeutschen Fernsehen*. Essen: Klartext, 2009.
Imre, Aniko, ed. *Companion to Eastern European Cinemas*. Malden, MA: Wiley-Blackwell, 2012.
Jameson, Frederic. "Foreword." In *On Meaning: Selected Writings in Semiotic Theory*, by Algirdas Julien Greimas, vi–xii. Minneapolis: University of Minnesota Press, 1987.

Jenkins, Henry. *Textual Poachers: Television Fans and Participatory Culture*. New York: Routledge, 2013.
Jinks, Rebecca. *Representing Genocide: The Holocaust as Paradigm?* London: Bloomsbury, 2016
Jordan, Raul. *Konfrontation mit der Vergangenheit: Das Medienereignis Holocaust und die politische Kultur der Bundesrepublik Deutschland*. Frankfurt: Lang, 2008.
Kael, Pauline. *Hooked*. New York: Dutton, 1989.
Kaes, Anton. *From Hitler to Heimat: The Return of History as Film*. Cambridge, MA: Harvard University Press, 1989.
Kansteiner, Wulf. "Aufstieg und Abschied der NS-Zeitzeugen in den Geschichtsdokumentationen des ZDF." In *Die Geburt des Zeitzeugen nach 1945*, edited by Martin Sabrow and Norbert Frei, 320–353. Göttingen: Wallstein Verlag, 2012.
———. "The Holocaust in the 21st Century: Digital Anxiety, Transnational Cosmopolitanism, and Never Again Genocide without Memory." In *Digital Memory Studies: Media Pasts in Transition*, edited by Andrew Hoskins, 110–140. New York: Routledge, 2017.
———. *In Pursuit of German Memory: History, Television, and Politics after Auschwitz*. Athens: Ohio University Press, 2006.
———. "What Is the Opposite of Genocide? Philosemitic Television in Germany, 1963–1995." In *Philosemitism in History*, edited by Jonathan Karp and Adam Sutcliffe 289–313. Cambridge: Cambridge University Press, 2011.
Keilbach, Judith. *Geschichtsbilder und Zeitzeugen: Zur Darstellung des Nationalsozialismus im Bundesdeutschen Fernsehen*. Münster: LIT, 2008.
Knoch, Habbo. *Die Tat als Bild: Fotografien des Holocaust in der deutschen Erinnerungskultur*. Hamburg: Hamburger Edition, 2001.
Kramp, Leif. *Gedächtnismaschine Fernsehen*. 2 vols. Berlin: Akademie-Verlag, 2011.
LaCapra, Dominick. *History and Memory after Auschwitz*. Ithaca, NY: Cornell University Press, 1998.
Lebow, Richard, Wulf Kansteiner, and Claudio Fogu, eds. *The Politics of Memory in Postwar Europe*. Durham, NC: Duke University Press, 2006.
Lersch, Edgar, and Reinhold Viehoff. *Geschichte im Fernsehen: Eine Untersuchung zur Entwicklung des Genres und der Gattungsästhetik geschichtlicher Darstellungen im Fernsehen 1995 bis 2003*. Düsseldorf: Vistas, 2007.
Loshitzky, Yosefa, ed. *Spielberg's Holocaust: Critical Perspectives on* Schindler's List. Bloomington: Indiana University Press, 1997.
Niethammer, Lutz. *Die Mitläuferfabrik: Die Entnazifizierung am Beispiel Bayerns*. Berlin: Dietz, 1972.
Novick, Peter, *The Holocaust in American Life*. Chicago: University of Chicago Press, 1999.
Olick, Jeffrey. *The Sins of the Fathers*. Chicago: University of Chicago Press, 2016.
Reichel, Peter. *Politik mit der Erinnerung: Gedächtnisorte im Streit um die nationalsozialistische Vergangenheit*. Munich: Hanser, 1995.
Reitz, Edgar. *Liebe zum Kino: Utopien und Gedanken zum Autorenfilm 1962–1983*. Cologne: Verlag Köln, 1984.
Rosenfeld, Alvin. "The Americanization of the Holocaust." In *Thinking about the Holocaust*, edited by Alvin Rosenfeld, 119–150. Bloomington: Indiana University Press, 1997.
Rothberg, Michael. *Multidirectional Memory: Remembering the Holocaust in the Age of Decolonization*. Stanford, CA: Stanford University Press, 2009.
Rothe, Anne. *Popular Trauma Culture: Selling the Pain of Others in the Mass Media*. New Brunswick, NJ: Rutgers University Press, 2011.

Rousso, Henri. *The Vichy Syndrome: History and Memory in France since 1944.* Cambridge, MA: Harvard University Press, 1994.
Schwab, Ulrike, ed. *Fiktionale Geschichtssendungen im DDR-Fernsehen.* Leipzig: Leipziger Universitätsverlag, 2007.
Shandler, Jeffrey. *While America Watches: Televising the Holocaust.* Oxford: Oxford University Press, 1999.
Steinmetz, Rüdiger and Reinhold Viehoff, eds. *Deutsches Fernsehen Ost: Eine Programmgeschichte des DDR-Fernsehens.* Berlin: vbb, 2008.
Todorov, Tzvetan. *Facing the Extreme: Moral Life in the Concentration Camp.* New York: Henry Holt & Co., 1996.
Weckel, Ulrike. *Beschämende Bilder: Deutsche Reaktionen auf alliierte Dokumentarfilme über befreite Konzentrationslager.* Stuttgart: Franz Steiner, 2012.
Wernecke, Klaus. "1968." In *Lexikon der Vergangenheitsbewältigung in Deutschland*, edited by Torben Fischer and Matthias Lorenz, 188–193. Bielefeld: Transcript, 2015.
Wilke, Jürgen. "Die Fernsehserie 'Holocaust' als Medienereignis." *Zeitgeschichte Online*, March 2004. http://zeitgeschichte-online.de/thema/die-fernsehserie-holocaust-als-medienereignis.
Wilke, Jürgen, Birgit Schenk, Akiba A. Cohen, and Tamar Zemach. *Holocaust und NS-Prozesse: Die Berichterstattung in Israel und Deutschland zwischen Aneignung und Abwehr.* Cologne: Böhlau, 1995.

Chapter 15

Stand by Your Man

(Self-)Representations of SS Wives after 1945

Susanne C. Knittel

The performance piece *The Woman at His Side: Careers, Crimes, and Female Complicity under National Socialism*, written and performed by the German actors Inga Dietrich, Joanne Gläsel, and Sabine Werner, explores the degree to which the wives of SS officers were implicated in National Socialist politics and crimes. Commissioned by the Haus der Wannseekonferenz, the piece premiered there in 2001 and has since been performed about forty times in more than thirty locations around Germany, including concentration camp memorials and other sites of Holocaust memory, theaters, schools, cultural centers, and academic conferences. In January 2007, a radio version was produced, directed by the American writer David Zane Mairowitz, which was broadcast in 2008 by the Norddeutscher Rundfunk and rebroadcast in 2015 by the Westdeutscher Rundfunk. In September 2016, *The Woman at His Side* saw its English-language debut at Utrecht University in the Netherlands.

The piece, which draws on Gudrun Schwarz's groundbreaking 1997 study *Eine Frau an seiner Seite*, is minimalist and highly self-reflexive in its staging and documentary in its approach: the script consists entirely of quotations taken from original sources. Ego-documents such as autobiographies, letters, and diaries but also other materials such as newspaper reports, legal documents, political speeches, and songs are arranged in such a manner that a narrative arc unfolds. The audience follows some of the most notorious "Nazi wives" such as Lina Heydrich, Ruth Kalder-Göth, Thea Stangl, Hedwig Höss, Irene Mengele, and Fanny Fritsch, as well as lesser-known women such as Eva Mennecke, from when they first met the men who would become their husbands, through courtship, engagement, and marriage. While their husbands organized the murder of the Jews, worked as concentration camp commanders, or selected patients for the "euthanasia" program, their wives fulfilled their duties as mothers and kept the household running. They were often well informed about the persecutory policies and plans of the Nazi regime. Many visited or lived with their husbands in or near the ghettos and concentration camps where they were stationed. There they profited from the persecutions by employing camp prisoners in their households and by enriching themselves with seized goods. Many actively supported their husbands' careers and helped them escape at the end of the war.[1]

The Woman at His Side is a meditation on guilt, complicity, responsibility, and representation. Given their intimate association with Nazi crimes, we would classify these women as perpetrators or, at the very least, accomplices. Nevertheless, this was not how they were seen after the end of the war. Most of them never faced legal prosecution, and postwar historical and cultural discourse construed them as innocent victims of or bystanders to Nazi crimes. Furthermore, the women themselves successfully exploited this idea in interviews and, in some cases, memoirs. The ambiguous status of these women in the discourse on the Holocaust is an illuminating example of the indeterminacy and fluidity of the categories of perpetrator and bystander, and, more importantly, of the strategic value of such categories within the discourse.

In this chapter, I will take the SS wives as a limit case for the construction and instrumentalization of the category of the bystander. To be clear: I am not suggesting that these women are or should be considered bystanders—on the contrary, by any reasonable definition they are perpetrators. Nevertheless, it has evidently been possible for them *to be cast* as bystanders, either by others or by themselves. What interests me is precisely how and why this was possible and what this reveals about the category of the bystander as such. "Bystander" is not a static a priori category but rather a discursive one that always entails a strategic or performative element. It is a label that is often applied only retroactively, often entirely divorced from historical facts and thus intrinsically unverifiable. Furthermore, as we shall see, it is this performative aspect that *The Woman at His Side* mobilizes and renders visible. As said, the performance consists almost entirely of statements by the SS wives. Minimal historical commentary provides context but never an interpretation or a judgment. This absence of explicit moralistic didacticism makes the piece valuable from an educational standpoint: precisely because it does not close on a single verdict, it leaves it up to the audience to form an opinion on these women and encounter them as human beings with hopes, desires, and fears.

In this way, *The Woman at His Side* can be seen as an example of practice-based research. The three actors do not merely read the texts aloud; they enliven them with gestures, movements, and facial expressions. At strategic moments, they play music or other sound recordings from the time (such as a speech by Heinrich Himmler). They do not, however, aim at a mimetic representation: they never imitate the voices of the historical persons, and they do not wear costumes. They always remain actors, firmly anchored in the present, exhibiting the words of these women. There are other distancing devices that minimize any auratic quality, such as the deliberately low-tech tape recorder they use to play the songs, the absence of dramatic light effects, and the laying open of all sources. Each passage is immediately followed by the bibliographic reference, read out by one of the actors.

The final section of the piece centers on the figures of Lina Heydrich and Thea Stangl, giving a glimpse of their postwar lives and in particular of their diametrically opposed perspectives on the past. Whereas Stangl, in a famous interview conducted by the historian Gitta Sereny, is clearly conflicted and finds it difficult to talk about that time, Heydrich, on the contrary, is entirely unapologetic and even proud of her achievements, as evinced by her 1976 autobiography. The actors read out substantial passages from both of these texts, ending with a long quotation from Sereny's book *Into That Darkness*, where at the end of their final interview in Brazil, Sereny asks Stangl whether, if she had issued her husband an ultimatum, "Treblinka—or me," he would have chosen her or the job.[2] Stangl at first responds, haltingly, that he would have chosen her, but later that night she writes a letter in which she retracts that answer, insisting that her husband would "never have destroyed himself or the family," the implication being that this would have been the consequence of resigning from his post. When Sereny calls Stangl about this letter, the latter begins to cry and says that she doesn't know which answer she wants Sereny to include in her book. Sereny tells her, "I would put in my book what she had said to me the previous day—which I thought was the truth. But that I would also add the letter, which only showed what we all know, which is that the truth can be a terrible thing, sometimes too terrible to live with."[3] These are also the final words of *The Woman at His Side*.

Beyond the question of truth and the difficulty of living with it, these two answers also highlight the active and passive dimensions of "standing by" that I would like to draw out in this chapter. Here it is important to distinguish between bystandership in the moment, when crimes are committed, and a secondary bystandership after the fact, in the moment of bearing witness. Both have passive and active connotations. The implication of Thea Stangl's first answer is that she could have intervened and that by not issuing an ultimatum she in fact actively (albeit through inaction) enabled her husband's crimes. In this way, she would be what Ernesto Verdeja has called a "moral bystander," bearing "some responsibility by virtue of being in a position to intercede and consequently alter the direction of events, and yet fail[ing] to act."[4] In her second answer, by contrast, Stangl insists that there was nothing she could have done to prevent her husband's crimes and that he was in fact merely following orders to protect himself and the family. In this answer, she fashions herself as an innocent and passive bystander to the crimes of the Third Reich, and even her husband's responsibility is diminished. In this scenario, she could not be described as a moral bystander, since she was unable to exercise morally significant agency, owing to external circumstances. It is important to emphasize that she is offering this interpretation of her capacity for agency in retrospect, so it cannot simply be considered neutral. Moreover, her retraction can also be seen as a consequence of her realization that with her first answer she had incriminated not only herself but also her husband. The revised answer, therefore, is itself a form of active bystandership in the sense that she "stood by" her man and his legacy.

The first form of bystandership has to do with the real or perceived scope for action available to an individual in the context of an atrocity. Applying this label, however, is an interpretation that is always on some level subjective and certainly not neutral or empirically verifiable. Therefore, labeling someone a bystander—or a perpetrator or victim, for that matter—is also always on some level strategic, that is, a means to a particular end. This strategy can be employed by the individuals themselves, as we see in the case of Thea Stangl. Here, I am principally interested in precisely this strategic dimension, which has more to do with representation and interpretation than with facts and empirical data. This is not to say that the facts are irrelevant but rather to insist that they are established, disseminated, and interpreted within a discursive field. In short, in what follows I will be less interested in the term "bystander" as an ontological category, that is, whether these women *really were* bystanders, perpetrators, or something else. Rather, I am more interested in the various ways in which they have been represented and have represented themselves, in what is at stake in applying labels such as bystander, and in how such labels may in fact obscure dynamics that are more complex.

In what follows, I will proceed in three stages corresponding to three different yet interrelated layers of representation regarding the SS wives. The first concerns the historical record: who were these women, what did they do, and what did they know? Here I will rely principally on Schwarz's study. Second, I will consider the representation of these women in scholarship, in the media, and in their own accounts, focusing particularly on Lina Heydrich's controversial autobiography. Finally, I will return to *The Woman at His Side*, which I read as a critical metacommentary on the previous layers: the piece integrates the insights and perspectives of current scholarship and brings them to bear on the representation of these women's lives.

More specifically, the use of quotation and repetition in the piece constitutes an affirmative critique, both of the women themselves and of the popular and scholarly discourse that surrounds them. These techniques create room for reflection and engagement that has the potential, paradoxically, to produce a difference. This is not to suggest that we endorse, rehabilitate, or assent to these women's words and actions. Rather, I am drawing here on the concept of the affirmative as it has been articulated in recent feminist philosophy as an alternative to traditional forms of critique, which tend, as Elizabeth Grosz writes, "to generate defensive self-representations" or else promote a dismissive stance toward the object of critique, presenting the moral and intellectual superiority of the critic as unassailable.[5] *The Woman at His Side* does not try to legislate in advance how the audience should respond to these women's words and in this way facilitates a more open-ended engagement with the profound questions their words and actions raise for us today.

The Historical Record: Who Were They, What Did They Do, What Did They Know?

Gudrun Schwarz's *Eine Frau an seiner Seite* (1997) is the only in-depth study of the important position of women in the SS.[6] Schwarz bases her study on the SS marriage files of the SS Race and Settlement Main Office (Rasse- und Siedlungshauptamt der SS), the files from the

Personal Staff of the Reich Leader of the SS (Hauptamt Persönlicher Stab Reichsführer-SS), including letters Himmler exchanged with the SS wives, and the Central Office of the State Justice Administrations (Zentrale Stelle der Landesjustizverwaltungen) in Ludwigsburg. She shows that, far from being a male-only elite organization, the SS under Himmler was actually a *Sippengemeinschaft* in which women played a crucial role, not only as the "keepers of the race" and mothers of future "Aryans" but also by normalizing of the crimes of the SS. From 1932 onward, all SS men were required to marry, and their would-be brides were subjected to rigorous vetting to determine their Aryan credentials as well as their moral and physical constitution. From 1931 to 1945, almost a quarter of a million women married into the SS.[7] Many lived with their families in the SS settlements at concentration camps, ghettos, and in towns and villages in the occupied territories, where they inevitably came into close contact with the workings of the Nazi persecution and extermination machine. They profited directly and indirectly from the persecutions.[8] Moreover, SS wives were "to establish a normal family life in the field in order to make the crimes their husbands committed there appear like an ordinary job. They were to mitigate the stress of the situation and thus enable their husbands to commit these terrible acts and to transform the place itself into something ordinary and everyday."[9] This involved hosting dinner parties, organizing leisure activities, and teaching children, but some wives took a more active part in the killing operations, for instance, by helping their husbands with the paperwork.[10]

In short, in the eyes of both the SS leadership and the wives themselves, the actions carried out by the SS would have been unthinkable without the support of the women in the *Sippengemeinschaft*. Thus, "the SS wives became perpetrators" themselves.[11] This loyalty continued after the end of the war when they helped their husbands hide and escape, and followed them into exile.[12] In the immediate postwar period, this loyalty was depoliticized and came to be seen as almost admirable and in some cases even served to rehabilitate the domestic values promoted by the *SS-Sippengemeinschaft* and National Socialism more generally.[13] Schwarz discusses a series of illustrated feature stories published in the weekly *Die Strasse* in 1950 entitled "My Husband—The War Criminal," each focusing on a different prominent SS family, and featuring interviews with the likes of Ilse Hess and Maria Frank. The image these women present of themselves and their family—unchallenged by the interviewer—is decidedly rose-tinted and fetishistic, imbued with a mixture of nostalgia and the cult of celebrity and notoriety. The term "war criminal" is presented almost as a badge of honor and/or as an ironic reference to the cliché that history is written by the victors.[14]

This stance is taken up even more clearly in the title of Lina Heydrich's autobiography, *Leben mit einem Kriegsverbrecher* (Life with a war criminal), which is overtly ironic, given her defiantly unapologetic stance. The SS wives were never put on trial. Evidently, Schwarz concludes, the court adhered to a traditional conception of gender roles whereby "the woman's place was in the home, far from any opportunity to commit crimes or to participate in them."[15] Nor was the court alone in this reductive view of female agency. In postwar German society, the steadfastness with which these women stood by their husbands "through thick and thin" made them appear as passive and apolitical bystanders. This was a role that many SS wives were only too eager to embrace. It was not until the late 1990s that this lenient appraisal of the SS wives' complicity came under critical scrutiny.

Representation in Scholarship, the Media, and Autobiography

Until quite recently, the discourse on women under National Socialism has overall been informed by a rather conservative understanding of femininity and gender roles. Indeed, there is a striking continuity between pre- and postwar representations of women, which tend to fall into the familiar dichotomy of innocence/depravity, mothers/whores.[16] This had profound implications not only for how the trials against female Nazi perpetrators were reported in the press but also on the trials themselves. As already mentioned, most women who were implicated in the crimes of the Nazis, including the SS wives, were never prosecuted because they failed to meet the criterion of demonstrable and deliberate criminal action and were hence not considered legally liable.[17] Those who *were* put on trial for their crimes, such as female concentration camp guards, were cast either as living proof of deviant femininity—the "beast," the *Mannweib* (she-man), or the "pervert"—or as victims of the circumstances, too young to understand what had truly been going on, or simply overwhelmed by the events.[18] This resulted in acquittals or lenient sentences for the latter group, in sharp contrast to the sensationalized trials of the women in the former group, such as, for example, Ilse Koch, the "Beast of Buchenwald," and Irma Grese, the "Hyena of Auschwitz." This kind of sensationalism is an enduring element of popular representations of women under National Socialism in the media, in films, and on television.[19]

Changing conceptions of femininity and gender dynamics have also left their mark on scholarship. Christina Herkommer has identified three dominant historiographical paradigms: the "victim thesis" of the 1980s, the "perpetrator thesis" of the 1990s, and the more recent approaches, which are ultimately a further development and refinement of the perpetrator thesis, exploring a multiplicity of roles, subject positions, and scopes for action (*Handlungsräume*), taking into account the social constructedness of gender categories and other insights from feminist theory and cultural studies.[20] The gray zones and more fluid lines between perpetrators, bystanders, and profiteers, however, still need further exploration and theorization. Other works have laid the foundation for a theory of agency based on the concept of the *Handlungsraum*.[21] Perhaps we might refer to this as the "bystander thesis." Studying the *Handlungsräume* of people during the Nazi regime, as well as their own perception, at the time and in retrospect, of the relative freedom to make decisions reveals how bystandership is not the product of a singular failure to act but rather depends on a series of contingent decisions and as such is not an ontological category defined by passivity but rather an actively reinforced, relational subject position that must be continually produced and performed.

Ernesto Verdeja's concept of the moral bystander can productively be read in conjunction with this "bystander thesis." Central to Verdeja's conception is the distinction between knowledge and acknowledgment. In order for an individual to be morally responsible for failing to act, they must have sufficient knowledge that an action or event in which they could potentially intervene is taking place. For this reason, the first line of defense against accusations of moral responsibility is the claim of ignorance. There is a difference, however, between knowledge of a crime and the acknowledgment that an action is in fact a crime. For Verdeja, this acknowledgment constitutes the criterion for moral bystanding. Thus, the category of the moral bystander depends on the subject's interpretation of the event in question. This raises intriguing questions with regard to the two SS wives Thea Stangl and Lina Heydrich.

In her interview with Sereny, Stangl recounts the moment at which it was no longer possible for her to remain ignorant of the genocide and, crucially, appears at least in retrospect to acknowledge, albeit reluctantly, that this was a crime and that she could have done something. Of the two answers she gives to Sereny's aforementioned question, the first, which Sereny judges to be the truth, is the one that makes her a moral bystander because she not only acknowledges that what was happening was a crime but also that she had the capacity to act. This answer might well be more satisfying for the reader and for Sereny as the interpretive authority, not only because it feels closer to the truth but also because it allows us to maintain our faith in the individual's capacity to act morally in the face of atrocity. This, too, is a function of the category of the bystander as such: it asserts the possibility of moral action *ex negativo*: a bystander is someone who could and more importantly should have done something to prevent a crime. Therefore, the category of the bystander holds open the individual's scope for action while acknowledging the various constraints and limitations within a social system.

The importance of Verdeja's distinction between knowledge and acknowledgment becomes very clear if we turn to Lina Heydrich's autobiography, published around the same time as Sereny's book, in which we find a diametrically opposed ratio of the two terms. Heydrich takes pride in her knowledge of her husband's activities but resolutely refuses to acknowledge them as crimes that she could or should have sought to prevent. This lack of acknowledgment above all makes her book so disturbing and morally repugnant. Published in 1976, *Leben mit einem Kriegsverbrecher* describes the years she spent as the wife and later widow of Reinhard Heydrich, the chief of the Reich Main Security Office and deputy *Reichsprotektor* of Bohemia and Moravia in Prague. The text gives detailed insight not only into the Heydrichs' personal life but also into their ambitions and political calculations, as well as the intrigues and manipulations among the Nazi leaders. In contrast to what the title suggests, the book is anything but a reckoning with Lina Heydrich's complicity in her husband's crimes. The tone is unapologetic—Heydrich certainly does not think of her husband as a war criminal—and she brazenly presents herself as a victim of postwar "injustice."[22]

The book is full of historical and chronological inaccuracies, most of which are nothing but deliberately exculpatory obfuscations. In order to draw attention to and compensate for these falsifications, the publisher asked the historian Werner Maser to provide an extensive commentary. Maser only reluctantly accepted the task, and his comments suggest that he does not take Heydrich very seriously. He states that the memoir should rather have been commented on by a psychiatrist, not a historian, and deplores the fact that she remained "inconvincible" by facts and documents, thus missing her chance at repentance.[23] To Maser, the memoir seems of value only insofar as it provides a glimpse into the personality of Reinhard Heydrich. The "politicizing widow" (as Himmler once disparagingly called Lina Heydrich) is for Maser, if anything, a pathological figure, alternately presented as an incorrigible liar or as a gullible housewife. He is decidedly uninterested in her as a person or a historical agent. Tellingly, while he goes to great lengths to point out the mistakes she makes when speaking about her husband, he fails to draw attention to the significant ambiguity surrounding her own involvement in the regime.

This peculiar lack of interest in and apparently deliberate misreading of the figure of Lina Heydrich is corroborated by the book's blurb, an excerpt from a review in the German newspaper *Die Welt*, which asks: "Is Lina Heydrich perhaps a deeply apolitical person, which would explain a lot, or is she just pretending to be?" Both Maser's and the reviewer's assessments are wide of the mark, and while autobiographies in general and especially self-justificatory texts by morally suspect people like Heydrich should not be taken at face value, it is clear to anyone who reads this memoir carefully that she neither is nor pretends to be apolitical. While she is unquestionably a highly unreliable witness, we should not dismiss her text outright but rather read it even more carefully. This is especially important because the assessment of Heydrich as either ignorant or psychopathic exemplifies the stereotypical postwar discourse on women who had been involved in the Nazi regime as either depraved and sadistic or obedient and naive.

When reading the memoir, it becomes clear that Heydrich was an intelligent and ambitious woman with firm political convictions. Her book is a success story and, in a different context, could almost be read as a narrative of female empowerment. She details the crucial role she played in her husband's career—as a staunch National Socialist and a fervent antisemite,[24] it was she who persuaded her husband to join the Nazi Party and to consider a career in the SS—but also her own achievements as estate manager and farming expert before and after 1945.

The historical errors in the memoir certainly cannot be ascribed to her ignorance of the persecutory politics of the Nazis—a fact that is perhaps best illustrated by her critical remarks about what she perceived to be the intellectualism and incompetence of Himmler. In her opinion, if it had not been for people such as her husband, Himmler would have been utterly lost.[25] In the passages in which she describes how she and her husband discussed political events, Heydrich reveals, almost in spite of herself, the extent of her knowledge. Nevertheless, at no point does she address or acknowledge her own active involvement in and responsibility for the crimes committed by the Nazis. Not surprisingly, Heydrich was not pleased with Maser's dismissive commentary on her memoir and tried repeatedly to have it removed by the publisher. When she failed, she took matters into her own hands and simply cut out the offending pages from the copies she sent to her friends and family. In 2012, on the seventieth anniversary of Reinhard Heydrich's death, the memoir was republished by their son Heider, with a new introduction, with amendments to the original text, and, most importantly, *without* the historical commentary included in the first edition. The title is now *Mein Leben mit Reinhard* (My life with Reinhard), and the publisher is the revisionist Druffel & Vowinckel, which is part of the Verlagsgruppe Berg, the biggest extreme-right publishing house in Germany.[26] However flawed one may find Maser's commentary of the first edition, it is even more problematic to have no critical framework at all.

Neither of the two editions facilitates the kind of engagement with this text and its author that might prompt critical self-reflection on the part of the reader. Maser clearly thinks that Heydrich has nothing worthwhile to tell us. He thus writes from a position of absolute moral superiority, but his refusal, to quote Grosz again, to "bother further with" her position is ultimately also a defensive attitude. How might one engage with the text without either endorsing or condemning it outright? Admittedly, her resolute lack of repentance and self-reflection make it difficult to read her text affirmatively, but it might still be worthwhile if it allows us to arrive at a deeper understanding of the worldview and motivations behind her actions—and perhaps even of our own assumptions, motivations, and agency.

The Woman at His Side

The Woman at His Side, I argue, can be read as an example of such an affirmative critique of SS wives' self-presentation. The performance is prefaced by a series of short statements, epigraphs almost, by some of the main protagonists. These statements were all given after the end of the war, either in interviews or in memoirs, and they return as leitmotifs over the course of the performance. They illustrate the different ways in which these women presented themselves to scholars and the public after the war.

Ruth Kalder-Göth, for example, was defiantly proud and still longed for her life with the KZ commandant Amon Göth: "Ah, yes, Göth—what a dream man. It was a beautiful time; we enjoyed being together. My Göth was the king, and I was his queen. Who wouldn't have traded places with us?" Fanny Fritsch, on the other hand, was in complete denial of the historical facts: "What they say about Auschwitz, about the extermination of the Jews, and all that—is a lie!" And Lina Heydrich presents herself and her husband as victims of the times: "Had the world not been so broken back then, today I would be not the wife of a war criminal but rather the wife of a brilliant violinist." Furthermore, these self-presentations functioned at the time as counternarratives to the supposed mischaracterizations and lies in the press and in the popular imagination. Each woman speaks out against what they perceive to be a false representation of themselves and their husbands.

These opening statements serve several functions. The most immediate is that of prolepsis, casting the trajectory that follows in a certain light. Second, and relatedly, the statements recur as a kind of refrain that continues to comment on the narrative as it unfolds, and with each repetition the words take on a slightly different hue. This can itself be read as a meta-reflection on repetition as a representational device, which then refers back to the performance as a whole, which consists entirely of quotations. Finally, the wives' insistence that the dominant narrative circulating about them and their husbands is false and must be set right alludes to the constructedness of all narratives. Throughout the performance, some of these quotations are replayed on a Dictaphone, whose small speaker distorts the sound, adding a ghostly dimension but also invoking the documentary, journalistic, and legal context in which these statements were originally made. The women's words come back to haunt them. Repeated in the new context, the words now appear to comment on the atrocities that these women witnessed and facilitated. In a form of dramatic irony, they are thus made to incriminate themselves.

At this point, one might ask what the difference is between simply reading these women's words and attending a performance of *The Woman at His Side*, which, after all, consists almost entirely of those same words read out loud. In what way can this performance be considered a critical intervention into the discourse on women under National Socialism if it refrains from critical commentary? The answer lies on the one hand in the embodied presence of the three actors on stage who give voice to these words. Crucially, these are not the voices of Thea Stangl, Lina Heydrich, and others. While we do hear some original sound recordings, they are not of the women themselves, but of songs, speeches, or radio features. This editorial decision is reinforced by the use of the Dictaphone: even when we hear a recording of their statements, it is a recording of one of the three actors speaking the line. This redoubling of mediation serves to heighten our awareness of the artificiality of the performance and simultaneously focuses our attention on the performance itself. The recording refers to the performance and not to the historical record. This leads into the second answer, which is that it deliberately refuses to grant the authority and aura of authenticity to the SS wives that hearing them speak might convey. In this way, their thoughts, opinions, and self-justifications become divorced from their specific historical persona and begin to circulate in the theater as floating signifiers that can attach themselves to new referents in new

Figure 15.1. *The Woman at His Side* (post-performance Q&A), Filmtheater 't Hoogt, Utrecht, 1 September 2016. *From left:* Sabine Werner, Inga Dietrich, Joanne Gläsel. (Photo: Kári Driscoll.)

configurations. This is reinforced by the fact that the epigraphs and several of the other returning statements are not "signed," that is, they are not followed by a name or attribution, which, given that each actor embodies multiple roles, means that it can be difficult or even impossible for the audience to know who exactly is speaking. Abstracted in this way from the individual biographies, these refrains become a kind of collage of the entire period.

In the writing, staging, and performance of the piece, the actors have taken great care to avoid indulging the kind of lurid fascination exemplified by the postwar magazine profiles on these women and their family life, as well as more recent popular representations on television and in other media, where the emphasis is always on the transgressive and illicit frisson of danger and evil that we may vicariously experience through these women and their stories. This is doubly important given that the piece is often performed at concentration camp memorials and other sites dedicated to the victims of Nazi persecution: in such a setting, any hint of glorification or voyeurism would be inappropriate and offensive.[27] It is equally important to avoid the opposite reaction, namely, immediate condemnation and repugnance, which likewise foreclose a genuine engagement with the complex moral, ethical, and representational questions at hand. *The Woman at His Side* aims to facilitate an encounter between the audience and these texts. And here it is important that this shared experience takes place in a specific location at a specific moment. We are invited to spend time with these women, albeit at a distance, not to condemn them outright but rather to affirm them, which, again, does not imply approval or endorsement but rather connotes an openness to the other and to one's encounter with it—a critical generosity. It means not taking one's own moral superiority for granted, at least not in a defensive attitude of the kind exhibited by Maser, for example. *The Woman at His Side* holds on to the idea that there is something to be learned from engaging with these women. At a minimum, this may serve to block the too-easy assertion that "I would have behaved differently," and this can be a valuable if uncomfortable insight. Conversely, it would be too easy to fall into the trap of moral relativism and say that, given the social and political circumstances at the time, there probably wasn't anything anyone could have done.

Virtually every performance is followed by an audience discussion with the actors, which is an important feature of the critical engagement with the material. It affords the audience an opportunity to ask questions pertaining to the creative process, the representational and aesthetic decisions that went into making the piece, as well as to discuss the questions of guilt and responsibility and scope for action. Conversely, these Q&A sessions enable the actors to gauge the audience's reaction, which can then help them revise the piece further. The reception has been overwhelmingly positive, in the press and among the audience, and on several occasions audience members have emphasized how the piece has prompted them to reevaluate their attitude toward their own family history. A performance of *The Woman at His Side* can be considered a success if it prompts this kind of critical reevaluation or reassessment, not only of the SS wives but also of the contemporary relevance of their biographies and actions. This reassessment hinges on the audience's willingness to be unsettled and to reevaluate their own position. In other words, the piece gives the audience credit and trusts them to be able to make up their own minds, albeit with clear guidance.

It is no coincidence, therefore, that the performance ends with Thea Stangl and not Lina Heydrich. This becomes very clear if we compare the stage play to the radio play, directed by Mairowitz, which preserves the narrative arc and many of the stylistic devices but omits the epigraphs and their repetition, as well as almost all of Stangl's account, including her reluctant acknowledgment of her own guilt. Instead, the radio play ends with Ruth Kalder-Göth's delusional description of Amon Göth as the perfect man, comparable only to Rhett Butler in *Gone with the Wind*, which, by implication, casts her as Scarlett O'Hara and their time at Plaszow as a romantic fantasy. As the music from the film swells, she declares that their life was glorious and that she has no regrets—that it was worth it to have soared like an eagle, if only for a brief moment. Thus, the radio play ends on a note of defiant pride and idealized nostalgia, which is bitterly ironic given the historical facts. We can only shake our heads in disbelief at this display of crass indifference and lack of self-awareness. This ending, together with the abundant use of original recordings and incidental music, certainly provides an immersive listening experience but ultimately limits the range of possible responses. Above all, the audience never needs to feel uncertain or insecure in their own moral superiority.

The Thea Stangl ending of the stage version, by contrast, performs a difficult and reluctant self-questioning, which, in turn, is harder for the audience to condemn. This is not to say that we automatically feel sympathy for her or uncritically accept her account, but the degree to which we should believe her is left open. Moreover, this ambiguity may prompt us to reflect on how we would have acted in her situation and come to terms with it after the fact. Whether we believe her or not, this ending makes it difficult to declare unequivocally either that one would certainly have taken action or that there was nothing that could have been done. In this way, Stangl's conflicted recognition of her own guilt serves to insist on the individual's capacity for moral agency. From this perspective, perhaps, it is also then necessary to affirm the category of the bystander as a figure of potentiality—not for its negative connotations of inaction and cowardice but rather for its implicit hope that things could have been otherwise.

Susanne C. Knittel is Assistant Professor of Comparative Literature at Utrecht University. Her research focuses on questions of memory, commemoration, and cultural amnesia across cultures and media. She is the author of *The Historical Uncanny: Disability, Ethnicity, and the Politics of Holocaust Memory* (Fordham University Press, 2015), a comparative study of German and Italian memory culture. Her current research focuses on the figure of the perpetrator in contemporary European memory culture. She is the founder of the Perpetrator Studies Network and editor-in-chief of the *Journal of Perpetrator Research*. For a list of publications, see https://www.uu.nl/medewerkers/SCKnittel/0.

Notes

The research for this chapter was supported by a VENI grant from the Netherlands Organisation for Scientific Research (NWO). I would like to thank the editors and Kári Driscoll, who translated all quotations from German, for their invaluable suggestions and comments.

1. Sabine Werner, Inga Dietrich, and Joanne Gläsel, *The Woman at His Side: Careers, Crimes, and Female Complicity under National Socialism*, trans. Kári Driscoll (unpublished manuscript, 2016); Gudrun Schwarz, *Eine Frau an seiner Seite: Ehefrauen in der SS-"Sippengemeinschaft"* (Berlin, 2001).
2. Gitta Sereny, *Into that Darkness: From Mercy Killing to Mass Murder* (1974; repr., London, 1995), 361.
3. Ibid., 362.
4. Ernesto Verdeja, "Moral Bystanders and Mass Violence," in *New Directions in Genocide Research*, ed. Adam Jones (New York, 2012), 154.
5. Elizabeth Grosz, *Time Travels: Feminism, Nature, Power* (Durham, NC, 2005), 3.
6. While more recent studies of women in the Third Reich do discuss some of the SS wives, they rely heavily on Schwarz's book; e.g., Kathrin Kompisch, *Täterinnen: Frauen im Nationalsozialismus* (Cologne, 2008) and Wendy Lower, *Hitler's Furies* (London, 2014),
7. Schwarz, *Eine Frau*, 11.
8. Ibid., 100.
9. Ibid., 102. All translations are by Kári Driscoll unless otherwise indicated.
10. Ibid., 229–237.
11. Ibid., 103.
12. Ibid., 239–269.
13. Ibid., 270–278.
14. Ibid., 272.
15. Ibid., 237.
16. See Elke Frietsch and Christina Herkommer, "Nationalsozialismus und Geschlecht: Eine Einführung," in *Nationalsozialismus und Geschlecht: Zur Politisierung und Ästhetisierung von Körper, "Rasse" und Sexualität im Dritten Reich und nach 1945*, ed. Elke Frietsch and Christina Herkommer (Bielefeld, 2009), 9–44; Susannah Heschel, "Does Atrocity Have a Gender? Feminist Interpretations of Women in the SS," in *Lessons and Legacies VI: New Currents in Holocaust Research*, ed. Jeffry M. Diefendorf (Evanston, IL, 2004), 300–321.
17. See Ulrike Weckel and Edgar Wolfrum, *"Bestien" und "Befehlsempfänger": Frauen und Männer in NS-Prozessen nach 1945* (Göttingen, 2003), 9–21.
18. See Insa Eschebach, "Gespaltene Frauenbilder: Geschlechterdramaturgien im juristischen Diskurs ostdeutscher Gerichte," in Weckel and Wolfrum, *"Bestien" und "Befehlsempfänger,"* 95–116; Kathrin Meyer, "'Die Frau ist der Frieden der Welt': Von Nutzen und Lasten eines Weiblichkeitsstereotyps in Spruchkammerentscheidungen gegen Frauen," in Weckel and Wolfrum, *"Bestien" und "Befehlsempfänger,"* 117–138.
19. See Johanna Gehmacher, "Im Umfeld der Macht: populäre Perspektiven auf Frauen der NS-Elite," in Frietsch and Herkommer, *Nationalsozialismus und Geschlecht*, 49–69; Elissa Mailänder, "Unsere Mütter, unsere Großmütter: Erforschung und Repräsentation weiblicher NS-Täterschaft in Wissenschaft und Gesellschaft," in *Nationalsozialistische Täterschaften: Nachwirkungen in Gesellschaft und Familie*, ed. Oliver von Wrochem and Christine Eckel (Berlin, 2016), 83–101; Anna Maria Sigmund, *Die Frauen der Nazis* (Munich, 1998).

20. Christina Herkommer, "Women under National Socialism: Women's Scope for Action and the Issue of Gender," in *Ordinary People as Mass Murderers: Perpetrators in Comparative Perspective*, ed. Olaf Jensen and Claus-Christian W. Szejnmann (Basingstoke, 2008), 100–107, 111–115.
21. Kirsten Heinsohn, Barbara Vogel, and Ulrike Weckel, eds., *Zwischen Karriere und Verfolgung: Handlungsräume von Frauen im nationalsozialistischen Deutschland* (Frankfurt, 1997); Sibylle Steinbacher, ed., *Volksgenossinnen: Frauen in der NS-Volksgemeinschaft* (Göttingen, 2007); Jutta Mühlenberg, "Die SS-Helferinnen und das weibliche Gefolge der SS: Tätigkeiten, Dienststellen und Einsätze von Frauen im Organisationsapparat der Waffen-SS," in *Die Waffen-SS: Neue Forschungen*, ed. Jan Erik Schulte, Peter Lieb, and Bernd Wegener (Paderborn, 2014), 99–114.
22. Lina Heydrich, *Leben mit einem Kriegsverbrecher* (Pfaffenhofen, 1976), 147.
23. Ibid., 161–162.
24. Robert Gerwarth, *Reinhard Heydrich: Biographie* (Munich, 2011), 61–62.
25. Heydrich, *Leben mit einem Kriegsverbrecher*, 85–86.
26. Lina Heydrich, *Mein Leben mit Reinhard: Die persönliche Biographie*, ed. Heider Heydrich (Gilching, 2012).
27. Personal communication with Sabine Werner, December 2016.

Bibliography

Eschebach, Insa. "Gespaltene Frauenbilder: Geschlechterdramaturgien im juristischen Diskurs ostdeutscher Gerichte." In Weckel and Wolfrum, *"Bestien" und "Befehlsempfänger,"* 95–116.

Frietsch, Elke and Christina Herkommer. "Nationalsozialismus und Geschlecht: Eine Einführung." In Frietsch and Herkommer, *Nationalsozialismus und Geschlecht*, 9–44.

———, eds. *Nationalsozialismus und Geschlecht: Zur Politisierung und Ästhetisierung von Körper, "Rasse" und Sexualität im Dritten Reich und nach 1945*. Bielefeld: Transcript, 2009.

Gehmacher, Johanna. "Im Umfeld der Macht: populäre Perspektiven auf Frauen der NS-Elite." In Frietsch and Herkommer, *Nationalsozialismus und Geschlecht*, 49–69.

Gerwarth, Robert. *Reinhard Heydrich: Biographie*. Munich, Siedler: 2011.

Grosz, Elizabeth. *Time Travels: Feminism, Nature, Power*. Durham, NC: Duke University Press, 2005.

Heinsohn, Kirsten, Barbara Vogel, and Ulrike Weckel, eds. *Zwischen Karriere und Verfolgung: Handlungsräume von Frauen im nationalsozialistischen Deutschland*. Frankfurt: Campus, 1997.

Herkommer, Christina. "Women under National Socialism: Women's Scope for Action and the Issue of Gender." In *Ordinary People as Mass Murderers: Perpetrators in Comparative Perspective*, edited by Olaf Jensen and Claus-Christian W. Szejnmann, 99–119. Basingstoke: Palgrave Macmillan, 2008.

Heschel, Susannah. "Does Atrocity Have a Gender? Feminist Interpretations of Women in the SS." In *Lessons and Legacies VI: New Currents in Holocaust Research*, edited by Jeffry M. Diefendorf, 300–321. Evanston, IL: Northwestern University Press, 2004.

Heydrich, Lina. *Leben mit einem Kriegsverbrecher*. Pfaffenhofen: Verlag W. Ludwig, 1976.

———. *Mein Leben mit Reinhard: Die persönliche Biographie*. Edited by Heider Heydrich. Gilching: Druffel & Vowinckel, 2012.

Kompisch, Kathrin. *Täterinnen: Frauen im Nationalsozialismus*. Cologne: Böhlau, 2008.

Lower, Wendy. *Hitler's Furies: German Women in the Nazi Killing Fields*. London: Vintage, 2014.
Mailänder, Elissa. "Unsere Mütter, unsere Großmütter: Erforschung und Repräsentation weiblicher NS-Täterschaft in Wissenschaft und Gesellschaft." In *Nationalsozialistische Täterschaften: Nachwirkungen in Gesellschaft und Familie*, edited by Oliver von Wrochem and Christine Eckel, 83–101. Berlin: Metropol, 2016.
Meyer, Kathrin. "'Die Frau ist der Frieden der Welt': Von Nutzen und Lasten eines Weiblichkeitsstereotyps in Spruchkammerentscheidungen gegen Frauen." In Weckel and Wolfrum, *"Bestien" und "Befehlsempfänger,"* 117–138.
Mühlenberg, Jutta. "Die SS-Helferinnen und das weibliche Gefolge der SS: Tätigkeiten, Dienststellen und Einsätze von Frauen im Organisationsapparat der Waffen-SS." In *Die Waffen-SS: Neue Forschungen*, edited by Jan Erik Schulte, Peter Lieb, and Bernd Wegener, 99–114. Paderborn: Schöningh, 2014.
Schwarz, Gudrun. *Eine Frau an seiner Seite: Ehefrauen in der SS-"Sippengemeinschaft."* 1997. Reprint, Berlin: Aufbau, 2001.
Sereny, Gitta. *Into That Darkness: From Mercy Killing to Mass Murder*. 1974. Reprint, London: Pimlico, 1995.
Sigmund, Anna Maria. *Die Frauen der Nazis*. Munich: Wilhelm Heyne Verlag, 1998.
Steinbacher, Sybille. *Volksgenossinnen: Frauen in der NS-Volksgemeinschaft*. Göttingen: Wallstein, 2007.
Verdeja, Ernesto. "Moral Bystanders and Mass Violence." In *New Directions in Genocide Research*, edited by Adam Jones, 153–168. New York: Routledge, 2012.
Weckel, Ulrike and Edgar Wolfrum, eds. *"Bestien" und "Befehlsempfänger": Frauen und Männer in NS-Prozessen nach 1945*. Göttingen: Vandenhoeck & Ruprecht, 2003.
Werner, Sabine, Inga Dietrich, and Joanne Gläsel. *The Woman at His Side: Careers, Crimes, and Female Complicity under National Socialism*, translated by Kári Driscoll. Unpublished manuscript, 2016.

CHAPTER 16

"BYSTANDERS" IN EXHIBITIONS AT THE UNITED STATES HOLOCAUST MEMORIAL MUSEUM

Susan Bachrach

The United States Holocaust Memorial Museum (USHMM) opened in April 1993 and has become a prominent feature in the landscape of the nation's capital, Washington, DC. The USHMM welcomes more than 1.5 million visitors every year, from students, educators, and tourists to foreign diplomats and leaders. In addition, the USHMM's scholarly wing, the Jack, Joseph and Morton Mandel Center for Advanced Holocaust Studies, attracts researchers from the United States and abroad drawn by workshops and seminars and by the museum's vast archival holdings and art and artifact collections.

Since the beginning, the "bystander" has been central to the USHMM's educational mission. In 1979, President Jimmy Carter's Commission on the Holocaust, chaired by the Holocaust survivor Elie Wiesel, recommended the creation of a museum to advance "an understanding of the Holocaust," beginning with "the roles of the bystanders as well as the perpetrators and victims."[1] Fifteen years later, the museum's first director, Jeshajahu Weinberg, said, "The most important lessons for visitors to take away from their museum experience are the insights that bystanders, by omission, became accomplices of the perpetrators."[2] Soon after, he added:

The Museum believes that one of the Holocaust's fundamental lessons is that to be a bystander is to share in the guilt. This lesson is applicable to the contemporary problems of society and to the behavior of individuals. Within any society, groups and individuals are constantly confronted with the destructive potential human beings possess. Only the intervention of the bystander can help society to become more human.[3]

Treatment of "Bystanders" in the Permanent Exhibition

The commissioners, Weinberg, and others who helped create the USHMM's permanent exhibition, *The Holocaust*, hoped that lessons about "bystanders" would emerge, in the first instance, from the power of the historical narrative. As Edward Linenthal, the chronicler of the museum's creation, explained in his book *Preserving Memory: The Struggle to Create America's Holocaust Museum*, "The commissioners assumed that it was important to arouse strong emotion in the visitor in order to bring about a moral transformation; their unspoken assumption was that enlightened attitudes toward others and wise public-policy decisions would emerge from an emotional encounter with the museum's Holocaust."[4] Advancing this overarching goal, the creators of the permanent exhibition also included explicit content about the "bystander." To begin with, wherever possible, they selected photographs of events documenting the persecution of Jews and other groups the Nazis targeted that also showed individuals who were onlookers or non-German collaborators.[5] The distinctions among participants may be lost on most visitors. Still, the inclusion of photographs showing individuals who were not German but involved in the events is considered important. Museum educators giving tours of the exhibition often point out the different actors present in the photographs, for example, onlookers who participated in the public humiliation of Jewish men accused of "racial defilement" for having relations with German women, or non-German police forces who assisted in the deportations of Jews and Roma from countries all over Europe to Nazi killing sites.

A second way that the permanent exhibition includes content devoted to "the roles of bystanders" is a "wall of rescuers" on which are inscribed the names by country of those recognized as "righteous gentiles" by Yad Vashem, the Israeli Holocaust memorial authority. For selected "righteous" persons, photographs and text have been included. The intention here was that the "righteous" serve as "role models for people who find themselves in the position of bystanders."[6] The wall stands adjacent to now iconic stories of rescue involving diplomats (Raoul Wallenberg),

Figure 16.1. The "wall of the rescuers" in the museum's permanent exhibition lists the names of the "righteous" who helped Jews. (United States Holocaust Memorial Museum. Photo: Miriam Lomaskin.)

communities (Le Chambon), organizations (Żegota), and nations (Denmark).

A third overt treatment of "bystanders" in the permanent exhibition is a text panel that stands alone with no visuals. It appears on the last floor of the exhibition near the segment "*Postwar Justice*," but it is often missed because it competes with audiovisual monitors showing excerpts of postwar trials of leading Nazi perpetrators. The text panel focuses on "the role of bystanders" as witnesses to the roundups, internment, and sometimes the murder of Jews within or near their communities. In the text, the "great majority of Europeans"—individuals in "France," "Poles," "citizens of the Soviet and Baltic republics," and "Germans"—are characterized as mostly passive and silent onlookers: "Some bystanders sought to exploit the situation of the Jews for personal gain, but most merely stood by, neither collaborating nor coming to the aid of the victims. This passivity amounted to acquiescence, and the planners and executors of the "Final Solution" counted on bystanders not intervening in the process of genocide.

Finally, the permanent exhibition highlights the "bystander" through the use of the now familiar words of Martin Niemöller, a German theologian and pastor, who, as the text points out, changed from a Nazi

Figure 16.2. Visitors study the Niemöller "bystander" quotation in the museum's permanent exhibition. (United States Holocaust Memorial Museum. Photo: Max Reid.)

supporter into an outspoken critic, for which the Nazis imprisoned him for more than seven years: "First they came for the socialists, and I did not speak out because I was not a socialist," its first line reads. This quotation—notably linked to a public, moral leader and not to any of the anonymous, ordinary individuals mentioned in the aforementioned "bystander" text panel—originally appeared in a location overlooked by most visitors. For this reason, it was moved to the wall by the gallery exit in early 2007. Now it is the last text all visitors sees as they leave the permanent exhibition, and many do indeed stop to read it. The same quote appears in a pamphlet distributed at the exit as part of a discussion on post-Holocaust efforts toward Christian-Jewish reconciliation.[7]

Apart from the above references to mostly European "bystanders," by far the most prominent "bystanders" in the USHMM's permanent exhibition are the US government and American society. This reflects the exhibition's Americanized presentation of the Holocaust that aimed to engage the primary audience by including content relevant to America's own history.[8] American soldiers who entered Nazi concentration camps and subcamps at the end of the war are seen on video and in large photomurals that open the exhibition. Visitors hear "How could this have happened?" spoken by a US Army veteran before returning to the beginning of the historical narrative starting with the Nazi rise to power. In addition to the US museum's creation by American citizens, the focus on the United States and its institutions and groups also fits with Holocaust scholarship of twenty-five years ago that identified many "bystanders" as nation-states and outside organizations and institutions such as the International Committee of the Red Cross and the churches.[9]

Critical discussions of "American responses" to events of the Holocaust appear in several places in the exhibition. The refugee question, and opposition to changing existing immigration law during the refugee crisis of the late 1930s in particular, is treated in several segments, including one on the fruitless international conference on the Jewish refugee crisis convened at Evian, France, in July 1938 and another on the ill-fated voyage of the MS *St. Louis* in 1939. Audiovisual programs present American responses to key events from the German boycott of Jewish businesses to the terror and violence of the 1938 November Pogrom (Kristallnacht). Regarding knowledge of the "final solution" and subsequent action or inaction, there are segments on the work of the War Refugee Board established by President Franklin D. Roosevelt in 1944 (described after the war by its first director, John Pehle, as an effort that was "late and little") and an audiovisual program on American responses to news of systematic mass murder.[10]

The museum's status as an independent establishment of the federal government, not as a private Jewish institution, influenced the prominent inclusion of this content, as did the location of the museum in the heart of Washington, DC, close to the seats of the US government. The USHMM seeks to remind visitors to the nation's capital of "their own responsibilities as citizens of a democracy."[11] Visitor evaluations show that many do leave the exhibition better informed about what Americans knew about events while they unfolded and the relative indifference of US leaders and most ordinary citizens to the fate of European Jews. The following are a few statements by unidentified visitors selected from interviews conducted at the museum in 2004:

> They tried to sweep it under the rug and ignore it; they knew but did nothing.
> The US was really aware of what was happening, but didn't act until too late.
> They were unwilling to help.
> The atrocities were reported in the press.
> It seems like we knew, was in all papers.
> The White House knew about the events but just sat by.
> Obviously we knew, but I don't think the American people were given all the truth; I can't imagine we could stand by, but we did![12]

Rationale for the *Some Were Neighbors* Exhibition

Treatment of "bystanders" in the USHMM's permanent exhibition, whether American or European, reflects Holocaust scholarship at the time, the late 1980s and early 1990s, when this exhibition was being conceived and produced. In the two decades since, more developed understandings have emerged both of "bystanders" in Europe and of American responses to the Holocaust. The creation of temporary exhibitions (and related programming on both topics)—*Some Were Neighbors: Collaboration and Complicity in the Holocaust* (2013–2017) and *Americans and the Holocaust* (2018–)—testifies to the museum's ongoing commitment to engage visitors on "the roles of the bystanders" and reflects its ability to benefit from new research that has advanced knowledge of the Holocaust.

The *Some Were Neighbors* exhibition provided the opportunity to explore a topic that was often referenced but with little nuance when the museum's permanent exhibition was created. As seen in previously referenced exhibition texts, discussions to that point tended to divide "bystanders" into those who did nothing to help the victims and the small minority of "rescuers." In most instances, historical analysis usually remained at the level of institutions—government, military, political, religious, cultural—and the elites who led them. Few local or grassroots studies had been conducted on the response of, say, ordinary German, Polish, French, or Dutch people. Studies of the expropriation and looting of Jewish property and of beneficiaries were few. Histories of the SS-organized mass shootings in Soviet territories relied primarily on German sources and delved little into what was happening on the ground in the hundreds of communities where Jews were slaughtered in mass executions, alongside prominent Communists, Roma, and other targeted groups. As a result, none of these important topics—the responses of "ordinary people" to the persecution of Jews within their communities, the looting of victims' property, or the mass shootings, with their implications for "the roles of the bystanders," were treated at much length in the museum's permanent exhibition.

Several developments that occurred since the USHMM opened have affected both Holocaust research and museum programs. These include the collapse of the Soviet Union, which opened up new archives and areas of research, such as the mass shootings, where so many indigenous helpers were involved in a variety of roles; research on looting as it spread complicity widely through populations; and events in Rwanda, Bosnia, and Sudan that triggered an attendant interest in comparative genocide and genocide prevention.[13] The role of "neighbors" and others in post-Holocaust crimes perpetrated in the name of "ethnic cleansing" has been one impetus in shifting focus to the grassroots. Another factor is the emergence of a new generation of scholars in countries from Poland to the Netherlands who have critically addressed their countries' dominant (often patriotic or nationalistic) narratives of local responses to the persecution of Jews during the war. ("We were also victims." "We were all resisters."). Finally, the shift reflects a natural progression in the historiography of the Holocaust from political history ("the view from the top") to social history ("the view from below").

The passage of time has also affected the museum's work. The Holocaust is being taught more in schools now than in 1993 and has been the subject of popular films, television shows, and books. Visitor evaluations confirm that many individuals enter the USHMM with at least some knowledge of the Holocaust.[14] Accordingly, in teacher-training programs, museum staff now encourage educators to move beyond the standard Holocaust narrative of the stages of persecution and mass murder. Museum programs, both those conducted for groups following visits to the permanent exhibition and those conducted off-site, explore the roles of individuals, groups, and institutions that were not leading Nazi perpetrators but bore some responsibility for the devastation. Special audiences for these programs include, among others, police forces, the FBI, the military, judges, church leaders, diplomats, teachers, government managers, and medical students.[15]

Most museum visitors do not benefit from such special programs, and for them, the momentous questions of how mass murder and genocide became the policies of a modern state in the twentieth century remain unanswered. Formal evaluations underscore missed educational opportunities. When asked by interviewers to state who and what was "responsible" for what happened during the Holocaust, visitors tend to respond, "Hitler," "the Nazis," or "antisemitism."[16] These have been common responses in both pre- and post-visit interviews. Although such answers cannot simply be judged as wrong, the unlikelihood that visitors will also refer to other social groups with lower but still significant level of responsibility such as the "German elites" or "ordinary people" reflects, in part, the natural tendency of individuals when confronting the Holocaust to distance themselves from such horrible events. This distancing occurs despite the best efforts of the permanent exhibition creators not to focus too much and exclusively on Hitler and other leading perpetrators.[17]

Clearly, while the exhibition does have an emotional impact on many visitors, such a response in and of itself does not appear sufficient to provoke most people into reflecting on their own responsibilities as citizens in a democracy. Shaking popular myths and misconceptions about the Holocaust presents great challenges. Peter Hayes has recently pointed out that as public knowledge of the Holocaust has spread, the chasm between scholarship and popular understandings has steadily grown.[18] Many people less familiar with its history continue to believe that ordinary people were completely powerless and that some pathology of Hitler's—his hatred of the Jews—explains the genocide.[19] Paul Salmons questions whether an "emotional experience, *when shorn of historical understanding*—no matter how powerful, memorable and engaging"—constitutes *"learning about the Holocaust* at all." Salmon promotes "restoring complexity" to the study of such categories as "perpetrators," "collaborators," "bystanders," "rescuers," and "resisters," an effort, he believes, helps students see "shocking" truths: for example, that "you do not need to hate anyone to be complicit in genocide" and that some rescuers held antisemitic views.[20]

In an effort to amplify aspects of the history underrepresented in the permanent exhibition, to indeed address its "complexity," and at the same time to help visitors *approach* the history instead of distancing themselves from it, the USHMM opened the *Some Were Neighbors* exhibition in April 2013. The title was taken from the testimony of a Holocaust survivor who used the phrase to recall the painful betrayal by people his family knew during the November Pogrom. (Some staff feared that the title might be confused with Jan Gross's provocative study *Neighbors*, about the 1941 pogrom in the Polish town of Jedwabne. As instrumental as that study has been in stirring scholars to look at grassroots responses to German-led persecution of Jews in occupied Poland and other countries, however, it is largely unknown to our mass audience.[21])

Treatment of "Bystanders" in *Some Were Neighbors*

The development of *Some Were Neighbors* presented many challenges.[22] First, the exhibition team needed to absorb and synthesize the findings of the growing but still sometimes frustratingly skimpy body of pertinent historical studies. In line with more recent scholarship, such as the work of Tim Cole and Jan Grabowski on ordinary people's responses to the persecution of Jewish neighbors in occupied Hungary and Poland, respectively, the exhibition eschews use of the category "bystanders" as too general, vague, and misleading in light of the actual range of actions taken by onlookers in response to events of the Holocaust.[23] Drawing on stories told through testimonies, objects, and photographs in the USHMM's and outside collections and on both published and unpublished research, the exhibition showed a *range* of behaviors involving Nazi perpetrators, active collaborators, and members of the wider German and other European populations.

The exhibition also presented a range of actors' motivations to help dispel the common misperception that antisemitism explains everything. (This belief is also another way for many visitors to distance themselves from this history by thinking that because they are not antisemites, the history is not pertinent to them personally.) The exhibition showed that while some individuals were ideological "true believers," many more were guided by opportunism or by shifting political considerations and social norms. Many benefited in lesser or greater ways from the persecution of Jews, thereby developing an investment in its continuation and an aggressive psychological stance toward the victims that carried over into the postwar era. At the same time, the exhibition showed that not all "rescuers" were motivated by altruism. The text purposely avoided the term "righteous," with its religious and moral connotations, to present a complex portrait of helpers and to complicate understandings of

Figure 16.3. A panel from *Some Were Neighbors* provokes visitors' reflection on the role of ordinary people—here, German customs and tax officials—in the Nazi persecution of Jews. (United States Holocaust Memorial Museum. Photo: David Y. Lee.)

motivations to include strategies ranging from seeking to survive in hard times—payment for food and lodging made the risk of harboring Jews worth taking—to acts out of sheer greed.[24]

The limitations of current scholarship and lack of answers to questions that we may never be able to find (such as what was going on inside someone's head at a certain moment) also presented, in one sense, an opportunity. Instead of pretending to offer a comprehensive treatment of the subject, the exhibition team rather focused on individual and human behavior from and toward a larger, sociological perspective, offering a kind of "think piece." Hoping to engage visitors and help them approach the history, the displays would raise thought-provoking or even rhetorical questions such as the following:

> **True Believers?** [linked to a photograph of SA men tormenting Jewish men and text about pressures to "jump on the bandwagon" by signing up after the Nazis took power]
>
> **Does Presence Make One Complicit?** [linked to a photograph showing a German girl entering a swimming facility that has a "No Jews Allowed" sign posted]
>
> **Benefiting from the Plight of Neighbors?** [linked to a photograph showing ghettoized Jews selling used belongings to Polish neighbors at fire sale prices]
>
> **Who Betrayed Anne Frank?** [linked to a photomural of the entrance to the "secret annex" and text discussing the range of possible answers]

Another challenge related to the scholarship derived from the wide geographical scope of the exhibition, covering all of Nazi-dominated Europe. Most research is carried out by country or locality. No recent synthetic overview on "bystanders" exists—a lacuna that this volume seeks to address at least partly. Many studies have been published on "ordinary Germans" over the past two decades,[25] whereas much work remains to be done for most other European countries.[26] The aim of the exhibition was not a comparative study of nations, say, between Poland and the Netherlands. Assessing relative blame for various nations is, after all, of little interest to most Americans. Further, the exhibition goal was not to confirm or undermine national narratives, though examples of unexpected behaviors help challenge such oversimplifications. Large, contrasting historical contexts (Nazi Germany, occupied Eastern Europe, countries allied with or occupied by Germany that were pressured to turn over Jews for deportation "to the East") were delineated not to judge but to highlight the different environments and points in time (prewar, before and after the Nazi turn to genocide, before and after the German defeat at Stalingrad) in which individuals responded to the events around them.

Notwithstanding these challenges regarding an adequate integration of the most recent scholarship, a much more daunting task loomed, one that sharply distinguishes an exhibition from a book or article. The message of complicity is difficult to communicate with visual evidence. How does one portray (often shifting) attitudes, prejudices, and dispositions and present these within varying contexts? Evaluations and anecdotal observations suggest that museum visitors are increasingly disinclined to spend much time perusing text panels and often miss the nuanced points buried in captions.[27] For this reason, the permanent exhibition relies heavily on large photographs and text headers, audiovisual programs, and immersive environments that include three-dimensional objects—the larger the better. The added challenge with regard to "bystanders," especially those living outside cities in rural settings, is that they often were not photographed (except as part of purposeful German documentation of events, including its use for propaganda). In many places such as occupied Poland and the Netherlands, the Germans confiscated cameras or prohibited independent photography, forcing some determined documenters to take clandestine photographs often at great risk to themselves.[28]

The first effort at a solution to these exhibition content and design challenges was to capture the attention of visitors when they are usually most attentive, namely, when they enter the gallery. *Some Were Neighbors* opened with a five-minute film that interwove short excerpts of the testimonies of Holocaust survivors recalling painful moments of betrayal, on the one hand, with key exhibition messages or visitor "takeaways" on the other. As the exhibition title suggests, the largest "takeaway" was that the Holocaust was not just the work of Hitler, the SS, and some radical ideologues. As the narrator of the opening program asks, "How could so many ordinary fellow human beings, even people they knew, have betrayed them? Taken pleasure in their persecution? Benefited in some way from their misfortune?" A corollary to this point about responsibility regards motivations. How much was owing to antisemitism? How much, the narrator asks, to other "pressures and motives—ones that affect individuals in less extreme circumstances ... ? Fears and pressures in school, work, and the community—roles as students, teachers, workers, police, soldiers, neighbors, friends influenced their choices to go along with their peers or to defer to authority, even when they had some moral qualms."

Discussion of the role of antisemitism versus other kinds of "pressures and motives" is explored in numerous places in the exhibition, beginning with testimonies. Most survivor testimony was found in the rich *Visual History Archives of the USC Shoah Foundation*. Stories of jealousy, revenge, going along with the crowd, or alternatively stepping out to show solidarity with the victims provided a glimpse into the diverse, often disturbingly venal impulses influencing peoples' behaviors. The USHMM's own collection of eyewitness interviews conducted in Europe since the 1990s provided an additional, unique perspective, one never before used in the museum's exhibitions. For example, one Lithuanian interviewee confessed with some discomfort that as an impressionable teenager, she had believed rumors about the blood libel myth, the incendiary allegation dating from the Middle Ages that Jews murdered Christians, especially children, for ritualistic purposes, such as to obtain blood for use in making unleavened bread at Passover. She later described the chain of looters of Jewish belongings in her community, from local collaborators to onlookers like herself. And she recalled having coveted a pair of red shoes that had belonged to a Jewish girl. In another testimony, a Polish woman recalled, with prodding, how, "unfortunately," local firefighters and local police officers had been involved in the search for Jews who hid during the roundup. In a third example, two men who had served in collaborating Lithuanian battalions under German command in Belarus offered an endless list of rationalizations for the horrible crimes they participated in.[29]

Visitors of all ages always seem willing to sit and watch testimony. Unfortunately, it appears from personal observation that visitors to *Some Were Neighbors* were less inclined to stand and listen to audio-only excerpts from the wartime diary of a Polish physician. The words of Zygmunt Klukowski provide a description unmatched in its vivid detail of how Poles, including the doctor himself, responded to the violence perpetrated on their Jewish neighbors during the Nazi-organized roundups. Yet they largely remained unheard by visitors.[30]

In addition to the responsibility of "ordinary people" and their motivations, the final "takeaway" of the opening film (and of the exhibition overall) focused on the question of choice: "While it might be comforting to think that people were simply forced to do what they did, or that they were even brainwashed, examples of individuals who did help those in danger suggest that people did have choices even in the face of great risks and temptations." The exhibition stressed this particular point because "fear" is so often used to deny responsibility. It did so by ending the program with words written by Raul Hilberg (these also appeared on a nearby gallery wall): "At crucial junctures, every individual makes decisions, and ... every decision is individual."³¹ Another method used to underscore the element of choice was to juxtapose stories of individuals who behaved differently in similar roles and contexts, for example, as police officers in Nazi Germany during the November Pogrom or neighbors of ghettoized Jews in occupied Poland. Videotaped survivor and witness testimonies of contrasting "bystander" behaviors were used one after the other for similar purposes. These juxtapositions were designed to show visitors that not everyone acted in the same way—that discretion for individual behavior existed.

A few other examples serve to illustrate efforts both to surmount challenges unique to a visual presentation and to transcend national histories. The exhibition displayed a graphically compelling map of Amsterdam, created by Dutch officials in 1941 on German orders to show the location of Jewish households, less to demonstrate "Dutch collaboration" than to highlight "administrative collaboration." We know this kind of cooperation was a common phenomenon in many occupied societies, provided most willingly when Germany seemed to be winning the war.³² Similarly, the exhibition designers created a physically prominent artistic evocation of the Paris police's notorious card file of Jewish names and addresses, created by the French official André Tulard (and his mostly female clerks) on German orders, less to show French collaboration than to illustrate a kind of collaboration that occurred in many places.³³

Both the Amsterdam map and the Tulard registry have become iconic symbols of collaboration in the Netherlands and France, respectively, but in an American exhibition, they assume a larger significance: they point to the pressures that humans may face to defer to authority or to earn a living for oneself and provide for one's family—and perhaps even to the inability to imagine the eventual nefarious use the Nazis would make of their work. The idea that the registration of a person's address with authorities might later be exploited for purposes harmful to those inscribed certainly resonates in a country divided over such questions as immigration and national security and debating whether these perceived problems merit the creation of a national identity card or even a registry of names based on religion or ethnicity—precisely the kinds of policy proposals that thus far have failed to progress because of persistent overriding concerns about individual rights and liberties.

Two other examples of strong visuals that evoked the response of "ordinary people" included the prominent display near the end of the exhibition of the words from a diary entry a Dutch shopkeeper wrote in September 1942: "Try not to think about it too much, because it only makes you miserable. At the moment, a human life does not count for

Figure 16.4. A display from *Some Were Neighbors* evokes the registries of cards containing the names and addresses of Jews. Such registries aided police during the roundups of Jews in France and other countries where officials collaborated with the Germans. (United States Holocaust Memorial Museum. Photo: Miriam Lomaskin.)

much, especially if it is a Jewish life."[34] This was shown less as a statement about Dutch responses to the persecution of Jews than as an illustration of quite normal human response.

The second example is rare film footage depicting the public humiliation of a young couple in a segment titled "Community Enforcement of Racial Laws"; it became one of the most viewed elements in *Some Were Neighbors*, owing to the film's inherent power and its location: it was shown on a large screen that jutted into the visitor pathway, literally stopping people in their tracks.[35] The extraordinary footage from 1941 showed citizens of Steindorf, a village in what was then German Silesia, helping to ostracize Bronia, a sixteen-year-old Polish farmworker, and nineteen-year-old Gerhard Greschok, her German lover.[36] A police decree of 1940 criminalized sexual relations between Germans and "racially inferior" Poles brought to Germany as forced laborers. Together, the two young people endured not only having their hair cut and burned and then being forced to march past neighbors but also the ugly taunts of some of their teenage peers, whom they may have personally known.

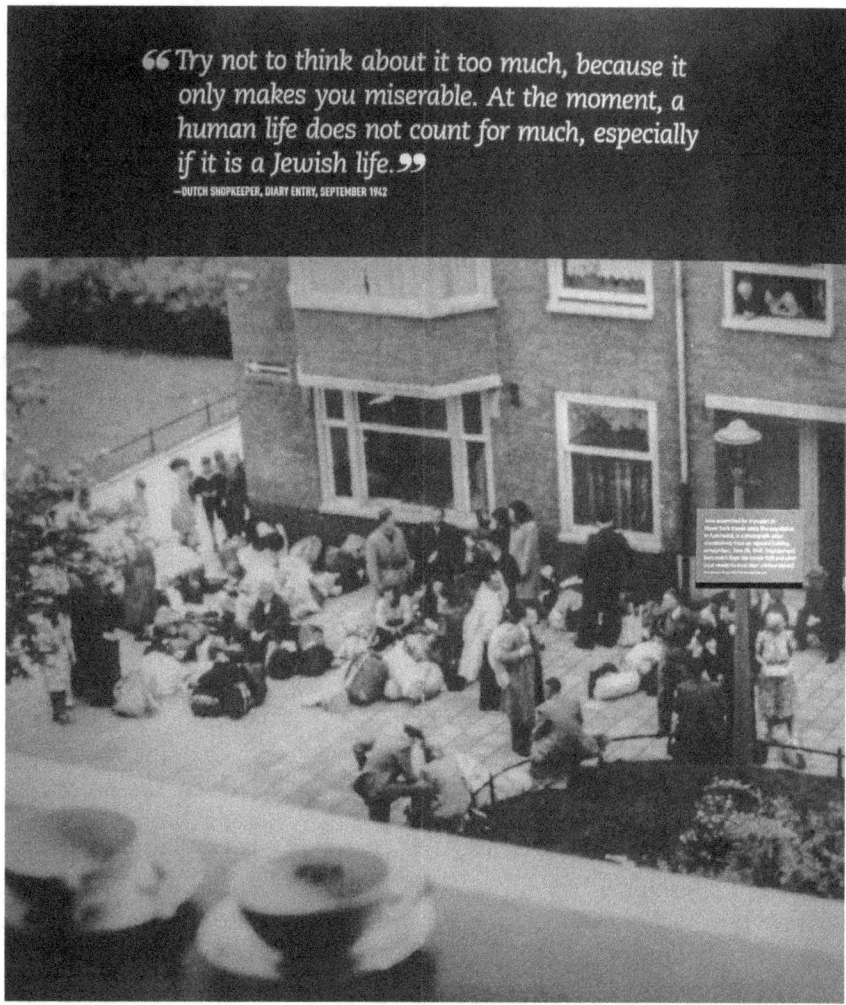

Figure 16.5. A display from *Some Were Neighbors* that includes a quotation from the diary of a Dutch shopkeeper imposed over a photograph of a roundup of Jews in Amsterdam. The shot was taken clandestinely from someone's apartment window. (United States Holocaust Memorial Museum. Photo: Joel Mason-Gaines.)

In addition to larger visual elements, *Some Were Neighbors* included small artifacts from the USHMM's collection that are linked to telling stories about "neighbors." Staff members giving tours highlighted some of these poignant but easy-to-miss displays. "Earrings Saved by Neighbor" was the caption header for gold jewelry that Bertha Herzfeld entrusted to a German neighbor before she and her husband were

Figure 16.6. One of the historic films in *Some Were Neighbors* showed young people participating in the shaming of their neighbors, Bronia and Gerhard, who violated racial decrees prohibiting their relationship. (United States Holocaust Memorial Museum, Photo: Miriam Lomaskin.)

deported. They did not return. The neighbor returned the objects to Bertha's surviving daughters after the war. A notebook holding handwritten old family recipes by Klara Fenjves, who did not survive deportation from occupied Hungarian territory to Auschwitz, was saved from looters by the family's cook. Visitors heard this story on an adjacent audiovisual monitor as told by survivor (and museum volunteer) Steven Fenves, Klara's son.

Reception of the *Some Were Neighbors* Exhibition

A formal evaluation of teenage students who visited *Some Were Neighbors* confirm the special challenges that Holocaust educators face in denting the dominant narrative about the Holocaust. Evaluators found "no difference between those who had not yet seen *Some Were Neighbors* and those who had just seen it" in the attribution of responsibility. Most teens in both instances focused on "Hitler and the Nazis." "Exposure to a variety of Holocaust materials" from inside and outside the classroom was correlated with more nuanced understandings of responsibility and the related linkage to one's own role in present-day society and potential new conflict situations.[37] But most students arrived with very limited knowledge about the history beyond "Hitler, Nazi, and concentration camps," "a view that does not include instances of choice and strongly favors a sense of oppression and fear with little or no [realistic] choice."[38] Bridging the gap between past and present, between historical bystander responsibility and current concepts of ideal citizenship, is especially difficult for educators of *American* teens as what happened was "on another continent, in a place with different attitudes, in a different language, with no names of anyone they know (except Hitler and Anne Frank)," as the writers of the visitor study concluded in 2015.[39]

The US Holocaust Memorial Museum and other institutions devoted to Holocaust education in the United States and abroad face the challenge of training and providing resources for educators so that they may integrate a fuller, more complex portrait of Holocaust history and "bystanders"—in all their shades of gray—into their thinking and teaching about the subject.[40] Public exhibitions and related catalogues, online resources, and other materials also have the capacity to influence adults in all walks of life, including professionals and leaders responsible for safeguarding democracy. New approaches can inform the work of creators of novels, television shows, films, and other forms of popular culture. Aiming to bridge the gap that has developed between current scholarship and the dominant popular narrative of the Holocaust, the *US Holocaust Memorial Museum* plans to incorporate new content on this and other underrepresented topics into the permanent exhibition. A multiyear project to revitalize the museum's influential core exhibition and its narrative of Holocaust history is currently under way.

In contrast to the measured responses of teenagers to the *Some Were Neighbors* exhibition, the responses of *adult* visitors, as revealed by statements written in a comment book placed at the gallery exit, show the exhibition's promising potential for altering standard understandings of the Holocaust. The comments, provided between April 2013 and November 2016, reflect a more nuanced view of history—one that apparently allows and inspires visitors to link the past to their lives today. Visitors wrote about a "new perspective" on a history that was "complex," "disturbing," "personal," and relevant to us as "humans." The remarks selected here are representative of their type, although they formed a minority of all the comments, many of which resemble those written in notebooks at the end of the permanent exhibition ("Never again!" "It made me so sad"). It is unknown how many individuals who wrote these comments had also visited the permanent exhibition.[41] Unless noted, the comments were unsigned and undated:

We always hear about the actual people who were [persecuted and killed] in the Holocaust, but not those who *knew* them. It was a new and interesting perspective I'd never seen before. The deepest I've thought about humanity in a long time.

No other Holocaust exhibit, movie, documentary or series has ever made me re-think the entire story so completely. —Marissa, Baltimore, Maryland

Important since many say the common citizen knew nothing—a harsh reality we need to confront as we live our daily lives. We should cultivate being brave lest we turn into cowards if evil should rear its head again near us and we have to choose.

I hope this never happens again. We are part of it. —Abe

There is a part of me that turns away from evil—I don't want to look. I am somehow threatened. I hope that this exhibit will be a good reminder to me, that when the time comes to stand up for what is right, when the time comes to do what is right for others, I will choose to do so, and not be the one who looks the other way. —Stephen B., Santa Paula, California

Neighbors exhibit is incredibly moving, a tale of *two* (possibly many more) sides of humanity. Powerful, and haunting knowing that the fate of so many often hinged on others. —A. B. K. (27 March 2015)

I could say that those who decided to turn in their friends, their neighbors, were cowards and morally corrupt, but I didn't live during that time. Given the same circumstances today, I hope I would be one who would help my friends and fight the regime (even if they threatened my family).

This exhibit, and the truth it contains, makes me more angry, more afraid, and more distraught than all else about the Holocaust. —Flynn B.

Such an eye-opening experience. Really makes you think, "What would I do?" —Sadie, Heath, Ohio

This is the first time the Holocaust felt deeply personal to me—the first time it left a textbook and really grabbed my mind and heart.

Sometimes, we forget they were people, just like us. Thank you for allowing me to see "the other side" of not-so-distant history.

The exhibit changed our view of what occurred throughout the course of the Holocaust. —Trey S.

I never thought of the regular community as being a part of this atrocity ... most enlightening. —T. M., Memphis, Tennessee

It's profound to realize that everyday citizens participated in the Holocaust. It wasn't just Hitler, Mengele, Himmler, etc.

These were average people. It makes you wonder how you would have acted.

A very poignant reminder that the evil of the Nazi regime was not confined to its leaders and soldiers. —E. C. (7 June 2013)

This subject makes two essential points that everyone should take with them: 1. The Holocaust was perpetrated and abetted by a much larger group of people than just the Nazi "true believers." 2. Within each of us there is the potential for participating in genocide and it is up to each of us to choose what we will do. —Kevin A. (1 November 2015)

Makes me question human nature. I'm convinced we really are just animals with big brains used to rationalize anything.

Promotes critical thinking on complex issues and encourages reflection. —C. P., Canada

A great understanding of "The Gray Zone."

How many of *you* would risk incarceration and death of *you* and *your families* for someone you've never met? I'm not defending what the collaborators and onlookers did. But are any of us strong enough to do the opposite? Great exhibition! —G. F., Budapest, Hungary

Every day [sic] regular people perpetuated the systematic persecution and mass murder of those in the Holocaust. People like you and me.

Gave me the understanding and knowledge I had no clue of. This really changed me and how I think about my life. —Tyler W.

Truly the Holocaust was complex in regards [sic] to those who collaborated and were complicit.

This should help us to reflect on our own lives! Are we willing to risk our comforts for the need of a fellow man? —Allan, UK

Would I have been any different or would I have collaborated? I don't know and that's scary. It was intriguing. —L. D. R.

Excellent exhibition with no concrete answers, which is how it really is. —G, England (8 July 2016)

Thanks for reminding me that as long as we are present, we are indeed taking part. —Y.S., Cuba

We are all humans. That is what we must never forget.

It makes you think ... more and more about responsibility.

Makes one look inward. —Suresh K.

Who are our neighbors today?

Susan Bachrach is a historian at the US Holocaust Memorial Museum in Washington, DC. She has curated several special exhibitions including *Deadly Medicine: Creating the Master Race* and, most recently, *Some Were Neighbors: Collaboration and Complicity in the Holocaust*, which explores the role of ordinary people in the persecution and mass murder of Jews and others in Nazi Germany and across Europe during World War II. She is currently the lead historian on the museum's project to revitalize its permanent exhibition on the history of the Holocaust.

Notes

The views expressed herein are those of the author's and not necessarily those of the United States Holocaust Memorial Museum. I would like to thank Krijn Thijs and

Christina Morina for their comments on an earlier version of this chapter, and Ted Phillips for editorial assistance.

1. Elie Wiesel, *Report to the President: President's Commission on the Holocaust*, 27 September 1979 (repr., Washington, DC, 2005), 11.
2. Jeshajahu Weinberg, "A Narrative History Museum," *Curator: The Museum Journal* 37, no. 4 (1994): 231.
3. Jeshajahu Weinberg and Rina Elieli, *The Holocaust Museum in Washington* (New York, 1995), 18.
4. Edward Linenthal, *Preserving Memory: The Struggle to Create America's Holocaust Museum* (New York, 1995), 112.
5. Interview with Sarah Ogilvie, Chief Program Officer, USHMM, 30 June 2016.
6. Linenthal, *Preserving Memory*, 55.
7. United States Holocaust Memorial Museum, *A Changed World: The Continuing Impact of the Holocaust* (Washington, DC, 2005).
8. Linenthal, *Preserving Memory*, 169.
9. For the historiography of early "bystander" discussions, see Michael Marrus, *The Holocaust in History* (New York, 1987), chaps. 4 and 5. For reevaluation of international "bystanders," see David Cesarani and Paul Levine, *Bystanders to the Holocaust: A Re-evaluation* (London and Portland, OR, 2002); Michael R. Marrus, "Holocaust Bystanders and Humanitarian Intervention," *Holocaust Studies: A Journal of Culture and History*, 13, no. 1 (2007): 1–18.
10. Linenthal, *Preserving Memory*, 217–224.
11. Weinberg and Elieli, *Holocaust Museum in Washington*, 23.
12. Jeff Hayward, Marilyn Rothenberg, and Brian Werner, "Evaluation of the Permanent Exhibition, United States Holocaust Memorial Museum, Washington, D.C.," unpublished report (2005), 99, 127–28.
13. Father Patrick Desbois, *The Holocaust by Bullets: A Priest's Journey to Uncover the Truth behind the Murder of 1.5 Million Jews* (New York, 2008); Martin Dean, *Robbing the Jews: The Confiscation of Jewish Property in the Holocaust, 1933–1945* (New York, 2008); on comparative genocide and prevention, see Scott Strauss, *Fundamentals of Genocide and Mass Atrocity Prevention* (Washington, DC, 2016).
14. Hayward, et al., "Evaluation of the Permanent Exhibition," 43–46, 50–71.
15. Jennifer Ciardelli and JoAnna Wasserman, "Inspiring Leaders: Unique Museum Programs Reinforce Professional Responsibility," *Journal of Museum Education* 36, no. 1 (2011): 45–56.
16. Hayward et al., "Evaluation of the Permanent Exhibition," 173: Findings "on the causes and circumstances of the Holocaust" show that "variations of 'Hitler' and 'Antisemitism' are the most common answers before seeing the PE [permanent exhibition] and months later."
17. Linenthal, *Preserving Memory*, 200.
18. Peter Hayes, *Why? Explaining the Holocaust* (New York, 2017).
19. William Meinecke, "Myths and Misconceptions about the Holocaust," in *Essentials of Holocaust Education: Fundamental Issues and Approaches*, ed. Samuel Totten and Stephen Feinberg (New York, 2016), 33–47.
20. Paul Salmons, "Universal Meaning or Historical Understanding? The Holocaust in History and History in the Curriculum," *Teaching History* 51, no. 141 (2010): 57–63, emphasis added.
21. Jan Gross, *Neighbors: The Destruction of the Jewish Community in Jedwabne, Poland* (Princeton, NJ, 2001).
22. Team members were Susan Bachrach (Curator); Belinda Blomberg, Nancy Gillette, Gregory Naranjo (Content Development and Coordination); Clare Cronin, Neal

Guthrie, Kassandra LaPrade-Seuthe, Kate O'Hare, Paul Rose (Research); Tim Kaiser (Educational Interpretation); Edward Phillips (Editor and Project Oversight, with Sarah Ogilvie). Gallagher & Associates provided the design and GToo Media the audiovisual productions.

23. Tim Cole, "Writing 'Bystanders' into Holocaust History in More Active Ways: 'Non-Jewish' Engagement with Ghettoisation, Hungary 1944," *Holocaust Studies: A Journal of Culture and History* 11, no. 1 (2005): 55–74; Jan Grabowski, *Rescue for Money: Paid Helpers in Poland, 1939–1945* (Jerusalem, 2008); Jan Grabowski, *Hunt for the Jews: Betrayal and Murder in German-Occupied Poland* (2011 in Polish; rev. ed., Bloomington, IN, 2013).

24. Research by social scientists was helpful on motivations and pressures, conscious and subconscious, which influence human behavior, including Ervin Staub, "The Evolution of Bystanders, German Psychoanalysts, and Lessons for Today," *Political Psychology* 10, no. 1 (1989): 42–45; Alan Rosenberg and Gerald E. Myers, eds., *Echoes from the Holocaust: Philosophical Reflections on a Dark Time* (Philadelphia, 1988); Rainer C. Baum, "Holocaust: Moral Indifference as the Form of Modern Evil," in *The Banality of Good and Evil: Moral Lessons from the Shoah and Jewish Tradition,* ed. David R. Blumenthal (Washington, DC, 1999), 53–90; James Waller, *Becoming Evil: How Ordinary People Commit Genocide and Mass Killing* (New York, 2007); Peter Lunt, *Stanley Milgram: Understanding Obedience and Its Implications* (New York, 2009).

25. The following were especially helpful: Frank Bajohr, "The 'Folk Community' and the Persecution of the Jews: German Society under National Socialist Dictatorship, 1933–1945," *Holocaust and Genocide Studies* 20, no. 2 (2006): 183–206; David Bankier, ed., *Probing the Depths of German Antisemitism: German Society and the Persecution of the Jews, 1933–1941* (New York, 2000); Christopher R. Browning, *Ordinary Men: Reserve Police Battalion 101 and the Final Solution in Poland* (1992; rev. ed., New York, 1998); Gerald D. Feldman and Wolfgang Seibel, *Networks of Nazi Persecution: Bureaucracy, Business and the Organization of the Holocaust* (New York, 2005); Peter Fritzsche, *Life and Death in the Third Reich* (Cambridge, MA, 2008); Mary Fulbrook, *A Small Town Near Auschwitz: Ordinary Nazis and the Holocaust* (Oxford, 2012); Robert Gellately, *The Gestapo and German Society: Enforcing Racial Policy 1933–1945* (Oxford, 1990); Elizabeth Harvey, *Women and the Nazi East: Agents and Witnesses of Germanization* (New Haven, CT, 2003); Eric A. Johnson, *Nazi Terror: The Gestapo, Jews, and Ordinary Germans* (London, 1999); Michael H. Kater, *Hitler Youth* (Cambridge, MA, 2004); Ian Kershaw, *Hitler, the Germans, and the Final Solution* (New Haven, CT, 2008); Thomas Kühne, *Belonging and Genocide: Hitler's Community, 1918–1945* (New Haven, CT, 2010); Alan E. Steinweis, *Kristallnacht 1938* (Cambridge, MA, 2009). Pertinent books that appeared after the exhibition opened include Wendy Lower, *Hitler's Furies: German Women in the Nazi Killing Fields* (New York, 2013); Nicholas Stargardt, *The German War: A Nation under Arms, 1939–1945* (New York, 2015).

26. France also has a large literature, including Michael Curtis, *Verdict on Vichy: Power and Prejudice in the Vichy France Regime* (New York, 2002); Julian Jackson, *France: The Dark Years, 1940–1944* (Oxford, 2001), chap. 15; Richard Vinen, *The Unfree French: Life under the Occupation* (New Haven, 2006), chap. 6. For other countries, see Karel C. Berkhoff, *Harvest of Despair: Life and Death in Ukraine under Nazi Rule* (Cambridge, MA, 2004); Peter Black, "Foot Soldiers of the Final Solution: The Trawniki Training Camp and Operation Reinhard," *Holocaust and Genocide Studies* 25, no. 1 (2011): 1–99; Martin Dean, *Collaboration in the Holocaust: Crimes of the Local Police in Belorussia and Ukraine, 1941–44* (London,

2000); Andrew Ezergailis, "'Neighbors' Did Not Kill Jews!" in *Collaboration and Resistance during the Holocaust: Belarus, Estonia, Latvia, Lithuania*, ed. David Gaunt, Paul A. Levine, and Laura Palosuo (Bern, 2004), 187–222; Michael MacQueen, "Lithuanian Collaboration in the 'Final Solution': Motivations and Case Studies," in Lithuania and the Jews: The Holocaust Chapter, ed. United States Holocaust Memorial Museum (Washington, DC, 2005), 1–16; Calel Perechodnik, *Am I A Murderer? Testament of a Jewish Ghetto Policeman*, ed. and trans. Frank Fox (Boulder, 1996); Antony Polonsky and Joanna B. Michlic, eds., *The Neighbors Respond: The Controversy over the Jedwabne Massacre in Poland* (Princeton, NJ, 2004); Leonid Rein, "Local Collaboration in the Execution of the 'Final Solution' in Nazi-Occupied Belorussia," *Holocaust and Genocide Studies* 20, no. 3 (2006): 381–409; Emmanuel Ringelblum, *Polish-Jewish Relations during the Second World War*, ed. Joseph Kermish and Shmuel Krakowski, trans. Dafna Allon, Danuta Dabrowska, and Dana Keren (Evanston, IL, 1992); Kazimierz Sakowicz, *Ponary Diary 1941–1943: A Bystander's Account of a Mass Murder*, ed. Yitzhak Arad (New Haven, 2005); Zoltán Vági, Lászlo Csösz, and Gábor Kádár, *The Holocaust in Hungary: Evolution of a Genocide* (Lanham, MD, 2013); Anton Weiss-Wendt, *Murder without Hatred: Estonians and the Holocaust* (Syracuse, NY, 2009). Appearing later were Wichert ten Have, *The Persecution of the Jews in the Netherlands, 1940–1945: New Perspectives* (Amsterdam, 2013); Agnes Grunwald-Spier, *Who Betrayed the Jew? The Realities of Nazi Persecution in the Holocaust* (Stroud, Gloucestershire, 2016). Two pertinent films are *Goodbye, Holland: The Destruction of Dutch Jewry*, dir. Willy Lindwer (Amstelveen: Ava-Dateline and Terra Film, 2004); *Human Failure* (DVD), dir. Michael Verhöven (Los Angeles: Menemsha Films Inc., 2008).
27. Hayward, et al., "Evaluation of the Permanent Exhibition," 131, 136.
28. Veronica Hekking and Flip Bool, *De illegale camera 1940–1945: Nederlandse fotografie tijdens de Duitse bezetting* (Naarden, 1995).
29. The interviews may be viewed in the original language at https//www.ushmm.org/search/collections.
30. Zygmunt Klukowski, *Diary from the Years of Occupation, 1939–44*, trans. George Klukowski, ed. Andrew Klukowski and Helen Klukowski May (Urbana, 1993). Colleague Jacek Nowakowski provided the voice of Klukowski and other important assistance to exhibition developers.
31. Raul Hilberg, *The Destruction of the European Jews*, vol. 3 (New York, 1985), 1012. The video may be seen at www.somewereneighbors.ushmm.org/about/exhibit.
32. USHMM thanks the NIOD Institute for War, Holocaust, and Genocide Studies for the loan of the map.
33. Laurent Joly, *L'antisémitisme de bureau: Enquête au cœur de la préfecture de Police de Paris et du commissariat général aux questions juives, 1940–1944* (Paris, 2011).
34. This quotation was originally seen in the exhibition of the Netherlands at the Auschwitz-Birkenau State Museum.
35. The source for the film is the Archiwum Państwowe w Krakowie. Museum colleague Victoria Barnett recommended this footage to show the "dynamics of bystander behavior" after she saw it at a conference in Uppsala, Sweden, in October 2008. See Henrik Edgren, ed., *Looking at the Onlookers and Bystanders: Interdisciplinary Approaches to the Causes and Consequences of Passivity* (Stockholm, 2012). The Living History Forum periodical booklet, no. 13 (2012). The film excerpt may be viewed at "Public Humiliation of a Teenage Couple," *Some Were Neighbors*, http://somewereneighbors.ushmm.org/#/exhibitions/teenagers/UN1967.
36. Today the town is Ścinawa Nyska. The clip (and its appearance in the exhibition) is discussed in Björn Krondorfer, "Book Review: Hitler's Volksgemeinschaft and the

Dynamics of Racial Exclusion: Violence against Jews in Provincial Germany, 1919–1939, by Michael Wildt," *Holocaust and Genocide Studies* 27, no. 3 (2013): 483–485.
37. People, Places & Design Research and MEM & Associates, "Understanding Teens' Perceptions of the Holocaust: Experiencing the *Some Were Neighbors* Exhibition," unpublished report for the US Holocaust Memorial Museum (2015), 11–12.
38. Ibid., 4.
39. Ibid., 87. Research on British teens' knowledge of the Holocaust shows similarly limited understandings, however. See Christopher Edwards and Siobhan O'Dowd, "The Edge of Knowing: Investigating Students' Prior Understandings of the Holocaust," *Teaching History* 51, no. 141 (2010): 20–26.
40. USHMM resources include an online exhibition called *Some Were Neighbors*, developed by a team led by Edna Friedberg, http://somewereneighbors.ushmm.org; "Bystanders," Holocaust Encyclopedia, www.ushmm.org/wlc/en/article.php?ModuleId=10008207; and a teaching module, "Ethical Leadership," https://www.ushmm.org/learn/introduction-to-the-holocaust/ethical-leaders/overview/ethical-leadership. See also the Yad Vashem resource: Irena Steinfeldt, *How Was It Humanly Possible? A Study of Perpetrators and Bystanders during the Holocaust* (Jerusalem, 2002).
41. Remarks taken from visitor comment books placed outside the gallery exit, 2013–2016.

Bibliography

Bajohr, Frank. "The 'Folk Community' and the Persecution of the Jews: German Society under National Socialist Dictatorship, 1933–1945." *Holocaust and Genocide Studies* 20, no. 2 (2006): 183–206.

Bankier, David, ed. *Probing the Depths of German Antisemitism: German Society and the Persecution of the Jews, 1933–1941*. New York: Berghahn Books, 2000.

Baum, Rainer C. "Holocaust: Moral Indifference as the Form of Modern Evil." In *The Banality of Good and Evil: Moral Lessons from the Shoah and Jewish Tradition*, edited by David R. Blumenthal, 53–90. Washington, DC: Georgetown University Press, 1999.

Berkhoff, Karel C. *Harvest of Despair: Life and Death in Ukraine under Nazi Rule*. Cambridge, MA: Belknap Press, 2004.

Black, Peter. "Foot Soldiers of the Final Solution: The Trawniki Training Camp and Operation Reinhard." *Holocaust and Genocide Studies* 25, no. 1 (2011): 1–99.

Browning, Christopher R. *Ordinary Men: Reserve Police Battalion 101 and the Final Solution in Poland*. 1992. Rev. ed., New York: Harper Perennial, 1998.

Cesarani, David, and Paul Levine. *Bystanders to the Holocaust: A Re-evaluation*. London: Frank Cass, 2002.

Ciardelli, Jennifer, and JoAnna Wasserman. "Inspiring Leaders: Unique Museum Programs Reinforce Professional Responsibility." *Journal of Museum Education* 36, no. 1 (2011): 45–56.

Cole, Tim. "Writing 'Bystanders' into Holocaust History in More Active Ways: 'Non-Jewish' Engagement with Ghettoisation, Hungary 1944." *Holocaust Studies: A Journal of Culture and History* 11, no. 1 (2005): 55–74.

Curtis, Michael. *Verdict on Vichy: Power and Prejudice in the Vichy France Regime*. New York: Arcade Publishing, 2002.

Dean, Martin. *Collaboration in the Holocaust: Crimes of the Local Police in Belorussia and Ukraine, 1941–44*. London: Macmillan, 2000.

———. *Robbing the Jews: The Confiscation of Jewish Property in the Holocaust, 1933–1945*. New York: Cambridge University Press, 2008.

Desbois, Father Patrick. *The Holocaust by Bullets: A Priest's Journey to Uncover the Truth behind the Murder of 1.5 Million Jews*. New York: Palgrave Macmillan, 2008.

Edgren, Henrik, ed. *Looking at the Onlookers and Bystanders: Interdisciplinary Approaches to the Causes and Consequences of Passivity*. Stockholm: Forum for Living History, 2012.

Edwards, Christopher, and Siobhan O'Dowd, "The Edge of Knowing: Investigating Students' Prior Understandings of the Holocaust," *Teaching History* 51, no. 141 (2010): 20–26.

Ezergailis, Andrew. "'Neighbors' Did Not Kill Jews!" in *Collaboration and Resistance during the Holocaust: Belarus, Estonia, Latvia, Lithuania*, edited by David Gaunt, Paul A. Levine, and Laura Palosuo, 187–222. Bern: Peter Lang, 2004.

Feldman, Gerald D., and Wolfgang Seibel. *Networks of Nazi Persecution: Bureaucracy, Business and the Organization of the Holocaust*. New York: Berghahn Books, 2005.

Fritzsche, Peter. *Life and Death in the Third Reich*. Cambridge, MA: Belknap Press, 2008.

Fulbrook, Mary. *A Small Town Near Auschwitz: Ordinary Nazis and the Holocaust*. Oxford: Oxford University Press, 2012.

Gellately, Robert. *The Gestapo and German Society: Enforcing Racial Policy 1933–1945*. Oxford: Clarendon Press, 1990.

Grabowski, Jan. *Hunt for the Jews: Betrayal and Murder in German-Occupied Poland*. Rev. ed. Bloomington: Indiana University Press, 2013. First published 2011 in Polish.

———. *Rescue for Money: Paid Helpers in Poland, 1939–1945*. Jerusalem: Yad Vashem, 2008.

Gross, Jan Tomasz, and Irena Grudzińska Gross. *Neighbors: The Destruction of the Jewish Community in Jedwabne, Poland*. Princeton, NJ: Princeton University Press, 2001.

Grunwald-Spier, Agnes. *Who Betrayed the Jew? The Realities of Nazi Persecution in the Holocaust*. Stroud, Gloucestershire: History Press, 2016.

Harvey, Elizabeth. *Women and the Nazi East: Agents and Witnesses of Germanization*. New Haven, CT: Yale University Press, 2003.

Have, Wichert ten. *The Persecution of the Jews in the Netherlands, 1940–1945: New Perspectives*. Amsterdam: Vossiuspers, 2013.

Hayes, Peter. *Why? Explaining the Holocaust*. New York: W.W. Norton & Company, 2017.

Hekking. Veronica, and Flip Bool. *De illegale camera 1940–1945: Nederlandse fotografie tijdens de Duitse bezetting*. Naarden: V+K Publishing, 1995.

Hilberg, Raul. *The Destruction of the European Jews*. Vol. 3. New York: Holmes & Meier, 1985.

Jackson, Julian. *France: The Dark Years, 1940–1944*. Oxford: Oxford University Press, 2001.

Johnson, Eric A. *Nazi Terror: The Gestapo, Jews, and Ordinary Germans*. London: John Murray, 1999.

Joly, Laurent. *L'antisémitisme de bureau: enquête au cœur de la préfecture de Police de Paris et du commissariat général aux questions juives, 1940–1944*. Paris: Grasset, 2011.

Kater, Michael H. *Hitler Youth*. Cambridge, MA: Harvard University Press, 2004.

Kershaw, Ian. *Hitler, the Germans, and the Final Solution*. New Haven, CT: Yale University Press, 2008.

Klukowski, Zygmunt. *Diary from the Years of Occupation, 1939–44*. Translated by George Klukowski, edited by Andrew Klukowski and Helen Klukowski May. Urbana: University of Illinois Press, 1993.

Krondorfer, Björn. "Book Review: Hitler's Volksgemeinschaft and the Dynamics of Racial Exclusion: Violence against Jews in Provincial Germany, 1919–1939, by Michael Wildt." *Holocaust and Genocide Studies* 27, no. 3 (2013): 483–485

Kühne, Thomas. *Belonging and Genocide: Hitler's Community, 1918–1945*. New Haven, CT: Yale University Press, 2010.

Linenthal, Edward T. *Preserving Memory: The Struggle to Create America's Holocaust Museum*. New York: Viking, 1995.

Lower, Wendy. *Hitler's Furies: German Women in the Nazi Killing Fields*. New York: Houghton Mifflin Harcourt, 2013.

Lunt, Peter. *Stanley Milgram: Understanding Obedience and Its Implications*. New York: Palgrave Macmillan, 2009.

MacQueen, Michael. "Lithuanian Collaboration in the 'Final Solution': Motivations and Case Studies." In Lithuania and the Jews: The Holocaust Chapter, edited by United States Holocaust Memorial Museum, 1–16. Washington, DC: US Holocaust Memorial Museum, 2005.

Marrus, Michael R. "Holocaust Bystanders and Humanitarian Intervention." *Holocaust Studies: A Journal of Culture and History* 13, no. 1 (2007): 1–18.

———. *The Holocaust in History*. New York: Meridian, 1987.

Meinecke, William. "Myths and Misconceptions about the Holocaust." In *Essentials of Holocaust Education: Fundamental Issues and Approaches*, edited by Samuel Totten and Stephen Feinberg, 33–47. New York: Routledge, 2016.

Perechodnik, Calel. *Am I A Murderer? Testament of a Jewish Ghetto Policeman*. Edited and translated by Frank Fox. Boulder, CO: Westview Press, 1996.

Polonsky, Antony, and Joanna B. Michlic, eds., *The Neighbors Respond: The Controversy over the Jedwabne Massacre in Poland*. Princeton, NJ: Princeton University Press, 2004.

Rein, Leonid. "Local Collaboration in the Execution of the 'Final Solution' in Nazi-Occupied Belorussia." *Holocaust and Genocide Studies* 20, no. 3 (2006): 381–409.

Ringelblum, Emmanuel. *Polish-Jewish Relations during the Second World War*. Edited by Joseph Kermish and Shmuel Krakowski. Translated by Dafna Allon, Danuta Dabrowska, and Dana Keren. Evanston, IL: Northwestern University Press, 1992.

Rosenberg, Alan, and Gerald E. Myers, eds. *Echoes from the Holocaust: Philosophical Reflections on a Dark Time*. Philadelphia: Temple University Press, 1988.

Sakowicz, Kazimierz. *Ponary Diary 1941–1943: A Bystander's Account of a Mass Murder*. Edited by Yitzhak Arad. New Haven, CT: Yale University Press, 2005.

Salmons, Paul. "Universal Meaning or Historical Understanding? The Holocaust in History and History in the Curriculum." *Teaching History* 51, no. 141 (2010): 57–63.

Stargardt, Nicholas. *The German War: A Nation under Arms, 1939–1945*. New York: Basic Books, 2015.

Staub, Ervin. "The Evolution of Bystanders, German Psychoanalysts, and Lessons for Today." *Political Psychology* 10, no. 1 (1989): 42–45.

Steinfeldt, Irena. *How Was It Humanly Possible? A Study of Perpetrators and Bystanders during the Holocaust*. Jerusalem: Yad Vashem, 2002.

Steinweis, Alan E. *Kristallnacht 1938*. Cambridge, MA: Belknap Press, 2009.

Strauss, Scott. *Fundamentals of Genocide and Mass Atrocity Prevention*. Washington, DC: US Holocaust Memorial Museum, 2016.

United States Holocaust Memorial Museum. *A Changed World: The Continuing Impact of the Holocaust*. Washington, DC: US Holocaust Memorial Museum, 2005.

Vági Zoltán, Lászlo Csösz, and Gábor Kádár. *The Holocaust in Hungary: Evolution of a Genocide*. Lanham, MD: Rowman & Littlefield, 2013.

Vinen, Richard. *The Unfree French: Life under the Occupation.* New Haven, CT: Yale University Press, 2006.
Waller, James. *Becoming Evil: How Ordinary People Commit Genocide and Mass Killing.* New York: Oxford University Press, 2007.
Weinberg, Jeshajahu. "A Narrative History Museum." *Curator: The Museum Journal* 37, no. 4 (1994): 231–239.
Weinberg, Jeshajahu, and Rina Elieli, *The Holocaust Museum in Washington.* New York, 1995.
Weiss-Wendt, Anton. *Murder without Hatred: Estonians and the Holocaust.* Syracuse, NY: Syracuse University Press, 2009.
Wiesel, Elie. *Report to the President: President's Commission on the Holocaust.* 27 September 1979. Reprint, Washington, DC: US Holocaust Memorial Museum, 2005.

Epilogue I
A Brief Plea for the Historicization of the Bystander

Norbert Frei

The privilege of being invited to contribute an epilogue to such a rich volume is also a burden. What can be said about the bystander—about their historical role and significance, about the concept and its development—that has not been dealt with in depth and detail in the previous pages? And what sense should it make to look for an all too easy conclusion or to "summarize" the full spectrum of ideas and findings that has just been displayed? The benefit of this book lies in its inspiring multidimensionality, not in a quasi-judicial verdict regarding the historical and/or the historiographical meaning of the bystander.

Perhaps it is because of a professional preoccupation with the aftermath of Nazi rule and of the Holocaust, but my overall impression from the contributions in this volume is that it would be worthwhile to proceed more consistently toward a full-fledged historicization of the bystander. In order to get an even more comprehensive and realistic picture, it might be useful to further connect the appearance of the bystander as a social phenomenon under Nazism with its post factum invention as a historiographical figure. In doing so, however, we might end up loosing Raul Hilberg as the main reference point (a notion that René Schlott's contribution to this volume seems to support anyway).

In fact, the bystander avant la lettre appears in the developing field of German *Zeitgeschichte* as early as in the 1950s. Most importantly, there was the report by SS Obersturmführer Kurt Gerstein that had already become publicly known during the International Military Tribunal at Nuremberg (Document PS-1553) and was printed in its second (German) version in the very first volume of the newly established *Vierteljahrshefte für Zeitgeschichte* in 1953.[1] As Schlott rightly emphasizes in this volume, in Hilberg's "Destruction of the European Jewry," Gerstein is present only as a "messenger."[2]

There is, however, another non-Jewish German who appears only as a briefly mentioned source in Hilberg's opus magnum but was granted the status of an important witness of the "final solution" in German historiography as early as in 1959: Wilhelm Cornides, a twenty-two-year-old descendant of a Munich publishing dynasty (R. Oldenbourg Verlag) who during an official trip as a sergeant of a Wehrmacht translator's unit in late August and early September 1942—that is, around the same time as Kurt Gerstein[3]—took the chance for private investigations in the territory of the *Generalgouvernement*. According to Hans Rothfels, the chief editor of the *Vierteljahrshefte für Zeitgeschichte* who wrote a brief introduction to Cornides's short document (and who had edited the Gerstein report six years earlier), the young man wanted to find out the truth about the "at that time in Germany circulating rumors about the 'resettlement' of the Jews."[4]

Around noon on 31 August 1942 at the train station of the Galician town of Rawa Ruska, Cornides witnessed the arrival of a deportation train escorted by SS guards:

Some of the doors were opened a crack, the windows barred with barbed wire. Among the trapped were only a few, mostly old men to see, everyone else were women, girls, and children. Many children crowded at the windows and the narrow doorways. The youngest were certainly not older than two years. As soon as the train stopped, the Jews tried to pass out bottles to get water. However, the train was surrounded by SS guards, so nobody could get near. At that moment, a train arrived from the direction of Jarosław, and the passengers streamed toward the exit, without bothering about the transport. A few Jews, busy loading a Wehrmacht lorry, waved their caps toward the trapped. I talked to a police officer who was on duty at the station. When I asked him where the Jews were coming from, he replied: "Those are probably the last ones of Lviv. This has been going on for three weeks without interruption. In Jarosław, they left only eight, no one knows why." I asked, "How far are they going?" He said: "To Bełżec." "And then?" "Poison." I asked, "Gas?" He shrugged. Then he just said: "In the beginning, they always shot them, I believe."[5]

During his early afternoon visit at the "German House" of Rawa Ruska, Cornides found out that Wehrmacht soldiers from the nearby Stalag 325 were well aware of the transports, although most trains passed the town by night. But when he was about to leave only a couple hours later, an empty deportation train just arrived: "I passed it two times and counted; it were fifty-six wagons. On the doors numbers were written in chalk, 60, 70, once 90, sometimes 40, probably the number of Jews who had been in."

In the compartment of his departing train, Cornides then talked to the wife of a railway police officer who was currently visiting her husband:

> She says that these transports come through daily, sometimes also with German Jews. Yesterday, the corpses of six children were found on the track. The woman says the Jews killed those children themselves, more likely they died on the trip. The railway police officer, who comes along as a train conductor, got into our compartment. He confirmed the woman's statements about the children's corpses found on the track yesterday. I asked: "Do the Jews know what is happening to them?" The woman replied: "Those who come from further away will probably not know anything, but those from around here know already. They try to run away if they notice that someone is coming for them."

During this conversation, the woman promised to Cornides to tell him when they would pass Bełżec. But while there was not much to see because of a hedge of firs, they both noticed an unpleasant sweet smell.

> "They are stinking already," said the woman. "Oh, nonsense, that's the gas," laughed the railway police officer. In the meantime—we had driven about two hundred meters—the sweet smell had turned into a sharp burning smell. "That is from the crematorium," the police officer said. Shortly thereafter, the fence ended. There was a guardhouse with SS guards in front of it, with a double track leading into the camp.[6]

Carefully separated from what he had seen with his own eyes, Cornides took down three additional "eyewitness reports" that he had collected during his trip. One had been given to him in the evening of 30 August in the "German House" at Rawa Ruska by an engineer ("a man of about twenty-six years, wearing the party badge") who according to Cornides concluded his story about POWs and Polish and Jewish forced laborers "with tears in his eyes." Obviously, the engineer was not very discreet, for a Sudeten German construction supervisor sitting at the same table felt encouraged to comment: "'The other day a drunken SS man sat in our staff canteen, he cried like a child. He said that he is doing service in Bełżec, and if that was to continue for another fourteen days he will kill himself because he cannot stand it anymore.'"[7]

Within hours, Cornides had made the direct or indirect acquaintance of more than half a dozen of bystanders—and had become one himself. His records, titled "1. Notes by a German sergeant of 31 August 1942" and "2. Additional eyewitness reports," came upon us as three pages of single-spaced typescript on thin paper. While Hilberg refers to them as a "diary,"[8] there is actually no indication that Cornides had written more than what he later gave to Hans Rothfels, respectively the *Vierteljahrshefte für Zeitgeschichte*, for publication.[9] It is unclear how Cornides, who used the opportunity of an official mission for this side trip "on his own" (Rothfels), ever reflected on his role as a bystander. As it appears both from the language of his notes and from the circumstances of their publication in 1959, at the time of the events he did not feel to be in a situation in which he could do anything to stop them. His style is extremely factual and sober, and he was very careful not to draw conclusions, to judge, or to show emotions. There are only interpretable traces of personal feelings—for instance, when he mentions twice that he walked alongside the deportation trains, the second time even twice, in order to count precisely the number of people who could have been carried in this now empty train.

Even after the war, Wilhelm Cornides, who would die young in 1966, does not seem to have felt the need to step out of his role taken in 1942. At the time of his report's publication, almost two decades after the events, the negative attitude of the West German public concerning the confrontation with the *jüngste Vergangenheit* (most recent past)[10] had just begun to change. In 1958, the Ulm Einsatzkommando trial and the subsequent establishment of the Zentrale Stelle der Landesjustizverwaltungen zur Aufklärung von NS-Verbrechen (Central Office of the State Justice Administrations for the Investigation of National Socialist Crimes) in Ludwigsburg marked a first caesura in Germany's *Vergangenheitsbewältigung* (coming to terms with the Nazi past). There is, however, no indication that Cornides tried to take advantage of this changing social climate. Despite—or probably because of—the fact that he had meanwhile become an experienced book author and an influential member of Bonn's foreign policy brain trust,[11] he decided not to personally edit his notes but to leave this to the renowned historian Hans Rothfels. As it seems, taking the notes in 1942 and having them published in 1959 was Cornides's cautious attempt to contribute to the educational impetus of the *Vierteljahrshefte* and to remind his fellow Germans about their past while not reflecting his—and their—role as bystanders.

Hans Rothfels, the German-Jewish remigrant historian and patron of the still young Institut für Zeitgeschichte, fell in line. Proportionally brief and in tone as sober as the document, his foreword provided no information about the author other than stating Cornides's military rank at the time of his observations in the *Generalgouvernement* and his recent professional function as editor of the foreign policy journal *Europa-Archiv*. Rothfels did not even try to emphasize the importance of the document—quite the contrary: "As far as the content is concerned, the fact, the scope, the form of the 'resettlement,' the notes offer nothing new," he stated. For Rothfels, the value of Cornides's notes became obvious by comparing them with those of Gerstein: "While Gerstein was told that [the "final solution"] was 'one of the most secret things' ('whoever speaks about it will be shot on the spot'), it is expressly stated below that the knowledge of the events—what one might suspect anyhow—was quite widespread in the *Generalgouvernement*, and that at any rate a relatively small effort was needed to track them down."[12]

Rothfels's final comment reflected what in 1959 could be said—but also had to be said about the bystanders, at least from the perspective of a scholarly journal and a research institute for contemporary history that was part and parcel of West Germany's emerging *Vergangenheitsbewältigung*: "Of course, only a few will have had the will or even the desire to set in writing what they have seen and heard. Thus, the notes have a certain documentary value in what they testify as to be known, as in the fact of being written down simultaneously."[13]

Norbert Frei is one of the most distinguished German scholars of the Third Reich and its legacies in postwar Germany and Europe. He is Professor of Contemporary History at the University of Jena and Director of the Jena Center 20th Century History. He was a visiting scholar at the Institute for Advanced Studies in Princeton, New Jersey; held the Theodor Heuss professorship at the New School for Social Research, New York; and was a guest professor at the Hebrew University of Jerusalem. His many publications on the subject include *A History of Jews in Germany since 1945: Politics, Culture, and Society*, with Michael Brenner et. al. (Indiana University Press, 2018); *1945 und wir: Das Dritte Reich im Bewußtsein der Deutschen* (Beck Verlag, 2005); and *Adenauer's Germany and the Nazi Past. The Politics of Amnesty and Integration*, foreword by Fritz Stern (Columbia University Press, 2002).

Notes

1. "Augenzeugenbericht zu den Massenvergasungen," intro. Hans Rothfels, *Vierteljahrshefte für Zeitgeschichte* 1 (1953): 177–194. Even more important for a general audience was certainly the early monograph by Saul Friedländer, *Kurt Gerstein oder die Zwiespältigkeit des Guten* (Munich, 1968).
2. I quote from the revised German paperback edition, Raul Hilberg: *Die Vernichtung der europäischen Juden*, 3 vols. (Frankfurt, 1990), 1030; a few more references relate to information derived from Gerstein's documents but not to his personality.
3. Gerstein refers to August 1942; see "Augenzeugenbericht," 192.
4. "Zur 'Umsiedlung' der Juden im Generalgouvernement," intro. Hans Rothfels, *Vierteljahrshefte für Zeitgeschichte* 7 (1959): 333; newly printed in Klaus-Peter Friedrich, ed., *Die Verfolgung und Ermordung der europäischen Juden durch das nationalsozialistische Deutschland 1933–1945, Bd. 9: Polen—Generalgouvernement August 1941–1945* (Munich, 2014), doc. 125, 397–400.
5. Ibid., 333–334; this and all the following quotes from Cornides's original German document are in my own translation; town and camp names differ from his Germanized spelling.
6. Ibid., 334.
7. Ibid., 335.
8. Hilberg, *Vernichtung*, 1307. This is particularly strange because Hilberg incorporated the Cornides document in his (not very well-known) collection of documents on the Holocaust, which appeared exactly a decade after the first edition of his major book; see Raul Hilberg, *Documents of Destruction: Germany and Jewry 1933–1945* (Chicago, 1971), 208–213.
9. Cornides seems to have contacted first Hans Rothfels; see Archive of the Institut für Zeitgeschichte (IfZ) ID 90-3, Rothfels to Kluke, 29 January 1959 and Rothfels to Krausnick, 29 May 1959. Two years later, upon Krausnick's request, Cornides provided the IfZ archive with his "original" document (which Rothfels had returned to him) and asked for a copy of it in return; IfZ, ID 103–57, Cornides to Krausnick, 5 July 1961 and Krausnick to Cornides, 17 October 1961. My special thanks go to Klaus Lankheit (IfZ) for providing me with this information.
10. Interestingly enough, Cornides used the term in the subtitle of his successful 1957 book on Germany's foreign policy situation; see Wilhelm Cornides, *Die Weltmächte und Deutschland: Geschichte der jüngsten Vergangenheit* (Tübingen, 1957).
11. In 1955, Wilhelm Cornides was a founding member of the Deutsche Gesellschaft für Auswärtige Politik (German Council on Foreign Relations) and served as the director of its research institute until his death.
12. "Zur 'Umsiedlung' der Juden im Generalgouvernement," 333.
13. Ibid.

Bibliography

"Augenzeugenbericht zu den Massenvergasungen." Introduction by Hans Rothfels. *Vierteljahrshefte für Zeitgeschichte* 1 (1953): 177–194.

Cornides, Wilhelm. *Die Weltmächte und Deutschland: Geschichte der jüngsten Vergangenheit*. Tübingen: Wunderlich Verlag, 1957.

Friedländer, Saul. *Kurt Gerstein oder die Zwiespältigkeit des Guten*. Munich: Bertelsmann Sachbuchverlag, 1968.

Friedrich, Klaus-Peter, ed. *Die Verfolgung und Ermordung der europäischen Juden durch das nationalsozialistische Deutschland 1933–1945, Bd. 9: Polen— Generalgouvernement August 1941–1945*. Munich, 2014.

Hilberg, Raul. *Die Vernichtung der europäischen Juden*. 3 vols. Frankfurt: Taschenbuch, 1990.

———. *Documents of Destruction: Germany and Jewry 1933–1945*. Chicago: Quadrangle, 1971.

"Zur 'Umsiedlung' der Juden im Generalgouvernement." Introduction by Rothfels. *Vierteljahrshefte für Zeitgeschichte* 7 (1959): 333–336.

Epilogue II
Saving the Bystander

Ido de Haan

One way to characterize the historiography of the bystander of the Holocaust, to which the chapters in this volume have made a substantial and challenging contribution, is to see it as a crime novel, *The Mystery of the Disappearing Bystander*. At first glance, bystanders are not just passive onlookers: they play an active part in the historical events in which they participate. First, they are witnesses, who willingly or unwillingly observe the events that are happening before their eyes. Whether they are looking or try to look away because they had a peek at the horror they refuse to see, their gaze adds to the reality of what they observe, even if what they see probes the limits of their imagination. Moreover, they are commentators of the events to which they are witness, who, like the chorus in the classical tragedy, contribute to the interpretations of the events, including the interpretation of the measure of responsibility and agency the circumstances allow. Therefore, bystanders are also actors who carry the burden of responsibility to intervene in, or to avoid, to condemn or to applaud, to resist or to support the action taking place before their eyes. As a bystander, one cannot avoid to witness, to interpret, and to act on your conclusions—even if that involves looking away, downplaying, and shying away from intervening.

While it is clear that in principle the repertoire of the bystander is very rich and varied, at a closer look the character of the bystander mysteriously disappears from the scene. As Mary Fulbrook argues in the opening chapter of this volume, "The bystander is by definition 'outside' the real dynamics of the situation," but in the context of systemic violence such as the Holocaust, "there is no 'outside.'" In the postwar debate about the role of the bystander, the category tended to dissolve into the two extremes of the spectrum of agency. Bystanders are either victims, whose failure to stop the events they condemn is excused by the forces that suppress their power to act, or perpetrators, whose failure to stop the events is an indication of their passive or active support of the situation they are part of. In both cases, the category of the bystander becomes a cover that is historically obsolete (covering the fact that there were not actual bystanders, only victims and perpetrators); analytically useless (covering a wide range of roles that need to be distinguished), and morally questionable (claiming the innocence of noninvolvement to cover up reprehensible acts). To use another literary allusion, the bystander is like the Lewis Carroll's Cheshire Cat, gradually dissolving into the background until nothing is left but his irritating grin, reminding us of the inescapable madness of the history all are implicated in.

As a witness to the spectacle offered in this volume, in which the bystander is so skillfully dissected until little is left of the category, one feels an academic as well as moral burden, to ask whether the bystander can still be saved and if there is any use in rescuing the bystander. This is, first of all, a historical question—were there, and if so, what were bystanders of the Holocaust? But it is also an analytical issue: does the category of the bystander help us to better understand the Holocaust? And it is maybe a moral challenge: doesn't the bystander have a claim to recognition as an individual that deserves attention or even respect? The contributions in the volume give reason to think the bystander can and needs to be saved but also that its meaning needs to be redressed before the bystander can be rehabilitated.

The Burden of Explanation

The first step to recover the bystander is to reduce the burden of explanation. In much of the recent historiography, the bystander is made responsible for much of the process and the outcome of the Holocaust. This can be seen as a side effect of the growing specialization and detail in the historiography of the Holocaust, in which local circumstances have come to be seen as decisive factors for the threats to the life and the opportunities for rescue of Jews in the various parts of Europe. It might also be the result of the incrementalism that dominates more recent interpretations of the overall process according to which a general antisemitic or genocidal mood only led to concrete murderous practices in the context of failed and shifting local policies aimed at "getting rid of the Jews." The murder of the Jews thus becomes the endpoint of a process of improvised bricolage, in which elements of the local social relations, culture, and practices come to play a defining role.[1] Finally, the emphasis on the role of the local population might be a function of the moral reckoning by which postwar social and political relations were rearranged, in which implication in the Holocaust became a most valuable asset (in case of rescue) or liability (for collaborators).[2]

The contributions in this volume present various examples of the historical as well as moral responsibility with which bystanders are burdened. In some cases, as in Jacques Semelin's discussion of "social reactivity" of the small gestures of French bystanders in response to the persecution of the Jews, they are presented in a positive role. But in other cases, bystanders are accused of aiding or abetting in the crimes committed against the Jews. This is most vividly presented in Remco Ensel and Evelien Gans's contribution about the Netherlands, and questioned by Bart van der Boom (a debate further analyzed by Krijn Thijs). Likewise, Froukje Demant points to the ways in which Jews' relations to non-Jews conditioned their persecution. Jan Grabowski also demonstrates the fatal role of bystanders in his discussion of the complicity of non-Jewish Poles in the extermination of the Jews. Not only was it "a public, terrifying spectacle, with millions of more or less engaged and fully aware spectators," as Grabowski puts it, but also "thousands of people from different walks of life and from various strata of Polish society" profited from the expropriation of Jews. Referring to Omer Bartov's notion of communal massacre, Grabowski characterizes the active involvement of bystanders as an act of "communal genocide."[3]

The inclusion of the bystander in the ranks of perpetrators, however, comes at the cost not only of discarding the notion of the bystander but also of obfuscating the concept of the perpetrator. By claiming, as Bartov does, that communal massacres "belie the very notion of passive bystanders: everyone becomes a protagonist, hunter and prey, resister and facilitator, loser and profiteer," it becomes more difficult to distinguish between the variety of acts and the different conditions of agency of the various actors in this tragedy.[4] Ironically, the accusation against scholars like Van der Boom, to efface the moral guilt of the bystander, comes back as a boomerang to scholars who by blaming the bystander in a sense relativize the guilt of more deliberate perpetrators. Even if the latter's responsibility is not denied, the almost exclusive focus on the failure of the bystander in much of the national debates on the Holocaust—be it on Vichy France, Dutch accommodation, Polish antisemitism, or by contrast, Danish heroism—tends to disregard the decisive impact of Nazi policies and actions on the initiation, course, and outcome of the Holocaust. This is not to deny agency on the part of bystanders. It is indisputably the case that perpetrators other than Nazis were involved in the persecution, expropriation, and destruction of Jews; moreover, the killing of Jews was often committed by neighbors, colleagues, and fellow townspeople. Yet, the motives, contexts, and conditions of these communal acts of violence differed fundamentally of that of soldiers, officers, and other professional killers who were assigned to eradicate European Jewry from the face of the earth.

Historical and Analytical Meanings

In order to get a better grip at the specific roles of the bystander, and to differentiate them from the various guises of the perpetrator, it is crucial to distinguish between historical and analytical meanings of the notion of the bystander. René Schlott is right to relativize the innovation of Hilberg's analysis of the bystander by pointing to earlier uses of the term or related concepts in previous scholarship. Yet the historical meaning of the concept emanates not from scholarship but from its use by the contemporaries of the Holocaust and, more importantly, its aftermath. As Christina Morina demonstrates in her chapter, non-Jewish Germans frequently manipulated the conceptualization of the bystander and instrumentalized its moral implication in order to forge personal culpability and innocence. But even more relevant, the construction of the bystander in the postwar years created what Fulbrook identifies as "alluring alibis" that could be used to dismiss accusations of moral guilt.

A crucial operation in this respect was the denial of personal knowledge; *"Wir haben davon nichts gewußt"* is still the central formula in many discussions about the Holocaust.[5] Yet there is more at stake than the cognitive dimension of the bystander, as further becomes clear from Fulbrook's analysis, not only in her contribution but even more masterly in her reflection on "ordinary Nazis" in *A Small Town near Auschwitz*.[6] Even if it was difficult to deny knowledge, it was always an option to deny actual involvement. And if that was hard to avoid, bystanders often claimed not to have had any agency, or if they had, to emphasize the pressures of military rank, social status, or material threat that caused them to become active against their will and moral judgment. And if that was all to no avail, there was still the moral argument that, given the conditions of the time, there was a reasonable expectation that Jews were a threat and therefore had to be neutralized. Overall, the historical notion of the bystander is morally suspicious.

When the notion of the bystander is used as an analytical category, it is hard to avoid the moral contamination implied in its troublesome history. This became clear, for instance, in the famous exchange between Martin Broszat and Saul Friedländer. While Broszat argued for a much broader spectrum of agency (introducing the notion of *Resistenz* between deliberate support for and active resistance against the Nazi persecution of the Jews) and for an explanatory framework that allowed for other social and cultural factors than the choice for or against Nazism, Friedländer rejected such historicization: it might help Germans to come to terms with their past, but "this type of perspective necessarily will differ considerably from that belonging to another group—and above all from the perspective of the victims." At the same time, Friedländer acknowledged the relevance of "restoring for the readers, i.e., for German society, a continuity in historical self-perception, not at the level of political institutions, but at that of the permanence of social reality."[7]

It is in the latter sense of the reconstruction of historical continuities that the focus on the bystander is crucial. One way to look at the Holocaust is to see it as a fundamental rupture in the social structure and as a breach in the course of history—or even as *Zivilisationsbruch*.[8] It is impossible to understand such transgression of normality without an analysis of the changing relations between Jews and non-Jews. But it also requires deeper insight in the traditions, practices, and institutions that constitutes the context of this event. Finally, these elements also form the structure that is affected by the impact of the Holocaust and are required to assess the aftermath. One might argue that in this way, the category also dissolves: understanding the Holocaust as an event that affects not only its victims and perpetrators but society as a whole. This underlines Fulbrook's point that in cases of systematic and large-scale violence, there are no outsiders who only observe a state of affairs that does not affect them in any other way. Yet, as an aspect of the context that is defined by much more than it being the context of the Holocaust, the notion of the bystander addresses an essential element for the evaluation of its meaning and impact.

Motives and Situations

This leads to a third and final step in this rescue operation. Considering that the bystander is relevant to understand not only agency in the Holocaust but also the structure in which the Holocaust emerges and impacts, it is useful to distinguish between motivational and situational aspects of the notion of the bystander. Much of the discussion of bystanders is focused on the first dimension. For instance, much time and effort has been spent on the moral makeup of the altruistic personality in order to answer the question what determines the decision to rescue Jews.[9] On the other hand, the failure to support Jews in their plight is generally discussed in terms of an individual or collective moral defect, be it manifest or covert antisemitism, self-interest, or moral indifference.[10]

As indicated earlier, a core concern in the debate about motives of bystanders is the issue of knowledge. Many of these debates start from the assumption that the bystander is subject to the mechanism of moral revelation: that seeing evil is not only a necessary but even a sufficient motive for assuming a moral responsibility to rescue Jews. This mechanism is, for instance, put to work in the core scene of Steven Spielberg's *Schindler's List*, when we see Schindler watching the liquidation of the Kraków Ghetto in June 1942. The moment of revelation is emphasized by a little girl's red coat in a scene filmed in black and white, indicating the sudden awareness of responsibility, not only of Schindler but at the same time of Spielberg's audience witnessing Schindler's witnessing. The scene is both manipulative—the audience is forced the assume Schindler's perspective—and deceptive: if only the assumption of moral responsibility was so easy.[11] Schindler and millions of others had already been aware of the injustice inflicted on the Jews before the beginning of Operation Reinhard. The signs banning Jews in the streets, the propaganda, the boasting, and the letters and pictures sent home made it clear for all to see that Jews were excluded, expropriated, humiliated, and abused. The true tragedy is not that so little was done to avoid the "final solution," but rather the widespread acceptance of the lesser evils inflicted on the Jews—an acceptance that continues today with the lack of protest against the treatment of refugees, racism, and genocide in many parts of the world.

From a moral perspective, this failure to act against what is blatantly unjust might lead to existential despair. Yet, from an analytical point of view, this failure makes it clear that a purely motivational understanding of the bystander needs to be expanded with a situational understanding that will help us to carve out the specific roles played by bystanders. For such an understanding, one must address the context, which conditions the perceptions, evaluations, and acts of the bystander. The nature of this context is very diverse—material, economic, social, cultural, political, institutional, and other of the usual suspects of sociological analysis—but the contributions in this volume point to two other contextual elements that might be specifically relevant for the understanding of the bystander: space and time.

Timothy Williams points to the relevance of spatiality: the attitude and behavior of bystanders can be analyzed by focusing on the proximity to the crime. Distance is a crucial category to understand how nearby a bystander actually is. However, other contributions make it clear that it is not distance as such but rather the way in which space is experienced and structured that makes a difference. A crucial insight in this respect is presented in this volume by Roma Sendyka, who draws our attention to the sensory aspects of the category of the bystander: watching the Holocaust is mediated by a variety of ways of seeing that require analysis to understand the perspective of the bystander. One can be blind to the crime that happens before one's eyes yet see the reality of the Holocaust through imaginations that emerge at far removed places.

A related issue is the analysis of the public nature of the Holocaust, not only in terms of the extent to which bystanders are able to witness these events but also with respect to the structure of the public sphere in which the Holocaust takes place. One obvious aspect to address here is the transparency of the public sphere, and even more the lack of it: the view of bystanders is obfuscated by manipulation and deceit, propaganda, and the various attempts to conceal the crime from the public eye. An additional way to analyze these dimensions of the public sphere is through theatrical metaphors: the bystanders form an audience who witness a scripted event. They are part of a chorus, commenting on the events. And the bystander is an actor, following established repertoires of collective action and contention. This also points to a theoretical source of inspiration that is so far little explored in bystander studies, which is the body of sociological theory on collective action. Bystanders of the Holocaust are mobilized to act in specific patterns that are derived from repertoires of contention (or the lack thereof) and developed in circumstances that had little to do with the Holocaust.[12]

Next to these spatial aspects of a contextual analysis, Froukje Demant adds a second, temporal dimension to this contextual understanding: the role of bystanders changes over time. Typical bystander behavior such as avoidance and exploitation of Jews emerged only over time, through a process of habituation and gradual acceptance of morally repulsive realities. Analyzing the bystander in such a dynamic context might help to explain not just bystander behavior but also changes in that behavior and, in the end, changes in the social structure as a result of the impact of the Holocaust. The focus on habituation emphasized by Demant can be expanded by other dynamic concepts, such as radicalization and de-identification. The first concept is currently a central notion in much of the research on collective violence and terror, emphasizing both the social environment and the institutional response as crucial factors that are conditioning the steps from observing and supporting to participating in and contributing to the Holocaust.[13] The second concept, of identification with the plight of the Jews, or the gradual distancing and de-identification, can be seen as instances of both spatial and emotional compartmentalization.[14] The analysis of such dynamic processes might help us to explain how bystanders can be near the destruction of Jews yet remain indifferent, passive, or otherwise unaffected. It might help us to understand why an event that from hindsight can only evoke moral outrage at the time was met with indifference, opportunistic acceptance, or even enthusiastic support. And finally, it could provide insight in the continuing divide between victims and bystanders, even after the crime, resulting in a failure to acknowledge the suffering of the victims and the responsibility of bystanders, if not to prevent the crime, then at least to recognize its horror.

Conclusion

Compared with the more straightforward concepts of victim and perpetrator, the bystander perhaps remains a more elusive category. But the contributions in this volume make it clear that it is worth the effort to rescue the bystander. From a historical perspective, it is clearly a relevant category, deployed to assume or avoid moral responsibility. In the footsteps of the contributors to this volume, one can envisage a conceptual history of the bystander, revealing its many transformations of its meaning in use.

As an analytical category, it draws our attention to the continuities of social relations within which the Holocaust needs to be located. It is evident that the Holocaust cannot be understood in the context of the genocidal policies of Nazi Germany alone—a wider canvas is needed to picture it. In this picture, bystanders are the neighbors, colleagues, schoolmates of the victims, both before and after the latter were victimized. These social relations and encounters need to be analyzed with all the tools and concepts of sociological analysis. In particular, the spatial and temporal aspects of these social relations are crucial to understand the specific dynamic—in the context of the Holocaust itself, as well as before and after the event.

Finally, there is also a moral obligation to rescue the bystander. They need to be acknowledged as human agents, with a specific responsibility to act, perhaps not in the overburdened sense of preventing a crime others committed but rather in the more limited sense, as people who witnessed and testified these crimes that happened in their presence.

Ido de Haan is Professor of Political History at Utrecht University. One of the Netherlands leading contemporary historians, he is a specialist on histories of citizenship, regime change and the aftermath of revolutions, and the repercussions of the Holocaust. Among his publications are "Imperialism, Colonialism and Genocide: The Dutch Case for an International History of the Holocaust," *BMGN-LCHR* 125, nos. 2–3 (2010); "The Paradox of Dutch History: Historiography of the Holocaust in the Netherlands" in *Holocaust Historiography in Context, Emergence, Challenges, Polemics and Achievements* (ed. David Bankier and Dan Michman, 2009); and "Paths of Normalization after the Persecution of the Jews: The Netherlands, France, and West Germany in the 1950s" in *Life after Death: Approaches to a Cultural and Social History of Europe During the 1940s and 1950s* (ed. Richard J. Bessel and Dirk Schumann, 2003). He is currently working on political reconstruction after large-scale violence in France and the Netherlands (1598, 1814, 1945), and on the role of silence in politics.

Notes

1. See, e.g., Ulrich Herbert, "Extermination Policy: New Answers and Questions about the History of the 'Holocaust' in German Historiography," in *National Socialist Extermination Policies: Contemporary Perspectives and Controversies*, ed. Ulrich Herbert (New York, 2000), 1–52; Christopher Browning, *The Origins of the Final Solution: The Evolution of Nazi Jewish Policy, September 1939–March 1942* (New York, 2014).
2. See Tony Judt, "From the House of the Dead: On Modern European Memory," *New York Review of Books* 52, no. 15 (2005): 12; on the Netherlands, see Ido de Haan, *Na de Ondergang: De herinnering aan de jodenvervolging in Nederland, 1945–1995* (The Hague, 1997).
3. Omer Bartov, "Wartime Lies and Other Testimonies: Jewish-Christian Relations in Buczacz, 1939–1944," *East European Politics and Societies* 25, no. 3 (2011): 486–511.
4. Ibid., 492.
5. E.g., Peter Longerich, *"Davon haben wir nichts gewusst!" Die Deutschen und die Judenverfolgung 1933–1945* (Munich, 2006); Bart van der Boom, *"Wij Weten Niets van hun Lot": Gewone Nederlanders en de Holocaust* (Amsterdam, 2012).

6. Mary Fulbrook, *A Small Town near Auschwitz: Ordinary Nazis and the Holocaust* (Oxford, 2013).
7. Martin Broszat and Saul Friedländer, "A Controversy about the Historicization of National Socialism," special issue on the Historikerstreit, *New German Critique* 44 (1988): 125.
8. Dan Diner, ed., *Zivilisationsbruch: Denken nach Auschwitz* (Frankfurt, 1988).
9. Samuel P. Oliner and Pearl M. Oliner, *The Altruistic Personality: Rescuers of Jews in Nazi Europe* (New York, 1988).
10. To name but a few remarkable titles in this context: antisemitism is emphasized in Jan T. Gross, *Neighbors: The Destruction of the Jewish Community in Jebwadne, Poland* (Princeton, NJ, 2001); collective and personal self-interest in Götz Aly, *Hitlers Volksstaat: Raub, Rassenkrieg und nationaler Sozialismus* (Frankfurt, 2005); indifference in Norman Geras, *The Contract of Mutual Indifference: Political Philosophy after the Holocaust* (London, 1998).
11. See Ido de Haan, "De morele kracht van de blik. Over de ooggetuigen van Steven Spielberg," *Krisis* 72 (1998): 25–41.
12. See, e.g., Charles Tilly, *Regimes and Repertoires* (Chicago, 2006).
13. See Randy Borum, "Radicalization into Violent Extremism I: A Review of Social Science Theories," *Journal of Strategic Security* 4, no. 4 (2012): 7–36.
14. Abram de Swaan. *The Killing Compartments: The Mentality of Mass Murder* (New Haven, CT, 2014).

Bibliography

Aly, Götz. *Hitlers Volksstaat: Raub, Rassenkrieg und nationaler Sozialismus*. Frankfurt: S. Fischer Verlag, 2005.
Bartov, Omer. "Wartime Lies and Other Testimonies: Jewish-Christian Relations in Buczacz, 1939–1944." *East European Politics and Societies* 25, no. 3 (2011): 486–511.
Boom, Bart van der. *"Wij Weten Niets van hun Lot": Gewone Nederlanders en de Holocaust*. Amsterdam: Boom, 2012.
Borum, Randy. "Radicalization into Violent Extremism I: A Review of Social Science Theories." *Journal of Strategic Security* 4, no. 4 (2012): 7–36.
Broszat, Martin, and Friedländer, Saul. "A Controversy about the Historicization of National Socialism." Special issue on the Historikerstreit, *New German Critique* 44 (1988): 85–126.
Browning, Christopher. *The Origins of the Final Solution*. New York: Random House, 2014.
Diner, Dan, ed. *Zivilisationsbruch: Denken nach Auschwitz*. Frankfurt: S. Fischer Verlag, 1988.
Fulbrook, Mary. *A Small Town near Auschwitz: Ordinary Nazis and the Holocaust*. Oxford: Oxford University Press, 2013.
Geras, Norman. *The Contract of Mutual Indifference: Political Philosophy after the Holocaust*. London: Verso, 1998.
Gross, Jan T. *Neighbors: The Destruction of the Jewish Community in Jebwadne, Poland*. Princeton, NJ: Princeton University Press, 2001.
Haan, Ido de. "De morele kracht van de blik. Over de ooggetuigen van Steven Spielberg." *Krisis* 72 (1998): 25–41.
———. *Na de Ondergang: De herinnering aan de jodenvervolging in Nederland, 1945-1995*. The Hague: Sdu Uitgevers, 1997.

Herbert, Ulrich. "Extermination Policy: New Answers and Questions about the History of the 'Holocaust' in German Historiography." In *National Socialist Extermination Policies: Contemporary Perspectives and Controversies*, edited by Ulrich Herbert, 1–52. New York, 2000.
Judt, Tony. "From the House of the Dead: On Modern European Memory." *New York Review of Books* 52, no. 15 (2005): 12.
Longerich, Peter. *"Davon haben wir nichts gewusst!" Die Deutschen und die Judenverfolgung 1933-1945*. Munich: Siedler Verlag, 2006.
Oliner, Samuel P., and Pearl M. Oliner. *The Altruistic Personality: Rescuers of Jews in Nazi Europe*. New York: Free Press, 1988.
Swaan, Abram de. *The Killing Compartments: The Mentality of Mass Murder*. New Haven, CT: Yale University Press, 2014.
Tilly, Charles. *Regimes and Repertoires*. Chicago: University of Chicago Press, 2006.

INDEX

Note: Page references with an *f* are figures.

accommodation: Denmark, 208–11; Netherlands, 213–15
accomplices, 2, 43, 54, 91, 107, 110, 119, 292, 309
The Accused (movie), 274
action roles, diversity of, 75–76
active encouraging, 80
active facilitating, 80
Adenauer, Konrad, 21
Adorno, Theodor W., 118, 168
agency, lack of, 22
Aktionen (ghettos), 189
alibis for innocence, 30
altruism, 317
Ambos, Kai, 76
Americanism, 181
American responses, 313
Amsterdam, Netherlands, 46–47, 107
analytical utility, 81–83
Andreas-Friedrich, Ruth, 26, 27, 30, 31
Anschluss (1938), 37
anti-Jewish measures: in Germany, 91; in the Netherlands, 211
anti-Jewish policies in Germany, 115
antisemitism, 90, 99, 109, 114, 174, 177, 255, 315, 317, 346; Danish opposition to, 216; in France, 224, 226; Germany, 249; in the Netherlands, 249; Poland, 194, 199; stereotypes, 118, 193
ARD (German TV station), 278, 283

Arendt, Hannah, 168, 216
Aryanization, stages of, 192
Aryans, 114, 116, 155, 157, 158, 169, 172, 191, 198, 211, 296
Ashes in the Wind: The Destruction of Dutch Jewry (Presser), 107, 108
assimilation, 151, 207
atrocities, bystanders reactions to, 116, 117
Auschwitz concentration camp, 109, 224, 230, 231, 272, 301
Austria, 37

Bachrach, Susan, 7
Baden-Baden, Germany, 131, 137*f*, 138*f*, 139*f*; November pogrom, 132, 134–36; onlookers, 140–43; photographing bystanders, 134–39
Baeumler, Alfred, 178, 182
Bajohr, Frank, 92, 149, 191
Bak, Sofie Lene, 208
Barnett, Victoria J., 17, 53, 112
Bar-On, Dan, 20
Bartov, Omer, 198, 345
Bauman, Zygmunt, 201
Becker, Annie, 232
behaviors, 317; bullying, 92 (*see also* bullying); bystanders, 20, 255; knowledge of, 253; of non-Jews toward Jews, 92, 93

Behrend-Rosenfeld, Else, 149, 150, 151, 152, 154, 155, 156, 158, 159, 160, 161
Being and Time (Heidegger), 168
Belguim, 226, 230, 237
bell curves, 200
Benayoun, Guy, 233, 234
Benayoun, Simon, 233, 234
beneficiaries, 19, 25, 31, 91, 112, 191, 314
Bergen-Belsen concentration camp, 115
Berger, John, 54
Bergmann, Werner, 117
Berlin, Germany, 159, 169, 212
Berlin Document Center, 136
Berr, Hélène, 232
Best, Werner, 210, 216
Beukert, Günter, 133
Bialas, Wolfgang, 178
Bielawski, Shraga Feivel, 196
Biélinky, Jacques, 231, 232
Black Notebooks (Heidegger), 169, 170, 171, 176, 181
Blom, Hans, 108, 109
Boekholt, Mrs., 111
Bon, Mr., 234
Bosnia, 314
Bousquet, René, 238
Bousquet-Oberg agreement (1942), 229
Brock, Werner, 173
Broszat, Martin, 259, 347
Browning, Christopher, 37, 38, 45, 75
Buchmann, Heinz, 75
Bulgaria, 229
bullying, 5, 16, 92, 93
Bund Deutscher Mädel, 22
bystanders, 1, 5, 15–35, 91; analysis of, 349; behaviors, 20, 255; *Camera Dropped from My Hands* (Józef Charyton), 59–66; catchall concept of, 16–21, 29; categories, 28; conceptualization of, 100, 343-53; critical clues, 23–29; definitions, 3, 16, 17, 19, 101, 248, 252, 292; Denmark, 215–18; Dutch, 107–27 (*see also* Dutch bystanders); in Dutch research (Netherlands), 247–73; dynamics of persecution, 148–67; fear and impunity, 195–99; France, 239–40; genealogy of visuality, 53–57; German television, 266–90 (*see also* German television); gray zones, 82; Heidegger, Martin, 183; Hilberg, Raul, 36–51 (*see also* Hilberg, Raul); historicization of, 1-4, 336–42; in history, 5; history of, 149; ignorance among, 188, 249-51; with influence, 73; innocence of, 17, 21; instability of, 20; introduction to term, 1-5; 37; mind-sets, 6; moral, 294; moralism, 256–60; in and out of concentration camps, 74; passive, 254; as perpetrators, 21–23; photographing, 131–47; Poland, 187–205; reactions to atrocities, 116, 117; research, 85–86; responses to the Nazi imperative, 154–59; responsibility of, 22; roles of, 310; situational nature of, 92; social dilemmas and passive participation, 90–106; solidarity, 159–62; SS wives as, 291–308; strength of unpopular norms, 98–99; temptation and greed, 191–95; treatment of (USHMM), 310–13; types of, 53, 95–98; violence and, 101; as visual subjects, 52–71; zones, 84

Cambodia, Khmer Rouge genocide in, 84–85
Camera Dropped from My Hands (Charyton), 59–66
Carter, Jimmy, 309
Cartwright, Lisa, 55
Central Committee, 199
Chabanaud, Mr., 234
Charpentier, Mr., 235
Charyton, Józef, 59–66
children, bullying, 93, 94
Children's Welfare Agency, 228
Christian X (King), 209
civil resistance (France), 231–39
Coeppicus, Josef Friedrich, 135, 136, 137*f*, 138*f*, 139, 139*f*
cohabitation, Jewish/non-Jewish, 97, 98, 100
Cohen, Asher, 226
Cohen, Jaap, 253
Cohn, Willy, 149, 150, 151, 153, 154, 155, 156, 157, 159
Cold War, 273, 274, 276
Cole, Tim, 316
Colijn, Hendrik, 115
collaboration, Danish policy of, 208, 210, 218, 321
Colombia, 133
Comité van Waakzaamheid (Commission of Vigilance), 115

complicity, 4, 77, 168, 169, 177, 183, 188, 200, 231, 283, 291, 292, 314, 319
concentration camps, 190, 250; Auschwitz, 109, 224, 230, 231, 272, 301; Bergen-Belsen, 115; bystanders in and out of, 74; Mauthausen, 214, 215; Ravensbrück, 72; Sobibór death camp, 81, 82; Treblinka death camp, 82
conscience (Nazi), 168–86
convictions: in Denmark, 206–7; in the Netherlands, 206–7
Cornides, Wilhelm, 337, 338, 339
Countrymen and the Rescue of Jews (Lidegaard), 4
Crary, Jonathan, 55, 57
crime fiction, 272
The Crisis of German Ideology (Mosse), 170
criticism, moral, 257
Cultural-Political Working Group of German University Professors, 171, 172
Czechoslovakia, 274, 275
Czerniaków, Adam, 28, 38

Darnand, Joseph, 230
death: of Jews in France, 225; methods of, 26
death camps, 29, 190, 214, 215. *See also* concentration camps
Debord, Guy, 55
de Chaunac, Christian, 227
De Groene Amsterdammer, 257
de Haan, Ido, 8, 109, 110
de Jong, Adolf, 96
de Jong, Loe, 108
de-Judification *(Entjudung)*, 191
Delegatura Rządu, 195
Demant, Froukje, 5, 349, 350
denazification, 177, 179, 182, 269
Denmark, 27, 237; accommodation, 208–11; attitudes toward Jews, 207–8; bystanders, 215–18; convictions in, 206–7; deportations in, 206–7, 210, 216, 217, 218; policy of collaboration, 321; protests in, 208; refugee policies, 207, 208; rescuers, 217
deportations, 281, 318; Auschwitz concentration camp, 231; in Denmark, 206–7, 210, 216, 217, 218; in France, 227; in the Netherlands, 206–7, 213, 218, 254

Der Israelit, 134
Der Kommissar (TV series), 270
Derrick (TV series), 270
Der Stellvertreter (Hochhuth), 38
Der Stürmer, 98
Desbois, Patrick, 52
The Destruction of the European Jews (Hilberg), 18, 27, 36, 37, 39
Deutsche Studentenschaft (German Student Union), 174
diaries, 24, 26, 30, 112, 171, 211, 231, 251; Frank, Anne, 215; Holocaust, 149, 151–54, 158, 196; Netherlands, 249–51; typologies, 252
Die Strasse, 296
Dietrich, Inga, 291, 303f
Die Welt, 300
discouraging, 81
diversity, tolerance of in the Netherlands, 211
documentaries, 39, 40, 57, 280, 291
Dostoyevsky, Fyodor, 134
Dreyfus Affair, 224
Dutch bystanders, 3, 4, 107–27, 206, 207, 211–215, 218, 219, 247–56, 261; after liberation, 117–18; in Dutch history, 110–13; prewar years, 113–15; years of occupation, 115–17
Dutch Criminal Code, 115
Dutch Jews: convictions in, 206–7; deportations in, 206–7; persecution of, 108; positioning of, 113. *See also* Denmark; the Netherlands
Dutch paradox, 3, 46

Eastern Europe, 189, 193, 200, 207, 273, 274
Eastern Front, 42, 197
Eastern Jews, 114
Egzekucja (Execution [Józef Charyton]), 1945–1963, 61f
Eichmann, Adolf, 82
Eine Frau an seiner Seite (Schwarz), 291, 295
Encyclopedia of Genocide (1999), 38
"*Endlösung*," 188. *See also* final solution
Ensel, Remco, 252, 256
Europa-Archiv, 340
evaders, 77
Evian, France, 313
eyewitnesses, 24, 320. *See also* witnesses

factor of time, 92
failure to intervene, 17
false enforcement, 6
family life, wives (SS), 296
February Strike of 1941, 213, 214
Feldpost letters (Germany), 251
fellow citizens *(Mitbürger)*, 158
fellow travelers *(Mitläufer)*, 2, 169
Fenjves, Klara, 324
fiction, crime, 272
filmmaking, 274. *See also* German television
final solution, 52, 187–205, 225, 311
First Polish Army, 199
Fivaz-Silbermann, Ruth, 225
Flehinger, Arthur, 135
Flinker, Moshe, 112, 113
Fotografowanie na pamija, tke (Photographing for a keepsake), 1945–1963, 64*f*
France, 321; antisemitism in, 224, 226; bystanders, 239–40; civil resistance, 231–39; deportations in, 227; factors for social reactivity, 225–31; rescuers in, 228; social reactivity, 224–44; survivors in, 229
Frank, Anne, 206, 215, 325
Frank, Maria, 296
free zones, 228, 229, 234
Frei, Norbert, 8, 21
French paradox, 224
French Revolution, 227
Friedländer, Saul, 110, 188, 259, 347
Friedrich, Ruth, 159
Fritsch, Fanny, 301
Fujii, Lee Ann, 77
Fulbrook, Mary, 5, 44, 66, 78, 92, 344, 346, 347

The Gambler (Dostoyevsky), 134
Gans, Evelien, 6, 252, 256, 257, 260, 345
gas chambers, 21, 110, 253, 256
Gaussian distribution, 200
gawkers, 54
Gawkers' Theatre, 56
genealogy of visuality, 53–57
Generalgouvernement, 190, 197, 337, 340
Generation War (movie), 280, 282
genocide, 278, 281, 283, 316; categorizing actors and action, 76–78; Khmer Rouge genocide in Cambodia, 84–85; process of, 73; typology of action in, 78–81
Gentiles, 113. *See also* non-Jews
Germanization, 28
German Student Union (Deutsche Studentenschaft), 174
German television, 266–90; *Der Kommissar,* 270; *Holocaust,* 38, 270, 273, 277, 278, 279, 280, 281, 283; narratives, 273, 279; *Sadowski Comes at Eight O'clock* (TV series), 270, 271, 272, 273, 277
Germany, 24; anti-Jewish policies in, 115; antisemitism, 249; Baden-Baden, 131 (*see also* Baden-Baden, Germany); Berlin, 159, 169, 212; dynamics of persecution, 148–67; *Feldpost* letters, 251; final solution, 52; Marburg, 172, 173; occupation policies, 209; repression, 238; victimhood, 270
Gerstein, Kurt, 42, 337, 340
Gestapo, 21, 43, 99, 134, 141, 156, 216
ghettos, 29, 159, 189; liquidation of, 192, 197; Litzmannstadt, 29; Warsaw Ghetto, 29, 38, 57
Gläsel, Joanne, 291, 303*f*
Glazema, Mrs., 111
Gleichschaltung, 173, 175, 182
Goebbels, Joseph, 78
Göth, Amon, 301, 305
Grabowski, Jan, 6, 316, 345
gray history, 3, 258
gray zones, 73, 82, 85
Great Deportation, 196
Greese, Irma, 297
Griffioen, Pim, 225
Gross, Jan T., 53, 190, 316
Grunberg, Albert, 231

Habermas, Jürgen, 168
half-Jews, 114
hangers-on *(Mitläufer)*, 2
HarperCollins, 42
Haus der Wannseekonferenz, 291
Heidegger, Martin, 6, 168–86; as a bystander, 183; as a Nazi bureaucrat, 171–77; as politically reliable professor, 177–82
Heidegger, Elfriede, 174
Heimat (movie), 280, 281
Heimatkunde (Germanic studies), 170, 179

helpers, 41, 91, 190, 217, 218, 317
Henry, Frances, 38
Herkommer, Christina, 298
Herz, Lotte, 97
Herzberg, Abel, 108, 115
Herzfeld, Bertha, 323
Hess, Ilse, 296
Hesse, Klaus, 134
Heydrich, Lina, 292, 293, 295, 297, 298, 299, 300, 301, 302, 304
Heydrich, Reinhard, 299, 300
Hilberg, Gwendolyn, 43
Hilberg, Raul, 2, 4, 5, 16, 18, 27, 187, 188, 239, 320, 336, 337, 339; Amsterdam, Netherlands, 46–47; composition, 40–42; concept of bystanders, 36–51; critics, 44–46; inspiration, 37–40; translation, 42–43; trichotomy of perpetrators, bystanders, and victims, 76, 91; types of bystanders, 53
Himmler, Heinrich, 293, 296, 299, 300
Historikerstreit (historians' controversy, Germany), 259
Hitler, Adolf, 171, 191, 315, 316, 319, 324, 325; assumption of power, 90; consent to violence, 134; genocide and, 78; Heidegger's proximity to, 168; Hitler Youth, 141, 271; *Mein Kampf,* 135; motives of, 153; national government in France, 228; National Socialism and, 179; as perpetrator, 21; speeches, 154; *Volksstaat,* 154
Hochhuth, Rolf, 38
Hoffnung, Marthe, 227, 235
Holland, 212, 226. *See also* the Netherlands
Holland deportatieland (the Netherlands, deportation country), 207
Holocaust, 2; act of killing during, 74; analytical utility, 81–83; attitudes to, 190; bystanders (*see* bystanders); categorizing actors and action, 76–78; diaries, 149, 151–54, 158, 196; German television, 266–90; history, 4, 5, 18, 40, 149, 259; individual inaction, 72–89; interpretation of ordinary Dutchmen, 247, 249; knowledge of, 255; memory, 278; research, 37, 46; survivors, 199; typology of action in genocide, 78–81; watching, 53 (*see also* bystanders); West German television, 266–90

Holocaust (TV series), 38, 270, 273, 277, 278, 279, 280, 281, 283
The Holocaust (USHMM exhibition), 310
Holocaust Resource Center (Yad Vashem), 19
Holokaust (documentary), 280, 282
Hondius, Dienke, 116
Hong, Nathaniel, 209
Horwitz, Gordon, 20
Höss, Hedwig, 292
Husserl, Edmund, 168
Husserl, Malvine, 174

Iconology: Image, Text, Ideology (Mitchell), 53
identification, 4, 111, 114, 248, 256–60, 282, 350
individual inaction, 72–89; analytical utility, 81–83; bystander research, 85–86; categorizing actors and action, 76–78; Khmer Rouge genocide in Cambodia, 84–85; Reserve Police Battalion 101, 74, 75–76; typology of action in genocide, 78–81
innocence of bystanders, 17
internment camps, Rivesaltes, 228. *See also* concentration camps
intervention, 17, 21
interviews, eyewitness, 320
intimidation, 207
Into That Darkness (Sereny), 293
Italy, 229

Jack, Joseph and Morton Mandel Center for Advanced Holocaust Studies, 309
Jäckel, Eberhard, 44
Jackson, Julian, 226
Jaensch, Erich, 172, 176, 177, 178, 182
Jaspers, Karl, 179, 181
Jeanne, Miss, 233
The Jerusalem Report, 45
Jewish branches, 114
Jewish Council, 214
Jewish *Gemeinde,* 152
Jewish gold, 193, 194
Jewish Historical Institute (JHI), 60
Jewish/non-Jewish cohabitation, 97, 98, 100, 149, 150, 159-62
Jews, 3; assimilation, 151; Denmark, 27; Denmark, attitudes toward, 207–8; *The Destruction of the European Jews*

Jews (*cont.*)
  (Hilberg), 18; Dutch (*see* Dutch Jews); dynamics of persecution, 148–67; full, 114; Netherlands, attitudes toward, 211–12; persecution of by Nazis, 94; persecution of in Netherlands, 108; Poland, 25, 26, 27; return of possessions after liberation, 117; risks, 258; self-identifications, 113; survival rates, 206 (*see also* survivors)
Joffo, Joseph, 233, 234, 235
Joffo, Maurice, 233
joiners, 77

Kadar, Jan, 274, 275
Kahn, Dennis, 94
Kalder-Göth, Ruth, 292, 301, 305
Kammerer, Arthur, 80
Kansteiner, Wulf, 7
Kaplan, Marion A., 152
Karski, Jan, 42, 44, 57–59
Kern, Eduard, 177
Khmer Rouge, genocide in Cambodia, 84–85
Kirchhoff, Hans, 217
Klarsfeld, Serge, 224, 225
Klemperer, Victor, 158
Klos, Elmar, 274, 275
Klukowski, Zygmunt, 24, 25, 26, 27, 30, 320
Knittel, Susanne, 7
Knochen, Helmut, 230
Knopp, Guido, 282
knowledge of the Holocaust: 4-7, 21, 109, 110, 163, 189, 219, 249-256, 298-300, 313-316, 340, 346, 348
Knowles, Adam, 6
Koch, Ilse, 297
Koegel, Anna, 72, 73, 75
Koegel, Max, 72
Koonz, Claudia, 170
Krammer, Arthur, 76
Kreutzmüller, Christoph, 6
Krieck, Ernst, 172, 176, 178, 182
Kriegel, Annie, 232
Kristallnacht. *See* November pogrom
Kushner, Tony, 111
Kuwabara, Ko, 94

labor conscription (the Netherlands), 213
Laborie, Pierre, 226

LaCapra, Dominick, 111, 260
Lanzmann, Claude, 5, 23, 39, 40, 43, 45, 57
Lassalle, Ferdinand, 151
Laval, Pierre, 230
League of German Girls (BDM), 156
Leben mit einem Kriegsverbrecher (Life with a war criminal [Heydrich]), 297, 299
Leder, Andrzej, 194
Leiden University, 249
Leo, Per, 175
leveling (*nivellering*), 119
liberation, Dutch bystanders after, 117–18
Lichtenberg, Bernhard, 43, 44
Lidegaard, Bo, 4, 207, 208
Life with a war criminal (*Leben mit einem Kriegsverbrecher* [Heydrich]), 297, 299
Linenthal, Edward, 310
Litzmannstadt, 29
Look at It, Look at It (Karski), 57–59
looting, 314
Löw, Andrea, 92

Macy, Michael, 94
Maier, Leonie, 154
Mairowitz, David Zane, 291, 304
Manchester Guardian, 133
Mannweib (she-man), 297
Marburg, Germany, 172, 173
Marcus, Michael, 18
Markusen, Eric, 77
Marrus, Michael, 38, 224, 226
Marx, Karl, 151
Maschmann, Melita, 22
Maser, Werner, 299, 300, 301, 304
mass shootings, 314
Mauthausen concentration camp, 214, 215
media, 266. *See also* German television
Meershoek, Guus, 253
Mein Kampf (Hitler), 135
Mein Leben mit Reinhard (My life with Reinhard [Heydrich]), 301
memory: bystanders in Dutch research (Netherlands), 247–73; collective, 207; criticism and controversy, 251–56; diaries and knowledge, 249–51; German television, 266–90; Holocaust, 278; moralism, 256–60; self-representations of SS wives, 291–308
Mengele, Eva, 292

Midgley, Mary, 20
Mitchell, J. T., 53, 54
Mitläufer (onlookers, or literally: hangers-on, fellow travelers), 2, 5, 169
moral bystanders, 294
moralism, 4, 5, 15-20, 30, 40, 101, 181, 256-60, 278, 283, 293, 304, 344, 348, 351
Morina, Christina, 6, 195, 249, 252, 346
Morrison, Jack, 20
Mosse, George L., 170
MS *St. Louis*, 313
My life with Reinhard (*Mein Leben mit Reinhard* [Heydrich]), 301

Na de Ondergang (de Haan), 109
narratives: German television, 273, 279; Third Reich, 269, 270. *See also* German television
Nationaal-Socialistische Beweging (NSB), 111
National Socialism, 168, 169, 170, 175, 176, 177, 180, 182, 296, 297-301
National Socialist German Students' League (Nationalsozialistischer Deutscher Studentenbund [NSDStB]), 174
Nazis, 2, 6, 21, 24, 315, 324, 325; antisemitic rhetoric of, 90; bystanders, 267 (*see also* bystanders); concept of a German folk community, 98; dynamics of persecution, 148-67; everyday life during Nazism, 269; final solution, 52; Heidegger, Martin, 168-86; *Hurrapatriot*, 157; invasion of Soviet Union (1941), 209; occupation of Poland, 25; persecution of Jews, 94; policies, 28; responses to the Nazi imperative, 154-59; takeover of power (1933), 95; years of occupation (Netherlands), 116
neighbors, 27, 320; diaries (Holocaust), 151-54; dynamics of persecution, 148-67; reactions, 39; responses to the Nazi imperative, 154-59; roles of, 315; solidarity, 159-62; *Some Were Neighbors* exhibition (USHMM), 314-16. *See also* bystanders
Neighbors (Gross), 4
the Netherlands, 6, 315; accommodation, 213-15; after liberation, 117-18; anti-Jewish measures in, 211; antisemitism in, 249; attitudes toward Jews, 211-12; bystanders in Dutch history, 110-13; bystanders in Dutch research, 247-73; convictions in, 206-7; criticism and controversy, 251-56; deportations in, 206-7, 213, 218, 254; diaries and knowledge, 249-51; Dutch Holocaust historiography, 256; February Strike of 1941, 213, 214; moralism, 256-60; non-Jews in, 109; persecution of Jews in, 108; prewar years, 113-15; resistance movements, 214; strikes in the, 212; Supreme Court of the, 213; tolerance, 260; years of occupation, 115-17
Neubauer, Rudolf, 133
New York Times, 44, 132
Niemöller, Martin, 311, 312*f*
The Night in Lisbon (Remarque), 1
Niziołek, Grzegorz, 56
non-Jews: after liberation, 117-18; bystanders in Dutch history, 110-13; Dutch bystanders, 107-27; in the Netherlands, 109; prewar years, 113-15; years of occupation, 115-17. *See also* Gentiles
normalization, 97
normative demarcation, 21
November pogrom (*"Kristallnacht"*), 91, 132, 313, 316, 321; Baden-Baden, Germany, 132, 134-36; photographing bystanders, 132-34
Nuremberg Laws (1935), 90, 99, 136
Nuremberg trials, 37

Oberg, Carl, 230
observation, 54, 55. *See also* visual subjects (bystanders as)
occupation policies (Germany), 209
Ohlendorf, Otto, 23
Ondergang (Presser), 107, 109
onlookers *(Mitläufer)*, 2, 5, 54, 91, 131, 140-43, 187
Ophuls, Marcel, 280
Ordinary Men (Browning), 45, 75
ostracization, 281
outsiders, 80

passiveness: bystanders, 25; encouraging, 80; facilitating, 80; passive participation, bystanders, 90-106
Paulsson, Gunnar, 210, 211, 216, 217, 218

Paxton, Robert, 224, 226
Pehle, John, 313
Pehle, Walter, 42
people's community *(Volksgemeinschaft)*, 4, 141, 150, 152, 268
perpetrators, 1, 5, 21–23, 30, 31, 39, 91, 149, 259, 309
Perpetrators Victims Bystanders (Hilberg), 5, 16, 18, 36, 37, 40; Bystander section, 41, 43; critics, 44–46; publishing of, 42; translations, 42–43
persecution, 19; diaries (Holocaust), 151–54; dynamics of, 148–67; of Jews, 94; of Jews in Netherlands, 108
Pétain, Marshal Philippe, 228, 230
photographing bystanders, 131–47; Baden-Baden, Germany, 134–39; November pogrom, 132–34; onlookers, 140–43
Picasso, Pablo, 39
Picture Theory (Mitchell), 54
Pius XII (Pope), 38
pluralistic ignorance, 5, 94
Polak, Henri, 115
Poland, 21, 22, 24, 25, 43, 315, 320; bystanders, 187–205; as bystanders, 25; Charyton, Józef, 59–66; fear and impunity, 195–99; responses of people, 26; temptation and greed, 191–95; visual subjects (bystanders as), 52–71
The Politics of Memory (Hilberg), 18
Pollock, Griselda, 55
Polski teatr Zagłady (Niziołek), 56
POW (prisoner of war) camps, 213, 276
Presser, Jacques, 107, 108, 109, 110, 119
prewar years, 113–15
Prinz, Joachim, 148, 149
properties, purchase of, 96
protests: anti-Jewish measures in the Netherlands, 211, 212; in Denmark, 208; of deportations, 210
psychological war *(Nervenkrieg)*, 153

The Question of German Guilt (Jaspers), 181
Quick, 136

Rabinbach, Anson, 178
Rampart *(Szaniec)*, 194
Rancière, Jacques, 55
rape, 16

Ravensbrück concentration camp, 72
refugee policies, Denmark, 207, 208
Regarding the Pain of Others (Sontag), 65
Reich Main Security Office, 299
Reich Ministry of Public Enlightenment and Propaganda (RMVP), 133
Reigner, Gerhart M., 44
Reinecker, Herbert, 270, 271, 272
Reitz, Edgar, 280, 281
Remarque, Erich Maria, 1, 2
Remco, Ensel, 6
rescuers, 5, 20, 77, 81, 83, 207, 317; Denmark, 217; in France, 228; gray zones, 82; wall of the rescuers (USHMM), 311*f*
research: bystanders in Dutch (Netherlands), 247–73; criticism and controversy, 251–56; diaries and knowledge, 249–51; moralism, 256–60
Reserve Police Battalion 101, 74, 75–76
resettlement, 340
resistance: France, 231–39; groups, 26; the Netherlands, 214
Resistenz, 347
resisters, 77
restitution efforts, West Germany, 277
risks, Jews, 258
Rivesaltes internment camp, 228
robbery, 16, 25
Romania, 229
Roosevelt, Franklin D., 313
Rosenfeld, Siegfried, 151
Roth, John K., 44
Rothberg, Michael, 112, 119
Rothfels, Hans, 337, 339, 340
roundups, 250, 311
Rumkowski, Chaim, 28
Rusina, Franciszek, 198
Rust, Bernhard, 176
Rwanda, 314

SA *(Sturmabteilung)*, 133
sabotage, 209; of deportations, 210; opposition to, 217
Sadowski Comes at Eight O'clock (TV series), 270, 271, 272, 273, 277
Saliège, Jules, 226, 227
Salmons, Paul, 316
Samuel, Vivette, 228
Sartre, Jean-Paul, 39

saving the bystanders, 343–53; burden of explanation, 344–46; historical and analytical meanings, 346–47; motives and situations, 348–50. See also bystanders
saviors, 236
Scali, Arlette, 233, 236
Scali, Elie, 236
Scavenius, Erik, 209
Schimke, Otto-Julius, 83
Schindler, Angelika, 141
Schindler, Oskar, 73, 75, 81
Schindler's List (movie), 280, 281, 348
Schlott, René, 5, 337
Schöffer, Ivo, 115
Schönfelder, Dr., 76, 80
Schubert, Heinz, 23
Schütz, Alfred, 150
Schwarz, Gudrun, 291, 295
Seible, Wolfgang, 230
self-representations of SS wives, 291–308; actions, identification, knowledge, 295–97; National Socialism and, 297–301; *The Woman at His Side: Careers, Crimes, and Female Complicity under National Socialism*, 291, 292, 293, 294, 295, 301–5
Semelin, Jacques, 7, 161, 229, 345
Sendyka, Roma, 5, 349
Sereny, Gitta, 293, 298, 299
Seyss-Inquart, Arthur, 212, 216
Shoah (Lanzmann), 5, 23, 39, 40, 45, 57, 280, 281
The Shop on Main Street (movie), 274, 275, 276, 277
A Small Town near Auschwitz (Fulbrook), 346
Snyder, Timothy, 189
Sobibór death camp, 81, 82
Social Democratic Party (SPD), 151
social dilemmas: bullying, 93, 94; bystanders, 90–106
social reactivity (France), 224–44; bystanders, 239–40; civil resistance, 231–39; factors for, 225–31
societal inclusiveness, 207
Society of the Spectacle (Debord), 55
solidarity, 159–62, 231
Some Were Neighbors (United States Holocaust Memorial Museum), 19, 317*f*, 322*f*, 323*f*, 324*f*; bystanders, 316–24; reception of, 324–28

Sontag, Susan, 65
The Sorrow and the Pity (documentary), 280
Soviet Union, 209, 273
Spain, 226, 228
spectators, 54, 55
Spielberg, Steven, 348
Springer, Philipp, 134
SS *(Schutzstaffel)*, 21, 27, 133, 134, 137, 139, 141, 238, 291–308. See also wives (SS)
stand by *(danebenstehen)*, 179
Stangl, Franz, 72, 75, 80, 82, 191
Stangl, Thea, 292, 293, 294, 298, 302, 304, 305
Star of David, 155, 212
Staub, Ervin, 45
Sterne (movie), 276
stigmatization, 227
Stimmungsberichte (reports on the mood of the population), 95
Stone, Dan, 110
strikes: February Strike of 1941, 213, 214
Sturken, Marita, 55
Sudan, 314
supporting, 81
Supreme Court of the Netherlands, 213
survivors, 77; in France, 225, 227, 229; Holocaust, 199; in the Netherlands, 206
Süskind, Alfred, 90, 91, 92, 101
Süskind, Sophie, 90, 91, 92, 101
Sweden, 42, 208, 216
Switzerland, 225, 226, 228
Szaniec (Rampart), 194
Szmajzner, Stan, 72, 81

Techniques of the Observer (Crary), 55
Teitelbaum, Mojżesz, 59
television. See German television
Thijs, Krijn, 7, 345
Third Reich, 91, 109, 114, 269; narratives, 269, 270. See also Germany
tolerance in the Netherlands, 260
Trapp, Wilhelm, 75, 80, 83
Treachery Act of 1934, 133
Treblinka death camp, 82
trials, 23, 37, 141, 191, 272, 297, 339; Nuremberg, 37; Ulm Einsatzkommando, 339
Tulard, André, 321

Ulm Einsatzkommando trial (1958), 339
Unarmed against Hitler (Semelin), 229
United Kingdom, 42
United States, 42, 313
United States Holocaust Memorial Museum (USHMM), 7, 19, 309–35; Niemöller, Martin, 311, 312*f*; *Some Were Neighbors* exhibition, 314–24; treatment of bystanders, 310–13; wall of the rescuers, 311*f*
University of Freiburg, 168, 169, 173, 179
University of Giessen, 148
University of Vermont, 41
unpopular norms, strength of, 98–99

Van der Boom, Bart, 4, 6, 109, 110, 111, 112, 247, 249, 250, 251, 252, 253, 254, 255, 256, 257, 258, 259, 345
van der Veen, Gerrit, 117
Verbannung (banishment), 152
Verdeja, Ernesto, 294, 298
Vergangenheitsbewältigung, 340
Verlang, S. Fischer, 42
Vichy France, 346
Vichy France and the Jews (Marrus and Paxton), 224
Vichy government, 226. *See also* France
Vichy Jewish Statute (3 October 1940), 227
victimhood, Germany, 270
victimization process, 20
victims, 1, 23, 39, 91
Vierteljahrshefte für Zeitgeschichte, 337, 339
violence: and bystanders, 101; collective, 28, 31; of concentration camps, 72; photographing bystanders, 133
Visual History Archives of the USC Shoah Foundation, 320
visuality, genealogy of, 53–57
visual subjects (bystanders as), 52–71; *Camera Dropped from My Hands* (Józef Charyton), 59–66; genealogy of visuality, 53–57; *Look at It, Look at It* (Jan Karski), 57–59
Volksgemeinschaft (people's community), 4, 141, 150, 152, 268
Volksgruppen, 156
vom Rath, Ernst, 134
Vor aller Augen (In plain view), 134
Vrije Universiteit Amsterdam, 47

Wallenberg, Raoul, 42, 310
war criminals, 296, 299
War Refugee Board, 313
Warsaw Ghetto, 29, 38, 57
Wasserstein, Bernard, 211
Weiller, Francine, 234
Weinberg, Jeshajahu, 309
Weltwende (universal turn), 153
Welzer, Harald, 45
Werner, Sabine, 291, 303*f*
Western Europe, 189
West Germany: restitution efforts, 277; television, 266–90 (*see also* German television); trials, 23
Wiener Library, 135
Wiesel, Elie, 309
Wij weten niets van hun lot: Gewone Nederlanders en de Holocaust (Van der Boom), 110
Willer, Robb, 94
Williams, Timothy, 5, 349
witnesses, 5, 43, 77, 80, 95, 256, 311
wives (SS), 291–308; actions, identification, knowledge, 295–97; family life, 296; National Socialism and, 297–301; *The Woman at His Side: Careers, Crimes, and Female Complicity under National Socialism*, 291, 292, 293, 294, 295, 301–5
Wolf, Konrad, 276
The Woman at His Side: Careers, Crimes, and Female Complicity under National Socialism, 291, 292, 293, 294, 295, 301–5, 303*f*
World War II, 4, 36, 42, 149, 153, 161, 171, 206, 224, 266, 274
Writing History, Writing Trauma (LaCapra), 111
Wyszyński, Franciszek, 196

Yad Vashem, 19, 60, 310

ZDF (German TV station), 270, 274, 275, 281, 283
Zeller, Ron, 225
Żemiński, Stanisław, 192
Zuccotti, Suzanne, 225
Zuroff, Efraim, 44
Żydówki przed egzekucją: Wys-Lit 1942 (Jewish women before the execution: Wys-Lit [Józef Charyton] 1942), 62*f*

www.ingramcontent.com/pod-product-compliance
Lightning Source LLC
Chambersburg PA
CBHW072142100526
44589CB00015B/2053